software project management

management

Third edition

BOB HUGHES AND MIKE COTTERELL

School of Information Management, University of Brighton

THE McGRAW-HILL COMPANIES

LONDON · BURR RIDGE IL · NEW YORK · ST LOUIS · SAN FRANCISCO · AUCKLAND
BOGOTÁ · CARACAS · LISBON · MADRID · MEXICO · MILAN · MONTREAL · NEW DELHI
PANAMA · PARIS · SAN JUAN · SÃO PAULO · SINGAPORE · SYDNEY · TOKYO · TORONTO

Published by McGraw-Hill Publishing Company
Shoppenhangers Road, Maidenhead, Berkshire, SL6 2QL, England
Telephone: +44(0) 1628 502500
Fax: +44(0) 1628 770224
Website: http://www.mcgraw-hill.co.uk

Editorial Director: Melissa Rosati
Acquisitions Editor: Conor Graham
Senior Marketing Manager: Jackie Harbor
Senior Production Manager: Max Elvey
New Media Developer: Doug Greenwood

Authors' website address: http://www.mcgraw-hill.co.uk/textbooks/hughes

Produced for McGraw-Hill by Steven Gardiner Ltd
Printed and bound in the United Kingdom by Bell and Bain Ltd, Glasgow
Cover design by Hybert Design

McGraw-Hill

A Division of The *McGraw·Hill* Companies

British Library Cataloguing in Publication Data
A catalogue record for this book is available from the British Library

Library of Congress Cataloging in Publication Data
The LOC data for this book has been applied for and may be obtained from the Library of
Congress, Washington, DC

ISBN 0 07 709834 X

1 2 3 4 5 BB 6 5 4 3 2

The road to hell is paved with works-in-progress.

Philip Roth

Contents

Preface to the third edition

The request for a third edition was initially met with some scepticism by the authors. This was especially the case as new editions are not necessarily welcomed by lecturers using the text if it means that references in the lecturers' materials to specific sections have to be modified. However, further consideration has suggested that there have been some developments in the discipline of software project management of which account should be taken. In particular, there has been:

- the more 'agile' approaches to software projects such as those of the Dynamic System Development Method (DSDM) and Extreme Programming (XP);
- a new version of the BS EN ISO 9000 family of standards and guidelines introduced in 2000;
- the increased awareness of the need to set project management in the context of programme management;
- development of new versions of the project management bodies of knowledge by both the Project Management Institute (PMI) in the United States and the Association of Project Management (APM) in the United Kingdom;
- a growing awareness of the issues of health and safety in general and of stress in particular within the project environment.

Other changes have been made as the result of using the text in teaching. In the initial chapters, particularly, some amendments and additions have been made to emphasize points that often seem to be misunderstood. We have, for example, added a typical contents list for a project plan as an Annex to Chapter 1 and an example of a Gantt chart in Chapter 2. This is because we have discovered that students find it helpful to have an idea of what the end-product will look like even if they do not yet understand the steps that create the product.

If some material is added then other material has to be dropped. For example, we have added an appendix on programme management, but, with some reluctance, dropped one on Euromethod that appeared in the second edition. Since the appearance of the previous edition, Bob Hughes's *Practical Software Measurement* has appeared and the section on the Goal/Question/Metric paradigm has been dropped from this text on the grounds that readers interested in GQM would be better off looking at the fuller treatment in the specifically measurement-related text.

During the course of preparing the three editions since 1995, we have received assistance from many people. These people have included: Ken I'Anson, Chris

Claire, David Howe, Martin Campbell Kelly, Barbara Kitchenham (for permission to use a project data set shown in Chapter 5), Paul Radford and Robyn Lawrie of Charismatek Software Metrics, Melbourne, David Garmus and David Herron (the last four, all for material in Chapter 10), David Purves, David Wynne, Dick Searles, John Pyman, Jim Watson, Mary Shepherd, Sunita Chulani, David Wilson, David Farthing, Charlie Svahnberg, Henk Koppelaar and Ian McChesney.

We would also like to thank the team at McGraw-Hill. In particular we would like to pay a special tribute to Dave Hatter who was our editor at International Thomson Press and then at McGraw-Hill and who was responsible for goading us into this third edition. We wish Dave a happy retirement in the groves and glades of Essex.

The first edition was dedicated to those former students of ours who were now grappling with problems of IT development in the 'real world' and that dedication seems to be just as appropriate today.

CHAPTER 1

Introduction to software project management

Objectives

When you have completed this chapter you will be able to:

- define the scope of 'software project management';
- distinguish between software and other types of development project;
- understand some problems and concerns of software project managers;
- define the usual stages of a software project;
- explain the main elements of the role of management;
- appreciate the need for careful planning, monitoring and control;
- identify the stakeholders of a project and their objectives and ways of defining the success in meeting those objectives.

1.1 Introduction

What is 'software project management'? What makes it different from management in general? Is *software* project management different from other types of project management? To answer these questions we need to look at some key ideas about the planning, monitoring and control of software projects. We will see that projects are largely about meeting objectives. Projects to produce software are only worthwhile if they satisfy real needs and so we will examine how we can identify the stakeholders in a project and their objectives. Having identified those objectives, ensuring that they are met is the basis of a successful project. This, however, cannot be done unless there is accurate information and how this is provided will be explored.

1.2 What is a project?

Dictionary definitions of 'project' include: 'A specific plan or design'; 'A planned undertaking'; 'A large undertaking: e.g. a public works scheme', *Longman Dictionary of the English Language*, 1991.

The dictionary definitions put a clear emphasis on the project being a *planned* activity.

The definition of a project as being planned assumes that to a large extent we can determine how we are going to carry out a task before we start. There may be some projects of an exploratory nature where this might be quite difficult. Planning is in essence thinking carefully about something before you do it – and even in the case of uncertain projects this is worth doing as long as it is accepted that the resulting plans will have provisional and speculative elements. Other activities, relating, for example, to routine maintenance, might have been performed so many times that everyone involved knows exactly what needs to be done. In these cases, planning hardly seems necessary, although procedures might need to be documented to ensure consistency and to help newcomers to the job.

The types of activity that will benefit most from conventional project management are likely to lie between these two extremes – see Figure 1.1.

Programme management is often used to coordinate activities on concurrent jobs – see Appendix C.

There is a hazy boundary between the non-routine project and the routine job. The first time you do a routine task it will be like a project. On the other hand, a project to develop a system similar to previous ones that you have developed will have a large element of the routine.

The characteristics which distinguish projects can be summarized as follows.

- non-routine tasks are involved;
- planning is required;
- specific objectives are to be met or a specified product is to be created;
- the project has a pre-determined time span;
- work is carried out for someone other than yourself;
- work involves several specialisms;
- work is carried out in several phases;
- the resources that are available for use on the project are constrained;
- the project is large or complex.

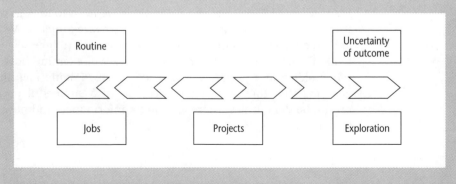

Figure 1.1   Activities most likely to benefit from project management

The more any of these factors apply to a task, the more difficult that task will be. Project size is particularly important. A project that employs 200 project personnel is going to be trickier to manage than one with just two people. The examples and exercises used in this book usually relate to smaller projects. This is just to make them more manageable from a learning point of view: the techniques and issues discussed are of equal relevance to larger projects.

Exercise 1.1

Consider the following:

- producing an edition of a newspaper
- building the Channel Tunnel
- getting married
- amending a financial computer system to deal with a common European currency
- a research project into what makes a good human–computer interface
- an investigation into the reason why a user has a problem with a computer system
- a second year programming assignment for a computing student
- writing an operating system for a new computer
- installing a new version of a word processing package in an organization.

Some would appear to merit the description 'project' more than others. Put them into an order that most closely matches your ideas of what constitutes a project. For each entry in the ordered list, describe the difference between it and the one above which makes it less worthy of the term 'project'.

There is no one correct answer to this exercise, but a possible solution to this and the other exercises you will come across may be found at the end of the book.

1.3 Software projects versus other types of project

Brooks, F. P. (1987). 'No silver bullet: essence and accidents of software engineering'. This essay has been included in *The Mythical Man-Month*, Anniversary Edition, Addision-Wesley, 1995.

Many of the techniques of general project management are applicable to software project management, but Fred Brooks pointed out that the products of software projects have certain characteristics which make them different.

One way of perceiving software project management is as the process of making visible that which is invisible.

Invisibility   When a physical artefact such as a bridge or road is being constructed the progress being made can actually be seen. With software, progress is not immediately visible.

Complexity   Per dollar, pound or euro spent, software products contain more complexity than other engineered artefacts.

Conformity   The 'traditional' engineer is usually working with physical systems and physical materials like cement and steel. These physical systems can have some complexity, but are governed by physical laws that are consistent. Software developers have to conform to the requirements of human clients. It is not just that individuals can be inconsistent. Organizations, because of lapses in collective memory, in internal communication or in effective decision-making can exhibit remarkable 'organizational stupidity' that developers have to cater for.

Flexibility   The ease with which software can be changed is usually seen as one of its strengths. However, this means that where the software system interfaces with a physical or organizational system, it is expected that, where necessary, the software will change to accommodate the other components rather than vice versa. This means the software systems are likely to be subject to a high degree of change.

1.4   Contract management and technical project management

Many organizations contract out IT development to outside specialist developers. In such cases, the client organization will often appoint a 'project manager' to supervise the contract. This project manager will be able to delegate many technically oriented decisions to the contractors. For instance, the project manager will not be concerned about estimating the effort needed to write individual software components as long as the overall project is fulfilled within budget and on time. On the supplier side, there will need to be project managers who are concerned with the more technical management issues. This book leans towards the concerns of these 'technical' project managers.

1.5   Activities covered by software project management

Chapter 4 on project analysis and technical planning looks at some alternative life cycles.

A software project is not only concerned with the actual writing of software. In fact, where a software application is bought in 'off the shelf', there may be no software writing as such. This is still fundamentally a software project because so many of the other elements associated with this type of project are present.

Usually there are three successive processes that bring a new system into being – see Figure 1.2.

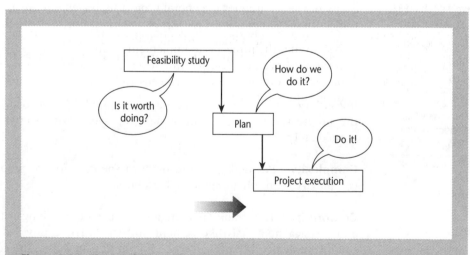

Figure 1.2   The feasibility study/plan/execution cycle

An outline of the content of a feasibility study is shown in Annex 1 to this chapter.

Appendix C contains a brief description of programme management.

The PRINCE2 method which is described in Appendix A takes this planning by stages approach.

Annex 2 to this chapter, has an outline of the content of a plan.

1. **The feasibility study**   This is an investigation into whether a prospective project is worth starting. Information is gathered about the requirements of the proposed application. The probable developmental and operational costs, along with the value of the benefits of the new system, are estimated. With a large system, the feasibility study could be treated as a project in its own right – and have its own planning sub-phase. The study could be part of a strategic planning exercise examining and prioritizing a range of potential software developments. Sometimes an organization has a policy where a group of projects is planned as a *programme* of development.

2. **Planning**   If the feasibility study produces results which indicate that the prospective project appears viable, planning of the project can take place. However, for a large project, we would not do all our detailed planning right at the beginning. We would formulate an outline plan for the whole project and a detailed one for the first stage. More detailed planning of the later stages would be done as they approached. This is because we would have more detailed and accurate information upon which to base our plans nearer to the start of the later stages.

3. **Project execution**   The project can now be executed. The execution of a project often contains *design* and *implementation* sub-phases. Students new to project planning often find it difficult to separate planning and design, and often the boundary between the two can be hazy. Essentially, design is thinking and making decisions about the precise form of the *products* that the project is to create. In the case of software, this could relate to the external appearance of the software, that is, the user interface, or the internal architecture. The plan lays down the *activities* that have to be carried out in order to create these products. Planning and design can be confused because at the most detailed level, planning decisions are influenced by design decisions. For example, if a software product is to have five major components, then it is likely that there will be five groups of activities that will create them.

Figure 1.3 suggests that these stages must be done strictly in sequence – we will see in Chapter 4 that other, iterative, approaches can be adopted. However, the actual activities listed here would still be done.

Individual projects are likely to differ considerably but a classic project life cycle is shown in Figure 1.3. The stages in the life cycle are described in a little more detail below:

● *Requirements analysis*   This is finding out in detail what the users require of the system that the project is to implement. Some work along these lines will almost certainly have been carried out when the project was evaluated, but now the original information obtained needs to be updated and supplemented. Several different approaches to the users' requirements may be explored. For example, a

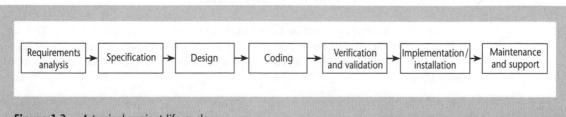

Figure 1.3   A typical project life cycle

small system which satisfies some, but not all, of the users' needs at a low price might be compared to a system with more functions but a higher price.

- *Specification* Detailed documentation of what the proposed system is to do.
- *Design* A design has to be drawn up which meets the specification. As noted earlier, this design will be in two stages. One will be the external or user design concerned with the external appearance of the application. The other produces the physical design which tackles the way that the data and software procedures are to be structured internally.
- *Coding* This may refer to writing code in a procedural language such as C or Ada, or could refer to the use of an application-builder such as Microsoft Access. Even where software is not being built from scratch, some modification to the base package could be required to meet the needs of the new application.
- *Verification and validation* Whether software is developed specially for the current application or not, careful testing will be needed to check that the proposed system meets its requirements.
- *Implementation/installation* Some system development practitioners refer to the whole of the project after design as 'implementation' (that is, the implementation of the design) while others insist that the term refers to the installation of the system after the software has been developed. In this latter case it includes setting up operational data files and system parameters, writing user manuals and training users of the new system.
- *Maintenance and support* Once the system has been implemented there is a continuing need for the correction of any errors that may have crept into the system and for extensions and improvements to the system. Maintenance and support activities may be seen as a series of minor software projects. In many environments, most software development is in fact maintenance.

Exercise 1.2 Brightmouth College is a higher education institution which used to be managed by a local government authority but has now become autonomous. Its payroll is still administered by the local authority and pay slips and other output are produced in the local authority's computer centre. The authority now charges the college for this service. The college management are of the opinion that it would be cheaper to obtain an 'off-the-shelf' payroll package and do the payroll processing themselves.

What would be the main stages of the project to convert to independent payroll processing by the college? Bearing in mind that an off-the-shelf package is to be used, how would this project differ from one where the software was to be written from scratch?

1.6 Plans, methods and methodologies

A plan for an activity must be based on some idea of a *method* of work. To take a simple example, if you were asked to test some software, even though you do not know anything about the software to be tested, you could assume that you would need to:

- analyse the requirements for the software;
- devise and write test cases that will check that each requirement has been satisfied;

- create test scripts and expected results for each test case;
- compare the actual results and the expected results and identify discrepancies.

While a *method* relates to a type of activity in general, a *plan* takes that method (and perhaps others) and converts it to real activities, identifying for each activity:

- its start and end dates;
- who will carry it out;
- what tools and materials will be used.

'Material' in this context could be information, for example, a requirements document.

With complex procedures, several methods may be deployed, in sequence or in parallel. The output from one method might be the input to another. Groups of methods or techniques are often referred to as *methodologies*. Object oriented design, for example, can be seen as a methodology made up of several component methods.

1.7 Some ways of categorizing software projects

See Simon Bennett, Steve McRobb and Ray Farmer, *Object Oriented Systems Analysis and Design using UML*, McGraw-Hill, 1999.

It is important to distinguish between the main types of software project because what is appropriate in one context may not be so in another. For example, some have suggested that the object-oriented approach, while useful in many contexts, might not be ideal for designing applications to be built around relational databases.

Information systems versus embedded systems

Embedded systems are also called real-time or industrial systems.

A distinction may be made between *information systems* and *embedded systems*. Very crudely, the difference is that in the former case the system interfaces with the organization, whereas in the latter case the system interfaces with a machine. A stock control system would be an information system that controls when the organization reorders stock. An embedded, or process control, system might control the air-conditioning equipment in a building. Some systems may have elements of both so that the stock control system might also control an automated warehouse.

Exercise 1.3

Would an operating system on a computer be an information system or an embedded system?

Objectives versus products

Projects may be distinguished by whether their aim is to produce a *product* or to meet certain *objectives*.

Service level agreements are becoming increasingly important as organizations contract out functions to external service suppliers.

A project might be to create a product the details of which have been specified by the client. The client has the responsibility for justifying the product.

On the other hand, the project may be required to meet certain objectives. There could be several ways of achieving these objectives. A new information system might be implemented to improve some service to users inside or outside an organization. The level of service that is the target would be the subject of an agreement rather than the characteristics of a particular information system.

Many software projects have two stages. The first stage is an objectives-driven project which results in a recommended course of action and may even specify a new software system to meet identified requirements. The next stage is a project actually to create the software product.

Exercise 1.4 Would the project to implement an independent payroll system at the Brightmouth College described in Exercise 1.2 above be an objectives-driven project or a product-driven project?

1.8 What is management?

The Open University Software Project Management module (1987) suggested that management involves the following activities:

A convenient way of accessing this OU material is in D. Ince, H. Sharp and M. Woodman, *Introduction to Software Project Management and Quality Assurance*, McGraw-Hill, 1993.

- Planning – deciding what is to be done;
- Organizing – making arrangements;
- Staffing – selecting the right people for the job, etc.;
- Directing – giving instructions;
- Monitoring – checking on progress;
- Controlling – taking action to remedy hold-ups;
- Innovating – coming up with new solutions;
- Representing – liaising with users, etc.

Exercise 1.5 Paul Duggan is the manager of a software development section. On Tuesday at 10.00 am he and his fellow section heads have a meeting with their group manager about the staffing requirements for the coming year. Paul has already drafted a document 'bidding' for staff. This is based on the work planned for his section for the next year. The document is discussed at the meeting. At 2.00 pm Paul has a meeting with his senior staff about an important project his section is undertaking. One of the programming staff has just had a road accident and will be in hospital for some time. It is decided that the project can be kept on schedule by transferring another team member from less urgent work to this project. A temporary replacement is to be brought in to do the less urgent work, but this may take a week or so to arrange. Paul has to phone both the personnel manager about getting a replacement and the user for whom the less urgent work is being done explaining why it is likely to be delayed.

Identify which of the eight management responsibilities listed above Paul was responding to at different points during his day.

1.9 Problems with software projects

One way of deciding what ought to be covered in 'software project management' is to consider what the problems are that it should address.

Traditionally, management has been seen as the preserve of a distinct class within the organization. As technology has made the tasks undertaken by an organization more sophisticated, many management tasks have become dispersed throughout the organization: there are management systems rather than managers.

Nevertheless the successful project will normally have one person who is charged with its success. Such people are focused on the overcoming of obstacles to success – they are primarily trouble-shooters and their job is likely to be shaped by the problems that confront the project. A survey of managers published by Thayer, Pyster and Wood identified the following commonly experienced problems:

Further details of the survey can be found in 'Major issues in software engineering project management', *IEEE Transactions on Software Engineering*, 7, 333–342, 1981.

- poor estimates and plans;
- lack of quality standards and measures;
- lack of guidance about making organizational decisions;
- lack of techniques to make progress visible;
- poor role definition – who does what?
- incorrect success criteria.

The above list looks at the project from the manager's point of view. What about the staff who make up the members of the project team? Below is a list of the problems identified by a number of students on a Computing and Information Systems course who had just completed a year's industrial placement:

- inadequate specification of work;
- management ignorance of IT;
- lack of knowledge of application area;
- lack of standards;
- lack of up-to-date documentation;
- preceding activities not completed on time – including late delivery of equipment;
- lack of communication between users and technicians;
- lack of communication leading to duplication of work;
- lack of commitment – especially when a project is tied to one person who then moves;
- narrow scope of technical expertise;
- changing statutory requirements;
- changing software environment;
- deadline pressure;
- lack of quality control;
- remote management;
- lack of training.

Many of the problems that were identified by the students stem from poor communications. A factor that contributes to this is the wide range of IT specialisms – an organization may be made up of lots of individuals each of whom is expert in one set of software techniques and tools but ignorant of those used by his or her colleagues. Communication problems are therefore bound to arise.

What about the problems faced by the customers of the products of computer projects? Here are some recent stories in the press:

Stephen Flower's *Software Failure, Management Failure,* Wiley, 1996, is an interesting survey of failed computer projects.

- The US Internal Revenue System was to abandon its tax system modernization programme after having spent $4 billion.
- The state of California spent $1 billion on its non-functional welfare database system.

- The £339 million UK air traffic control system was reported as being two years behind schedule.

- A discount stock brokerage company had 50 people working 14 hours or more a day to correct clerically three months of records – the report commented that the new system had been rushed into operation without adequate testing.

- In the United Kingdom, a Home Office immigration service computerization project was reported as having missed two deadlines and was nine months late.

- The Public Accounts Committee of the House of Commons in the United Kingdom blamed software bugs and management errors for £12 million of project costs in relation to an implementation of a Ministry of Agriculture computer system to administer farm subsidies.

Most of the stories above relate to public sector organizations. This may be misleading – private sector organizations tend to conceal their disasters and in any case many of the public projects above were actually carried out by private sector contractors. Any lingering faith by users in the innate ability of IT people to plan ahead properly will have been removed by the 'millennium bug', a purely self-inflicted IT problem. On balance it might be a good idea *not* to survey users about their problems with IT projects!

1.10   Setting objectives

Project objectives should be clearly defined.

To have a successful software project, the manager and the project team members must know what will constitute success. This will make them concentrate on what is essential to project success.

There may be several sets of users of a system and there may be several different groups of specialists involved in its development. There is a need for well-defined objectives that are accepted by all these people. Where there is more than one user group then a *project authority* needs to be identified which has overall authority over what the project is to achieve.

This committee is likely to contain user, development and management representatives.

This authority is often held by a *project steering committee* (or *project board*) which has overall responsibility for setting, monitoring and modifying objectives. The project manager still has responsibility for running the project on a day-to-day basis, but has to report to the steering committee at regular intervals. Only the steering committee can authorize changes to the project objectives and resources.

Sub-objectives and goals

Defining sub-objectives requires assumptions about how the main objective is to be achieved.

Setting objectives can be used to guide and motivate individuals and groups of staff. To be useful, though, the objective set for an individual must be something that is within the control of that individual. An objective might be set that the software application to be produced must pay for itself by reducing staff costs over two years. As an overall business objective this might be reasonable. For software developers it would be unreasonable as, though they can control development costs, any reduction in operational staff costs depends not just on them, but also on the operational management after the application has 'gone live'. What would be appropriate would be to set a *goal* or sub-objective for the software developers to keep development costs within a certain budget.

Thus, objectives will need to be broken down into goals or sub-objectives. Here we say that in order to achieve the objective we must achieve certain goals first. These goals are steps on the way to achieving an objective, just as goals scored in a football match are steps towards the objective of winning the match.

Exercise 1.6

Bearing in mind the above discussion of objectives, comment on the appropriateness of the wording of each of the following 'objectives' for software developers:

(i)   to implement the new application on time and within budget;

(ii) to implement the new software application with as few software errors as possible that might lead to operational failures;

(iii) to design a system that is user friendly;

(iv) to produce full documentation for the new system.

Measures of effectiveness

Effective objectives are concrete and well defined. Vague aspirations such as 'to improve customer relations' are unsatisfactory. Objectives should be such that it is obvious to all whether the project has been successful or not. Ideally there should be *measures of effectiveness* which tell us how successful the project has been. For example, 'to reduce customer complaints by 50%' would be more satisfactory as an objective than 'to improve customer relations'. The measure can, in some cases, be an answer to simple yes/no question, e.g. 'Did we install the new software by 1st June?'

One of the authors, Bob Hughes, explores measurement issues in detail in the companion textbook *Practical Software Measurement*, McGraw-Hill, 2000.

A measure of effectiveness will usually be related to the installed operational system. 'Mean time between failures' (mtbf) might, for example, be used to measure reliability. Such measures are *performance* measures and, as such, can only be taken once the system is operational. Project managers will want to get some idea of the likely performance of the completed system as it is being constructed. They will therefore be seeking *predictive* measures. For example. a large number of errors found during code inspections might indicate potential problems later with reliability.

Exercise 1.7

Identify the objectives and sub-objectives of the Brightmouth College payroll project. What measures of effectiveness could be used to check the success in achieving the objectives of the project?

1.11 Stakeholders

These are people who have a stake or interest in the project. It is important that they be identified as early as possible, because you need to set up adequate communication channels with them right from the start. The project leader also has to be aware that not everybody who is involved with a project has the same motivation and objectives. The end-users might, for instance, be concerned about the ease of use of the system while their managers might be interested in the staff savings the new system will allow.

Stakeholders might be internal to the project team, external to the project team but in the same organization, or totally external to the organization.

- *Internal to the project team* This means that they will be under the direct managerial control of the project leader.
- *External to the project team but within the same organization* For example, the project leader might need the assistance of the information management group in order to add some additional data types to a data base or the assistance of the users to carry out systems testing. Here the commitment of the people involved has to be negotiated.
- *External to both the project team and the organization* External stakeholders may be customers (or users) who will benefit from the system that the project implements or contractors who will carry out work for the project. One feature of the relationship with these people is that it is likely to be based on a legally binding contract.

B. W. Boehm and R. Ross 'Theory W Software Project Management: Principles and Examples', in B. W. Boehm (ed.) *Software Risk Management*, CS Press, Los Alamitos, CA, 1989.

Within each of the general categories there will be various groups. For example, there will be different types of user with different types of interests.

Different types of stakeholder may have different objectives and one of the jobs of the successful project leader is to recognize these different interests and to be able to reconcile them. It should therefore come as no surprise that the project leader needs to be a good communicator and negotiator. Boehm and Ross proposed a 'Theory W' of software project management where the manager concentrates on creating situations where all parties involved in a project benefit from it and therefore have an interest in its success. (The 'W' stands for Everyone a Winner.)

Exercise 1.8 Identify the stakeholders in the Brightmouth College payroll project.

1.12 The business case

Most projects need to have a justification or business case: the effort and expense of pushing the project through must be seen to be worthwhile in terms of the benefits that will eventually be felt. A cost–benefit analysis will often be part of the project's feasibility study. This will itemize and quantify the project's costs and benefits. The benefits will be affected by the completion date: the sooner the project is completed, the sooner the benefits can be experienced. The quantification of benefits will often require the formulation of a *business model* which explains how the new application can generate the claimed benefits.

A simple example of a business model is that a new web-based application might allow customers from all over the world to order a firm's products via the internet, increasing sales and thus increasing revenue and profits.

Any project plan must ensure that the business case is kept intact, for example:

- that development costs are not allowed to rise to a level which threatens to exceed the value of benefits;
- that the features of the system are not reduced to a level that the expected benefits cannot be realized;
- that the delivery date is not delayed so that there is an unacceptable loss of benefits.

1.13 Requirement specification

Very often, especially in the case of product-driven projects, the objectives of the project are carefully defined in terms of functional requirements, quality requirements and resource requirements.

- *Functional requirements* These define what the end-product of the project is to do. Systems analysis and design methods, such as SADT and Information Engineering, are designed primarily to provide functional requirements.

These are sometimes called non-functional requirements.

- *Quality requirements* There will be other attributes of the application to be implemented that do not relate so much to what the system is to do but how it is to do it. These are still things that the user will be able to experience. They include, for example, response time, the ease of using the system and its reliability.

- *Resource requirements* A record of how much the organization is willing to spend on the system. There may be a trade-off between this and the time it takes to implement the system. In general it costs disproportionately more to implement a system by an earlier date than a later one. There may also be a trade-off between the functional and quality requirements and cost. We would all like exceptionally reliable and user-friendly systems which do exactly what we want but we may not be able to afford them.

All these requirements must be consistent with the business case.

1.14 Management control

In general, management can be seen as the process of setting objectives for a system and then monitoring the system to see what its true performance is. In Figure 1.4 the 'real world' is shown as being rather formless. Especially in the case of large undertakings there will be a lot going on about which management should be aware.

Exercise 1.9 An IT project is to replace locally held paper-based records with a centrally organized database. Staff in a large number of offices that are geographically dispersed need training and then need to use the new IT system to set up the back-log of manual records on the new database. The system cannot be properly operational until the last record has been transferred. The new system will only be successful if new transactions can be processed within certain time cycles.

Identify the data that you would collect to ensure that during execution of the project things were going to plan.

This will involve the local managers in *data collection*. Bare details, such as 'location X has processed 2000 documents' will not be very useful to higher management: *data processing* will be needed to transform this raw *data* into useful *information*. This might be in such forms as 'percentage of records processed', 'average documents processed per day per person' and 'estimated completion date'.

In our example, the project management might examine the 'estimated completion date' for completing data transfer for each branch. These can be checked against the overall target date for completion of this phase of the project. In effect they are comparing actual performance with one aspect of the overall project objectives. They might find that one or two branches will fail to complete the transfer of details in time. They would then need to consider what to do (this is represented in Figure 1.4 by the box 'making decisions/plans'). One possibility would be to move staff temporarily from one branch to another. If this is done, there is always the danger that while the completion date for the one branch is pulled back to before the overall target date, the date for the branch from which staff are being moved is pushed forward beyond that date. The project manager would need to calculate carefully what the impact would be of moving staff from particular branches. This is *modelling* the consequences of a potential solution. Several different proposals could be modelled in this way before one was chosen for *implementation*.

Having implemented the decision, the situation needs to be kept under review by collecting and processing further progress details. For instance, the next time that progress is reported, a branch to which staff have been transferred could still be behind in transferring details. The reason why the branch has got behind in transferring details may be because the manual records are incomplete and another department, for whom the project has a low priority, has to be involved in providing the missing information. In this case, transferring extra staff to do data inputting will not have accelerated data transfer.

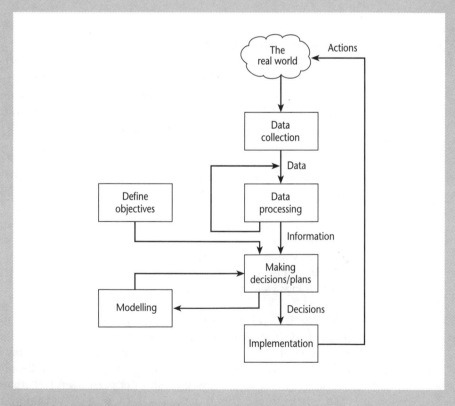

Figure 1.4   The project control cycle

It can be seen that a project plan is dynamic and will need constant adjustment during the execution of the project.

1.15 Conclusion

This chapter has laid a foundation for the remainder of the book by defining what is meant by various terms such as 'software project' and 'management'. Among some of the more important points that have been made are the following:

- Projects are by definition non-routine and therefore more uncertain than normal undertakings.
- Software projects are similar to other projects, but have some attributes that present particular difficulties, e.g. the relative invisibility of many of their products.
- A key factor in project success is having clear objectives. Different stakeholders in a project, however, are likely to have different objectives. This points to the need for a recognized overall project authority.
- For objectives to be effective there must be practical ways of testing that the objectives have been met.
- Where projects involve many different people, effective channels of information have to be established. Having objective measures of success helps unambiguous communication between the various parties to a project.

Annex 1 Contents list for a feasibility study

- Introduction: identifies what the document is;
- Description of current situation;
- Problem description;
- Proposed development
  - business and financial aspects
  - technical aspects
  - organizational aspects;
- Estimated costs
  - development costs
  - operational costs;
- Envisaged benefits;
- Recommendation.

Annex 2 Contents list for a project plan

- Introduction;
- Background: including reference to the business case;
- Project objectives;
- Constraints: these could be included with project objectives;

The detail that goes into these sections will be explained in later chapters. For example, Chapter 7 relates to risk while Chapter 12 explains aspects of the management of quality.

- Project products: both deliverable products that the client will receive and intermediate products;
- Methods;
- Activities to be carried out;
- Resources to be used;
- Risks to the project;
- Management of the project, including
  - organizational responsibilities
  - management of quality
  - configuration management.

1.16 Further exercises

1. List the problems you experienced when you carried out a recent IT-related assignment. Try to put these problems into some order of magnitude. For each problem consider whether there was some way in which the problem could have been reduced by better organization and planning by yourself.

2. Identify the main types of personnel employed in an information systems department. For each stage of a typical IS development project, list the types of personnel who are likely to be involved.

3. A public library is considering the implementation of a computer-based system to help administer book loans at libraries. Identify the stakeholders in such a project. What might be the objectives of such a project and how might the success of the project be measured in practical terms?

4. A software house has developed a customized order processing system for a client. You are an employee of the software house that has been asked to organize a training course for the end-users of the system. At present, a user handbook has been produced, but no specific training material. A plan is now needed for the project which will set up the delivery of the training courses. The project can be assumed to have been completed when the first training course starts. Among the things that will need to be considered are the following:

   - Training materials will need to be designed and created;
   - A timetable will need to be drafted and agreed;
   - Date(s) for the course will need to be arranged;
   - The people attending the course will need to be identified and notified;
   - Rooms and computer facilities for the course will need to be provided for.

   (a) Identify the stakeholders for this project.
   (b) Draw up a list of the stakeholders for this project.
   (c) For each of the objectives, identify the measures of effectivness.
   (d) For each objective, write down the stakeholders who will be responsible for the achievement of that objective.
   (e) For each objective/stakeholder pair identified in (d), draft a statement of their goal or sub-objective.

5. A manager is in charge of a sub-project of a larger project. The sub-project requires the transfer of paper documents into a computer-based document retrieval system and their subsequent indexing so that they can be accessed via key words. Optical

character readers are to be used for the initial transfer but the text then needs to be clerically checked and corrected by staff. The project is currently scheduled to take twelve months using permanent staff. A small budget is available to hire temporary staff in the case of staff absences through holidays, sickness or temporary transfer to other, more urgent, jobs. Discuss the control system that will need to be in place to control this sub-project.

CHAPTER 2

Step Wise: an overview of project planning

Objectives

When you have completed this chapter you will be able to:

- approach project planning in an organized step-by-step manner;
- see where the techniques described in other chapters fit into an overall planning approach;
- repeat the planning process in more detail for sets of activities within a project as the time comes to execute them.

2.1 Introduction to Step Wise project planning

This chapter describes a framework of basic steps in project planning upon which the following chapters build. There are many different techniques which can be used in project planning and this chapter gives an overview of the points at which these techniques can be used during project planning. Chapter 4 will illustrate how different projects might be different approaches, but this framework should always apply to the planning process used.

Appendix A adds some further details about the PRINCE 2 approach.

The framework described is called the Step Wise method to help to distinguish it from other methods such as PRINCE 2. PRINCE 2 is a set of project management standards that were originally sponsored by the Central Computing and Telecommunications Agency (CCTA) for use on British government IT projects. The standards are also widely used on non-government projects in the United Kingdom. Step Wise should be compatible with PRINCE 2. It should be noted, however, that Step Wise only covers the planning stages of a project and not monitoring and control.

In order to illustrate the Step Wise approach and how it might have to be adapted to deal with different circumstances, two parallel examples are used. Let us assume that there are two former Computing and Information Systems students who now have several years of software development experience under their belts.

Brightmouth College Payroll and International Office Equipment Group Maintenance Accounts

Brigette has been working for the Management Services department of a local authority when she sees an advertisement for the position of Information Systems Development Officer at Brightmouth College. She is attracted to the idea of being her own boss, working in a relatively small organization and helping them to set up appropriate information systems from scratch. She applies for the job and gets it. One of the first tasks that confronts her is the implementation of independent payroll processing! (This scenario has already been used as the basis of some examples in Chapter 1.)

Amanda works for International Office Equipment (IOE), which manufactures and supplies various items of high-technology office equipment. An expanding area of their work is the maintenance of IT equipment. They have now started to undertake maintenance of equipment for which they were not originally the suppliers. A computer-based batch processing system deals with invoicing on a job-by-job basis. An organization might have to call IOE out several times to deal with different bits of equipment and there is a need to be able to group the invoice details for work done into 'group accounts' for which monthly statements will be produced. Amanda has been given her first project management role, the task of implementing this extension to the invoicing system.

In Table 2.1 we outline the general approach that might be taken to planning these projects. Figure 2.1 provides an outline of the main planning activities. Steps 1 and 2 'Identify project scope and objectives' and 'Identify project infrastructure' could be tackled in parallel in some cases. Steps 5 and 6 will need to be repeated for each activity in the project.

A major principle of project planning is to plan in outline first and then in more detail as the time to carry out an activity approaches. Hence the lists of products and activities that are the result of Step 4 will be reviewed when the tasks connected with a particular phase of a project are considered in more detail. This will be followed by a more detailed iteration of Steps 5 to 8 for the phase under consideration.

2.2 Step 0: Select project

Chapter 3 discusses project evaluation in more detail.

This is called Step 0 because in a way it is outside the main project planning process. Projects are not initiated out of thin air – some process must decide to start this project rather than some other. While a feasibility study might suggest that the project is worthwhile, it would still need to be established that it should be done before other projects also found to be worthwhile. This project evaluation may be done on an individual basis or as part of strategic planning.

Table 2.1 An outline of Step Wise planning activities

Step	Activities within step
0	Select project
1	Identify project scope and objectives
	1.1 Identify objectives and measures of effectiveness in meeting them
	1.2 Establish a project authority
	1.3 Identify stakeholders
	1.4 Modify objectives in the light of stakeholder analysis
	1.5 Establish methods of communications with all parties
2	Identify project infrastructure
	2.1 Establish relationship between project and strategic planning
	2.2 Identify installation standards and procedures
	2.3 Identify project team organization
3	Analyse project characteristics
	3.1 Distinguish the project as either objective or product driven
	3.2 Analyse other project characteristics
	3.3 Identify high-level project risks
	3.4 Take into account user requirements concerning implementation
	3.5 Select general life cycle approach
	3.6 Review overall resource estimates
4	Identify project products and activities
	4.1 Identify and describe project products (including quality criteria)
	4.2 Document generic product flows
	4.3 Recognize product instances
	4.4 Produce ideal activity network
	4.5 Modify ideal to take into account need for stages and checkpoints
5	Estimate effort for each activity
	5.1 Carry out bottom-up estimates
	5.2 Revise plan to create controllable activities
6	Identify activity risks
	6.1 Identify and quantify activity-based risks
	6.2 Plan risk reduction and contingency measures where appropriate
	6.3 Adjust plans and estimates to take account of risks
7	Allocate resources
	7.1 Identify and allocate resources
	7.2 Revise plans and estimates to account for resource constraints
8	Review/publicize plan
	8.1 Review quality aspects of project plan
	8.2 Document plans and obtain agreement
9/10	Execute plan/lower levels of planning
	This may require the reiteration of the planning process at a lower level

2.3 Step 1: Identify project scope and objectives

The activities in this step ensure that all the parties to the project agree on the objectives and are committed to the success of the project. A danger to be avoided is overlooking people who are affected by the project.

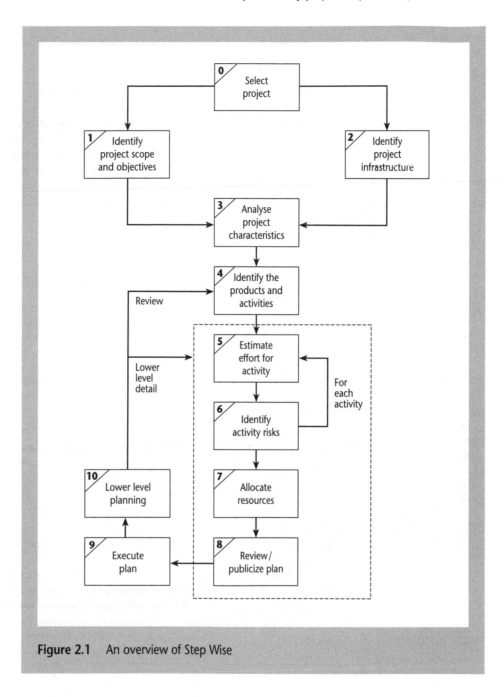

Figure 2.1   An overview of Step Wise

Step 1.1   Identify objectives and practical measures of the effectiveness in meeting those objectives

We discussed in Chapter 1 the need for agreed objectives for a project and ways of measuring the success in achieving those objectives.

Project objectives

The project objectives for the Brightmouth College payroll project have already been discussed in Exercise 1.7.

Amanda at IOE has the objectives clearly laid down for her in the recommendations of a feasibility study report which have been accepted by IOE management. The main objectives are to allow a detailed monthly statement to be sent to group account clients and to be able to reallocate the cash received to individual jobs when the client has paid on the monthly statement. Other objectives are laid down that refer to expected timescales and the resources that might be used.

Step 1.2 Establish a project authority

We have already noted in Chapter 1 that a single overall project authority needs to be established so that there is unity of purpose among all those concerned.

Throughout the text we use capitalized initial letters to indicate a term that has a precise meaning in the PRINCE 2 standards, e.g. Project Board.

Project authorities

Amanda finds that her manager and the main user management have already set up a Project Board which will have overall direction of the project. She is a little concerned as the equipment maintenance staff are organized with different sections dealing with different types of equipment. This means that a customer could have work done by several different sections. Not all the sections are represented on the Project Board and Amanda is aware that there are some differences of opinion between some sections. It is left to the user representatives on the board to resolve those differences and to present an agreed policy to the systems developers.

Brigette finds that effectively she has two different clients for the payroll system: the finance and personnel departments. To help resolve conflicts, it is agreed that the managers of both departments should attend a monthly meeting with the Vice-Principal which Brigette has arranged in order to steer the project.

Step 1.3 Stakeholder analysis – identify all stakeholders in the project and their interests

Recall that this was the basis of a discussion in Chapter 1. Essentially all the parties who have an interest in the project need to be identified. In that chapter we listed as an example the stakeholders in the Brightmouth College Payroll project.

Exercise 2.1 What important stakeholders outside the IOE organization might be considered in the case of the IOE Maintenance Group Accounts System?

Step 1.4 **Modify objectives in the light of stakeholder analysis**

In order to gain the full cooperation of all concerned, it might be necessary to modify the project objectives. This could mean adding new features to the system which give a benefit to some stakeholders as a means of assuring their commitment to the project. This is potentially dangerous as the system size may be increased and the original objectives obscured. Because of these dangers, it is suggested that this process be done consciously and in a controlled manner.

CASE STUDY
EXAMPLES

Modified project objectives

The IOE maintenance staff are to be given the extra task of entering data about completed jobs. They do not benefit from this additional work. To give some benefit, the system is to be extended to automatically reorder spare parts when required.

At Brightmouth College, the personnel department has a lot of work preparing payroll details for finance. It would be tactful to agree to produce some management information reports for personnel from the payroll details held on the computer.

Step 1.5 **Establish methods of communication with all parties**

For internal staff this should be fairly straightforward, but a project leader implementing a payroll system would need to find a contact point with BACS (Bankers Automated Clearing Scheme) for instance.

2.4 Step 2: Identify project infrastructure

Projects are rarely initiated in a vacuum. There is usually some kind of existing infrastructure into which the project can fit. If they do not know already, project leaders must find out the precise nature of this infrastructure.

Step 2.1 **Identify relationship between the project and strategic planning**

Some of the issues of strategic planning are addressed in Chapter 3.

As well as identifying projects to be carried out, an organization needs to decide in what order these projects are to be carried out. It also needs to establish the framework within which the proposed new systems are to fit. Hardware and software standards, for example, are needed so that various systems can communicate with each other. These strategic decisions must be documented in a strategic business plan or in an information technology plan that is developed from the business plan.

Step 2.2 **Identify installation standards and procedures**

Any organization that develops software should define their development procedures. As a minimum, the normal stages in the software life cycle to be carried out should be documented along with the products created at each stage.

CASE STUDY
EXAMPLES

Role of existing strategic plans

Amanda finds at IOE that there is a well-defined rolling strategic plan which has identified her group accounts subsystem as an important required development. Because it is an extension of an existing system, the hardware and software platforms upon which the application are to run are dictated.

Brigette at Brightmouth College finds that there is an overall college strategic plan which describes new courses to be developed, and so on, and mentions in passing the need for 'appropriate administrative procedures' to be in place. There is a recommendation that independent payroll processing be undertaken in a short section in a consultant's report from an accountancy firm concerning the implications of financial autonomy. Although the college has quite a lot of IT equipment for teaching purposes, there is no machine set aside for payroll processing and the intention is that the hardware to run the payroll will be acquired at the same time as the software.

See Chapter 9 on Monitoring and Control.

Change control and *configuration management* standards should be in place to ensure that changes to requirements are implemented in a safe and orderly way.

The procedural standards may lay down the quality checks that need to be done at each point of the project life cycle or these may be documented in a separate *quality standards and procedures* manual.

The organization as part of its monitoring and control policy may have a *measurement programme* in place which dictates that certain statistics have to be collected at various stages of a project.

Finally the project manager should be aware of any *project planning and control standards*. These will relate to how the project is controlled: for example, the way that the hours spent by team members on individual tasks are recorded on timesheets

CASE STUDY
EXAMPLES

Identifying standards

Amanda at IOE finds that there is a very weighty volume of development standards which, among other things, specifies that SSADM will be the analysis and design method used. She finds that a separate document has been prepared which lays down quality procedures. This specifies when the reviews of work will be carried out and describes detailed procedures about how the reviews are to be done. Amanda also finds a set of project management guidelines modelled closely on PRINCE 2.

Brigette finds no documents of the nature that Amanda found at IOE except for some handouts for students that have been produced by different lecturers at different times and which seem to contradict each other.

CASE STUDY EXAMPLES
CONTINUED ▶

As a stopgap measure, Brigette writes a brief document which states what the main stages of a 'project' (perhaps 'job for the user' would be a better term in this context) should be. This happens to be very similar to the list given in Chapter 1. She stresses that:

● no job of work to change a system or implement a new one is to be done without there being a detailed specification first;

● the users must record agreement to each specification in writing before the work is carried out.

She draws up a simple procedure for recording all changes to user requirements.

Brigette, of course, has no organizational quality procedures, but she dictates that each person in the group (including herself) has to get someone else to check through their work when they finish a major task and that, before any new or amended software is handed over to the users, someone other than the original producer should test it. She sets up a simple system to record errors found in system testing and their resolution. She also creates a log file of reported user problems with operational systems.

Brigette does not worry about time sheets but arranges an informal meeting with her colleagues each Monday morning to discuss how things are going and also arranges to see the Vice-Principal, who is her official boss, and the heads of the finance and personnel sections each month to review progress in general terms.

Step 2.3   Identify project team organization

Some of these issues will be discussed in Chapter 11 – Managing people and organizing teams.

Project leaders, especially in the case of large projects, might have some control over the organizational structure of the project team. More often, though, the organizational structure will be dictated to them. For example, a high-level managerial decision might have been taken that programmers and systems analysts will be in different groups, or that the development of PC applications will be done within a separate group from that responsible for 'traditional' main frame applications.

If the project leader does have some control over the project team organization then this would best be considered at a later stage (see Step 7: Allocate resources).

CASE STUDY
EXAMPLES

Project organization

At IOE, there are groups of systems analysts set up as teams that deal with individual user departments. Hence the users always know whom they should contact within the information systems department if they have a problem. Programmers, however, work in a 'pool' and are allocated to specific projects on an *ad hoc* basis.

CASE STUDY EXAMPLES
CONTINUED

> At Brightmouth College, a programmer has been seconded to Brigette from the technicians supporting the computing courses in the college. She is also allowed to recruit a trainee analyst/programmer. She is not unduly worried about the organizational structure needed.

2.5 Step 3: Analyse project characteristics

The general purpose of this part of the planning operation is to ensure that the appropriate methods are used for the project.

Step 3.1 Distinguish the project as either objective or product driven

Chapter 4 elaborates on the process of analysing project characteristics.

This has already been discussed in the first chapter. As system development advances it tends to become more product driven, although the underlying objectives always remain and must be respected.

Step 3.2 Analyse other project characteristics (including quality-based ones)

For example, is an information system to be developed or a process control system, or will there be elements of both? Will the system be safety critical, where human life could be threatened by a malfunction?

Step 3.3 Identify high-level project risks

Consideration must be given to the risks that threaten the successful outcome of the project. Generally speaking most risks can be attributed to the operational or development environment, the technical nature of the project or the type of product being created.

CASE STUDY
EXAMPLES

High-level risks

At IOE Amanda identifies the danger of there being resistance to the new system by maintenance engineers, especially as a new centralized group accounts office is to be set up. Amanda decides therefore that additional efforts are needed to consult all sections involved and that the new procedures should be introduced in small increments to accustom staff to them gradually.

Brigette at Brightmouth College considers the application area to be very well defined. There is a risk, however, that there might be no package on the market which caters for the way that things are done at the moment. Brigette therefore decides that an early task in the project is to obtain information about the features of the main payroll packages that are available.

Step 3.4 Take into account user requirements concerning implementation

The clients will sometimes have their own procedural requirements. For example, work for UK government departments might require the use of SSADM.

Step 3.5 Select development methodology and life-cycle approach

Chapter 4 discusses life cycles in more detail.

The development methodology and project life cycle to be used for the project will be influenced by the issues raised above. The idea of a methodology, that is, the group of methods to be used in a project, was discussed in Chapter 1. For many software developers, the choice of methods will seem obvious: they will use the ones that they have always used in the past. In Chapter 4 we recommend caution in assuming that the current project is really similar to previous ones.

As well as the methods to be used, there are generic ways of structuring projects, such as the use of the life cycle outlined in Chapter 1, that need to be considered. If the setting of objectives involves identifying the problems to be solved, this part of planning is working out the ways in which these problems are to be solved. For a project that is novel to the planner, some research into the methods typically used in the problem domain is worthwhile. For example, sometimes, as part of a project, a questionnaire survey has to be conducted. There are lots of books on the techniques used in such surveys and a wise move would be to look at one or two of them at the planning stage.

Step 3.6 Review overall resource estimates

Chapter 5 goes into more detail on this topic. Function points are an attempt to measure system size without using lines of code.

Once the major risks have been identified and the broad project approach has been decided upon, this would be a good point at which to re-estimate the effort and other resources required to implement the project. Where enough information is available a function point-based estimate might be appropriate.

2.6 Step 4: Identify project products and activities

The more detailed planning of the individual activities now takes place. The longer term planning is broad and in outline, while the more immediate tasks are planned in some detail.

Step 4.1 Identify and describe project products (or deliverables)

In general there can be no project products which do not have activities which create them. Wherever possible, we ought also to ensure the reverse: that there are no activities that do not produce a tangible product. Identifying all the things the project is to create helps us to ensure that all the activities we need to carry out are accounted for. Some of these products will be handed over to the client at the end of the project – these are *deliverables*. Other products might not be in the final configuration, but are needed as *intermediate* products used in the process of creating the deliverables.

These products will include a large number of *technical* products including training material and operating instructions, but also products to do with the *management* and the *quality* of the project. Planning documents would, for example, be management products.

PRINCE 2 suggests that the PBS be presented as a hierarchy diagram. In practice it may be more convenient to produce a structured list.

The products will form a hierarchy. The main products will have sets of component products which in turn may have sub-component products and so on. These relationships can be documented in a Product Breakdown Structure (PBS).

Some products are created from scratch, for example, new software components. A product could quite easily be a document, like a software design document. It might be a new, modified, version of something that already exists, such as an amended piece of code. A product could even be a person, such as a 'trained user', a product of the process of training. Always remember that a product is the result of an activity. A common error is to identify as products things that are really activities such as 'training', 'design' and 'testing'. Specifying 'documentation' as a product should also be avoided – by itself this term is just too vague.

This part of the planning process draws heavily on the standards laid down in PRINCE 2. These specify that products at the bottom of the PBS should be documented by *Product Descriptions* which contain:

- the *name/identity* of the product
- the *purpose* of the product
- the *derivation* of the product (that is, the other products from which it is derived)
- the *composition* of the product
- the *form* of the product
- the relevant *standards*
- the *quality* criteria that should apply to it.

Product Breakdown Structures

At IOE, Amanda finds that there is a standard PBS that she can use as a checklist for her own project.

Brigette at Brightmouth College has no installation standard PBS, although she can, of course, refer to various books for standard checklists. She decides that one part of the PBS should contain the products needed to help select the appropriate hardware and software for the payroll application (Figure 2.2).

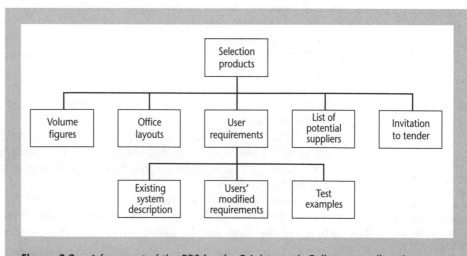

Figure 2.2 A fragment of the PBS for the Brightmouth College payroll project

Step 4.2 Document generic product flows

The PFD effectively documents, in outline, the methodology (see Chapter 1) for the project.

Some products will need one or more other products to exist first before they can be created. For example, a program design must be created before the program can be written and the program specification must exist before the design can be commenced. These relationships can be portrayed in a *Product Flow Diagram* (PFD). Figure 2.3 gives an example. Note that the 'flow' in the diagram is assumed to be from top to bottom and left to right. In the example in Figure 2.3, 'overall system specification' is in an oval as it is used by the project but is not created by it. It is often convenient to identify an overall product at the bottom of the diagram, 'operational system', say, into which all the other products feed.

Exercise 2.2

Draw up a possible Product Flow Diagram (PFD) based on the Product Breakdown Structure (PBS) shown in Figure 2.2. This represents the products generated when gathering information to be presented to potential suppliers of the hardware. The volume figures are for such things as the number of employees for whom records will have to be maintained.

CASE STUDY EXAMPLES

IOE has standard PFD

At IOE, Amanda has a standard installation PFD for software development projects. This is because a recognized software development method is used which lays down a sequence of documents that have to be produced. This sequence of products can be straightforwardly documented as a PFD.

Step 4.3 Recognize product instances

This may be delayed to later in the project when more information is known.

Where the same generic PFD fragment relates to more than one instance of a particular type of product, an attempt should be made to identify each of those instances.

CASE STUDY EXAMPLES

Identifying product instances

Amanda decides that there are likely to be four major software modules needed in her application for which the PFD fragment in Figure 2.3 would be appropriate
   The products that Brigette can identify at the present are all unique.

Step 4.4 Produce ideal activity network

In order to generate one product from another there must be one or more activities which carry out the transformation. By identifying these activities we can create an activity network which shows the tasks that have to be carried out and the order in which they have to be executed.

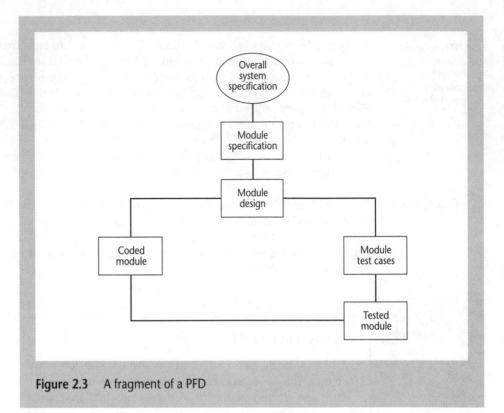

Figure 2.3 A fragment of a PFD

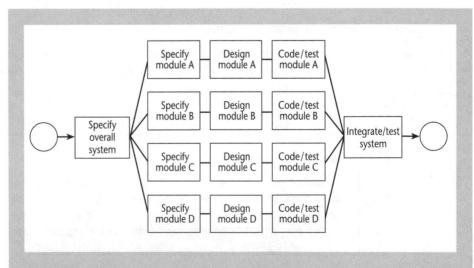

Figure 2.4 An activity network fragment for the IOE Maintenance Group Accounts project

CASE STUDY EXAMPLES

Activity network for IOE Maintenance Accounts

Part of the initial activity network for the IOE Maintenance Group Accounts project might look like Figure 2.4.

Exercise 2.3

Draw up an Activity Network for the Product Flow Diagram that you created in Exercise 2.2 (or the PFD given in the solution if you prefer!).

The activity networks are 'ideal' in the sense that no account has been taken of resource constraints. For example in Figure 2.4, it is assumed that resources are available for all four software modules to be developed in parallel.

Step 4.5 Modify the ideal to take into account need for stages and checkpoints

The approach to sequencing activities described above encourages the formulation of a plan that will minimize the overall duration, or 'elapsed time', for the project. It assumes that an activity will start as soon as the preceding ones upon which it depends have been completed.

There might, however, be a need to modify this by dividing the project into stages and introducing checkpoint activities. These are activities which draw together the products of preceding activities to check that they are compatible. This could potentially delay work on some elements of the project – there has to be a trade-off between efficiency and quality.

The people to whom the project manager reports could decide to leave the routine monitoring of activities to the project manager. However, there could be some key activities, or *milestones*, which represent the completion of important stages of the project of which they would want to take particular note. Checkpoint activities are often useful milestones.

Exercise 2.4

Amanda decides that after the four modules have been specified, the four specifications need to be carefully checked to see that they are consistent and compatible. Redraw the activity network in Figure 2.4 to reflect this.

2.7 Step 5: Estimate effort for each activity

Step 5.1 Carry out bottom-up estimates

Chapter 5 on Software effort estimation deals with this topic in more detail.

Some top-down estimates of effort, cost and duration will already have been done in the feasibility study and have been revisited in Step 3.6.

At this point, estimates of the staff effort required, the probable elapsed time and the non-staff resources needed for each activity will need to be produced. The method of arriving at each of these estimates will vary depending on the type of activity.

The difference between *elapsed time* and *effort* should be noted. Effort is the amount of work that needs to be done. If a task requires three members of staff to work for two full days each, the effort expended is six days. Elapsed time is the time between the start and end of a task. In our example above, if the three members of staff start and finish at the same time then the elapsed time for the activity would be two days.

The individual activity estimates of effort should be summed to get an overall bottom-up estimate which can be reconciled with the previous top-down estimate.

The activities on the activity network can be annotated with their elapsed times so that the overall duration of the project can be calculated.

Step 5.2   Revise plan to create controllable activities

The estimates for individual activities could reveal that some are going to take quite a long time. Long activities make a project difficult to control. If an activity involving system testing is to take 12 weeks, it would be difficult after six weeks to judge accurately whether 50% of the work is completed. It would be better to break this down into a series of smaller sub-tasks.

CASE STUDY EXAMPLES

IOE Maintenance Group Accounts – breaking activities down into manageable tasks

At IOE, Amanda has to estimate the lines of code for each of the software modules. She looks at programs that have been coded for similar types of application at IOE in the past to get some idea of the size of the new modules. She then refers to some conversion tables that the information systems development department at IOE have produced that convert the lines of code into estimates of effort. Other tables allow her to allocate the estimated effort to the various stages of the project.

Although Brigette is aware that some additional programs might have to be written to deal with local requirements, the main software is to be obtained 'off-the-shelf' and so estimating based on lines of code would clearly be inappropriate. Instead, she looks at each individual task and allocates a time. She realizes that in many cases these represent 'targets' as she is uncertain at the moment how long these tasks will really take (see Step 6 below).

There might be a number of activities that are important, but individually take up very little time. For a training course, there might be a need to book rooms and equipment, notify those attending, register students on the training system, order refreshments, copy training materials and so on. In a situation like this it would be easier to bundle the activities into a portmanteau activity 'make training course arrangements' which could be supplemented with a checklist.

In general, try to make activities about the length of the reporting period used for monitoring and controlling the project. If you have a progress meeting every two weeks, it would convenient to have activities of two weeks' duration on average, so that progress meetings would normally be made aware of completed tasks each time they are held.

2.8 Step 6: Identify activity risks

Step 6.1 Identify and quantify activity-based risks

Chapter 7 on Risk touches on this topic in more detail.

Risks inherent in the overall nature of the project have already been considered in Step 3. We now want to look at each activity in turn and assess the risks to its successful outcome. Any plan is always based on certain assumptions. Say the design of a component is planned to take five days. This is based on the assumption that the client's requirement is clear and unambiguous. If it is not then additional effort to clarify the requirement would be needed. The possibility that an assumption upon which a plan is based could be wrong constitutes a risk. In this example, one way of expressing the uncertainty would be to express the estimate of effort as a range of values.

A project plan will be based on a huge number of assumptions, and so some way of picking out the risks that are most important is needed. The damage that each risk could cause and the likelihood of it occurring have to be gauged. This assessment can draw attention to the most serious risks. The general effect if a problem materializes is to make the task longer or more costly.

Step 6.2 Plan risk reduction and contingency measures where appropriate

It may be possible to avoid or at least reduce some of the identified risks. Contingency plans specify action that is to be taken if a risk materializes. For example, a contingency plan could be to use contract staff if a member of the project team is unavailable at a key time because of serious illness.

Step 6.3 Adjust overall plans and estimates to take account of risks

We may change our plans, by adding new activities which reduce risks. For example, a new programming language might mean we schedule training courses and time for the programmers to practise their new programming skills on some non-essential work.

CASE STUDY EXAMPLES

Identifying risks

As well as the four new software modules that will have to be written, Amanda has identified several existing modules that will need to be amended. The ease with which the modules can be amended will depend upon the way that they were originally written. There is therefore a risk that they may take longer than expected to modify. Amanda takes no risk reduction measures as such, but notes a pessimistic elapsed time for the amendment activity.

Brigette identifies as a risk the possible absence of key staff when investigating the user requirements as this activity will take place over the holiday period. To reduce this risk, she adds a new activity, 'arrange user interviews', at the beginning of the project. This will give her advance notice of any likely problems of this nature.

2.9 Step 7: Allocate resources

Step 7.1 Identify and allocate resources

Chapter 8 on Resource allocation covers this topic in more detail.

The type of staff needed for each activity is recorded. The staff available for the project are identified and are provisionally allocated to tasks.

Step 7.2 Revise plans and estimates to take into account resource constraints

Some staff may be needed for more than one task at the same time and, in this case, an order of priority is established. The decisions made here might have an effect on the overall duration of the project when some tasks are delayed while waiting for staff to become free.

Gantt charts are named after Henry Gantt and 'Gantt' should therefore *not* be written in capital letters as if it stood for something!

Ensuring staff are available to start work on activities as soon as the preceding activities have been completed might mean that they are idle while waiting for the job to start and are therefore used inefficiently.

The product of steps 7.1 and 7.2 would typically be a Gantt chart – see Figure 2.5. The Gantt chart is not unlike the holiday planners that are on the walls of most offices and so is in a format that will be familiar to both developers and clients.

CASE STUDY EXAMPLES

Taking resource constraints into account

Amanda has now identified four major software modules plus two existing software modules that will need extensive amendment. At IOE the specification of modules is carried out by the lead systems analyst for the project (who in this case is Amanda) assisted by junior analyst/designers. Four analyst/programmers are available to carry out the design, coding and unit testing of the individual modules. After careful consideration and discussion with her manager, Amanda decides to use only three analyst/programmers so as to minimize the risk of staff waiting between tasks. It is accepted that this decision, while reducing the cost of the project, will delay its end.

Brigette finds that she herself will have to carry out many important activities. She can reduce the workload on herself by delegating some work to her two colleagues, but she realizes that she will have to devote more time to specifying exactly what they will have to do and to checking their work. She adjusts her plan accordingly.

2.10 Step 8: Review/publicize plan

Step 8.1 Review quality aspects of the project plan

A danger when controlling any project is that an activity can reveal that an earlier activity was not properly completed and needs to be reworked. This, at a stroke, can transform a project that appears to be progressing satisfactorily into one that is badly out of control. It is important to know that when a task is reported as completed, it

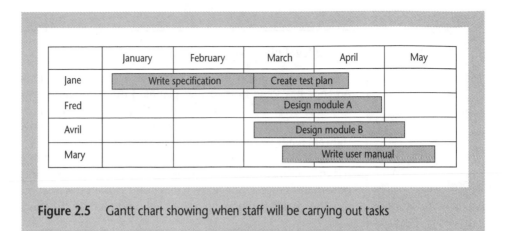

Figure 2.5   Gantt chart showing when staff will be carrying out tasks

really is – hence the importance of quality reviews. Each task should have 'exit requirements'. These are quality checks that have to be passed before the activity can be 'signed off' as completed.

IOE existing quality standards

Amanda finds that at IOE, the Quality Standards and Procedures Manual lays down quality criteria for each type of task. For example, all module design documentation has to be reviewed by a group of colleagues before the coding of that module can commence.

Exercise 2.5   Brigette has no installation standards to help her apart from the minimal ones she has written herself. What quality checks might Brigette introduce to ensure that she has understood the users requirements properly?

Step 8.2   Document plans and obtain agreement

It is important that the plans be carefully documented and that all the parties to the project understand and agree to the commitments required of them in the plan. This may sound obvious, but it is amazing how often this is not done.

Exercise 2.6   At the end of Chapter 1 the main sections of a project plan document were listed. Draw up a table showing which Step Wise activities provide material for which sections of the project plan

2.11   Steps 9 and 10: Execute plan and lower levels of planning

Once the project is under way, plans will need to be drawn up in greater detail for each stage as it becomes due. Detailed planning of the later stages will need to be

CASE STUDY
EXAMPLES

Lower level planning

While work is going on with the specification of the individual modules, Amanda has some time to start planning the integration tests in some detail. She finds that, in fact, integration testing of two of the six new or amended modules will be independent of the others. Testing of these two can start when they are ready without waiting for the remainder.

When Brigette comes to consider the activity 'draft invitation to tender', she has to familiarize herself with the detailed institutional rules and procedures that govern this process. She finds that in order to draft this document she will need to obtain some additional pieces of information from the users.

delayed because more information will be available nearer the start of the stage. Of course, it is necessary to make provisional plans for the more distant tasks, because thinking about what needs to be done can help unearth potential problems, but sight should not be lost of the fact that these plans are provisional.

2.12 Conclusion

This chapter has presented a framework into which the techniques described in the other parts of the book should slot. It is suggested that any planning approach should have the following elements:

- the establishment of project objectives;
- the analysis of the characteristics of the project;
- the establishment of an infrastructure consisting of an appropriate organization and set of standards, methods and tools;
- the identification of the products of the project and the activities needed to generate those products;
- the allocation of resources to activities;
- the establishment of quality controls.

Project planning is an iterative process. As the time approaches for particular activities to be carried out they should be replanned in more detail.

2.13 Further exercises

1. List the products created by the Step Wise planning process.
2. What products must exist before the activity 'test program' can take place? What products does this activity create?
3. An employee of a training organization has the task of creating case study exercises and solutions for a training course which teaches a new systems analysis and design method. The person's work plan has a three-week task 'learn new method'. A

colleague suggests that this is unsatisfactory as a task as there are no concrete deliverables or products from the activity. What can be done about this?

4. In order to carry out usability tests for a new word processing package, the software has to be written and debugged. User instructions have to be available describing how the package is to be used. These have to be scrutinized in order to plan and design the tests. Subjects who will use the package in the tests will need to be selected. As part of this selection process, they will have to complete a questionnaire giving details of their past experience of, and training in, typing and using word processing packages. The subjects will carry out the required tasks using the word processing package. The tasks will be timed and any problems the subjects encounter with the package will be noted. After the test, the subjects will complete another questionnaire about what they felt about the package. All the data from the tests will be analysed and a report containing recommendations for changes to the package will be drawn up. Draw up a Product Breakdown Structure, a Product Flow Diagram and a preliminary activity network for the above.

5. Question 4 in the further exercises for Chapter 1 refers to a scenario relating to a training exercise. Using that scenario, draw up a Product Breakdown Structure, a Product Flow Diagram and a preliminary activity network.

6. Identify the actions that could prevent each of the following risks from materializing or could reduce the impact if it did occur:

   (a) a key member of the programming team leaving;
   (b) a new version of the operating system being introduced which has errors in it;
   (c) a disk containing copies of the most up-to-date version of the software under development being corrupted;
   (d) system testing unearths more errors than were expected and takes longer than planned;
   (e) the government changes the taxation rules which alter the way that VAT is to be calculated in an order processing system under development.

CHAPTER **3**

Project evaluation

Objectives

When you have completed this chapter you will be able to:

● carry out an evaluation and selection of projects against strategic, technical and economic criteria;

● use a variety of cost–benefit evaluation techniques for choosing among competing project proposals;

● evaluate the risk involved in a project and select appropriate strategies for minimizing potential costs.

3.1 Introduction

'Do nothing' is an option which should always be considered.

Deciding whether or not to go ahead with a project is really a case of comparing a proposed project with the alternatives and deciding whether to proceed with it. That evaluation will be based on strategic, technical and economic criteria and will normally be undertaken as part of strategic planning or a feasibility study for any information system development. The risks involved also need to be evaluated.

The BS 6079 guidelines (see Appendix B) use the term *project* in this way.

In this chapter we shall be using the term *project* in a broader sense than elsewhere in the book. Our decision as to whether or not to proceed with a project needs to be based upon whether or not it is desirable to carry out the development *and operation* of a software system. The term project may therefore be used, in this context, to describe the whole life cycle of a system from conception through to final decommissioning.

Project evaluation is normally carried out in Step 0 of Step Wise (Figure 3.1). The subsequent steps of Step Wise are then concerned with managing the development project that stems from this project selection.

3.2 Strategic assessment

Programme management

It is being increasingly recognized that individual projects need to be seen as components of a *programme* and should be evaluated and managed as such. A

D. C. Ferns defined a programme as 'a group of projects that are managed in a co-ordinated way to gain benefits that would not be possible were the projects to be managed independently' in a seminal article in the *International Journal of Project Management*, August 1991.

programme, in this context, is a collection of projects that all contribute to the same overall organizational goals. Effective programme management requires that there is a well-defined *programme goal* and that all the organization's projects are selected and tuned to contribute to this goal. A project must be evaluated according to how it contributes to this programme goal and its viability, timing, resourcing and final worth can be affected by the programme as a whole. It is to be expected that the

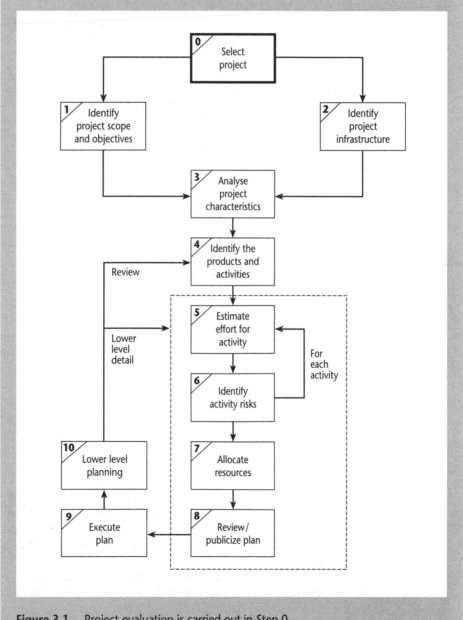

Figure 3.1   Project evaluation is carried out in Step 0

Table 3.1 Typical issues and questions to be considered during strategic assessment

Issue	Typical questions
Objectives	How will the proposed system contribute to the organization's stated objectives? How, for example, might it contribute to an increase in market share?
IS plan	How does the proposed system fit into the IS plan? Which existing system(s) will it replace/interface with? How will it interact with systems proposed for later development?
Organization structure	What effect will the new system have on the existing departmental and organization structure? Will, for example, a new sales order processing system overlap existing sales and stock control functions?
MIS	What information will the system provide and at what levels in the organization? In what ways will it complement or enhance existing management information systems?
Personnel	In what way will the proposed system affect manning levels and the existing employee skill base? What are the implications for the organization's overall policy on staff development?
Image	What, if any, will be the effect on customers' attitudes towards the organization? Will the adoption of, say, automated systems conflict with the objectives of providing a friendly service?

value of any project is increased by the fact that it is part of a programme – the whole, as they say, being greater than the sum of the parts.

In order to carry out a successful strategic assessment of a potential project there should therefore be a strategic plan clearly defining the organization's objectives. This provides the context for defining the programme and programme goals and, hence, the context for assessing the individual project. It is likely, particularly in a large organization, that there will be an organizational structure for programme management and it will be, for example, the *programme director* and *programme executive*, rather than, say, a project manager, who will be responsible for the strategic assessment of a proposed project.

Even where there is no explicitly defined programme, any proposed project must be evaluated within the context of the organization's overall business objectives. Moreover, any potential software system will form part of the user organization's overall information system and must be evaluated within the context of the existing information system and the organization's information strategy. Table 3.1 illustrates typical issues that must be addressed as part of the strategic assessment of a project.

Where a well-defined information systems strategy does not exist, system development and the assessment of project proposals will be based on a more piece-meal approach – each project being individually assessed early in its life cycle. In such cases it is likely that cost–benefit analysis will have more importance and some of the questions of Table 3.1 will be more difficult to answer.

Portfolio management

Where an organization such as a software house is developing a software system they could be asked to carry out a strategic and operational assessment on behalf of the customer. Whether or not this should be the case, they will require an assessment of any proposed project themselves. They will need to ensure that carrying out the development of a system is consistent with their own strategic plan – it is unlikely, for example, that a software house specializing in financial and accounting systems would wish to undertake development of a factory control system unless their strategic plan placed an emphasis on diversification.

The proposed project will form part of a *portfolio* of ongoing and planned projects and the selection of projects must take account of the possible effects on other projects in the portfolio (competition for resources, for example) and the overall portfolio profile (for example, specialization versus diversification).

3.3 Technical assessment

Technical assessment of a proposed system consists of evaluating the required functionality against the hardware and software available. Where an organization has a strategic information systems plan, this is likely to place limitations on the nature of solutions that might be considered. The constraints will, of course, influence the cost of the solution and this must be taken into account in the cost–benefit analysis.

3.4 Cost–benefit analysis

The most common way of carrying out an economic assessment of a proposed information system, or other development, is by comparing the expected costs of development and operation of the system with the benefits of having it in place.

Assessment is based upon the question of whether the estimated costs are exceeded by the estimated income and other benefits. Additionally, it is usually necessary to ask whether or not the project under consideration is the best of a number of options. There might be more candidate projects than can be undertaken at any one time and, in any case, projects will need to be prioritized so that any scarce resources may be allocated effectively.

The standard way of evaluating the economic benefits of any project is to carry out a cost–benefit analysis, which consists of two steps.

- *Identifying and estimating all of the costs and benefits of carrying out the project and operating the system*   These include the development costs of the system, the operating costs and the benefits that are expected to accrue from the operation of the new system. Where the proposed system is replacing an existing one, these estimates should reflect the change in costs and benefits due to the new system. A new sales order processing system, for example, could not claim to benefit an organization by the total value of sales – only by the increase due to the use of the new system.

- *Expressing these costs and benefits in common units*   We need to evaluate the net benefit, that is, the difference between the total benefit accruing from the system and the total cost of creating and operating it. To do this, we must express each cost and each benefit in some common unit. The fundamental common unit of measurement is money. We therefore need to express each of the expected benefits and costs in monetary terms.

Many costs are easy to identify and measure in monetary terms.

Most direct costs are relatively easy to identify and quantify in approximate monetary terms. It is helpful to categorize costs according to where they originate in the life of the project.

- *Development costs*   Include the salaries and other employment costs of the staff involved in the development project and all associated costs.
- *Setup costs*   Include the costs of putting the system into place. These consist mainly of the costs of any new hardware and ancillary equipment, but will also include costs of file conversion, recruitment and staff training.
- *Operational costs*   Consist of the costs of operating the system once it has been installed.

Benefits, on the other hand, are often quite difficult to quantify in monetary terms even once they have been identified. Benefits may be categorized as follows.

- *Direct benefits*   These accrue directly from the operation of the proposed system. These could, for example, include the reduction in salary bills through the introduction of a new, computerized system.

Indirect benefits, which are difficult to estimate, are sometimes known as 'intangible benefits'.

- *Assessable indirect benefits*   These are generally secondary benefits, such as increased accuracy through the introduction of a more user-friendly screen design where we might be able to estimate the reduction in errors, and hence costs, of the proposed system.
- *Intangible benefits*   These are generally longer term or benefits that are considered very difficult to quantify. Enhanced job interest can lead to reduced staff turnover and, hence, lower recruitment costs.

Exercise 3.1

Brightmouth College are considering the replacement of the existing payroll service, operated by a third party, with a tailored, off-the-shelf computer-based system. List some of the costs and benefits they might consider under each of the six headings given above. For each cost or benefit, explain how, in principle, it might be measured in monetary terms.

If a proposal shows an excess of benefits over costs then it is a candidate for further consideration.

Any project that shows an excess of benefits over costs is clearly worth considering for implementation. However, as we shall see later, it is not a sufficient justification for going ahead: we might not be able to afford the costs; there might be even better projects we could allocate our resources to instead; the project might be too risky.

3.5 Cash flow forecasting

As important as estimating the overall costs and benefits of a project is the forecasting of the cash flows that will take place and their timing. A cash flow forecast will indicate when expenditure and income will take place (Figure 3.2).

We need to spend money, such as staff wages, during the development stages of a project. Such expenditure cannot be deferred until income is received (either

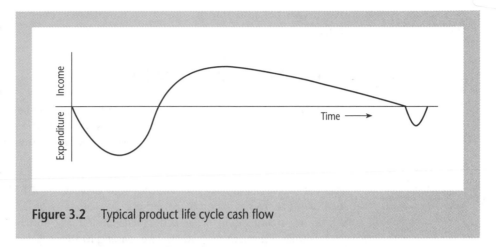

Figure 3.2 Typical product life cycle cash flow

Typically products generate a negative cash flow during their development followed by a positive cash flow over their operating life. There might be decommissioning costs at the end of a product's life.

Cash flows take place at the end of each year. The year 0 figure represents the initial investment made at the start of the project.

Table 3.2 Four project cash flow projections – figures are end of year totals (£)

Year	Project 1	Project 2	Project 3	Project 4
0	−100,000	−1,000,000	−100,000	−120,000
1	10,000	200,000	30,000	30,000
2	10,000	200,000	30,000	30,000
3	10,000	200,000	30,000	30,000
4	20,000	200,000	30,000	30,000
5	100,000	300,000	30,000	75,000
Net profit	50,000	100,000	50,000	75,000

from using the software if it is being developed for in-house use or from selling it). It is important that we know that we can fund the development expenditure either from the company's own resources or by borrowing from the bank. In any event, it is vital to have some forecast of when expenditure such as the payment of salaries and bank interest will take place and when any income is to be expected, such as payment on completion or, possibly, stage payments.

Accurate cash flow forecasting is not easy, as it generally needs to be done early in the project's life cycle (at least before any significant expenditure is committed) and many items to be estimated (particularly the benefits of using software or decommissioning costs) might be some years in the future.

The difficulty and importance of cash flow forecasting is evidenced by the number of companies that suffer bankruptcy because, although they are developing profitable products or services, they cannot sustain an unplanned negative cash flow.

When estimating future cash flows, it is usual to ignore the effects of inflation. Trying to forecast the effects of inflation increases the uncertainty of the forecasts. Moreover, if expenditure is increased due to inflation it is likely that income will increase proportionately. However, measures to deal with increases in costs where work is being done for an external customer must be in place – for example index-linked prices where work involves use of raw materials – see Chapter 10 on contract management.

Table 3.2 illustrates cash flow forecasts for four projects. In each case it is assumed that the cash flows take place at the end of each year. For short-term projects or where candidate projects demonstrate significant seasonal cash flow patterns it can be advisable to produce quarterly, or even monthly, cash flow forecasts.

3.6 Cost–benefit evaluation techniques

We would consider proceeding with a project only where the benefits outweigh the costs. However, in order to choose among projects, we need to take into account the timing of the costs and benefits as well as the benefits relative to the size of the investment.

Exercise 3.2   Consider the project cash flow estimates for four projects at IOE shown in Table 3.2. Negative values represent expenditure and positive values income.

Rank the four projects in order of financial desirability and make a note of your reasons for ranking them in that way before reading further.

In the following sections we will take a brief look at some common methods for comparing projects on the basis of their cash flow forecasts.

Net profit

The net profit of a project is the difference between the total costs and the total income over the life of the project. Project 2 in Table 3.2 shows the greatest net profit but this is at the expense of a large investment. Indeed, if we had £1m to invest, we might undertake all of the other three projects and obtain an even greater net profit. Note also, that all projects contain an element of risk and we might not be prepared to risk £1m. We shall look at the effects of risk and investment later in this chapter.

Moreover, the simple net profit takes no account of the timing of the cash flows. Projects 1 and 3 each have a net profit of £50,000 and therefore, according to this selection criterion, would be equally preferable. The bulk of the income occurs late in the life of project 1, whereas project 3 returns a steady income throughout its life. Having to wait for a return has the disadvantage that the investment must be funded for longer. Add to that the fact that, other things being equal, estimates in the more distant future are less reliable that short-term estimates and we can see that the two projects are not equally preferable.

Payback period

The *payback period* is the time taken to break even or pay back the initial investment. Normally, the project with the shortest payback period will be chosen on the basis that an organization will wish to minimize the time that a project is 'in debt'.

Exercise 3.3   Consider the four project cash flows given in Table 3.2 and calculate the payback period for each of them.

The advantage of the payback period is that it is simple to calculate and is not particularly sensitive to small forecasting errors. Its disadvantage as a selection technique is that it ignores the overall profitability of the project – in fact, it totally ignores any income (or expenditure) once the project has broken even. Thus the fact that projects 2 and 4 are, overall, more profitable than project 3 is ignored.

Return on investment

The *return on investment* (ROI), also known as the *accounting rate of return* (ARR), provides a way of comparing the net profitability to the investment required. There are some variations on the formula used to calculate the return on investment, but a straightforward common version is

$$ROI = \frac{\text{average annual profit}}{\text{total investment}} \times 100$$

Exercise 3.4

Calculating the ROI for project 1, the net profit is £50,000 and the total investment is £100,000. The return on investment is therefore calculated as

$$ROI = \frac{\text{average annual profit}}{\text{total investment}} \times 100$$

$$= \frac{10,000}{100,000} \times 100 = 10\%$$

Calculate the ROI for each of the other projects shown in Table 3.2 and decide which, on the basis of this criterion, is the most worthwhile.

The return on investment provides a simple, easy to calculate measure of return on capital and is therefore quite popular. Unfortunately it suffers from two severe disadvantages. Like the net profitability, it takes no account of the timing of the cash flows. More importantly, it is tempting to compare the rate of return with current interest rates. However, this rate of return bears no relationship to the interest rates offered or charged by banks (or any other normal interest rate) since it takes no account of the timing of the cash flows or of the compounding of interest. It is therefore, potentially, very misleading.

Net present value

Net present value (NPV) and internal rate of return (IRR) are collectively known as discounted cash flow (DCF) techniques.

The calculation of *net present value* (NPV) is a project evaluation technique that takes into account the profitability of a project and the timing of the cash flows that are produced. It does so by discounting future cash flows by a percentage known as the discount rate. This is based on the view that receiving £100 today is better than having to wait until next year to receive it, because the £100 next year is worth less than £100 now. We could, for example, invest the £100 in a bank today and have £100 plus the interest in a year's time. If we say that the present value of £100 in a year's time is £91, we mean that £100 in a year's time is the equivalent of £91 now.

Note that this example uses approximate figures – when you have finished reading this section you should be able to calculate the exact figures yourself.

The equivalence of £91 now and £100 in a year's time means we are discounting the future income by approximately 10% – that is, we would need an extra 10% to make it worthwhile waiting for a year. An alternative way of considering the equivalence of the two is to consider that, if we received £91 now and invested for a year at an annual interest rate of 10%, it would be worth £100 in a year's time. The annual rate by which we discount future earnings is known as the *discount rate*: 10% in the above example.

Similarly, £100 received in 2 years' time would have a present value of approximately £83 – in other words, £83 invested at an interest rate of 10% would yield approximately £100 in 2 years' time.

The present value of any future cash flow may be obtained by applying the following formula

$$\text{Present value} = \frac{\text{value in year } t}{(1 + r)^t}$$

where r is the discount rate, expressed as a decimal value and t is the number of years into the future that the cash flow occurs.

Alternatively, and rather more easily, the present value of a cash flow may be calculated by multiplying the cash flow by the appropriate discount factor. A small table of discount factors is given in Table 3.3.

The NPV for a project is obtained by discounting each cash flow (both negative and positive) and summing the discounted values. It is normally assumed that any initial investment takes place immediately (indicated as year 0) and is not discounted. Later cash flows are normally assumed to take place at the end of each year and are discounted by the appropriate amount.

Exercise 3.5

Assuming a 10% discount rate, the NPV for project 1 (Table 3.2) would be calculated as in Table 3.4. The net present value for project 1, using a 10% discount rate is therefore £618. Using a 10% discount rate, calculate the net present values for projects 2, 3 and 4 and decide which, on the basis of this, is the most beneficial to pursue.

It is interesting to note that the net present values for projects 1 and 3 are significantly different – even though they both yield the same net profit and both have the same return on investment. The difference in NPV reflects the fact that, with project 1, we must wait longer for the bulk of the income.

More extensive or detailed tables may be constructed using the formula

$$\text{discount factor} = \frac{1}{(1 + r)^t}$$

for various values of r (the discount rate) and t (the number of years from now).

Table 3.3 Table of NPV discount factors

| Year | \multicolumn{6}{c}{Discount rate (%)} | | | | | |
	5	6	8	10	12	15
1	0.9524	0.9434	0.9259	0.9091	0.8929	0.8696
2	0.9070	0.8900	0.8573	0.8264	0.7972	0.7561
3	0.8638	0.8396	0.7938	0.7513	0.7118	0.6575
4	0.8227	0.7921	0.7350	0.6830	0.6355	0.5718
5	0.7835	0.7473	0.6806	0.6209	0.5674	0.4972
6	0.7462	0.7050	0.6302	0.5645	0.5066	0.4323
7	0.7107	0.6651	0.5835	0.5132	0.4523	0.3759
8	0.6768	0.6274	0.5403	0.4665	0.4039	0.3269
9	0.6446	0.5919	0.5002	0.4241	0.3606	0.2843
10	0.6139	0.5584	0.4632	0.3855	0.3220	0.2472
15	0.4810	0.4173	0.3152	0.2394	0.1827	0.1229
20	0.3769	0.3118	0.2145	0.1486	0.1037	0.0611
25	0.2953	0.2330	0.1460	0.0923	0.0588	0.0304

Table 3.4 Applying the discount factors to project 1

Year	Project 1 cash flow (£)	Discount factor @ 10%	Discounted cash flow (£)
0	−100,000	1.0000	−100,000
1	10,000	0.9091	9,091
2	10,000	0.8264	8,264
3	10,000	0.7513	7,513
4	20,000	0.6830	13,660
5	100,000	0.6209	62,090
Net Profit:	£50,000		NPV: £618

Table 3.5 Three estimated project cash flows

Year	Project A (£)	Project B (£)	Project C (£)
0	−8,000	−8,000	−10,000
1	4,000	1,000	2,000
2	4,000	2,000	2,000
3	2,000	4,000	6,000
4	1,000	3,000	2,000
5	500	9,000	2,000
6	500	−6,000	2,000
Net Profit:	4,000	5,000	6,000

The main difficulty with NPV for deciding between projects is selecting an appropriate discount rate. Some organizations have a standard rate but, where this is not the case, then the discount rate should be chosen to reflect available interest rates (borrowing costs where the project must be funded from loans) plus some premium to reflect the fact that software projects are inherently more risky than lending money to a bank. The exact discount rate is normally less important than ensuring that the same discount rate is used for all projects being compared. However, it is important to check that the ranking of projects is not sensitive to small changes in the discount rate – have a look at the following exercise.

Exercise 3.6 Calculate the NPV for each of the projects A, B and C shown in Table 3.5 using each of the discount rates 8%, 10% and 12%.

For each of the discount rates, decide which is the best project. What can you conclude from these results?

Alternatively, the discount rate can be thought of as a target rate of return. If, for example, we set a target rate of return of 15% we would reject any project that did not display a positive NPV using a 15% discount rate. Any project that displayed a positive NPV would be considered for selection – perhaps by using an additional set of criteria where candidate projects were competing for resources.

Internal rate of return

One disadvantage of NPV as a measure of profitability is that, although it may be used to compare projects, it might not be directly comparable with earnings from other investments or the costs of borrowing capital. Such costs are usually quoted as a percentage interest rate. The internal rate of return (IRR) attempts to provide a profitability measure as a percentage return that is directly comparable with interest rates. Thus, a project that showed an estimated IRR of 10% would be worthwhile if the capital could be borrowed for less than 10% or if the capital could not be invested elsewhere for a return greater than 10%.

The IRR is calculated as that percentage discount rate that would produce an NPV of zero. It is most easily calculated using a spreadsheet or other computer program that provides functions for calculating the IRR. Microsoft Excel and Lotus, for example, both provide IRR functions which, provided with an initial guess or seed value (which may be zero), will search for and return an IRR.

Manually, it must be calculated by trial and error or estimated using the technique illustrated in Figure 3.3. This technique consists of guessing two values (one either side of the true value) and using the resulting NPVs (one of which must be positive and the other negative) to estimate the correct value. Note that this technique will provide only an approximate value but, in many cases that can be sufficient to dismiss a project that has a small IRR or indicate that it is worth making a more precise evaluation.

The IRR is a convenient and useful measure of the value of a project in that it is a single percentage figure that may be directly compared with rates of return on other projects or interest rates quoted elsewhere.

Table 3.6 illustrates the way in which a project with an IRR of 10% may be directly compared with other interest rates. The cash flow for the project is shown in column (a). Columns (b) to (e) show that if we were to invest £100,000 now at

The IRR may be estimated by plotting a series of guesses:
For a particular project, a discount rate of 8% gives a positive NPV of £7,898; a discount rate of 12% gives a negative NPV of −£5,829. The IRR is therefore somewhere between these two values. Plotting the two values on a chart and joining the points with a straight line suggests that the IRR is about 10.25%. The true IRR (calculated with a spreadsheet) is 10.167%.

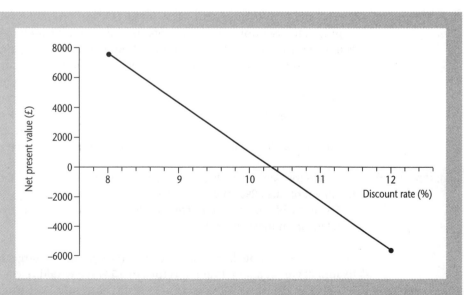

Figure 3.3 Estimating the internal rate of return for project 1

£100,000 invested at 10% may be used to generate the cash flows shown. At the end of the five-year period the capital and the interest payments will be entirely consumed leaving a net balance of zero.

Table 3.6 A project cash flow treated as an investment at 10%

| | (a) Project cash flow forecast (£) | Equivalent investment at 10% | | | |
| | | (b) Capital at start of year (£) | (c) Interest during year (£) | (d) Capital at end of year (£) | (e) End of year withdrawal (£) |
Year					
0	−100,000	–	–	–	–
1	10,000	100,000	10,000	110,000	10,000
2	10,000	100,000	10,000	110,000	10,000
3	10,000	100,000	10,000	110,000	10,000
4	20,000	100,000	10,000	110,000	20,000
5	99,000	90,000	9,000	99,000	99,000
6		0	0	0	0

an annual interest rate of 10% in, say, a bank, we could withdraw the same amounts as we would earn from the project at the end of each year, column (e), and we would be left with a net balance of zero at the end. In other words, investing in a project that has an IRR of 10% can produce exactly the same cash flow as lending the money to a bank at a 10% interest rate. We can therefore reason that a project with an IRR greater than current interest rates will provide a better rate of return than lending the investment to a bank. We can also say that it will be worth borrowing to finance the project if it has an IRR greater than the interest rate charged on the loan.

One deficiency of the IRR is that it does not indicate the absolute size of the return. A project with an NPV of £100,000 and an IRR of 15% can be more attractive than one with an NPV of £10,000 and an IRR of 18% – the return on capital is lower but the net benefits greater.

An often quoted objection to the internal rate of return is that, under certain conditions, it is possible to find more than one rate that will produce a zero NPV. This is not a valid objection since, if there are multiple solutions, it is always appropriate to take the lowest value and ignore the others. Spreadsheets will normally always return the lowest value if provided with zero as a seed value.

The NPV and IRR are not, however, a complete answer to economic project evaluation.

● A total evaluation must also take into account the problems of funding the cash flows – will we, for example, be able to repay the interest on any borrowed money and pay development staff salaries at the appropriate time?

● While a project's IRR might indicate a profitable project, future earnings from a project might be far less reliable than earnings from, say, investing with a bank. To take account of the risk inherent in investing in a project, we might require that a project earn a 'risk premium' (that is, it must earn, say, at least 15% more than current interest rates) or we might undertake a more detailed risk analysis as described in the following sections of this chapter.

- We must also consider any one project within the financial and economic framework of the organization as a whole – if we fund this one, will we also be able to fund other worthy projects?

3.7 Risk evaluation

There is a risk that software might exceed the original specification and that a project will be completed early and under budget. That is not a risk that need concern us.

Every project involves risk of some form. When assessing and planning a project, we are concerned with the risk of the project not meeting its objectives. In Chapter 8 we shall discuss ways of analysing and minimizing risk during the development of a software system. In this chapter, we are concerned with taking risk into account when deciding whether to proceed with a proposed project.

Risk identification and ranking

In any project evaluation we should attempt to identify the risks and quantify their potential effects. One common approach to risk analysis is to construct a project risk matrix utilizing a checklist of possible risks and to classify each risk according to its relative importance and likelihood. Note that the importance and likelihood need to be separately assessed – we might be less concerned with something that, although serious, is very unlikely to occur than with something less serious that is almost certain. Table 3.7 illustrates a basic project risk matrix listing some of the risks that might be considered for a project, with their importance and likelihood classified as high (H), medium (M), low (L) or exceedingly unlikely (–). So that projects may be compared the list of risks must be the same for each project being assessed. It is likely, in reality, that it would be somewhat longer than shown and more precisely defined.

The project risk matrix may be used as a way of evaluating projects (those with high risks being less favoured) or as a means of identifying and ranking the risks for a specific project. In Chapter 7 we shall consider a method for scoring the importance and likelihood of risks that may be used in conjunction with the project risk matrix to score and rank projects.

Risk and net present value

Where a project is relatively risky it is common practice to use a higher discount rate to calculate NPV. This addition or risk premium, might, for example, be an

A more detailed analysis would identify the causes as well as the damage caused by each risk.

Table 3.7 A fragment of a basic project risk matrix

Risk	Importance	Likelihood
Software never completed or delivered	H	–
Project cancelled after design stage	H	–
Software delivered late	M	M
Development budget exceeded ⩽20%	L	M
Development budget exceeded >20%	M	L
Maintenance costs higher than estimated	L	L
Response time targets not met	L	H

additional 2% for a reasonably safe project or 5% for a fairly risky one. Projects may be categorized as high, medium or low risk using a scoring method and risk premiums designated for each category. The premiums, even if arbitrary, provide a consistent method of taking risk into account.

Cost–benefit analysis

A rather more sophisticated approach to the evaluation of risk is to consider each possible outcome and estimate the probability of its occurring and the corresponding value of the outcome. Rather than a single cash flow forecast for a project, we will then have a set of cash flow forecasts, each with an associated probability of occurring. The value of the project is then obtained by summing the cost or benefit for each possible outcome weighted by its corresponding probability. Exercise 3.7 illustrates how this may be done.

| Exercise 3.7 | BuyRight, a software house, is considering developing a payroll application for use in academic institutions and is currently engaged in a cost–benefit analysis. Study of the market has shown that, if they can target it efficiently and no competing products become available, they will obtain a high level of sales generating an annual income of £800,000. They estimate that there is a 1 in 10 chance of this happening. However, a competitor might launch a competing application before their own launch date and then sales might generate only £100,000 per year. They estimate that there is a 30% chance of this happening. The most likely outcome, they believe, is somewhere in between these two extremes – they will gain a market lead by launching before any competing product becomes available and achieve an annual income of £650,000. BuyRight have therefore calculated their expected sales income as in Table 3.8.

Total development costs are estimated at £750,000 and sales are expected to be maintained at a reasonably constant level for at least four years. Annual costs of marketing and product maintenance are estimated at £200,000, irrespective of the market share gained. Would you advise them to go ahead with the project?

This approach is frequently used in the evaluation of large projects such as the building of new motorways, where variables such as future traffic volumes, and hence the total benefit of shorter journey times, are subject to uncertainty. The technique does, of course, rely on our being able to assign probabilities of occurrence to each scenario and, without extensive study, this can be difficult.

When used to evaluate a single project, the cost–benefit approach, by 'averaging out' the effects of the different scenarios, does not take account an organization's

Table 3.8 BuyRight's income forecasts

Sales	Annual sales income (£) i	Probability p	Expected value (£) $i \times p$
High	800,000	0.1	80,000
Medium	650,000	0.6	390,000
Low	100,000	0.3	30,000
Expected income			500,000

reluctance to risk damaging outcomes. Because of this, where overall profitability is the primary concern, it is often considered more appropriate for the evaluation of a portfolio of projects.

Risk profile analysis

An approach which attempts to overcome some of the objections to cost–benefit averaging is the construction of risk profiles using sensitivity analysis.

This involves varying each of the parameters that affect the project's cost or benefits to ascertain how sensitive the project's profitability is to each factor. We might, for example, vary one of our original estimates by plus or minus 5% and recalculate the expected costs and benefits for the project. By repeating this exercise for each of our estimates in turn we can evaluate the sensitivity of the project to each factor.

By studying the results of a sensitivity analysis we can identify those factors that are most important to the success of the project. We then need to decide whether we can exercise greater control over them or otherwise mitigate their effects. If neither is the case, then we must live with the risk or abandon the project.

For an explanation of the Monte Carlo technique see any textbook on operational research.

Sensitivity analysis demands that we vary each factor one at a time. It does not easily allow us to consider the effects of combinations of circumstances, neither does it evaluate the chances of a particular outcome occurring. In order to do this we need to use a more sophisticated tool such as Monte Carlo simulation. There are a number of risk analysis applications available (such as @*Risk* from Palisade) that use Monte Carlo simulation and produce risk profiles of the type shown in Figure 3.4.

Projects may be compared as in Figure 3.4, which compares three projects with the same expected profitability. Project A is unlikely to depart far from this expected

All three projects have the same expected profitability. The profitability of project A is unlikely to depart greatly from its expected value (indicated by the vertical axis) compared to the likely variations for project B. Project A is therefore less risky than project B.

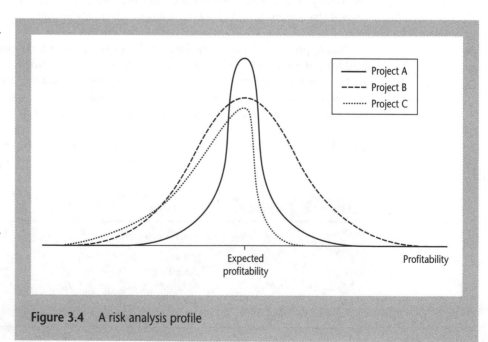

Figure 3.4 A risk analysis profile

value compared to project B, which exhibits a larger variance. Both of these have symmetric profiles, which contrast with project C. Project C has a skewed distribution, which indicates that although it is unlikely ever to be much more profitable than expected, it is quite likely to be far worse.

Using decision trees

The approaches to risk analysis discussed previously rather assume that we are passive bystanders allowing nature to take its own course – the best we can do is to reject over-risky projects or choose those with the best risk profile. There are many situations, however, where we can evaluate whether a risk is important and, if it is, indicate a suitable course of action.

Many such decisions will limit or affect future options and, at any point, it is important to be able to see into the future to assess how a decision will affect the future profitability of the project.

Prior to giving Amanda the job of extending their invoicing system, IOE must consider the alternative of completely replacing the existing system – which they will have to do at some point in the future. The decision largely rests upon the rate at which their equipment maintenance business expands – if their market share significantly increases (which they believe will happen if rumours of a competitor's imminent bankruptcy are fulfilled) the existing system might need to be replaced within two years. Not replacing the system in time could be an expensive option as it could lead to lost revenue if they cannot cope with the increase in invoicing demand. Replacing it immediately will, however, be expensive as it will mean deferring other projects that have already been scheduled.

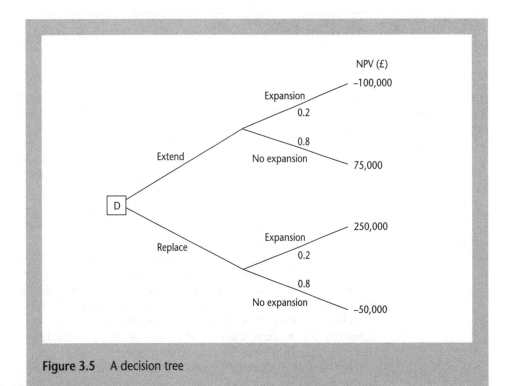

Figure 3.5 A decision tree

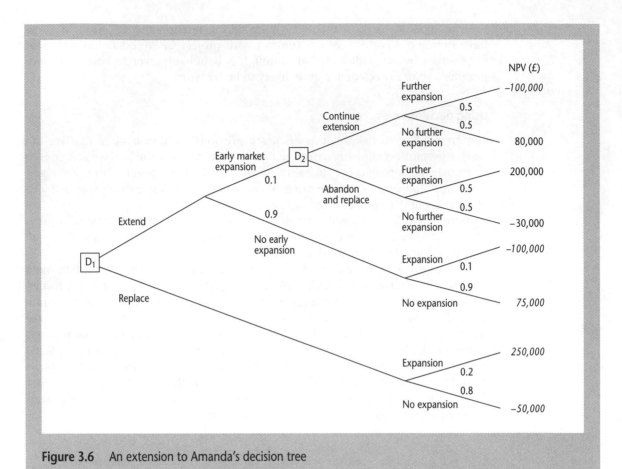

Figure 3.6 An extension to Amanda's decision tree

The NPVs shown in italic are those identified in Amanda's original decision tree shown in Figure 3.5.

They have calculated that extending the existing system will have an NPV of £57,000, although if the market expands significantly, this will be turned into a loss with an NPV of −£100,000 due to lost revenue. If the market does expand, replacing the system now has an NPV of £250,000 due to the benefits of being able to handle increased sales and other benefits such as improved management information. If sales do not increase, however, the benefits will be severely reduced and the project will suffer a loss with an NPV of −£50,000.

The company estimate the likelihood of the market increasing significantly at 20% – and, hence, the probability that it will not increase as 80%. This scenario can be represented as a tree structure as shown in Figure 3.5.

The analysis of a decision tree consists of evaluating the expected benefit of taking each path from a decision point (denoted by D in Figure 3.5). The expected value of each path is the sum of the value of each possible outcome multiplied by its probability of occurrence. The expected value of extending the system is therefore £40,000 (75,000 × 0.8 − 100,000 × 0.2) and the expected value of replacing the system £10,000 (250,000 × 0.2 − 50,000 × 0.8). IOE should therefore choose the option of extending the existing system.

This example illustrates the use of a decision tree to evaluate a simple decision at the start of a project. One of the great advantages of using decision trees to model and analyse problems is the ease with which they can be extended. Figure 3.6 illustrates an extended version of Amanda's decision tree, which includes the possibility of a later decision should they decide to extend the system and then find there is an early market expansion.

3.8 Conclusion

Some of the key points in this chapter are:

- projects must be evaluated on strategic, technical and economic grounds;
- economic assessment involves the identification of all costs and income over the lifetime of the system, including its development and operation and checking that the total value of benefits exceeds total expenditure;
- money received in the future is worth less than the same amount of money in hand now, which may be invested to earn interest;
- the uncertainty surrounding estimates of future returns lowers their real value measured now;
- discounted cash flow techniques may be used to evaluate the present value of future cash flows taking account of interest rates and uncertainty;
- cost–benefit analysis techniques and decision trees provide tools for evaluating expected outcomes and choosing between alternative strategies.

3.9 Further exercises

1. Identify the major risks that could affect the success of the Brightmouth College payroll project and try to rank them in order of importance.

2. Working in a group of three or four, imagine that you are about to embark upon a programming assignment as part of the assessed work for your course. Draw up a list of the risks that might affect the assignment outcome. Individually classify the importance and likelihood of each of those risk as high, medium or low. When you have done this compare your results and try to come up with an agreed project risk matrix.

3. Explain why discounted cash flow techniques provide better criteria for project selection than net profit or return on investment.

4. Consider the decision tree shown in Figure 3.6 and decide, given the additional possibilities, which option(s) IOE should choose.

CHAPTER 4

Selection of an appropriate project approach

Objectives

When you have completed this chapter you will be able to:

- take account of the characteristics of the system to be developed when planning a project;
- select an appropriate process model;
- make best use of the 'waterfall' process model where appropriate;
- reduce risks by the creation of appropriate prototypes;
- reduce other risks by implementing of the project in increments;
- identify where unnecessary organizational obstacles can be removed by using 'agile' development methods.

4.1 Introduction

The development of software in-house usually means that:

- the project team and the users belong to the same organization;
- the applications being considered slot into a portfolio of existing computer-based systems;
- the methodologies and technologies to be used are not selected by the project manager, but are dictated by local standards.

See Martyn Ould's *Managing Software Quality and Business Risk*, Wiley, 1999.

However, where successive development projects are carried out by a software house for different external customers, the methodologies and technologies to be used need to be reviewed for each individual project. This decision-making process has been called 'technical planning' by some, although here we use the term 'project analysis'. Even where development is in-house, any characteristics of the new project requiring a different approach from previous projects need to be considered. It is this analysis that is the subject of this chapter.

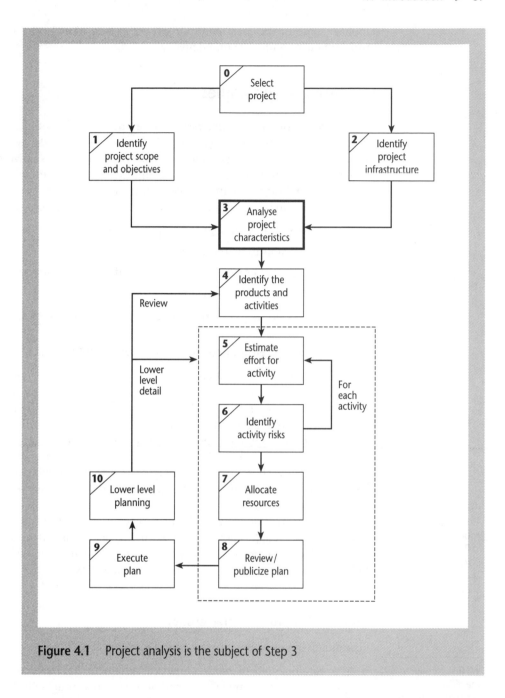

Figure 4.1   Project analysis is the subject of Step 3

The relevant part of the Step Wise approach is Step 3: Analyse project characteristics. The selection of a particular process model will add new products to the Project Breakdown Structure or new activities to the activity network. This will create outputs for Step 4: Identify the products and activities of the project (see Figure 4.1).

In the remainder of this chapter we will look at how the characteristics of a project will influence the approach to the planning of a project. We will then look at some of the most common *process models*, namely the waterfall approach, prototyping and incremental delivery.

4.2 Choosing technologies

An outcome of project analysis will be the selection of the most appropriate methodologies and technologies. Methodologies include techniques like the various flavours of object-oriented (OO) development, SSADM and JSP (Jackson Structured Programming) while technologies might include an appropriate application-building and automated testing environments.

As well as the products and activities, the chosen technology will influence:

- the training requirements for development staff;
- the types of staff to be recruited;
- the development environment – both hardware and software;
- system maintenance arrangements.

We are now going to describe some of the steps of project analysis.

Identify project as either objectives driven or product driven

In Chapter 1 we distinguished between *objectives driven* and *product driven* projects. Often a product driven project will have been preceded by an objective driven project which chose the general software solution that is to be implemented.

The project manager's ideal situation is to have well-defined objectives, but as much freedom as possible about the way those objectives are to be satisfied. For example, the objective might be to pay staff in a start-up company reliably, accurately and with low administrative costs. Use of a particular packaged software solution does not have to be specified at the outset – but as we will see later there can be exceptions to this.

The soft systems approach is described in P Checkland, and J. Scholes, *Soft Systems Methodology in Action*, Wiley 1990.

Sometimes the objectives of the project are uncertain or are the subject of disagreement. People might be experiencing problems but no-one knows exactly how to solve these problems. IT specialists might provide help with some problems but assistance from other specialisms is needed with others. In these kinds of situation a *soft systems* approach may need to be considered.

Analyse other project characteristics

The following questions can be usefully asked.

We first introduced the difference between information systems and embedded systems in Chapter 1.

- *Is a data-oriented or process-oriented system to be implemented?* *Data-oriented* systems generally mean information systems that will have a substantial database. *Process oriented* systems refer to embedded control systems. It is not uncommon to have systems with elements of both. Some writers suggest that the OO approach is more suitable for process oriented systems where control is important than for systems dominated by a relational database.

Note that here we are talking about writing the software tool, not its use.

- *Will the software that is to be produced be a general tool or application specific?* An example of a general tool would be a spreadsheet or a word processing package. An application specific package could be, for example, an airline seat reservation system.

- *Is the application to be implemented of a particular type for which specific tools have been developed?* For example:
  - *Does it involve concurrent processing?* The use of techniques appropriate to the analysis and design of such systems would be considered;
  - *Will the system to be created be knowledge based?* Expert systems have rules which result in some 'expert advice' when applied to a problem, and specific methods and tools exist for developing such systems;
  - *Will the system to be produced make heavy use of computer graphics?*
- *Is the system to be created safety critical?* For instance, could a malfunction in the system endanger human life? If so, testing would, for example, become very important.
- *What is the nature of the hardware/software environment in which the system will operate?* The environment in which the final software will operate could be different from that in which it is to be developed. Embedded software might be developed on a large development machine which has lots of supporting software tools in the way of compilers, debuggers, static analysers and so on, but then be downloaded to a small processor in the larger engineered product. A standalone desk-top application needs a different approach to one for a main-frame or a client-server environment.

Exercise 4.1 How would you categorize each of the following systems according to the classification above?

(a) a payroll system;

(b) a system to control a bottling plant;

(c) a system which holds details of the plans of plant used by a water company to supply water to consumers;

(d) a software package to support project managers;

(e) a system used by lawyers to get hold of case law relating to company taxation.

Identify high level project risks

Chapter 3 has already touched on some aspects of risk which are developed further in Chapter 7.

At the beginning of a project, management might expect elaborate plans even though we are ignorant of many important factors affecting the project. For example, until we investigate in detail the users' requirements we cannot estimate the effort needed to build a system to meet those requirements. The greater the uncertainties at the beginning, the greater the risk that the project will be unsuccessful. Once we recognize a particular area of uncertainty we can, however, take steps to reduce its uncertainty.

One suggestion is that uncertainty can be associated with the *products*, *processes*, or *resources* of a project.

- *Product uncertainty* How well the requirements are understood? The users themselves could be uncertain about what a proposed information system is to do. The government, say, might introduce a new form of taxation but its detailed operation might not be known until case law has been built up. Some environments change so quickly that a seemingly precise and valid statement of requirements rapidly becomes out of date.

DSDM™ stands for Dynamic Systems Development Method.

- *Process uncertainty*   The project under consideration might be the first where an organization is using a method such as DSDM. A new application building tool might be used. Any change in the way that the systems are developed introduces uncertainty.

- *Resource uncertainty*   The main area of uncertainty here will be the availability of staff of the right ability and experience. The larger the number of resources needed or the longer the duration of the project, the more inherently risky it will be.

Some factors increase *uncertainty*, e.g. continually changing requirements, while others increase *complexity*, e.g. software size. Different strategies are needed to deal with the two distinct types of risks.

Of course, some risk factors can increase both *uncertainty* and *complexity*.

Exercise 4.2

At IOE, Amanda has identified possible user resistance as a risk to the maintenance group accounts project. Would you classify this as a product, process or resource risk? It may be that it does not fit into any of these categories and some other is needed.

Brigette at Brightmouth College has identified the possibility that no suitable payroll package would be available on the market as a risk. What other risks might be inherent in the Brightmouth College payroll project?

Take into account user requirements concerning implementation

Chapter 12 on Software quality discusses BS EN ISO 9001 and TickIT.

We suggested earlier that staff planning a project should try to ensure that unnecessary assumptions or constraints are not imposed on the way that a project's objectives are to be met. The example given was the specification of the exact payroll package to be deployed. Sometimes, such constraints are needed, however. It might be that a company is a subsidiary of some larger group and the same package has to be used throughout the group to ensure compatibility.

A client organization often lays down standards that have to be adopted by any contractor providing software for them. It is common for organizations to specify that suppliers of software have BS EN ISO 9001:2000 or TickIT accreditation. This will affect the way projects are conducted.

Select general life-cycle approach

- *Control systems*   An embedded real-time system will need to be implemented using an appropriate methodology. Real-time systems that employ concurrent processing may have to use techniques such as Petri nets.

- *Information systems*   Similarly, an information system will need a methodology, such as SSADM or Information Engineering, that matches that type of environment. SSADM will be especially appropriate where there are a large number of development staff whose work will need to be co-ordinated: the method lays down in detail the activities and products needed at each step. Team members would therefore know exactly what is expected.

- *General tools*   Where the software is for the general market rather than application and user specific, then a methodology such as SSADM would have to be thought about very carefully. The framers of this method make the assumption that a specific user exists. Some parts in the method also assume an existing clerical system which can be analysed to yield the logical features of a new, computer-based, system.

- *Specialized techniques*   For example, expert system shells and logic-based programming languages have been invented to expedite the development of *knowledge-based systems*. Similarly a number of specialized techniques and tools are available to assist in the development of *graphics-based systems*.

- *Hardware environment*   The environment in which the system is to operate could put constraints on the way it is to be implemented. For instance, the need for a fast response time or restricted computer memory might mean that only low-level programming languages can be used.

- *Safety-critical systems*   Where safety and reliability are essential, the additional expense of a formal specification using a notation such as Z or VDM might be justified. Really critical systems could justify the cost of having independent teams develop parallel systems with the same functionality. The operational systems can then run concurrently with continuous cross-checking.

The implications of prototyping and the incremental approach are explored later in the chapter.

- *Imprecise requirements*   Uncertainties or a *novel hardware/software platform* mean that a prototyping approach should be considered. If the environment in which the system is to be implemented is a rapidly changing one, then serious consideration would need to be given to *incremental delivery*. If the users have *uncertain objectives* in connection with the project, then a *soft systems* approach may be desirable.

Exercise 4.3   Bearing in mind the discussion above, what, in broad outline, is the most suitable approach for each of the following?

(a) a system which calculates the amount of a drug that should be administered to a patient who has a particular complaint;

(b) a system to administer a student loans scheme;

(c) a system to control trains in the Channel Tunnel.

4.3   Technical plan contents list

Project analysis will produce practical requirements to be fed into the next stage of the planning process. These requirements might involve additional activities, the acquisition of items of software or hardware, or special staff training. As these will imply certain costs, they should be recorded formally.

A software house might produce a preliminary technical plan to help prepare a bid for a contract. Sometimes, the plan might actually be shown to the potential customer in order to explain the basis for the bid price and to impress the customer with the soundness of the intended approach.

The technical plan is likely to have the following contents:

1. **Introduction and summary constraints:**
   (a) character of the system to be developed;
   (b) risks and uncertainties of the project;
   (c) user requirements concerning implementation.

2. **Recommended approach:**
   (a) selected methodology or process model;
   (b) development methods;
   (c) required software tools;
   (d) target hardware/software environment.

3. Implementation:
(a) required development environment;
(b) required maintenance environment;
(c) required training.

4. Implications:
(a) project products and activities – this will have an effect on the schedule and staff-time;
(b) financial – this report will be used to produce costings.

The content of such a report could be incorporated into a general planning document which has the general format outlined in Annex 2 of Chapter 1. The *Recommended approach* could be absorbed into the *Methods* section of the project plan. *Development details* would be incorporated into the *Resources* section of the plan.

One outcome of project analysis could be the abandonment of the project if the costs of its implementation is now seen to exceed the expected benefits.

4.4 Choice of process models

The word 'process' is sometimes used to emphasize the idea of a system *in action*. In order to achieve an outcome, the system will have to execute one or more activities: this is its process. This idea can be applied to the development of computer-based systems where a number of interrelated activities have to be undertaken to create a final product. These activities can be organized in different ways and we can call these *process models*.

A major part of the planning will be choosing development methods and slotting them into an overall process model.

The planner needs not only to select methods, but also to specify how each method is to be applied. With methods such as SSADM, there is a considerable degree of choice about how it is to be applied: not all parts of SSADM are compulsory. Many student projects have the rather basic failing that at the planning stage they claim that, say, SSADM is to be used: in the event all that is produced are a few SSADM fragments such as a top-level data flow diagram and a preliminary logical data structure diagram. If this is all the particular project requires, it should be stated at the outset.

4.5 Structure versus speed of delivery

The principle behind structured methods is 'get it right first time'.

Although some 'object-oriented' specialists might object(!), we include the OO approach as a structured method – after all, we hope it is not unstructured. Structured methods are made up of sets of steps and rules which when applied produce system products such as data flow diagrams. Each of these products is carefully documented. Such methods are often time consuming compared to more intuitive approaches and this implies some additional cost. The pay-off, it is hoped, is a less error prone and more maintainable final system. This balance of costs and benefits is more likely to be justified on a large project involving many developers and users. This is not to say that smaller projects cannot justify the use of such methods.

It might be thought that users would generally welcome the more professional approach that structured methods imply. However, customers of IS/IT are concerned with getting working business applications delivered quickly and at less cost and often see structured methods as unnecessarily bureaucratic and slow. A response to this has been *rapid application development* (RAD) which puts the emphasis on quickly producing prototypes of the software for users to evaluate.

The RAD approach does not preclude the use of some elements of structured methods such as Logical Data Structure diagrams but also adopts tactics such as *joint application development* (JAD) workshops. In these workshops, developers and users work together intensively for, say, three to five days and identify and agree fully documented business requirements. Often these workshops are conducted away from the normal business and development environments in *clean rooms*, special conference rooms free from outside interruption and suitably furnished with white boards and other aids to communication. Advocates of JAD believe these hot-house conditions can speed up communication and negotiation that might take several weeks or months via a conventional approach of formal reports containing proposals and counter-proposals.

Joint Application Development, Jane Wood and Denise Silver, Wiley, 1995 is a useful introduction to JAD.

Just because a project uses JAD does not mean that it is not structured. The definition of the scope of the project, the initial research involving the interviewing of key personnel and the creation of preliminary data and process models would need to be planned and executed before the JAD sessions were organized. The results of JAD sessions could be implemented using quite conventional methods.

Two competing pressures can be seen. One is to get the job done as quickly and cheaply as possible, and the other is to make sure that the final product has a robust structure which will be able to meet evolving needs. Some of these ideas will be returned to in our later discussions on prototyping and the incremental approach.

4.6 The waterfall model

The first description of this approach is said to be that of H. D. Bennington in 'Production of Large Computer Programs' in 1956. This was reprinted in 1983 in *Annals of the History of Computing* 5(4).

This is the 'classical' model of system development. Alternative names for this model are *one-shot* or *once-through*. As can be seen from the example in Figure 4.2, there is a sequence of activities working from top to bottom. The diagram shows some arrows pointing upwards and backwards. This indicates that a later stage may reveal the need for some extra work at an earlier stage, but this should definitely be the exception rather than the rule. After all, the flow of a waterfall should be downwards with the possibility of just a little water splashing back. The limited scope for iteration is in fact one of the strengths of this process model. With a large project you want to avoid reworking tasks previously thought to be completed. Having to reopen completed activities plays havoc with promised completion dates.

We contend that there is nothing intrinsically wrong with the waterfall approach, even though writers often advocate alternative models. It is the ideal for which the project manager strives. When it works well, the waterfall approach allows project completion times to be forecast with more confidence than with some more iterative approaches allowing projects to be controlled effectively. However, where there is uncertainty about how a system is to be implemented, and unfortunately there very often is, a more flexible, iterative, approach might be required.

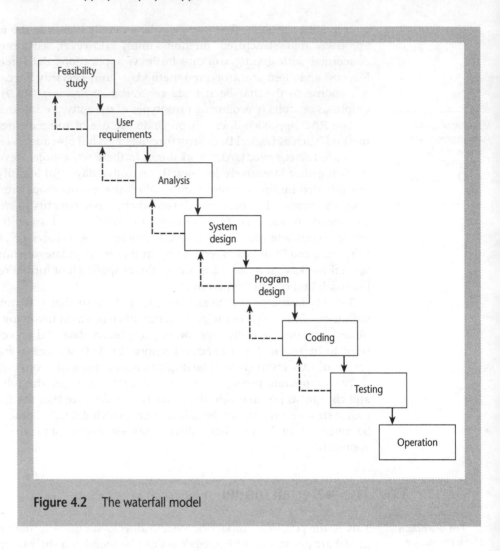

Figure 4.2 The waterfall model

4.7 The V-process model

Figure 4.3 gives a diagrammatic representation of this model. This is an elaboration of the waterfall model and stresses the necessity for validation activities that match the activities that create the products of the project.

The V-process model can be seen as expanding the activity *testing* in the waterfall model. Each step has a matching validation process which can, where defects are found, cause a loop back to the corresponding development stage and a reworking of the following steps. Ideally this feeding back should only occur where a discrepancy has been found between what was specified by a particular activity and what was actually implemented in the next lower activity on the descent of the V loop. For example, the system designer might have written that a calculation be carried out in a certain way. A second developer building code to meet this design might have misunderstood what was required. At system testing stage, the original designer would be responsible for checking that the software is doing what was

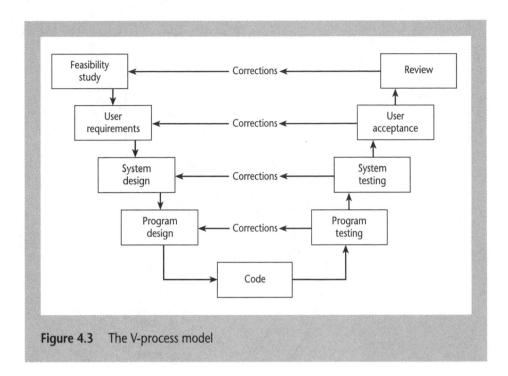

Figure 4.3   The V-process model

specified and this would discover the coder's misreading of that document. Only corrections should be fed back, not the system designer's second thoughts, otherwise the project would slip into 'evolutionary prototyping'.

Exercise 4.4   Figure 4.3 shows the V-process model. The review that is held after the system has been implemented is shown as possibly feeding corrections back to the feasibility study which may have been conducted months or years before. How would this work in practice?

4.8   The spiral model

The original ideas behind the spiral model can be found in B. W. Boehm's 1988 paper 'A spiral model of software development and enhancement' in *IEEE Computer* 21(5).

It could be argued that this is another way of looking at the waterfall model. In the waterfall model, it is possible to escape at the end of any activity in the sequence. A feasibility study might decide that the implementation of a proposed system would be beneficial. The management therefore authorize work on the detailed analysis of user requirements. Some analysis, for instance the interviewing of users, might already have taken place at the feasibility stage, but a more thorough investigation is now launched. This could reveal that the costs of implementing the system would be higher than projected benefits and lead to a decision to abandon the project.

A greater level of detail is considered at each stage of the project and a greater degree of confidence about the probability of success for the project should be justified. This can be portrayed as a loop or a spiral where the system to be implemented is considered in more detail in each sweep. Each sweep terminates with an evaluation before the next iteration is embarked upon. Figure 4.4 illustrates how SSADM can be interpreted in such a way.

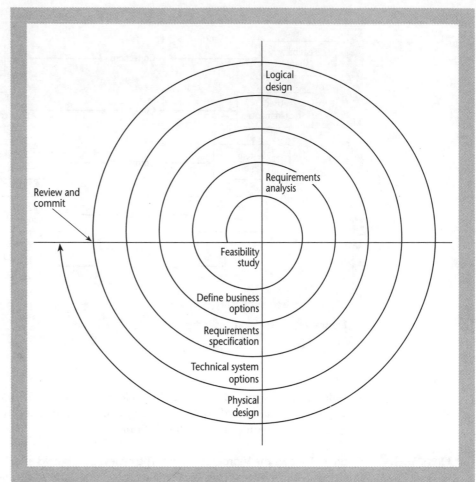

Figure 4.4 The application of the spiral model to SSADM version 4

4.9 Software prototyping

A prototype is a working model of one or more aspects of the projected system. It is constructed and tested quickly and inexpensively in order to test out assumptions.

Prototypes can be classified as throw-away or evolutionary.

- *Throw-away prototypes* Here the prototype is used only to test out some ideas and is then discarded when the true development of the operational system is commenced. The prototype could be developed using a different software environment (for example, a desk-top application builder as opposed to a procedural programming language for the final system where machine efficiency might be important) or even on a different kind of hardware platform.

- *Evolutionary prototypes* The prototype is developed and modified until it is finally in a state where it can become the operational system. In this case the standards that are used to develop the software have to be carefully considered.

Some of the reasons that have been put forward for prototyping are the following:

- *Learning by doing*   When we have just done something for the first time we can usually look back and see where we have made mistakes.

- *Improved communication*   Even if users do read system specifications, they do not get a feel for how the system is likely to work in practice.

- *Improved user involvement*   The users can be more actively involved in design decisions about the new system.

- *Clarification of partially known requirements*   Where there is no existing system to mimic, users can often get a better idea of what might be useful to them by trying out prototypes.

- *Demonstration of the consistency and completeness of a specification*   Any mechanism that attempts to implement a specification on a computer is likely to uncover ambiguities and omissions. The humble spreadsheet can, for instance, check that calculations have been specified correctly.

- *Reduced need for documentation*   Because a working prototype can be examined there is less need for detailed documentation of requirements.

- *Reduced maintenance costs*   If the user is unable to suggest modifications at the prototyping stage they are more likely to ask for changes to the operational system. This reduction of maintenance costs is the core of the financial case for prototypes.

- *Feature constraint*   If an application building tool is used, then the prototype will tend to have features that are easily implemented by that tool. A paper-based design might suggest features that are expensive to implement.

- *Production of expected results*   The problem with creating test cases is generally not the creation of the test input but the accurate calculation of the expected results. A prototype can help here.

Software prototyping is not without its drawbacks and dangers, however.

- *Users can misunderstand the role of the prototype*   For example, they might expect the prototype to have as stringent input validation or as fast a response as the operational system although this was not intended.

- *Lack of project standards possible*   Evolutionary prototyping could just be an excuse for a sloppy 'hack it out and see what happens' approach.

- *Lack of control*   It can be difficult to control the prototyping cycle if the driving force is the users' propensity to try out new things.

- *Additional expense*   Building and exercising a prototype will incur additional expenses. However, this should not be overestimated as many analysis and design tasks have to be undertaken whatever the approach.

- *Machine efficiency*   A system built through prototyping, while sensitive to the users' needs, might not be as efficient in machine terms as one developed using more conventional methods.

- *Close proximity of developers*   Prototyping could mean that code developers have to be sited close to the users. One trend is for organizations in developed countries to transfer software development to developing countries with lower costs such as India. Prototyping might prevent this.

The most important justification for a prototype is the need to reduce uncertainty by conducting an experiment.

Some may argue, however, that this is a very dangerous suggestion.

4.10 Other ways of categorizing prototypes

What is being learnt?

The most important reason for prototyping is a need to learn about an area of uncertainty. Thus it is essential to identify at the outset what is to be learned from the prototype.

Computing students often realize that the software that they are to write as part of their final-year project could not safely be used by real users. They therefore call the software a 'prototype'. However, if it is a real prototype then they must:

- specify what they hope to learn from the prototype;
- plan how the prototype is to be evaluated;
- report on what has actually been learnt.

Prototypes can be used to find out about new development techniques, by using them in a pilot project. Alternatively, the development methods might be well known, but the nature of the application uncertain.

Different projects will have uncertainties at different stages. Prototypes can therefore be used at different stages. A prototype might be used, for instance, at the requirements gathering stage to pin down requirements that seem blurred and shifting. A prototype might, on the other hand, be used at the design stage to test out the users' ability to navigate through a sequence of input screens.

To what extent is the prototyping to be done?

It would be unusual for the whole of the application to be prototyped. The prototyping usually only simulates some aspects of the target application. For example there might be:

- *Mock-ups*   As when copies of input screens are shown to the users on a workstation, but the screens cannot actually be used.

- *Simulated interaction*   For example, the user can type in a request to access a record and the system will show the details of a record, but the details shown are always the same and no access is made to a database.

- Partial working model:
  Vertical   Some, but not all, features are prototyped fully;
  Horizontal   All features are prototyped but not in detail – perhaps there is not full validation of input.

What is being prototyped?

- *The human–computer interface*   With business applications, processing requirements have usually been established at an early stage. Prototyping tends, therefore, to be confined to the nature of operator interaction. Here the physical vehicle for the prototype should be as similar as possible to the operational system.

- *The functionality of the system*   Here the precise way the system should function internally is not known. For example, a computer model of some real-world phenomenon is being developed. The algorithms used might need to be repeatedly adjusted until they satisfactorily imitate the real-world behaviour.

Exercise 4.5 At what stage of a system development project (for example, feasibility study, requirements analysis, etc.) would a prototype be useful as a means of reducing the following uncertainties.

(a) There is a proposal that the senior managers of an insurance company have personal access to management information through an executive information system installed on personal computers located on their desks. Such a system would be costly to set up and there is some doubt about whether the managers would actually use the system.

(b) A computer system is to support sales office staff taking phone calls from members of the public enquiring about motor insurance and giving quotations over the phone.

(c) The insurance company is considering implementing the telephone sales system using the system development features supplied by the Microsoft Access. They are not sure, at the moment, that it can provide the kind of interface that would be needed and are also concerned about the possible response times of a system developed using Microsoft Access.

4.11 Controlling changes during prototyping

A major problem with prototyping is controlling changes to the prototype following suggestions by the users. One approach has been to categorize changes as belonging to one of three types:

- *Cosmetic* (about 35% of changes)
  These are simply changes to the layout of the screen. They are:
  (a) implemented;
  (b) recorded.

- *Local* (about 60% of changes)
  These involve changes to the way that the screen is processed but do not affect other parts of the system. They are:
  (a) implemented;
  (b) recorded;
  (c) backed-up so that they can be removed at a later stage if necessary;
  (d) inspected retrospectively.

Inspections are discussed in Chapter 12.

- *Global* (about 5% of changes)
  These are changes that affect more than one part of the processing. All changes here have to be the subject of a design review before they can be implemented.

4.12 Incremental delivery

Tom Gilb whose *Principles of Software Engineering Management* was published by Addison-Wesley in 1988 is a prominent advocate of this approach.

This approach involves breaking the application down into small components which are then implemented and delivered in sequence. Each component delivered must give some benefit to the user. Figure 4.5 gives a general idea of the approach.

Time boxing is often associated with an incremental approach. Here the scope of the deliverables for an increment is rigidly constrained by an agreed deadline. This deadline has to be met, even at the expense of dropping some

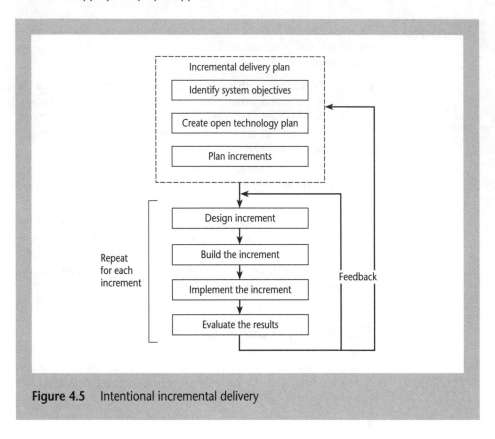

Figure 4.5 Intentional incremental delivery

of the planned functionality. Omitted features can be transferred to later increments.

Advantages of this approach

These are some of the justifications given for the approach.

- The feedback from early increments improve the later stages.
- The possibility of changes in requirements is reduced because of the shorter timespan between the design of a component and its delivery.
- Users get benefits earlier than with a conventional approach.
- Early delivery of some useful components improves cash flow, because you get some return on investment early on.
- Smaller sub-projects are easier to control and manage.
- 'Gold-plating', that is the requesting of features that are unnecessary and not in fact used, is less as users will know that they get more than one bite of the cherry – if a feature is not in the current increment then it can be included in the next.
- The project can be temporarily abandoned if more urgent work crops up.
- Job satisfaction is increased for developers who see their labours bearing fruit at regular, short, intervals.

Disadvantages

On the other hand these disadvantages have been put forward.

- Software breakage, that is, later increments may require modifications to earlier increments.
- Programmers may be more productive working on one large system than on a series of smaller ones.
- Grady Booch, an authority on OO, suggests that with what he calls 'requirements driven' projects (which equate to incremental delivery) *'Conceptual integrity sometimes suffers because there is little motivation to deal with scalability, extensibility, portability or reusability beyond what any vague requirements might imply'*. Booch also suggests there might be a tendency towards a large number of discrete functions with little common infrastructure.

This quotation is from Grady Booch's *Object Solutions: Managing the Object Oriented Project*, Addison-Wesley, 1996.

The incremental delivery plan

The nature and order of each increment to be delivered to the users have to be planned at the outset.

The process is similar to strategic planning, but at a more detailed level. Attention is given to increments of a user application rather than whole applications. The elements of the incremental plan are the *system objectives, open technology plan* and the *incremental plan*.

The process of planning the increments of a project as described by Gilb has similarities with stratetic planning described in the previous chapter.

Identify system objectives

Recall that earlier we suggested that project planners ideally want well-defined objectives, but as much freedom as possible about how these are to be met. These overall objectives can then expanded into more specific functional goals and quality goals.

Functional goals will include:

- objectives it is intended to achieve;
- jobs the system is to do;
- computer/non-computer functions to achieve them.

Chapter 12 discusses software quality characteristics.

In addition, measurable quality characteristics should be defined such as reliability, response and security. If this is done properly, these overarching quality requirements can go some way to meeting the concerns, expressed by Grady Booch, that these might get lost through the concentration on the functional requirements at increment level. It also reflects Tom Gilb's concern that system developers always keep sight of the objectives that they are trying to achieve on behalf of their clients. In the changing environment of an application individual requirements could change over the course of the project, but the objectives should not.

Create open technology plan

If the system is to be able to cope with new components being continually added, it needs to be extendible, portable and maintainable.

As a minimum this will require the use of:

- a standard high-level language;
- a standard operating system;

- small modules;
- variable parameters, for example, items such as the names of an organization and its departments, charge rates and so on are held in a parameter file that can be amended without programmer intervention;
- standard database management system.

These are all things that might be expected as a matter of course in a modern IS development environment.

Although Gilb does not suggest this, following Booch's hints, it would be desirable to draw up an initial logical data model or object model for the whole system. It is difficult to see how the next stage of planning the nature and order of the increments could be done without this foundation.

Plan increments

Having defined the overall objectives and formulated an open technology plan, the next stage is to plan the increments using the following guidelines:

- steps typically should consist of 1% to 5% of the total project;
- non-computer steps should be included;
- an increment should, ideally, not exceed one month and should not, at worst, take more than three months;
- each increment should deliver some benefit to the user;
- some increments will be physically dependent on others;
- value-to-cost ratios may be used to decide priorities (see below).

A new system might be replacing an old computer system and the first increments could use parts of the old system. For example, the data for the database of the new system could initially be obtained from the old system's standing files.

Which steps should be first? Some steps will be prerequisites because of physical dependencies, but others may be in any order. Value-to-cost ratios (see Table 4.1) can be used to establish the order in which increments are to be developed. The customer is asked to rate the value of each increment with a score in the range 1–10. The developers also rate the cost of developing each of the increments with a score in the range 0–10. This might seem rather crude, but people are often

A zero cost would mean the change can be implemented without software development – some costs might be incurred by users in changing procedures.

The value-to-cost ratio = V/C where V is a score 1–10 representing value to customer and C is a score 0–10 representing cost.

Table 4.1 Ranking by value-to-cost ratio

Step	Value	Cost	Ratio	Rank
Profit reports	9	1	9	(2nd)
Online database	1	9	0·11	(6th)
Ad hoc enquiry	5	5	1	(4th)
Production sequence plans	2	8	0·25	(5th)
Purchasing profit factors	9	4	2·25	(3rd)
Clerical procedures	0	7	0	(7th)
Profit-based pay for managers	9	0	∞	(1st)

unwilling to be more precise. By then dividing the value rating by the cost rating, a rating which indicates the relative 'value for money' of each increment may be derived.

An incremental example

Tom Gilb describes a project where a software house negotiated a fixed price contract with a three-month delivery time with the Swedish Government to supply a system to support map making. It later became apparent that the original estimate of effort upon which the bid was based was probably about half the real effort.

The project was replanned so that it was divided into 10 increments, each supplying something of use to the customer. The final increments were not available until three months after the contract's delivery date. The customer was not in fact unhappy about this as the most important parts of the system had actually been delivered early.

4.13 Dynamic Systems Development Method

A fuller explanation of DSDM can be found in Jennifer Stapleton's *DSDM Dynamic Systems Development Method*, Addison-Wesley, 1997.

In the United Kingdom, SSADM (Structured Systems Analysis Design Method) has until recently been a predominant methodology. In no small part, this has been because of sponsorship by the United Kingdom government. More recently, however, it has lost some of its favour, partly because it has been perceived as overly bureaucratic and prescriptive. In contrast there has been an increased interest in the iterative and incremental approaches we have outlined above. As a consequence, a consortium has developed guidelines for the use of such techniques and has packaged the overall approach as the Dynamic Systems Development Method (DSDM). It is possible to attend courses on the method and to become an accredited DSDM practitioner.

Nine core DSDM principles have been enunciated:

1. Active user involvement is imperative;
2. DSDM teams must be empowered to make decisions;
3. Focus on frequent delivery of products;
4. Fitness for *business purpose* is the essential criterion for acceptance of deliverables;
5. Iterative and incremental delivery is necessary to converge on an accurate business solution;
6. All changes during development are reversible;
7. Requirements are base-lined at a *high level*;
8. Testing is integrated throughout the life cycle;
9. A collaborative and co-operative approach between all stakeholders is essential.

JAD, Joint Application Development was discussed in Section 4.5.

Figure 4.6 outlines the general approach. Before development starts, a feasibility study needs to be conducted as with any other project. This will consider not just the business case for the project, but also its suitability for DSDM. A business requirement is then developed, probably using JAD. Prototypes might then be created which explore the functional requirements. These may be followed by

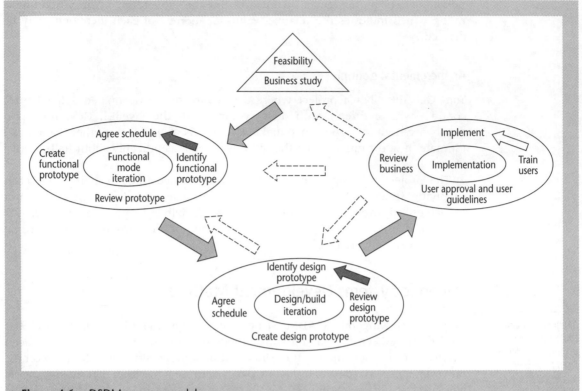

Figure 4.6 DSDM process model
(Reproduced by permission of DSDM Consortium. DSDM is a registered trademark of Dynamic Systems Development Method Limited)

further prototypes that establish the detailed design, particularly of the interfaces. Implementation of the components can then follow. The arrows between the various functions that are shown in Figure 4.6 illustrate how this order of activities is very flexible and iterative.

DSDM encourages the use of time boxes. It is suggested that these should typically be between two and six weeks. This short time-span should make participants focus on what is really needed. It will be recalled that in order to meet the deadline imposed by a time box, the implementation of less important features may be held over to later increments (or even dropped altogether). In order to prioritize the relative importance of requirements, they can be categorized using the 'MoSCoW' classification:

- *Must have*: that is, essential features.
- *Should have*: these would probably be mandatory if you were using a conventional development approach – but the system can operate without them.
- *Could have*: these requirements can be delayed with some inconvenience.
- *Won't have*: these features are wanted, but their delay to a later increment is readily accepted.

The possibility of requirements being reallocated to different increments means that project plans will need to be constantly updated if the project is to be successfully controlled.

4.14 Extreme programming

See Kent Beck's *Extreme Programming Explained: Embrace Change*, Addison-Wesley, 1999.

The concept of extreme programming (XP) is particularly associated with Kent Beck and has its origins with Chrysler C3 payroll project with which Beck was associated. Extreme programming is a further development of many of the RAD and DSDM principles that have been explored above. In some ways XP can be seen as 'super-programmers' describing their idea of coding heaven. It belongs to a cluster of similar methodologies (including Jim Highsmith's Adaptive Software Development and Alistair Cockburn's Crystal Light methods) which have collectively been called *agile* methods.

As with DSDM, XP advocates argue that applications should be written in increments of working software that should take a matter of weeks to complete. If anything, they seem to go further than DSDM and talk of increments ideally taking only one to three weeks. The customer for the software can at any stage suggest improvements to the functionality.

XP seems to argue against Booch's view that software development needs to be based on a careful preliminary design of a robust underlying structure. For a start, distinctions between designing the software structure and building the software are argued to be artificial. The principle adopted is that code should be developed simply to meet existing requirements and not possible future extensions to the application as future requirements tend to be uncertain. Clearly such an approach could lead to very unstructured code as an application develops in an *ad hoc* fashion. This is countered by the use of frequent redesigns of the code (or *refactoring*) which tidies up the code for existing features.

Perhaps the most interesting aspect of XP is the emphasis on testing. Test cases and expected results are devised before the design takes place. To do this, the developer and user must agree exactly what should happen given specific circumstances. As well as generating test cases, this helps to clarify the user's exact requirements. When the code is complete and tested, the test cases are merged with a consolidated set of test cases. After each new increment, this consolidated set of test cases is executed to ensure that the additions to functionality or the refactoring of old code has not introduced errors into what had previously worked correctly.

4.15 Managing iterative processes

This discussion of agile methods may be confusing as it seems to turn many of our previous planning concepts on their head.

Approaches such as XP correctly emphasize the importance of communication and of removing artificial barriers to development productivity. Extreme programming to many might seem to be simply a 'licence to hack'. However, a more detailed examination of the techniques of XP shows that many (such as pair programming and installation standards) are conscious techniques to counter the excesses of hacking and to ensure that good maintainable code is written.

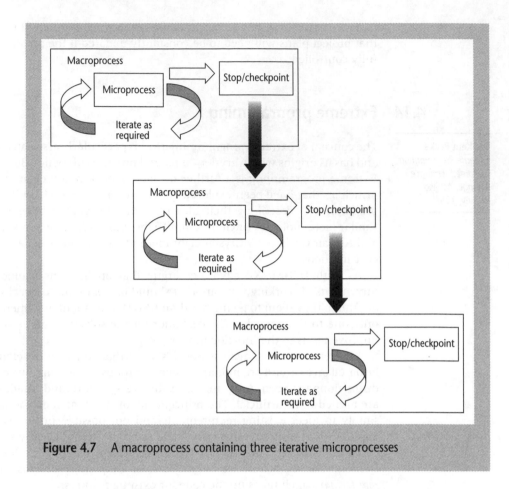

Figure 4.7   A macroprocess containing three iterative microprocesses

Booch suggests that there are two levels of development: the *macroprocess* and the *microprocess*. The macroprocess is closely related to the waterfall process model. At this level, a range of activities carried out by a variety of specialist groups has to be coordinated. We need to have some dates when we know that major activities will be finished so that we know when we will need to bring in staff to work on subsequent activities. Within this macroprocess there will be microprocess activities which might involve iterative working. Systems testing has always been one. Figure 4.7 illustrates how a sequential macroprocess can be imposed on a number of iterative sub-process. With iterative microprocesses, the use of time boxes is needed for control at the macro level.

There are cases where the macroprocess itself can be iterative. It might be that a prototype for a complex technical system is produced in two or three successive versions, each taking several months to create and evaluate. In these circumstances, each iteration might be treated as a project in its own right.

4.16   Selecting the most appropriate process model

Construction of an application can be distinguished from its *installation*. It is possible to use different approaches for these two stages. For example, an application could

See Appendix C for
an overview of
ISO 12207, which
offers advice on
process model
selection.

be constructed using a one-shot strategy, but then be released to its users in
increments. The only combinations of construction and installation strategies that
are not feasible are the evolutionary installation with any other construction
approach than evolutionary.

Where uncertainty is high then an evolutionary approach is to be favoured. An
example of uncertainty would be where the users' requirements are not clearly
defined. Where the requirements are relatively certain but there are many
complexities, as with a large embedded system needing a large amount of code,
then an incremental approach might be favoured. Where deadlines are tight, then
either an evolutionary or an incremental approach is favoured over a one-shot
strategy, as both tactics should allow at least something to be delivered at the
deadline, even if it is not all that was originally promised. Students about to plan
final-year projects would do well to note this.

4.17 Conclusion

This chapter has stressed the need to examine each project carefully to see whether
it has characteristics that suggest a particular approach or process model.
These characteristics might suggest the addition of specific activities to the project
plan.

The classic waterfall process model that attempts to minimize iteration should lead
to projects that are easy to control. Unfortunately many projects do not lend themselves to this structure. Prototyping may be able to reduce project uncertainties by
allowing knowledge to be bought through experimentation. The incremental
approach encourages the execution of a series of small, manageable, 'mini-projects',
but does have some costs.

4.18 Further exercises

1. A building society has a long history of implementing computer-based information
   systems to support the work of its branches. It uses a proprietary structured systems
   analysis and design method. It has been decided to create a computer model of the
   property market. This would attempt, for example, to calculate the effect of changes
   of interest rates on house values. There is some concern that the usual methodology
   used for IS development would not be appropriate for the new project.

   (a) Why might there be this concern and what alternative approaches should be
       considered?
   (b) Outline a plan for the development of the system which illustrates the application
       of your preferred methodology for this project.

2. A software package is to be designed and built to assist in software cost estimation. It
   will input certain parameters and produce initial cost estimates to be used at bidding
   time.

   (a) It has been suggested that a software prototype would be of value in these
       circumstances. Explain why this might be.
   (b) Discuss how such prototyping could be controlled to ensure that it is conducted
       in an orderly and effective way and within a specified time span.

3. An invoicing system is to have the following components: amend invoice, produce invoice, produce monthly statements, record cash payment, clear paid invoices from database, create customer records, delete customer.

   (a) What physical dependencies govern the order in which these transactions are implemented?

   (b) How could the system be broken down into increments that would be of some value to the users. (Hint – think about the problems of taking existing details onto a database when a system is first implemented.)

4. In Section 4.10 we stressed the need to define what is to be learned from a prototype and the way that it will be evaluated to obtain the new knowledge. Outline the learning outcomes and evaluation for the following:

   (a) A final-year degree student is to build an application that will act as a 'suggestions box' in a factory. The application will allow employees to make suggestions about process improvements, and will track the subsequent progress of the suggestion as it is evaluated. The student wants to use a web-based front-end with a conventional database. The student has not previously developed any applications using this mix of technologies.

   (b) An engineering company has to maintain a large number of different types of document relating to current and previous projects. It has decided to evaluate the use of a computer-based document retrieval system and wishes to try it out on a trial basis.

   (c) A business that specializes in 'e-solutions', that is, the development of business applications that exploit the World Wide Web has been approached by the computing school of a local university. The school is investigating setting up a special website for its former students. The website's core will be information about job and training opportunities, and it is hoped that this will generate income through advertising. It agreed that some kind of pilot to evaluate the scheme is needed.

5. In a college environment, an intranet for students that holds information about courses, such as lecture programmes, reading lists and assignment briefs, is often set up. As a 'real' exercise, plan, organize and carry out a JAD session to design (or improve the design) of an intranet facility.

   This will require:

   ● preliminary investigation to identify representative key stakeholders (for example, staff who might be supplying information for the intranet);
   ● creation of documents for use in the JAD proceedings;
   ● recording of the JAD proceedings;
   ● creating a report which will present the findings of the JAD session.

CHAPTER 5

Software effort estimation

Objectives

When you have completed this chapter you will be able to:

- avoid the dangers of unrealistic estimates;
- understand the range of estimating methods that can be used;
- estimate projects using a bottom-up approach;
- count the function points and object points for a system;
- estimate the effort needed to implement software using a procedural programming language;
- understand the COCOMO approach to developing effort models.

5.1 Introduction

One definition of a successful project is that the system is delivered 'on time and within budget and with the required quality', which implies that targets are set and the project leader then tries to meet those targets. This assumes that the targets are reasonable – the possibility of a project leader achieving record levels of productivity from the team, but still not meeting a deadline because of incorrect initial estimates is not recognized. Realistic estimates are therefore crucial to the project leader.

In Chapter 1, the special characteristics of software identified by Brooks, i.e. complexity, conformity, changeability and invisibility, were discussed.

What sorts of problem might a project leader such as Amanda, who is in charge of the IOE Maintenance Group Accounts project, encounter when trying to do estimates? Estimating the effort required to implement software is notoriously difficult. Some of the difficulties of estimating are inherent in the very nature of software, especially its complexity and invisibility. In addition the intensely human activities that make up system development cannot be treated in a purely mechanistic way. Other difficulties include:

- *Novel applications of software* With traditional engineering projects, it is often the case that the system to be created is similar to one constructed previously but for a different customer or in a different location. The estimates for such a project can therefore be based on previous experience. With software, in most major projects the product will in some way be unique and will therefore be clouded with doubts and uncertainties.

79

The figures are taken from B. A. Kitchenham and N. R. Taylor 'Software Project Development Cost Estimation, *Journal of Systems and Software*, 5, 1985.

The abbreviation SLOC stands for 'source lines of code'. SLOC is one way of indicating the size of a system.

Table 5.1 Some project data – effort in work months (as percentage of total effort in brackets)

Project	Design wm	Design (%)	Coding wm	Coding (%)	Testing wm	Testing (%)	Total wm	Total SLOC
a	3.9	(23)	5.3	(32)	7.4	(44)	16.7	6050
b	2.7	(12)	13.4	(59)	6.5	(26)	22.6	8363
c	3.5	(11)	26.8	(83)	1.9	(6)	32.2	13334
d	0.8	(21)	2.4	(62)	0.7	(18)	3.9	5942
e	1.8	(10)	7.7	(44)	7.8	(45)	17.3	3315
f	19.0	(28)	29.7	(44)	19.0	(28)	67.7	38988
g	2.1	(21)	7.4	(74)	0.5	(5)	10.1	38614
h	1.3	(7)	12.7	(66)	5.3	(27)	19.3	12762
i	8.5	(14)	22.7	(38)	28.2	(47)	59.5	26500

● *Changing technology* For example, at IOE the original maintenance billing system might have been written in Cobol, while the new extension for group accounts that Amanda is directing might be developed using an application building environment such as that provided by Oracle.

● *Lack of homogeneity of project experience* As we will see, effective estimating should be based on information about how past projects have performed. It is surprising how many organizations do not make this data available to staff. Amanda might also find that even where the previous project data is available, it might not be that useful.

Table 5.1 shows a set of figures recorded for actual projects carried out by the same organization.

Exercise 5.1 Calculate the productivity (that is, SLOC per work month) of each of the projects in Table 5.1 and also for the organization as a whole. If the project leaders for projects a and d had correctly estimated the number of source lines of code (SLOC) and then used the average productivity of the organization to calculate the effort needed to complete the projects, how far out would their estimates have been from the actual effort?

It would be very difficult on the basis of this information to advise a project manager about what sort of productivity to expect, or about the probable distribution of effort among the phases of design, coding and testing that could be expected from a new project.

There have been some attempts to set up industry-wide databases of past projects. However, this data seems to be of limited use to estimators as there are uncertainties in the way that various terms can be interpreted. For example, what exactly is meant by the term 'testing'? Does it cover the activity of the software developer when debugging code? Does 'design' include drawing up program structure diagrams or does this come under the heading of 'programming'?

Subjective nature of estimating Some research shows that people tend to underestimate the difficulty of small tasks and overestimate that of large ones. In the world of software development this is perhaps justifiable, as large projects are usually disproportionately more complex and more difficult than smaller ones.

Political implications   Different groups within an organization have different objectives. The IOE information systems development managers might, for example, want to see as many systems as possible implemented and will therefore put pressure on estimators to reduce cost estimates. As Amanda is responsible for the development of the maintenance group accounts subsystem, she might be concerned that the project does not exceed its budget and is not delivered late, because this will reflect badly on herself. She might therefore try to increase the estimates. One suggestion is that all estimates within an organization should be carried out by a specialist estimating group, independent of both the users and the project team. Not all agree with this, as staff involved in a project are more likely to be committed to targets where they have participated in formulating them.

> The possibility of the different groups with stakes in a project having different and possibly conflicting objectives was discussed in Chapter 1.

5.2   Where are estimates done?

Estimates are carried out at various stages of a software project. At each stage, the reasons for the estimate and the methods used will vary.

> Chapter 3 discusses strategic planning in some detail.

Strategic planning   The costs of computerizing potential applications as well as the benefits of doing so might need to be estimated to help decide what priority to give to each project. Such estimates might also influence the numbers of various types of development staff to be recruited by the organization.

Feasibility study   This ascertains that the benefits of the potential system will justify the costs.

System specification   Most system development methodologies usefully distinguish between the definition of the users' requirements and the design that documents how those requirements are to be fulfilled. The effort needed to implement different design proposals will need to be estimated. Estimates at the design stage will also confirm that the feasibility study is still valid, taking into account all that has been learnt during detailed requirements analysis.

> The estimate at this stage cannot be based only on the user requirement: some kind of technical plan is also needed – see Chapter 4.

Evaluation of suppliers' proposals   In the case of the IOE maintenance group accounts sub-system, for example, IOE might consider putting the actual system building out to tender. Staff in the software houses that are considering a bid would need to scrutinize the system specification and produce estimates on which to base proposals. Amanda might still be required to carry out her own estimate to help judge the bids received. IOE might wish to question a proposal that seems too low: they might wonder, for example, whether the proposer had properly understood the requirements. If, on the other hand, the bids seem too high, they might reconsider in-house development.

Project planning   As the planning and implementation of the project progresses to greater levels of detail, more detailed estimates of smaller work components will be made. As well as confirming the earlier and more broad-brush estimates, these will help answer questions about, for example, when staff will have completed particular tasks and be available for new activities. Two general points can be made here:

● as the project proceeds, so the accuracy of the estimates should improve as knowledge about the nature of the project increases;

● conventional wisdom is that at the beginning of the project the user requirement (that is, a logical model of the required system) is of paramount importance and that premature consideration of the physical implementation is to be avoided. In order to do an estimate, however, the estimator will have to speculate about this physical implementation, for instance about the number of software modules to be written.

To set estimating into the context of the Step Wise framework (Figure 5.1) presented in Chapter 1, re-estimating might take place at almost any step, but specific provision is made for it at Step 3: Analyse project characteristics, where a relatively high-level estimate will be produced, and in Step 5 for each individual activity. As Steps 5–8 are repeated at progressively lower levels, so estimates will be done at a finer degree of detail. As we will see later in this chapter, different methods of estimating are needed at these different planning steps.

5.3 Problems with over- and under-estimates

A project leader such as Amanda will need to be aware that the estimate itself, if known to the development team, will influence the time required to implement the application. An over-estimate might cause the project to take longer than it would otherwise. This can be explained by the application of two 'laws'.

Parkinson's law was originally expounded in C. Northcote Parkinson's tongue-in-cheek book *Parkinson's Law*, John Murray, 1957.

Parkinson's Law   *'Work expands to fill the time available'*, which implies that given an easy target staff will work less hard.

Brooks' law comes from *The Mythical Man-month* that has been referred to in Chapter 1.

Brooks' Law   The effort required to implement a project will go up disproportionately with the number of staff assigned to the project. As the project team grows in size so will the effort that has to go into management, coordination and communication. This has given rise, in extreme cases, to the notion of Brooks' Law: *'putting more people on a late job makes it later'*. If there is an over-estimate of the effort required then this might lead to more staff being allocated than are needed and managerial overheads will be increased. This is more likely to be of significance with large projects.

See T. K. Hamid and S. E. Madnick 'Lessons learnt from modeling the dynamics of software development' in C. F. Kemerer (ed.) *Software Project Management*, Irwin, 1997.

Some have suggested that while the under-estimated project might not be completed on time or to cost, it might still be implemented in a shorter time than a project with a more generous estimate. There must, however, be limits to this phenomenon where all the slack in the project is taken up.

The danger with the under-estimate is the effect on quality. Staff, particularly those with less experience, might respond to pressing deadlines by producing work which is sub-standard. Since we are into laws, this might be seen as a manifestation of Weinberg's zeroth law of reliability: *'if a system does not have to be reliable, it can meet any other objective'*. In other words, if there is no need for the program actually to work, you can meet any programming deadline that might be set! Sub-standard work might only become visible at the later, testing, phases of a project, which are

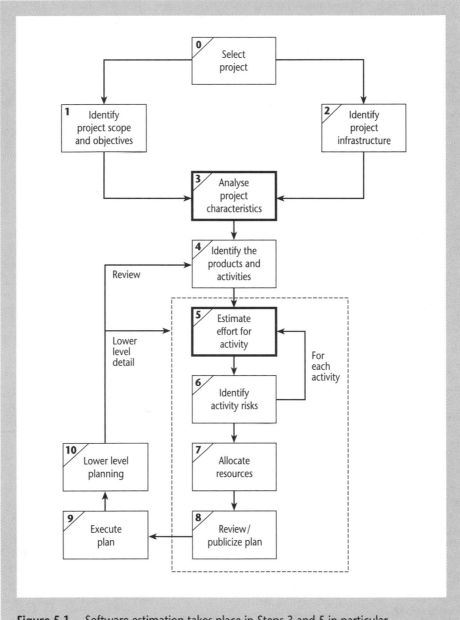

Figure 5.1   Software estimation takes place in Steps 3 and 5 in particular

particularly difficult to control and where extensive rework can have catastrophic consequences for the project completion date.

Because of the possible effects on the behaviour of development staff caused by the size of estimates, they might be artificially reduced by their managers to increase pressure on staff. This will work only where staff are unaware that this has been done. Research has found that motivation and morale are enhanced where targets are achievable. If, over a period of time, staff become aware that the targets set are unattainable and that projects are routinely not meeting their published targets, then this will help to destroy motivation. Furthermore, people like to think of themselves as winners and there is a general tendency to put success down to our own efforts, while failure is blamed on the organization.

In the end, an estimate is not really a prediction, it is a *management goal*. Barry Boehm has suggested that if a software development cost is within 20% of the estimated cost estimate for the job then a good manager can turn it into a self-fulfilling prophecy. A project leader like Amanda will work hard to make the actual performance conform to the estimate.

Barry Boehm devised the COCOMO COnstructive COst MOdel estimating models, which are described later in this chapter.

5.4 The basis for software estimating

The need for historical data

Nearly all estimating methods need information about how projects have been implemented in the past. However, care needs to be taken in judging the applicability of data to the estimator's own circumstances because of possible differences in environmental factors such as the programming languages used, the software tools available, the standards enforced and the experience of the staff.

Measure of work

SLOC has already been used in Table 5.1.

It is normally not possible to calculate directly the actual cost or time required to implement a project. The time taken to write a program might vary according to the competence or experience of the programmer. Implementation times might also vary because of environmental factors such as the software tools available. The usual practice is therefore to express the work content of the system to be implemented independently of effort, using a measure such as source lines of code (SLOC). The reader might also come across the abbreviation KLOC which refers to thousands of lines of code.

R. E. Park has devised a standard for counting source statements that has been widely adopted – see *Software Size Measurement: a Framework for Counting Source Statements*, Software Engineering Institute, 1992.

As can be imagined, SLOC is a very imprecise measure. Does it include comment lines? Are data declarations to be included? Unfortunately, researchers have not been consistent on these points. The writers' view is that comment lines are excluded, but data declarations are included. The argument for including data declarations is that, in Cobol especially, it is possible to transfer much of the specification of processing to the DATA DIVISION, by using, for example, the report writer facility. Others might argue over this, but the main point is that consistency is essential.

Counting SLOC is difficult when employing application-building tools, which often use tables or diagrams to record processing rules. Different measures of size are needed, such as object or function points, that are explained further on in this chapter.

Complexity

Differences in complexity might be one of the reasons for the inconsistencies in Table 5.1.

Two programs with the same KLOC will not necessarily take the same time to write, even if done by the same developer in the same environment. One program might be more complex. Because of this, SLOC estimates have to be modified to take complexity into account. Attempts have been made to find objective measures of complexity, but often it will depend on the subjective judgement of the estimator.

5.5 Software effort estimation techniques

See B. W. Boehm 'Software engineering economics' in C. F. Kemerer (ed.), *Software Project Management*, Irwin, 1997.

Barry Boehm, in his classic work on software effort models, identified the main ways of deriving estimates of software development effort as:

- *algorithmic models* which use 'effort drivers' representing characteristics of the target system and the implementation environment to predict effort;
- *expert judgement* where the advice of knowledgeable staff is solicited;
- *analogy* where a similar, completed, project is identified and its actual effort is used as a basis for the new project;
- *Parkinson* which identifies the staff effort available to do a project and uses that as the 'estimate';
- *price to win* where the 'estimate' is a figure that appears to be sufficiently low to win a contract;
- *top-down* where an overall estimate is formulated for the whole project and is then broken down into the effort required for component tasks;
- *bottom-up* where component tasks are identified and sized and these individual estimates are aggregated.

Clearly, the 'Parkinson' method is not really an effort prediction method, but a method of setting the scope of a project. Similarly, 'price to win' is a way of deciding a price and not a prediction method. On these grounds, Boehm rejects them as prediction techniques although they might have some value as management techniques. There is, for example, a perfectly acceptable engineering practice of 'design to cost' which is one example of the broader approach of 'design by objectives'.

We will now look at some of these techniques more closely. First we will examine the difference between top-down and bottom-up estimating.

Bottom-up estimating

Estimating methods can be generally divided into bottom-up and top-down approaches. With the bottom-up approach, the estimator breaks the project into its component tasks and then estimates how much effort will be required to carry out each task. With a large project, the process of breaking down into tasks would be a repetitive one: each task would be analysed into its component sub-tasks and these in turn would be further analysed. This is repeated until you get to components that can be executed by a single person in about a week or two. The reader might wonder why this is not called a top-down approach: after all you are starting from the top and working down! Although this top-down analysis is an essential precursor to bottom-up estimating, it is really a separate one – that of producing a Work Breakdown Structure (WBS). The bottom-up part comes in adding up the calculated effort for each activity to get an overall estimate.

The bottom-up approach is most appropriate at the later, more detailed, stages of project planning. If this method is used early on in the project cycle, the estimator will have to make some assumptions about the characteristics of the final system, for example the number and size of software modules. These will be working assumptions that imply no commitment when it comes to the actual design of the system.

Where a project is completely novel or there is no historical data available, the estimator would be well advised to use the bottom-up approach.

Exercise 5.2

Brigette at Brightmouth College has been told that there is a requirement, now that the payroll system has been successfully installed, to create a sub-system that analyses the staffing costs for each course. Details of the pay that each member of staff receives can be obtained from the payroll standing data. The number of hours that each member of staff spends teaching on each course can be obtained from standing files in a computer-based time-tabling system.

What tasks would have to be undertaken to implement this requirement? Try to identify tasks that would take one person about one or two weeks.

Which tasks are the ones whose durations are most difficult to estimate?

The top-down approach and parametric models

The top-down approach is normally associated with parametric (or algorithmic) models. These may be explained using the analogy of estimating the cost of rebuilding a house. This would be of practical concern to a house-owner who needs sufficient insurance cover to allow for rebuilding the property if it were destroyed. Unless the house-owner happens to be in the building trade it is unlikely that he or she would be able to work out how many bricklayer-hours, how many carpenter-hours, electrician-hours and so on would be required. Insurance companies, however, produce convenient tables where the house-owner can find an estimate of rebuilding costs based on such *parameters* as the number of storeys and the floor space that a house has. This is a simple parametric model.

The effort needed to implement a project will be related mainly to variables associated with characteristics of the final system. The form of the parametric model will normally be one or more formulae in the form:

$$effort = (system\ size) \times (productivity\ rate)$$

For example, system size might be in the form 'thousands of lines of code' (KLOC) and the productivity rate 40 days per KLOC. The values to be used will often be matters of subjective judgement.

A model to forecast software development effort therefore has two key components. The first is a method of assessing the size of the software development task to be undertaken. The second assesses the rate of work at which the task can be done. For example, Amanda at IOE might estimate that the first software module to be constructed is 2 KLOC. She might then judge that if Kate undertook the development of the code, with her expertise she could work at a rate of 40 days per KLOC and complete the work in 2×40 days, that is, 80 days, while Ken, who is less experienced, would need 55 days per KLOC and take 2×55 that is, 110 days to complete the task.

Some parametric models, such as that implied by function points, are focused on system or task size, while others, such are COCOMO, are more concerned with productivity factors.

At the earlier stages of a project, the top-down approach would tend to be used, while at later stages the bottom-up approach might be preferred.

Having calculated the overall effort required, the problem is then to allocate proportions of that effort to the various activities within that project.

The top-down and bottom-up approaches are not mutually exclusive. Project managers will probably try to get a number of different estimates from different people using different methods. Some parts of an overall estimate could be derived using a top-down approach while other parts could be calculated using a bottom-up method.

Exercise 5.3

Students on a course are required to produce a written report on an IT-related topic each semester. If you wanted to create a model to estimate how long it should take a student to complete such an assignment, what measure of work content would you use? Some reports might be more difficult to produce than others: what factors might affect the degree of difficulty?

5.6 Expert judgement

This is asking someone who is knowledgeable about either the application area or the development environment to give an estimate of the effort needed to carry out a task. This method will most likely be used when estimating the effort needed to change an existing piece of software. The estimator would have to carry out some kind of impact analysis in order to judge the proportion of code that would be affected and from that derive an estimate. Someone already familiar with the software would be in the best position to do this.

See R. T. Hughes, 'Expert judgement as an estimating method', *Information and Software Technology*, 38(3), 67–75, 1996.

Some have suggested that expert judgement is simply a matter of guessing, but our own research has shown that experts tend to use a combination of an informal analogy approach where similar projects from the past are identified (see below), and bottom-up estimating.

5.7 Estimating by analogy

The use of analogy is also called *case-based reasoning*. The estimator seeks out projects that have been completed (*source cases*) and that have similar characteristics to the new project (the *target case*). The effort that has been recorded for the matching source case can then be used as a base estimate for the target. The estimator should then try to identify any differences between the target and the source and make adjustments to the base estimate for the new project.

This might be a good approach where you have information about some previous projects but not enough to draw generalized conclusions about what variables might make good size parameters.

See M. Shepperd and C. Schofield 'Estimating software project effort using analogies' in *IEEE Transactions in Software Engineering*, SE-23(11), 736–743, 1997.

A problem here is how you actually identify the similarities and differences between the different systems. Attempts have been made to automate this process. One software application that has been developed to do this is ANGEL. This identifies the source case that is nearest the target by measuring the Euclidean distance between cases. The source case that is at the shortest Euclidean distance from the target is deemed to be the closest match. The Euclidean distance is calculated:

$$distance = \text{square-root of } [(target\_parameter_1 - source\_parameter_1)^2 + \ldots + (target\_parameter_n - source\_parameter_n)^2]$$

CASE STUDY
EXAMPLES

Calculating Euclidean distance

Say that the cases are being matched on the basis of two parameters, the number of inputs to and the number of outputs from the system to be built. The new project is known to require 7 inputs and 15 outputs. One of the past cases, project A, has 8 inputs and 17 outputs. The Euclidean distance between the source and the target is therefore the square-root of $[(7 - 8)^2 + (15 - 17)^2]$, that is 2.24.

Exercise 5.4

Project B has 5 inputs and 10 outputs. What would be the Euclidean distance between this project and the target new project being considered above? Is project B a better analogy with the target than project A?

The above explanation is simply to give an idea of how Euclidean distance might be calculated. The ANGEL package uses rather more sophisticated algorithms based on this principle.

5.8 Albrecht function point analysis

See A. J. Albrecht and J. E. Gaffney Jr, 'Software function, source lines of code, and development effort prediction: a software science validation' in M. Shepperd (ed.), *Software Engineering Metrics*, Volume 1, McGraw-Hill, 1993.

This is a top-down method that was devised by Allan Albrecht when he worked for IBM. Albrecht was investigating programming productivity and needed some way to quantify the functional size of programs independently of the programming languages in which they had been coded. He developed the idea of *function points* (FPs).

The basis of function point analysis is that computer-based information systems comprise five major components, or *external user types* in Albrecht's terminology, that are of benefit to the users:

● *External input types* are input transactions that update internal computer files.

● *External output types* are transactions where data is output to the user. Typically these would be printed reports, since screen displays would come under external inquiry types (see below).

● *Logical internal file types* are the standing files used by the system. The term 'file' does not sit easily with modern information systems. It refers to a group of data that is usually accessed together. It might be made up of one or more *record types*. For example, a purchase order file might be made up of a record type *PurchaseOrder* plus a second that is repeated for each item ordered on the purchase order – *PurchaseOrderItem*.

Albrecht also specifies that outgoing external interface files should be double counted as logical internal file types as well.

● *External interface file types* allow for output and input that might pass to and from other computer applications. Examples of this would be the transmission of accounting data from an order processing system to the main ledger system or the production of a file of direct debit details on a magnetic or electronic medium to be passed to the Bankers Automated Clearing System (BACS). Files shared among applications would also be counted here.

Table 5.2 Albrecht complexity multipliers

	Multiplier		
External user type	*Low*	*Average*	*High*
External input type	3	4	6
External output type	4	5	7
Logical internal file type	7	10	15
External interface file type	5	7	10
External inquiry type	3	4	6

● *External inquiry types* – note the US spelling of inquiry – are transactions initiated by the user that provide information but do not update the internal files. The user inputs some information that directs the system to the details required.

The International FP User Group (IFPUG) have developed and published extensive rules governing FP counting. Hence Albrecht FPs are now often referred to as IFPUG FPs.

The analyst has to identify each instance of each external user type in the projected system. Each component is then classified as having either high, average or low complexity. The counts of each external user type in each complexity band are multiplied by specified weights (see Table 5.2) to get FP scores, which are summed to obtain an overall FP count, which indicates the information processing size.

Exercise 5.5

The task for which Brigette has been made responsible in Exercise 5.2 needs a program that will extract yearly salaries from the payroll file, and the details of courses and hours taught on each course by each member of staff from two files maintained by the time-tabling system. The program will calculate the staff costs for each course and put the results into a file that will then be read by the main accounting system. The program will also produce a report showing for each course the hours taught by each member of staff and the cost of those hours.

Using the method described above, calculate the Albrecht function points for this subsystem, assuming that the report is of high complexity, but that all the other elements are of average complexity.

One problem with FPs as originally defined by Albrecht was that the question of whether the external user type was of high, low or average complexity was rather subjective. The International FP User Group (IFPUG) have now promulgated rules on how this is to be judged. For example, in the case of logical internal files and external interface files, the boundaries shown in Table 5.3 are used to decide the complexity level.

Tables 5.4 and 5.5 are used to allocate scores to external inputs and external outputs. Each external inquiry has to be counted both as if it were an external input and an external output and whichever score is higher is used.

Function point analysis now goes on to take into account the fact that the effort required to implement a computer-based information system will relate not just to the number and complexity of the features to be provided but also to the environment in which the system is to operate.

Fourteen factors have been identified that can influence the degree of difficulty associated with implementing a system. The list that Albrecht produced related

CASE STUDY
EXAMPLES

Assesing the complexity of a logical internal file

A logical internal file might contain data about purchase orders. These purchase orders might be organized into two separate record types: the main *PurchaseOrder* details, namely purchase order number, supplier reference and purchase order date and then details for each *PurchaseOrderItem* specified in the order, namely the product code, the unit price and number ordered. The number of record types for that file would therefore be 2 and the number of data types would be 6. According to Table 5.3, this file type would be rated as 'low'. This would mean that according to Table 5.2, the FP count would be seven for this file.

particularly to the concerns of information system developers in the late 1970s and early 1980s. Some technology that was then new and relatively threatening is now well established.

Further details on TCA can be found in the Albrecht and Gaffney paper.

The technical complexity adjustment (TCA) calculation has had lots of problems. Some have even found that it produces less accurate estimates than using the unadjusted function point count. Because of these difficulties, we are going to omit further discussion of the TCA.

Tables have been calculated to convert the FPs to lines of code for various languages. For example, it is suggested that 91 lines of Cobol are needed on average to implement an FP, while for C the figure is 128 and for QuickBasic is 64.

Exercise 5.6

In the case of the sub-system described in Exercise 5.5 for which Brigette is responsible at Brightmouth College, how many lines of Cobol code should be needed to implement this sub-system, according to the standard conversion?

5.9 Function points Mark II

This method has come into the public domain with the publication of the book by Charles R. Symons, *Software Sizing and Estimating – Mark II FPA*, Wiley, 1991.

The Mark II method has been recommended by the CCTA (Central Computer and Telecommunications Agency), which lays down standards for UK government projects. At one time this Mark II approach seemed to be a good method to use with SSADM but some difficulties are now apparent. The 'Mark II' label implies an improvement and replacement of the Albrecht method. The Albrecht (now IFPUG) method, however, has had many refinements made to it and FPA Mark II remains a minority method used mainly in the United Kingdom.

As with Albrecht, the information processing size is initially measured in unadjusted function points (UFPs) to which a technical complexity adjustment can then be applied (TCA). The assumption here is that an information system comprises transactions that have the basic structure shown in Figure 5.2.

For each transaction the UFPs are calculated:

$$W_i \times \text{(number of input data element types)} +$$
$$W_e \times \text{(number of entity types referenced)} +$$
$$W_o \times \text{(number of output data element types)}$$

Table 5.3 IFPUG file type complexity

Number of record types	Number of data types		
	<20	20–50	>50
1	Low	Low	Average
2 to 5	Low	Average	High
>5	Average	High	High

Table 5.4 IFPUG External input complexity

Number of file types accessed	Number of data types accessed		
	<5	5–15	>15
0 or 1	Low	Low	Average
2	Low	Average	High
>2	Average	High	High

Table 5.5 IFPUG External output complexity

Number of file types	Number of data types		
	<6	6–19	>19
0 or 1	Low	Low	Average
2 or 3	Low	Average	High
>3	Average	High	High

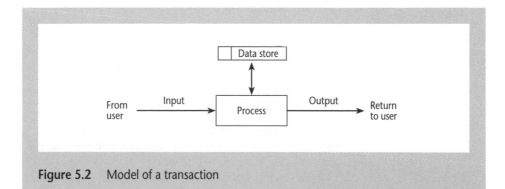

Figure 5.2 Model of a transaction

Here, W_i, W_e, and W_o are weightings that might be derived by asking developers what proportion of effort has been spent in previous projects developing those parts of the software that deal with processing inputs, accessing and modifying stored data and processing outputs. From this it should be possible to work out the average hours of work generated by instances of each type of element.

The averages are then normalized into ratios, or weightings, which add up to 2.5. If this way of getting hold of the weightings seems too time-consuming then some industry averages are available, which are currently (2002) 0.58 for W_i, 1.66 for W_e and 0.26 for W_o.

The only reason why 2.5 was adopted here was to produce FP counts similar to the Albrecht equivalents.

CASE STUDY EXAMPLES

Calculating Mark II function points

A cash receipt transaction in the IOE maintenance accounts system accesses two entity types – *Invoice* and *CashReceipt*.

The data elements that are input are:

- *InvoiceNumber*
- *DateReceived*
- *CashReceived*

If an *Invoice* record is not found for the invoice number, then an error message is issued. If the invoice number is found, then a *CashReceipt* record is created.

The error message constitutes the only output data element that the transaction has to cater for.

The unadjusted function points, using the industry average weightings, for this transaction would therefore be:

$$(0.58 \times 3) + (1.66 \times 2) + (0.26 \times 1) = 5.32$$

Exercise 5.7

One of the transactions that will be part of the IOE maintenance group accounts subsystem for which Amanda is responsible will be used to set up details of new group account customers.

The operator will input:

- CustomerAccountNumber
- CustomerName
- Address
- Postcode
- CustomerType
- StatementProductionDate

All this information will be set up in a *Customer* record on the system's database. If a *Customer* account already exists for the account number that has been input, an error message will be displayed to the operator.

Calculate the number of unadjusted Mark II function points for this transaction, using the industry average weightings.

Mark II FPs follow the Albrecht method in recognizing that one system delivering the same functionality as another might be more difficult to implement (but also more valuable to the users) because of additional technical requirements. For example, the incorporation of additional security measures would increase the amount of effort to deliver the system. The original Albrecht FP method identified 14 technical complexity adjustment factors – Mark II FPs identify five more factors:

- interfaces to other applications;
- special security features;
- direct access for third parties;
- user training features;
- documentation requirements.

The addition of other factors to suit local circumstances is encouraged.

With both the Albrecht and Symons methods, FPs can be counted for previous projects where actual effort is known. If you have figures for the effort expended on past projects (in work-days for instance) and also the system sizes in FPs, you should be able to work out a productivity rate, that is:

$$Productivity = size/effort.$$

For new projects, the function points can be counted and then the effort can be projected using the productivity rate derived above:

$$Effort = size/productivity.$$

A more sophisticated way of doing this would be by using the statistical technique, least squares regression, to derive an equation in the form:

$$Effort = constant_1 + size \times constant_2.$$

Symons is very much against the idea of using function points to estimate SLOC rather than effort. One finding by Symons is that productivity, that is, the effort per function point to implement a system, is influenced very much by the size of the project. In general, larger projects, up to a certain point, tend to be more productive because of economies of scale. However, beyond a certain size they tend to become less productive because of additional management overheads.

Some of the rules and weightings used in FP counting, especially in the case of the Albrecht flavour, are rather arbitrary and have been criticized by academic writers on this account. FPs, however, are widely used in practice because of the lack of other methods of gauging the functional size of information systems.

This simplified approach assumes rather unrealistically that the factors affecting productivity are the same for each project.

5.10 Object points

This approach was devised at the Leonard N. Stern School of Business, New York University. It has similarities with the FP approach, but takes account of features that might be more readily identifiable if you are building a system using a high-level application building tool. The reader should be warned that despite its name, the technique has no direct bearing on object-oriented techniques. The approach uses counts of the screens, reports and 3GL components that an application might

See R. D. Banker, R. Kauffman and R. Kumar, 'An empirical test of object-based output measurement metrics', *Journal of MIS*, 8(3), 1992.

In other development environments, other types of object and other weightings would be more appropriate.

possess – it is these that are referred to as *objects*. Each object has to be classified as one of the following:

- simple;
- medium;
- difficult.

Tables 5.6 and 5.7 show the scheme used to make this classification. The numbers of objects at each level are multiplied by the appropriate complexity weighting shown in Table 5.8. The weighted sub-totals are then summed to get an overall score for the application.

Some of these objects might not need to be developed as there are already existing components that can be utilized. The object point score can be adjusted to take this into account. Say that in an application containing 840 object points, 20%

Further details can be found in R. Kauffman and R. Kumar's report 'Modelling estimation expertise in object based ICASE environments', Stern School of Business, 1993.

Table 5.6 Object points for screens

	Number and source of data tables		
Number of views contained	Total <4 (<2 servers <3 clients)	Total <8 (<3 servers 3–5 clients)	Total >7 (>3 servers >5 clients)
<3	Simple	Simple	Medium
3–7	Simple	Medium	Difficult
>7	Medium	Difficult	Difficult

Table 5.7 Object points for reports

	Number and source of data tables		
Number of sections contained	Total <4 (<2 servers <3 clients)	Total <8 (<3 servers 3–5 clients)	Total >7 (>3 servers >5 clients)
<2	Simple	Simple	Medium
2 or 3	Simple	Medium	Difficult
>3	Medium	Difficult	Difficult

Table 5.8 Object points complexity weightings

	Complexity weighting		
Object type	Simple	Medium	Difficult
Screen	1	2	3
Report	2	5	8
3GL component	–	–	10

Table 5.9 Object point effort conversion					
Developer's experience and capability/ICASE maturity and capability	Very low	Low	Nominal	High	Very high
PROD	4	7	13	25	50

can be supplied by using existing components, then the adjusted new object points (NOP) score would be:

$$NOP = 840 \times (100 - 20)/100 = 672$$

Finally a productivity rate (PROD) has to be identified. It would be best if the estimator could use details of past projects to derive this. As an example, the developers of object points have published the details in Table 5.9 to calculate PROD. In the situation where this information was gathered, as the CASE tool's features were improving with successive releases, so the experience of the developers with the tool was growing too.

An estimate of the person-months needed to carry out the project is then calculated by dividing PROD into NOP. For example, given the 672 new object points above and a development environment where productivity was nominal, then the estimated effort for the project would be 672/13 = 52 months.

5.11 A procedural code-oriented approach

The previous approach would be useful at the design stage of a project and where a procedural programming language is not the primary vehicle for development. However, how could you estimate the effort to develop a software application using a procedural language? An approach might be based on the following steps.

1. Envisage the number and type of programs in the final system
This is easiest where the system is of a conventional and well understood nature. Most information systems are built from a small set of system operations, such as insert, amend, update, display, delete, print. The same principle should equally apply to embedded systems, albeit with a different set of primitive functions.

2. Estimate the SLOC of each identified program
The estimator must have a particular implementation language in mind for this step.

One way to judge the number of instructions likely to be in a program is to draw up a program structure diagram and to visualize how many instructions would be needed to implement each identified procedure. The estimator might look at existing programs that have a similar functional description to help in this process.

Where programs for an information system are similar (for instance, they are data validation programs) then the number of data item types processed by each program is likely to be the major influence on size.

Function point analysis Mark II is also based on the idea that the number of data item types processed influences program size.

3. Estimate the work content, taking into account complexity and technical difficulty

The practice is to multiply the SLOC estimate by a factor for complexity and technical difficulty. This factor will depend largely on the subjective judgement of the estimator. For example, the requirement to meet particular highly constrained performance targets can greatly increase programming effort.

A weighting can be given when there is uncertainty, for example about a new technique used in particular module, but this should not be excessive. Where there is a large amount of uncertainty then specific measures should be taken to reduce this by such means as the use of exploratory prototypes.

See Chapter 4 for a discussion of prototypes.

4. Calculate the work-days effort

Historical data can be used to provide ratios to convert weighted SLOC to effort. These conversion factors are often based on the productivity of a 'standard programmer' of about 15–18 months of experience. In installations where the rate of turnover is lower and the average programmer experience is higher this might be reflected in the conversion rate employed.

Note that the steps above can be used to derive an estimate of lines of code that can be used as an input to one of the COCOMO models, which are now about to be described.

Exercise 5.8

Draw up an outline program structure diagram for a program to do the processing described in Exercise 5.7, which sets up *Customer* records. For each box on your diagram, estimate the number of lines of code needed to implement the routine in a third generation language such as Cobol.

5.12 COCOMO: a parametric model

Because there is now a newer COCOMO II, the older version is now referred to as COCOMO 81.

Boehm's COCOMO (COnstructive COst MOdel) is often referred to in the literature on software project management, particularly in connection with software estimating. The term COCOMO really refers to a group of models.

Boehm originally based his models in the late 1970s on a study of 63 projects. Of these only seven were business systems and so they could be used with applications other than information systems. The basic model was built around the equation

$$effort = c \times size^k$$

Boehm originally used mm (for man-months) when he wrote Software Engineering Economics.

where effort is measured in *pm*, or the number of 'person-months' consisting of units of 152 working hours, size is measured in *kdsi*, thousands of delivered source code instructions, and *c* and *k* are constants.

The first step was to derive an estimate of the system size in terms of *kdsi*. The constants, *c* and *k* (see Table 5.10), depended on whether the system could be classified, in Boehm's terms, as 'organic', 'semi-detached' or 'embedded'. These related to the technical nature of the system and the development environment.

Generally, information systems were regarded as organic while real-time systems were embedded.

- *Organic mode* This would typically be the case when relatively small teams developed software in a highly familiar in-house environment and when the system being developed was small and the interface requirements were flexible.

- *Embedded mode* Tthis meant the product being developed had to operate within very tight constraints and changes to the system were very costly.

Table 5.10 COCOMO constants

System type	c	k
Organic	2.4	1.05
Semi-detached	3.0	1.12
Embedded	3.6	1.20

● *Semi-detached mode*   This combined elements of the organic and the embedded modes or had characteristics that came between the two.

The exponent value *k*, when it is greater than 1, means that larger projects are seen as requiring disproportionately more effort than smaller ones. This reflected Boehm's finding that larger projects tended to be less productive than smaller ones because they needed more effort for management and co-ordination.

Exercise 5.9   Apply the basic COCOMO model to the lines of code figures in Table 5.1 to generate estimated work-months of effort, assuming an organic mode. Compare the calculated figures with the actuals.

As well as the intermediate model, a further, detailed, COCOMO model attempts to allocate effort to individual project phases.

Boehm in fact found this, by itself, to be a poor predictor of the effort required and so went on to develop the intermediate version of COCOMO, which took into account 15 cost drivers. In the intermediate model, a nominal effort estimate, (pm_{nom}) is derived in a similar way as for the basic model.

The nominal estimate is then adjusted by a development effort multiplier (*dem*):

$$pm_{est} = pm_{nom} \times dem$$

where *dem* is calculated by taking into account multipliers based on the effort drivers in Table 5.11.

These multipliers take into account such influences on productivity as Boehm's suggestion that having a programming team fully conversant with the programming language to be used could reduce the effort required to implement the project by up to 20% compared to a team with a very low or initially non-existent familiarity with the programming language. In fact, the biggest influence on productivity according to Boehm is the capability of the implementation team.

As an example of the approach, an organization might decide to use the following multipliers for assessing the effect of analyst capability (ACAP):

Very low	1.46
Low	1.19
Nominal	1.00
High	0.80
Very High	0.71

If the analysts involved in a project, taken as a whole, generally possess above average talent and productivity then the estimator might rate the ACAP as high and use a multiplier of 0.8, effectively reducing the nominal estimate by 20%.

The overall *dem* is calculated by multiplying the multipliers selected for each cost driver in Table 5.11 to create a single combined multiplier.

Table 5.11 COCOMO81 intermediate cost drivers

Driver type	Code	Cost driver
Product attributes	RELY	Required software reliability
	DATA	Database size
	CPLX	Product complexity
Computer attributes	TIME	Execution time constraints
	STOR	Main storage constraints
	VIRT	Virtual machine volatility – degree to which the operating system changes
	TURN	Computer turn around time
Personnel attributes	ACAP	Analyst capability
	AEXP	Application experience
	PCAP	Programmer capability
	VEXP	Virtual machine (i.e. operating system) experience
	LEXP	Programming language experience
Project attributes	MODP	Use of modern programming practices
	TOOL	Use of software tools
	SCED	Required development schedule.

Exercise 5.10

At IOE, most of the systems that are developed are technically similar, so that the product, computer and project attributes, as listed in Table 5.11 do not change from one project to another and are given a unit multiplier of 1.0. Only personnel attributes differ and the following table is used by the organization to take this into account.

Attribute	Very low	Low	Nominal	High	Very high
ACAP	1.46	1.19	1.00	0.86	0.71
AEXP	1.29	1.13	1.00	0.91	0.82
PCAP	1.42	1.17	1.00	0.80	0.70
VEXP	1.21	1.10	1.00	0.90	–
LEXP	1.14	1.07	1.00	0.95	–

On the new IOE group maintenance accounts project, the analyst is regarded as being of exceptionally high quality. The programmers are of high quality but have little experience of the particular application area and are going to use a programming language that is new to them. They are however familiar with the operating system environment and thus can be rated as high on VEXP.

What would be the *dem* for this project? If the nominal estimate for this project was four person-months, what would be the final estimate?

A new family of models, COCOMO II, is currently (2002) being refined by Barry Boehm and his co-workers. This approach uses various multipliers and exponents,

The detailed *COCOMO II Model Definition Manual* has been published by the Centre for Software Engineering, University of Southern California.

the values of which have been set initially by experts. However, a database containing the performance details of executed projects is being built up and periodically analysed so that the expert judgements can be progressively replaced by values derived from actual projects. The new models take into account that there is now a wider range of process models in common use for software development projects than in the late 1970s and early 1980s. As we noted earlier, estimates are required at different stages in the system life cycle and COCOMO II has been designed to accommodate this by having models for three different stages.

Application composition   Here the external features of the system that the users will experience are designed. Prototyping will typically be employed to do this. With small applications that can be built using high-productivity application-building tools, development can stop at this point.

Early design   Where the fundamental software structures are designed. With larger, more demanding systems, where, for example, there will be large volumes of transactions and performance is important, careful attention will need to be paid to the architecture to be adopted.

Post architecture   Where the software structures undergo final construction, modification and tuning to create a system that will perform as required.

To estimate the effort for *application composition*, the counting of object points, which were described earlier, is recommended by the developers of COCOMO II.

At the *early design* stage, FPs are recommended as the way of gauging a basic system size. An FP count might be converted to a SLOC equivalent by multiplying the FPs by a factor for the programming language that is to be used.

The following model can then be used to calculate an estimate of person-months.

$$pm = A \times size^{sf} \times em_1 \times em_2 \times \ldots \times em_n$$

Note that where COCOMO 81 used 'man-months', COCOMO II uses 'person-months'.

Where *pm* is the effort in 'person-months', *A* is a constant (in 1998 it was 2.45), size is measured in SLOC (which might have been derived from an FP count as explained above), and *sf* is exponent scale factor.

The scale factor is derived thus:

$$sf = 0.91 + 0.01 \times \Sigma(exponent\ driver\ ratings)$$

Exercise 5.11   What is the maximum value that the scale factor (*sf*) can have, given that there are five exponent drivers and the maximum rating for an individual driver is five and the minimum is zero?

The qualities that govern the exponent drivers used to calculate the scale factor are listed below. Note that the less each quality is applicable, the bigger the value given to the exponent driver. The fact that these factors are used to calculate an exponent implies that the *lack* of these qualities will *increase* the effort required disproportionately more on larger projects.

- *Precedentedness*   This quality refers to the degree to which there are *precedents*, similar cases in the past, for the project that is being planned. The greater the novelty of the new system, the more uncertainty there is and the higher the value given to the exponent driver.

- *Development flexibility*   This is the degree to which the requirements can be met in a number of different ways. The less flexibility there is, the higher the value of the exponent driver.

- *Architecture/risk resolution*   This relates to the degree of uncertainty there is about the requirements. If they are not firmly fixed and are liable to change then this would lead to a high value being given to this exponent driver.

- *Team cohesion*   This reflects the degree to which there is a large dispersed team (perhaps in several countries) as opposed to there being a small tightly knit team.

- *Process maturity*   The chapter on software quality explains the process maturity model. The more structured and organized the way the software is produced, the lower uncertainty and the lower the rating will be for this exponent driver.

Exercise 5.12

A new project has 'average' novelty for the software house that is going to execute it and is thus given a 3 rating on this account for precedentedness. Development flexibility is high to the extent that this generates a zero rating, but requirements might change radically and so the risk resolution exponent is rated at 4. The team is very cohesive and this generates a rating of 1, but the software house as a whole tends to be very informal in its standards and procedures and the process maturity driver has there-fore been given a value of 4.

What would be the scale factor, *sf*, that would be applicable in this case?

In the COCOMO II model the *effort multipliers, em,* are similar in nature to the development effort multipliers, *dem,* used in the original COCOMO. There are 7 of these multipliers that are relevant to early design and 17 that can be used at the post architecture stage. Table 5.12 lists the effort multipliers for early design and Table 5.13 for post architecture. As with COCOMO 81, each of these multipliers might, for a particular application, be given a rating of very low, low, nominal, high or very high. Each rating for each effort multiplier has a value associated with it. A value greater than 1 means that development effort is increased, while a value less than 1 causes effort to be decreased. The nominal rating means that the multiplier has no effect on the estimate, that is, it is 1. The intention is that the ratings that these and other values use in COCOMO II will be modified and refined over time as details of actual projects are added to the database.

Table 5.12 COCOMO II early design effort multipliers

Code	Effort multiplier
RCPX	Product reliability and complexity
RUSE	Required reusability
PDIF	Platform difficulty
PERS	Personnel capability
PREX	Personnel experience
FCIL	Facilities available
SCED	Schedule pressure

Table 5.13 COCOMO II Post Architecture effort multipliers

Modifier type	Code	Effort multiplier
Product attributes	RELY	Required software reliability
	DATA	Database size
	DOCU	Documentation match to life-cycle needs
	CPLX	Product complexity
	RUSE	Required reusability
Platform attributes	TIME	Execution time constraint
	STOR	Main storage constraint
	PVOL	Platform volatility
Personnel attributes	ACAP	Analyst capabilities
	AEXP	Application experience
	PCAP	Programmer capabilities
	PEXP	Platform experience
	LEXP	Programming language experience
	PCON	Personnel continuity
Project attributes	TOOL	Use of software tools
	SITE	Multisite development
	SCED	Schedule pressure

5.13 Conclusion

To summarize some key points:

● estimates are really management targets;

● collect as much information about previous projects as possible;

● use more than one method of estimating;

● top-down approaches will be used at the earlier stages of project planning while bottom-up approaches will be more prominent later on;

● be careful about using other people's historical productivity data as a basis for your estimates, especially if it comes from a different environment (this includes COCOMO!);

● seek a range of opinions;

● document your method of doing estimates and record all your assumptions.

5.14 Further exercises

1. Identify size and productivity effort drivers for the following activities:
   ● installing computer workstations in a new office;
   ● transporting assembled personal computers from the factory where they were assembled to warehouses distributed in different parts of the country;
   ● typing in and checking the correctness of data that is populating a new database;
   ● system testing a newly written software application.

2. If you were asked as an expert to provide an estimate of the effort needed to make certain changes to an existing piece of software, what information would you like to have to hand to assist you in making that estimate?

3. Consider the details held about previously developed software modules shown in Table 5.14. A new module has seven inputs, one entity type access and seven outputs. Which of the modules a to e is the closest analogy in terms of Euclidean distance?

Table 5.14 Data concerning previously developed modules

module	inputs	entity types accessed	outputs	days
a	1	2	10	2.60
b	10	2	1	3.90
c	5	1	1	1.83
d	2	3	11	3.50
e	1	3	20	4.30

4. Using the data in Table 5.14, calculate the Simons Mark II FPs for each module. Using the results, calculate the effort needed for the new module described in question 3. How does this estimate compare to the one based on analogy?

5. A report in a college time-tabling system produces a report showing the students who should be attending each time-tabled teaching activity. Four files are accessed: the *Staff* file, the *Student* file, the *StudentOption* file and the *TeachingActivity* file. The report contains the following information:

For each teaching activity:
   Teaching Activity Reference
   Topic Name
   Staff Forename
   Staff Surname
   Title
   Semester (1 or 2)
   Day Of Week
   Time
   Duration
   Location
For each student:
   Student Forename
   Student Surname

Calculate both IFPUG and Mark II FPs that this transaction would generate. Can you identify the factors that would tend to make the two methods generate divergent counts?

Activity planning

Objectives

When you have completed this chapter you will be able to:

- produce an activity plan for a project;
- estimate the overall duration of a project;
- create a critical path and a precedence network for a project.

6.1 Introduction

In earlier chapters we looked at methods for forecasting the effort required for a project – both for the project as a whole and for individual activities. A detailed plan for the project, however, must also include a schedule indicating the start and completion times for each activity. This will enable us to:

- ensure that the appropriate resources will be available precisely when required;
- avoid different activities competing for the same resources at the same time;
- produce a detailed schedule showing which staff carry out each activity;
- produce a detailed plan against which actual achievement may be measured;
- produce a timed cash flow forecast;
- replan the project during its life to correct drift from the target.

Project monitoring is discussed in more detail in Chapter 9.

To be effective, a plan must be stated as a set of targets, the achievement or non-achievement of which can be unambiguously measured. The activity plan does this by providing a target start and completion date for each activity (or a window within which each activity may be carried out). The starts and completions of activities must be clearly visible and this is one of the reasons why it is advisable to ensure that each and every project activity produces some tangible product or 'deliverable'. Monitoring the project's progress is then, at least in part, a case of ensuring that the products of each activity are delivered on time.

As a project progresses it is unlikely that everything will go according to plan. Much of the job of project management concerns recognizing when something has gone wrong, identifying its causes and revising the plan to mitigate its effects. The activity plan should provide a means of evaluating the consequences of not meeting any of the activity target dates and guidance as to how the plan might most effectively be modified to bring the project back to target. We shall see that the activity plan may well also offer guidance as to which components of a project should be most closely monitored.

6.2 The objectives of activity planning

In addition to providing project and resource schedules, activity planning aims to achieve a number of other objectives which may be summarized as follows:

- **Feasibility assessment**   Is the project possible within required timescales and resource constraints? It is not until we have constructed a detailed plan that we can forecast a completion date with any reasonable knowledge of its achievability. The fact that a project may have been estimated as requiring two work-years effort might not mean that it would be feasible to complete it within, say, three months were eight people to work on it – that will depend upon the availability of staff and the degree to which activities may be undertaken in parallel.

- **Resource allocation**   What are the most effective ways of allocating resources to the project and when should they be available? The project plan allows us to investigate the relationship between timescales and resource availability (in general, allocating additional resources to a project shortens its duration) and the efficacy of additional spending on resource procurement.

- **Detailed costing**   How much will the project cost and when is that expenditure likely to take place? After producing an activity plan and allocating specific resources, we can obtain more detailed estimates of costs and their timing.

- **Motivation**   Providing targets and being seen to monitor achievement against targets is an effective way of motivating staff, particularly where they have been involved in setting those targets in the first place.

- **Co-ordination**   When do the staff in different departments need to be available to work on a particular project and when do staff need to be transferred between projects? The project plan, particularly with large projects involving more than a single project team, provides an effective vehicle for communication and co-ordination among teams. In situations where staff may need to be transferred between project teams (or work concurrently on more than one project), a set of integrated project schedules should ensure that such staff are available when required and do not suffer periods of enforced idleness.

Activity planning and scheduling techniques place an emphasis on completing the project in a minimum time at an acceptable cost or, alternatively, meeting an arbitrarily set target date at minimum cost. These are not, in themselves, concerned with meeting quality targets, which generally impose constraints on the scheduling process.

One effective way of shortening project durations is to carry out activities in parallel. Clearly we cannot undertake all the activities at the same time – some require the completion of others before they can start and there are likely to be resource constraints limiting how much may be done simultaneously. Activity

---

Chapter 11 discusses motivation in more detail.

This co-ordination will normally form part of Programme Management.

In Chapter 2 we saw that Amanda's wish to check that four module specifications were correct, while increasing the likely quality of the product, created a constraint that could potentially delay the next stage of the project.

scheduling will, however, give us an indication of the cost of these constraints in terms of lengthening timescales and provide us with an indication of how timescales may be shortened by relaxing those constraints. It is up to us, if we try relaxing precedence constraints by, for example, allowing a program coding task to commence before the design has been completed, to ensure that we are clear about the potential effects on product quality

6.3 When to plan

Planning is an ongoing process of refinement, each iteration becoming more detailed and more accurate than the last. Over successive iterations, the emphasis and purpose of planning will shift.

During the feasibility study and project start-up, the main purpose of planning will be to estimate timescales and the risks of not achieving target completion dates or keeping within budget. As the project proceeds beyond the feasibility study, the emphasis will be placed upon the production of activity plans for ensuring resource availability and cash flow control.

Throughout the project, until the final deliverable has reached the customer, monitoring and replanning must continue to correct any drift that might prevent meeting time or cost targets.

6.4 Project schedules

On a large project, detailed plans for the later stages will be delayed until information about the work required has emerged from the earlier stages.

Before work commences on a project or, possibly, a stage of a larger project, the project plan must be developed to the level of showing dates when each activity should start and finish and when and how much of each resource will be required. Once the plan has been refined to this level of detail we call it a *project schedule*. Creating a project schedule comprises four main stages.

The first step in producing the plan is to decide what activities need to be carried out and in what order they are to be done. From this we can construct an *ideal activity plan* – that is, a plan of when each activity would ideally be undertaken were resources not a constraint. It is the creation of the ideal activity plan that we shall discuss in this chapter. This activity plan is generated by Steps 4 and 5 of Step Wise (Figure 6.1).

The ideal activity plan will then be the subject of an *activity risk analysis*, aimed at identifying potential problems. This might suggest alterations to the ideal activity plan and will almost certainly have implications for resource allocation. Activity risk analysis is the subject of Chapter 7.

The third step is *resource allocation*. The expected availability of resources might place constraints on when certain activities can be carried out, and our ideal plan might need to be adapted to take account of this. Resource allocation is covered in Chapter 8.

The final step is *schedule production*. Once resources have been allocated to each activity, we will be in a position to draw up and publish a project schedule, which indicates planned start and completion dates and a resource requirements statement for each activity. Chapter 9 discusses how this is done and the role of the schedule in managing a project.

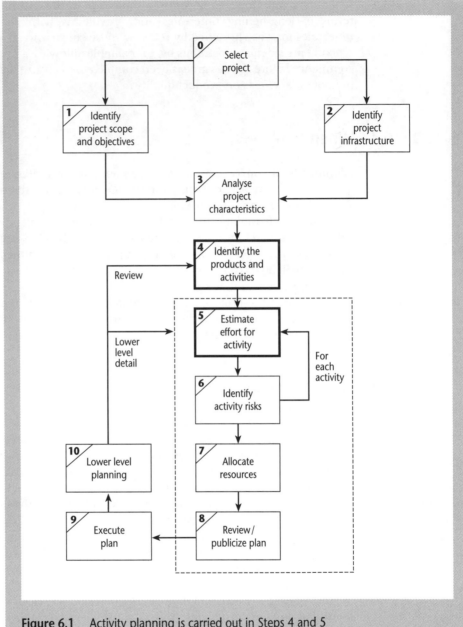

Figure 6.1 Activity planning is carried out in Steps 4 and 5

6.5 Projects and activities

Defining activities

Before we try to identify the activities that make up a project it is worth reviewing what we mean by a project and its activities and adding some assumptions that will be relevant when we start to produce an activity plan.

Activities must be defined so that they meet these criteria. Any activity that does not meet these criteria must be redefined.

- a project is composed of a number of interrelated activities;
- a project may start when at least one of its activities is ready to start;
- a project will be completed when all of the activities it encompasses have been completed;
- an activity must have a clearly defined start and a clearly defined end-point, normally marked by the production of a tangible deliverable;
- if an activity requires a resource (as most do) then that resource requirement must be forecastable and is assumed to be required at a constant level throughout the duration of the activity;
- the duration of an activity must be forecastable – assuming normal circumstances, and the reasonable availability of resources;
- some activities might require that others are completed before they can begin (these are known as *precedence requirements*).

Identifying activities

Essentially there are three approaches to identifying the activities or tasks that make up a project – we shall call them the *activity-based approach*, the *product-based approach* and the *hybrid approach*.

The activity-based approach The activity-based approach consists of creating a list of all the activities that the project is thought to involve. This might involve a brainstorming session involving the whole project team or it might stem from an analysis of similar past projects. When listing activities, particularly for a large project, it might be helpful to subdivide the project into the main life-style stages and consider each of these separately.

WBSs are advocated by BS 6079, which is discussed in Appendix B.

Rather than doing this in an *ad hoc* manner, with the obvious risks of omitting or double-counting tasks, a much favoured way of generating a task list is to create a Work Breakdown Structure (WBS). This involves identifying the main (or high-level) tasks required to complete a project and then breaking each of these down into a set of lower level tasks. Figure 6.2 shows a fragment of a WBS where the design task has been broken down into three tasks and one of these has been further decomposed into two tasks.

Activities are added to a branch in the structure if they directly contribute to the task immediately above – if they do not contribute to the parent task, then they should not be added to that branch. The tasks at each level in any branch should include everything that is required to complete the task at the higher level – if they are not a comprehensive definition of the parent task, then something is missing.

When preparing a WBS, consideration must be given to the final level of detail or depth of the structure. Too great a depth will result in a large number of small tasks that will be difficult to manage, whereas a too shallow structure will provide insufficient detail for project control. Each branch should, however, be broken down at least to a level where each leaf may be assigned to an individual or responsible section within the organization.

A complete task catalogue will normally include task definitions along with task input and output products and other task-related information.

Advantages claimed for the WBS approach include the belief that it is much more likely to result in a task catalogue that is complete and is composed of non-overlapping activities. Note that it is only the leaves of the structure that comprise the list of activities comprising the project – higher level nodes merely represent collections of activities.

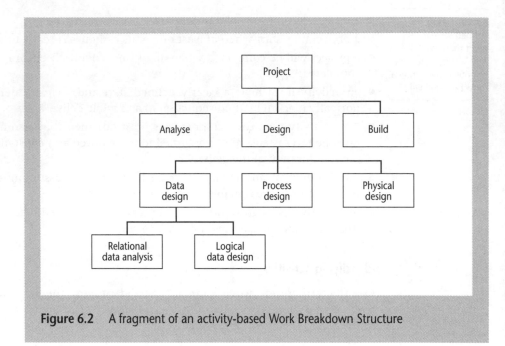

Figure 6.2   A fragment of an activity-based Work Breakdown Structure

The WBS also represents a structure that may be refined as the project proceeds. In the early part of a project we might use a relatively high-level or shallow WBS, which can be developed as information becomes available, typically during the project's analysis and specification phases.

Once the project's activities have been identified (whether or not by using a WBS) they need to be sequenced in the sense of deciding which activities need to be completed before others can start.

The product-based approach   The product-based approach, used in PRINCE 2 and Step Wise, has already been described in Chapter 2. It consists of producing a Product Breakdown Structure and a Product Flow Diagram. The PFD indicates, for each product, which other products are required as inputs. The PFD can therefore be easily transformed into an ordered list of activities by identifying the transformations that turn some products into others. Proponents of this approach claim that it is less likely that a product will be left out of a PBS than that an activity might be omitted from an unstructured activity list.

This approach is particularly appropriate if using a methodology such as SSADM, which clearly specifies, for each step or task, each of the products required and the activities required to produce it. The SSADM Reference Manual provides a set of generic PBSs for each stage in SSADM (such as that shown in Figure 6.3), which can be used as a basis for generating a project-specific PBS.

The SSADM Reference Manual also supplies generic activity networks and, using the project-specific PBS and derived PFD, these may be used as a basis for developing a project-specific activity network. Figure 6.4 illustrates an activity network for the activities required to create the products in Figure 6.3.

Most good texts on SSADM will explain the tailoring of the generic PBSs and Activity Networks. The illustrations here are taken from M. Goodland and C. Slater, *SSADM Version 4: A Practical Approach*, McGraw-Hill, 1995.

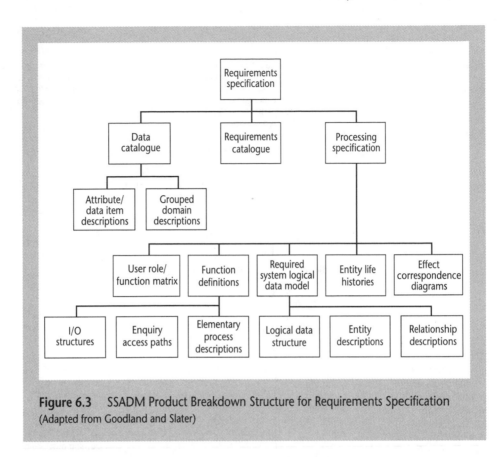

Figure 6.3 SSADM Product Breakdown Structure for Requirements Specification (Adapted from Goodland and Slater)

The activity numbers in Figure 6.4 are the step numbers used by SSADM version 4.

Notice how the development of a PFD leads directly to an activity network that indicates the sequencing of activities – in Figure 6.4, activity 340 (Enhance required data model) requires products from activity 330 and activity 360 needs products from both activities 330 and 340.

BS 6079 states that WBSs may be product-based, cost-centre-based, task-based or function-based but states that product-based WBSs are preferred.

The hybrid approach The WBS illustrated in Figure 6.2 is based entirely on a structuring of activities. Alternatively, and perhaps more commonly, a WBS may be based upon the project's products as illustrated in Figure 6.5, which is in turn based on a simple list of final deliverables and, for each deliverable, a set of activities required to produce that product. Figure 6.5 illustrates a flat WBS and it is likely that, in a project of any size, it would be beneficial to introduce additional levels – structuring both products and activities. The degree to which the structuring is product-based or activity-based might be influenced by the nature of the project and the particular development method adopted. As with a purely activity-based WBS, having identified the activities we are then left with the task of sequencing them.

A framework dictating the number of levels and the nature of each level in the structure may be imposed on a WBS. For example, in their MITP methodology, IBM recommend that the following five levels should be used in a WBS:

● *Level 1: Project.*
● *Level 2: Deliverables* such as software, manuals and training courses.

Not all of the products in this activity structuring will be final products. Some will be further refined in subsequent steps.

The current version of the SSADM reference manual provides generic PBSs and generic activity networks but not generic PFDs. Stress is placed on the fact that these are *generic* structures and it is important that project-specific versions are created. A project-specific PFD would be produced as part of this process.

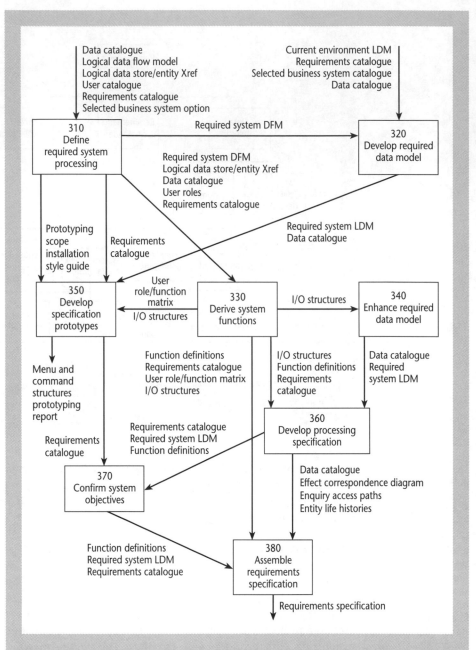

Figure 6.4 A structuring of activities for the SSADM Requirements Specification stage

(From Goodland and Slater)

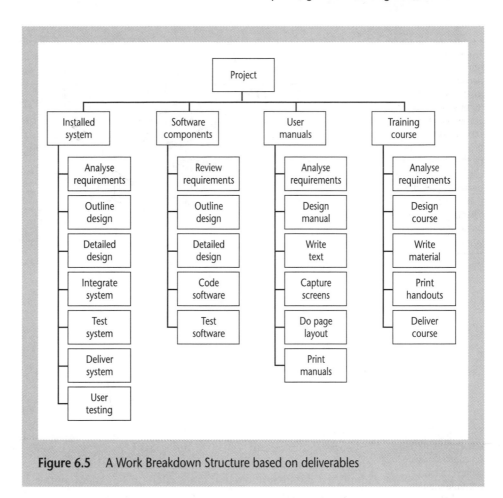

Figure 6.5   A Work Breakdown Structure based on deliverables

- *Level 3: Components* which are the key work items needed to produce deliverables, such as the modules and tests required to produce the system software.
- *Level 4: Work-packages* which are major work items, or collections of related tasks, required to produce a component.
- *Level 5: Tasks* which are tasks that will normally be the responsibility of a single person.

6.6   Sequencing and scheduling activities

Throughout a project, we will require a schedule that clearly indicates when each of the project's activities is planned to occur and what resources it will need. We shall be considering scheduling in more detail in Chapter 8, but let us consider in outline how we might present a schedule for a small project. One way of presenting such a plan is to use a bar chart as shown in Figure 6.6.

The chart shown has been drawn up taking account of the nature of the development process (that is, certain tasks must be completed before others may

The bar chart does not show why certain decisions have been made. It is not clear, for example, why activity H is not scheduled to start until week 9. It could be that it cannot start until activity F has been completed or it might be because Charlie is going to be on holiday during week 8.

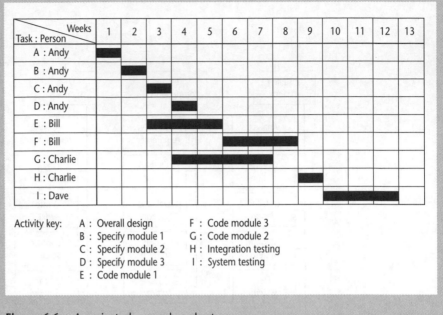

Figure 6.6   A project plan as a bar chart

Separating the logical sequencing from the scheduling may be likened to the principle used in SSADM of separating the logical system from its physical implementation.

start) and the resources that are available (for example, activity C follows activity B because Andy cannot work on both tasks at the same time). In drawing up the chart, we have therefore done two things – we have sequenced the tasks (that is, identified the dependencies among activities dictated by the development process) and scheduled them (that is, specified when they should take place). The scheduling has had to take account of the availability of staff and the ways in which the activities have been allocated to them. The schedule might look quite different were there a different number of staff or were we to allocate the activities differently.

In the case of small projects, this combined sequencing–scheduling approach might be quite suitable, particularly where we wish to allocate individuals to particular tasks at an early planning stage. However, on larger projects it is better to separate out these two activities: to sequence the task according to their logical relationships and then to schedule them taking into account resources and other factors.

Approaches to scheduling that achieve this separation between the *logical* and the *physical* use networks to model the project and it is these approaches that we will consider in subsequent sections of this chapter.

6.7 Network planning models

These project scheduling techniques model the project's activities and their relationships as a network. In the network, time flows from left to right. These techniques were originally developed in the 1950s – the two best known being CPM (Critical Path Method) and PERT (Program Evaluation Review Technique).

CPM was developed by the Du Pont Chemical Company who published the method in 1958, claiming that it had saved them $1 million in its first year of use.

Both of these techniques used an activity-on-arrow approach to visualizing the project as a network where activities are drawn as arrows joining circles, or *nodes*, which represented the possible start and/or completion of an activity or set of activities. More recently a variation on these techniques, called *precedence networks*, has become popular. This method uses *activity-on-node* networks where activities are represented as nodes and the links between nodes represent precedence or sequencing requirements. This latter approach avoids some of the problems inherent in the activity-on-arrow representation and provides more scope for easily representing certain situations. It is this method that is adopted in the majority of computer applications currently available. These three methods are very similar, and it must be admitted that many people use the same name (particularly CPM) indiscriminately to refer to any or all of the methods.

In the following sections of this chapter, we will look at the critical path method applied to precedence (activity-on-node) networks followed by a brief introduction to activity-on-arrow networks – a discussion of PERT will be reserved for Chapter 7 when we look at risk analysis.

6.8 Formulating a network model

The first stage in creating a network model is to represent the activities and their interrelationships as a graph. In activity-on-node we do this by representing activities as links (arrowed lines) in the graph – the nodes (circles) representing the events of activities starting and finishing.

Constructing precedence networks

Before we look at how networks are used, it is worth spending a few moments considering some rules for their construction.

A project network should have only one start node Although it is logically possible to draw a network with more than one starting node it is undesirable to do so as it is a potential source of confusion. In such cases (for example, where more than one activity can start immediately the project starts) it is normal to invent a 'start' activity which has zero duration but may have, for example, an actual start date.

A project network should have only one end node The end node designates the completion of the project and a project may only finish once! Although it is possible to draw a network with more than one end node it will almost certainly lead to confusion if this is done. Where the completion of a project depends upon more than one 'final' activity it is normal to invent a 'finish' activity.

A node has duration A node represents an activity and, in general, activities take time to execute. Notice, however, that the network in Figure 6.7 does not contain any reference to durations. This network drawing merely represents the logic of the project – the rules governing the order in which activities are to be carried out.

Links normally have no duration Links represent the relationships between activities. In Figure 6.9 neither installation cannot start until program testing is

In Chapter 2 we saw how Amanda used her Product Breakdown to obtain an activity network. Figure 6.7 shows the fragment of her network that was discussed in that chapter as an activity-on-node network. Figure 6.8 shows how this network would look represented as an activity-on-arrow network. Study each of the networks briefly to verify that there, are indeed, merely different graphical representations of the same thing.

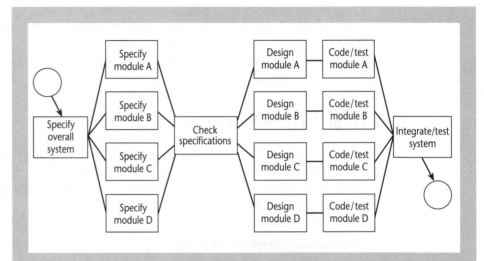

Figure 6.7   The IOE maintenance group accounts project activity network fragment with a checkpoint activity added

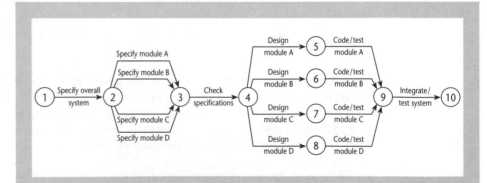

Figure 6.8   The IOE maintenance group accounts project activity network fragment represented as a CPM network

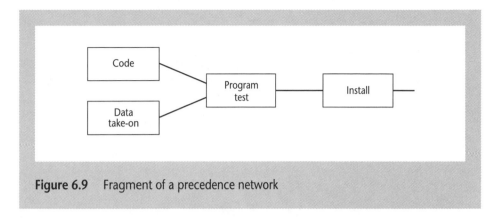

Figure 6.9   Fragment of a precedence network

Figure 6.10   A loop represents an impossible sequence

complete. Program testing cannot start until both coding and data take-on have been completed.

Precedents are the immediate preceding activities   In Figure 6.9, the activity *Program test* cannot start until both *Code* and *Data take-on* have been completed and activity *Install* cannot start until *Program test* has finished. *Code* and *Data take-on* can therefore be said to be precedents of *Program test*, and *Program test* is a precedent of *Install*. Note that we do not speak of *Code* and *Data take-on* as precedents of *Install* – that relationship is implicit in the previous statement.

Time moves from left to right   If at all possible, networks are drawn so that time moves from left to right. It is rare that this convention needs to be flouted, but some people add arrows to the lines to give a stronger visual indication of the time flow of the project.

A network may not contain loops   Figure 6.10 demonstrates a loop in a network. A loop is an error in that it represents a situation that cannot occur in practice. While loops, in the sense of iteration, may occur in practice, they cannot be directly represented in a project network. Note that the logic of Figure 6.10 suggests that program testing cannot start until the errors have been corrected.

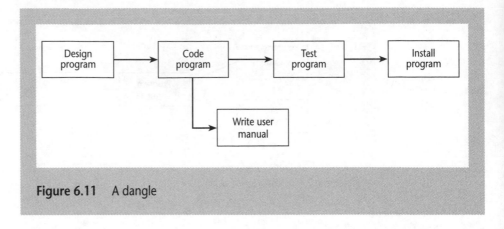

Figure 6.11   A dangle

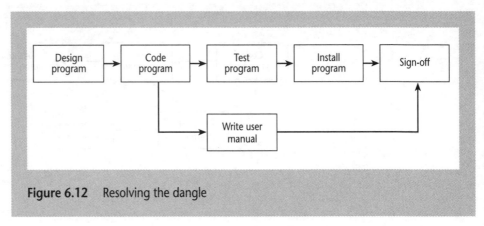

Figure 6.12   Resolving the dangle

If we know the number of times we expect to repeat a set of activities, a test–diagnose–correct sequence, for example, then we can draw that set of activities as a straight sequence, repeating it the appropriate number of times. If we do not know how many times a sequence is going to be repeated then we cannot calculate the duration of the project unless we adopt an alternative strategy such as redefining the complete sequence as a single activity and estimating how long it will take to complete it.

Although it is easy to see the loop in this simple network fragment, very large networks can easily contain complex loops which are difficult to spot when they are initially constructed. Fortunately, all network planning applications will detect loops and generate error messages when they are found.

A network should not contain dangles   A dangling activity such as *Write user manual* in Figure 6.11 should not exist as it is likely to lead to errors in subsequent analysis. Indeed, in many cases dangling activities indicate errors in logic when activities are added as an afterthought. If, in Figure 6.11, we mean to indicate that the project is complete once the software has been installed *and* the user manual written then we should redraw the network with a final completion activity – which, at least in this case, is probably a more accurate representation of what should happen. The redrawn network is shown in Figure 6.12.

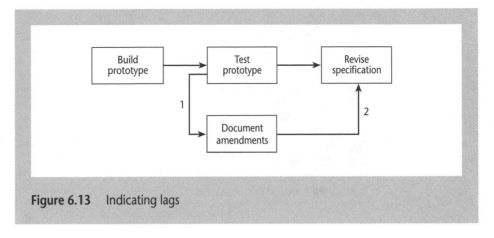

Figure 6.13   Indicating lags

Documenting amendments may take place alongside prototype testing so long as it starts at least one day later and finishes two days later.

Representing lagged activities

We might come across situations where we wished to undertake two activities in parallel so long as there is a lag between the two. We might wish to document amendments to a program as it was being tested – particularly if evaluating a prototype. In such a case we could designate an activity 'test and document amendments'. This would, however, make it impossible to show that amendment recording could start, say, one day after testing had begun and finishing a little after the completion of testing.

Where activities can occur in parallel with a time lag between them we represent the lag with a duration on the linking arrow as shown in Figure 6.13. This indicates that documenting amendments can start one day after the start of prototype testing and will be completed two days after prototype testing is completed.

Hammock activities

Hammock activities are activities which, in themselves, have zero duration but are assumed to start at the same time as the first 'hammocked' activity and to end at the same time as the last one. They are normally used for representing overhead costs or other resources that will be incurred or used at a constant rate over the duration of a set of activities.

Labelling conventions

Activity label	Duration
Earliest start	Earliest finish
Latest start	Activity description	Latest finish
Activity span	Float

There are a number of differing conventions that have been adopted for entering information on an activity-on-node network. One of the more common conventions for labelling nodes, and the one adopted here is shown on the left.

The activity label is usually a code developed to uniquely identify the activity and may incorporate a project code (for example, InvExt/P/3 to designate one of the programming activities for IOE's invoice extension project). The activity description will normally be a brief activity name such as 'Test take-on module'. The other items in our activity node will be explained as we discuss the analysis of a project network.

Table 6.1 An example project specification with estimated activity durations and precedence requirements

Activity		Duration (weeks)	Precedents
A	Hardware selection	6	
B	Software design	4	
C	Install hardware	3	A
D	Code and test software	4	B
E	File take-on	3	B
F	Write user manuals	10	
G	User training	3	E, F
H	Install and test system	2	C, D

6.9 Adding the time dimension

Having created the logical network model indicating what needs to be done and the interrelationships between those activities, we are now ready to start thinking about when each activity should be undertaken.

The critical path approach is concerned with two primary objectives: planning the project in such a way that it is completed as quickly as possible; and identifying those activities where a delay in their execution is likely to affect the overall end date of the project or later activities' start dates.

The method requires that for each activity we have an estimate of its duration. The network is then analysed by carrying out a *forward pass*, to calculate the earliest dates at which activities may commence and the project be completed, and a *backward pass*, to calculate the latest start dates for activities and the *critical path*.

In practice we would use a software application to carry out these calculations for anything but the smallest of projects. It is important, though, that we understand how the calculations are carried out in order to interpret the results correctly and understand the limitations of the method.

The description and example that follow use the small example project outlined in Table 6.1 – a project composed of eight activities whose durations have been estimated as shown in the table.

Exercise 6.1 Draw an activity network using precedence network conventions for the project specified in Table 6.1. When you have completed it, compare your result with that shown in Figure 6.14.

6.10 The forward pass

During the forward pass, earliest dates are recorded as they are calculated.

The forward pass is carried out to calculate the earliest dates on which each activity may be started and completed.

Where an actual start date is known, the calculations may be carried out using actual dates. Alternatively we can use day or week numbers and that is the approach we shall adopt here. By convention, dates indicate the end of the period

Figure 6.14 illustrates the network for the project specified in Table 6.1.

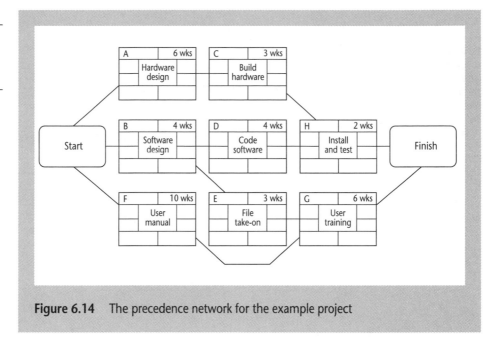

Figure 6.14 The precedence network for the example project

and the project is therefore shown as starting in week zero (or the beginning of week 1).

The forward pass and the calculation of earliest start dates is calculated according to the following reasoning.

- Activities A, B and F may start immediately, so the earliest date for their start is zero.

- Activity A will take 6 weeks, so the earliest it can finish is week 6.

- Activity B will take 4 weeks, so the earliest it can finish is week 4.

- Activity F will take 10 weeks, so the earliest it can finish is week 10.

- Activity C can start as soon as A has finished so its earliest start date is week 6. It will take 3 weeks so the earliest it can finish is week 9. The earliest it can finish is therefore week 9.

- Activities D and E can start as soon as B is complete so the earliest they can each start is week 4. Activity D, which will take 4 weeks, can therefore finish by week 8 and activity E, which will take 3 weeks, can therefore finish by week 7.

- Activity G cannot start until both E and F have been completed. It cannot therefore start until week 10 – the later of week 7 (for activity E and 10 for activity F).

- Similarly, Activity H cannot start until week 9 – the later of the two earliest finished dates for the preceding activities C and D.

- The project will be complete when both activities H and G have been completed. Thus the earliest project completion date will be the later of weeks 11 and 13 – that is, week 13.

The results of the forward pass are shown in Figure 6.15.

The forward pass rule: the earliest start date for an activity is the earliest finish date for the preceding activity. Where there is more than one immediately preceding activity we take the *latest* of the *earliest finish dates* for those activities.

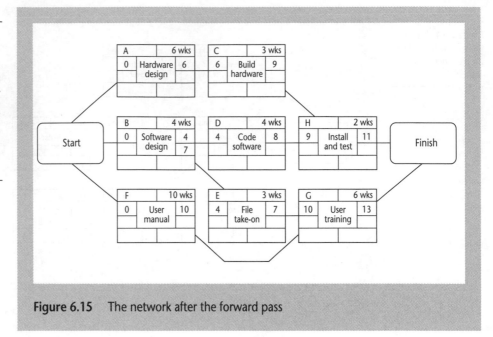

Figure 6.15 The network after the forward pass

6.11 The backward pass

The second stage in the analysis of a critical path network is to carry out a backward pass to calculate the latest date at which each activity may be started and finished without delaying the end date of the project. In calculating the latest dates, we assume that the latest finish date for the project is the same as the earliest finish date – that is, we wish to complete the project as early as possible.

Figure 6.16 illustrates our network after carrying out the backward pass.

The latest activity dates are calculated as follows:

- The latest completion date for activities G and H is assumed to be week 13.

- Activity H must therefore start at week 9 at the latest (13–2) and the latest start date for activity G is week 10 (13–3).

- The latest completion date for activities C and D is the latest date at which activity H must start – that is, week 11. They therefore have latest start dates of week 8 (11–3) and week 7 (11–4) respectively.

- Activities E and F must be completed by week 10 so their earliest start dates are weeks 7 (10–3) and 0 (10–10) respectively.

- Activity B must be completed by week 7 (the latest start date for both activities D and E) so its latest start is week 3 (7–4).

- Activity A must be completed by week 8 (the latest start date for activity C) so its latest start is week 2 (8–6).

- The latest start date for the project start is the earliest of the latest start dates for activities A, B and F. This is week zero. This is, of course, not very surprising since it tells us that if the project does not start on time it won't finish on time.

The backward pass rule: the latest finish date for an activity is the latest start date for all the activities that may commence immediately that activity is complete. Where more than one activity can commence we take the *earliest* of the *latest start dates* for those activities.

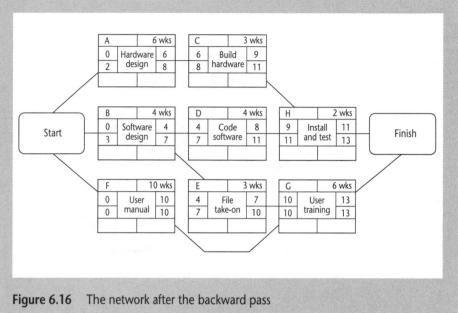

Figure 6.16 The network after the backward pass

6.12 Identifying the critical path

There will be at least one path through the network (that is, one set of successive activities) that defines the duration of the project. This is known as the *critical path*. Any delay to any activity on this critical path will delay the completion of the project.

The difference between an activity's earliest start date and its latest start date (or, equally, the difference between its earliest and latest finish dates) is known as the activity's *float* – it is a measure of how much the start or completion of an activity may be delayed without affecting the end date of the project. Any activity with a float of zero is critical in the sense that any delay in carrying out the activity will delay the completion date of the project as a whole. There will always be at least one path through the network joining those critical activities; this is the *critical path* and is shown bold in Figure 6.17.

This float is also known as *total float* to distinguish it from other forms of float – see Section 6.13.

The significance of the critical path is twofold.

● In managing the project, we must pay particular attention to monitoring activities on the critical path so that the effects of any delay or resource unavailability are detected and corrected at the earliest opportunity.

● In planning the project, it is the critical path that we must shorten if we are to reduce the overall duration of the project.

Figure 6.17 also shows the *activity span*. This is the difference between the earliest start date and the latest finish date and is a measure of the maximum time allowable for the activity. However, it is subject to the same conditions of interpretation as activity float which is discussed in the next section.

The critical path is the longest path through the network.

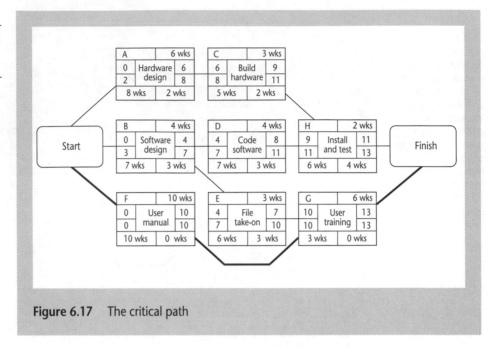

Figure 6.17 The critical path

Table 6.2 Estimated activity durations for Amanda's network

Activity	Estimated duration (days)	Activity	Estimated duration (days)
Specify overall	34	Design module C	4
Specify module A	20	Design module D	4
Specify module B	15	Code/test module A	30
Specify module C	25	Code/test module B	28
Specify module D	15	Code/test module C	15
Check specification	2	Code/test module D	25
Design module A	7	System integration	6
Design module B	6		

Exercise 6.2

Refer back to Amanda's CPM network illustrated in Figure 6.7.

Using the activity durations given in Table 6.2, calculate the earliest completion date for the project and identify the critical path on your network.

6.13 Activity float

Total float may only be used once.

Although the total float is shown for each activity, it really 'belongs' to a path through the network. Activities A and C each have 2 weeks total float. If, however, activity A uses up its float (that is, it is not completed until week 8) then activity B will have zero float (it will have become critical). In such circumstances it may be misleading and detrimental to the project's success to publicize total float!

There are a number of other measures of activity float, including the following:

● **Free float**   The time by which an activity may be delayed without affecting any subsequent activity. It is calculated as the difference between the earliest completion date for the activity and the earliest start date of the succeeding activity. This might be considered a more satisfactory measure of float for publicizing to the staff involved in undertaking the activities.

● **Interfering float**   The difference between total float and free float. This is quite commonly used, particularly in association with the free float. Once the free float has been used (or if it is zero), the interfering float tells us by how much the activity may be delayed without delaying the project end date – even though it will delay the start of subsequent activities.

Exercise 6.3   Calculate the free float and interfering float for each of the activities shown in the activity network (Figure 6.17).

6.14   Shortening the project duration

If we wish to shorten the overall duration of a project we would normally consider attempting to reduce activity durations. In many cases this can be done by applying more resources to the task – working overtime or procuring additional staff, for example. The critical path indicates where we must look to save time – if we are trying to bring forward the end date of the project, there is clearly no point in attempting to shorten non-critical activities. Referring to Figure 6.17 it can be seen that we could complete the project in week 12 by reducing the duration of activity F by one week (to nine weeks).

Exercise 6.4   Referring to Figure 6.17, suppose that the duration for activity F is shortened to eight weeks. Calculate the end date for the project.

What would the end date for the project be if activity F were shortened to seven weeks? Why?

As we reduce activity times along the critical path we must continually check for any new critical path emerging and redirect our attention where necessary.

There will come a point when we can no longer safely, or cost-effectively, reduce critical activity durations in an attempt to bring forward the project end date. Further savings, if needed, must be sought in a consideration of our work methods and by questioning the logical sequencing of activities. Generally, time savings are to be found by increasing the amount of parallelism in the network and the removal of bottlenecks (subject always, of course, to resource and quality constraints).

6.15   Identifying critical activities

The critical path identifies those activities which are critical to the end date of the project; however, activities that are not on the critical path may become critical. As the project proceeds, activities will invariably use up some of their float and this

For a more in-depth discussion of the role of the critical path in project monitoring, see Chapter 9.

will require a periodic recalculation of the network. As soon as the activities along a particular path use up their total float then that path will become a critical path and a number of hitherto non-critical activities will suddenly become critical.

It is therefore common practice to identify 'near-critical' paths – those whose lengths are within, say, 10–20% of the duration of the critical path or those with a total float of less than, say, 10% of the project's uncompleted duration.

The importance of identifying critical and near-critical activities is that it is they that are most likely to be the cause of delays in completing the project. We shall see, in the next three chapters, that identifying these activities is an important step in risk analysis, resource allocation and project monitoring.

6.16 Activity-on-arrow networks

The developers of the CPM and PERT methods both originally used activity-on-arrow networks. Although now less common than activity-on-node networks, they are still used and introduce an additional useful concept – that of *events*. We will therefore take a brief look at how they are drawn and analysed using the same project example shown in Table 6.1.

In activity-on-arrow network activities are represented by links (or arrows) and the nodes represent events of activities (or groups of activities) starting or finishing. Figure 6.18 illustrates our previous example drawn as an activity-on-arrow network.

Activity-on-arrow network rules and conventions

A project network may have only one start node This is a requirement of activity-on-arrow networks rather than merely desirable as is the case with activity-on-node networks.

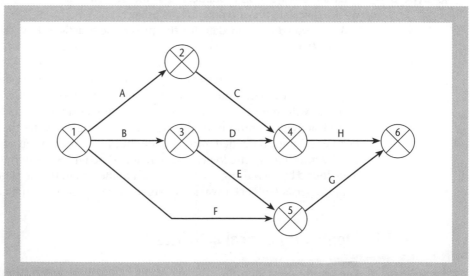

Figure 6.18 An activity-on-arrow network

A project network may have only one end node   Again, this is a requirement for activity-on-arrow networks.

A link has duration   A link represents an activity and, in general, activities take time to execute. Notice, however, that the network in Figure 6.18 does not contain any reference to durations. The links are not drawn in any way to represent the activity durations. The network drawing merely represents the logic of the project – the rules governing the order in which activities are to be carried out.

Nodes have no duration   Nodes are events and, as such, are instantaneous points in time. The *source node* is the event of the project becoming ready to start and the *sink node* is the event of the project becoming completed. Intermediate nodes represent two simultaneous events – the event of all activities leading into a node having been completed and the event of all activities leading out of that node being in a position to be started.

In Figure 6.19 node 3 is the event that both coding and data take-on have been completed and activity program testing is free to start. Installation may be started only when event 4 has been achieved, that is, as soon as program testing has been completed.

Time moves from left to right   As with activity-on-node networks, activity-on-arrow networks are drawn, if at all possible, so that time moves from left to right.

Nodes are numbered sequentially   There are no precise rules about node numbering, but nodes should be numbered so that head nodes (those at the 'arrow' end of an activity) always have a higher number than tail events (those at the 'non-arrow' end of an activity. This convention makes it easy to spot loops.

A network may not contain loops   Figure 6.20 demonstrates a loop in an activity-on-arrow network. As discussed in the context of precedence networks, loops are either an error of logic or a situation that must be resolved by itemizing iterations of activity groups.

A network may not contain dangles   A dangling activity such as *Write user manual* in Figure 6.21 cannot exist, as it would suggest there are two completion

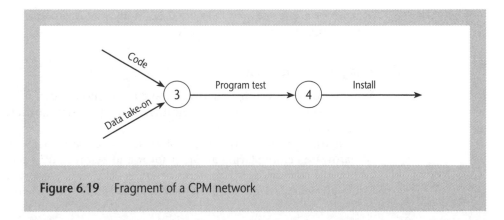

Figure 6.19   Fragment of a CPM network

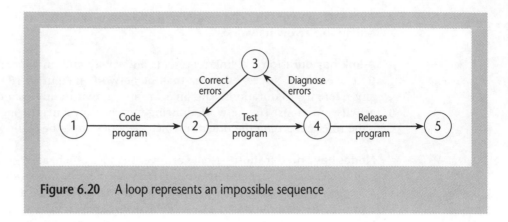

Figure 6.20 A loop represents an impossible sequence

Dangles are not allowed in activity-on-arrow networks.

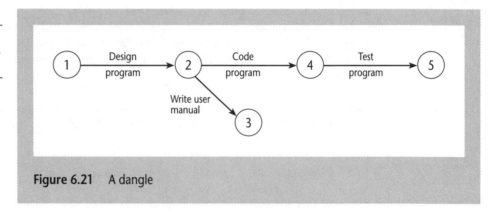

Figure 6.21 A dangle

points for the project. If, in Figure 6.21 node 5 represents the true project completion point and there are no activities dependent on activity *Write user manual*, then the network should be redrawn so that activity *Write user manual* starts at node 2 and terminates at node 5 – in practice, we would need to insert a dummy activity between nodes 3 and 5. In other words, all events, except the first and the last, must have at least one activity entering them and at least one activity leaving them and all activities must start and end with an event.

Exercise 6.5 Take a look at the networks in Figure 6.22. State what is wrong with each of them and where possible redraw them correctly.

Using dummy activities

When two paths within a network have a common event although they are, in other respects, independent, a logical error such as that illustrated in Figure 6.23 might occur.

Suppose that, in a particular project, it is necessary to specify a certain piece of hardware before placing an order for it and before coding the software. Before coding the software it is also necessary to specify the appropriate data structures, although clearly we do not need to wait for this to be done before the hardware is ordered.

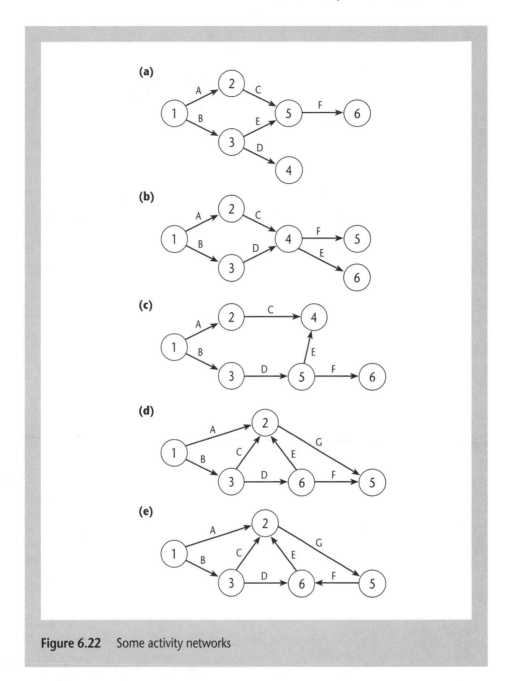

Figure 6.22 Some activity networks

Figure 6.23 is an attempt to model the situation described above, although it is incorrect in that it requires both hardware specification and data structure design to be completed before either an order may be placed or software coding may commence.

We can resolve this problem by separating the two (more or less) independent paths and introducing a dummy activity to link the completion of data structure design to the start of the activity placing an order. This effectively breaks the link between data structure design and placing the order and is shown in Figure 6.24.

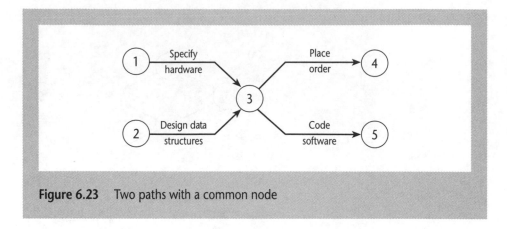

Figure 6.23　Two paths with a common node

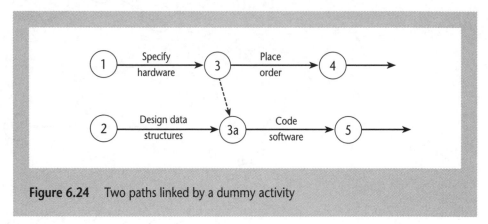

Figure 6.24　Two paths linked by a dummy activity

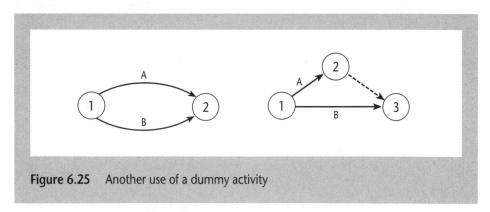

Figure 6.25　Another use of a dummy activity

Dummy activities, shown as dotted lines on the network diagram, have a zero duration and use no resources. They are often used to aid in the layout of network drawings as in Figure 6.25. The use of a dummy activity where two activities share the same start and end nodes makes it easier to distinguish the activity end-points. These are problems that do not occur with activity-on-node networks.

Where parallel activities have a time lag we may show this as a 'ladder' of activities: documentation may proceed alongside prototype testing so long as it starts at least a day later and will finish two days after the completion of prototype testing.

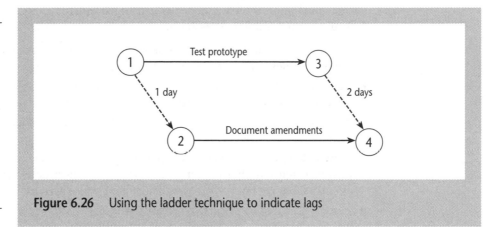

Figure 6.26 Using the ladder technique to indicate lags

Exercise 6.6   Take another look at Brigette's college payroll activity network fragment, which you developed in Exercise 2.3 (or take a look at the model answer in Figure F.3). Redraw this as an activity-on-arrow network.

Representing lagged activities

Activity-on-arrow networks are less elegant when it comes to representing lagged parallel activities. We need to represent these with pairs of dummy activities as shown in Figure 6.26. Where the activities are lagged because a stage in one activity must be completed before the other may proceed, it is likely to be better to show each stage as a separate activity.

Activity labelling

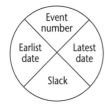

There are a number of differing conventions that have been adopted for entering information on an activity-on-arrow network. Typically the diagram is used to record information about the events rather than the activities – activity-based information (other than labels or descriptions) is generally held on a separate activity table.

One of the more common conventions for labelling nodes, and the one adopted here, is to divide the node circle into quadrants and use those quadrants to show the event number, the latest and earliest dates by which the event should occur, and the event slack (which will be explained later).

Network analysis

During the forward pass, earliest dates are recorded as they are calculated. For events, they are recorded on the network diagram and for activities they are recorded on the activity table.

Analysis proceeds in the same way as with activity-on-node networks although the discussion places emphasis on the events rather than activity start and completion times.

The forward pass   The forward pass is carried out to calculate the earliest date on which each event may be achieved and the earliest date on which each activity may be started and completed. The earliest date for an event is the earliest date by which all activities upon which it depends can be completed. The calculation proceeds according to the following reasoning.

- Activities A, B and F may start immediately, so the earliest date for event 1 is zero and the earliest start date for these three activities is also zero.

- Activity A will take 6 weeks, so the earliest it can finish is week 6 (recorded in the activity table). Therefore the earliest we can achieve event 2 is week 6.

- Activity B will take 4 weeks, so the earliest it can finish and the earliest we can achieve event 3 is week 4.

- Activity F will take 10 weeks, so the earliest it can finish is week 10 – we cannot, however, tell whether or not this is also the earliest date that we can achieve event 5 since we have not, as yet, calculated when activity E will finish.

- Activity E can start as early as week 4 (the earliest date for event 3) and, since it is forecasted to take 3 weeks, will be completed, at the earliest, at the end of week 7.

- Event 5 may be achieved when both E and F have been completed, that is, week 10 (the later of 7 and 10).

- Similarly we can reason that event 4 will have an earliest date of week 9. This is the later of the earliest finish for activity D (week 8) and the earliest finish for activity C (week 9).

- The earliest date for the completion of the project, event 6, is therefore the end of week 13 – the later of 11 (the earliest finish for H) and 13 (the earliest finish for G).

The results of the forward pass are shown in Figure 6.27 and Table 6.3.

The backward pass The second stage is to carry out a backward pass to calculate the latest date at which each event may be achieved, and each activity started and finished, without delaying the end date of the project. The latest date for an event

The forward pass rule: the earliest date for an event is the earliest finish date for all the activities terminating at that event. Where more than one activity terminates at a common event we take the latest of the earliest finish dates for those activities.

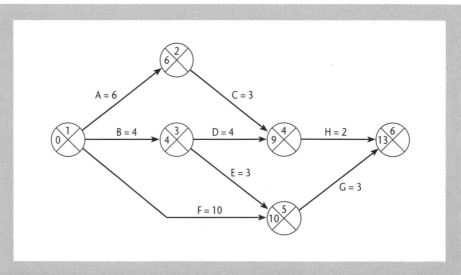

Figure 6.27   A CPM network after the forward pass

Table 6.3 The activity table after the forward pass

Activity	Duration (weeks)	Earliest start date	Latest start date	Earliest finish date	Latest finish date	Total float
A	6	0		6		
B	4	0		4		
C	3	6		9		
D	4	4		8		
E	3	4		7		
F	10	0		10		
G	3	10		13		
H	2	9		11		

The backward pass rule: the latest date for an event is the latest start date for all the activities that may commence from that event. Where more than one activity commences at a common event we take the earliest of the latest start dates for those activities.

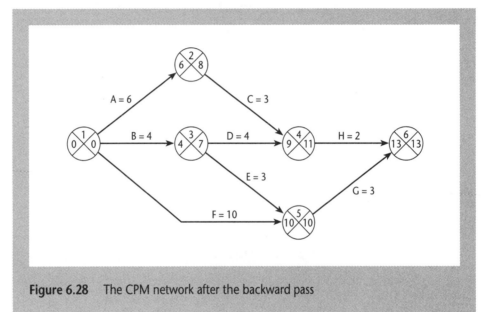

Figure 6.28 The CPM network after the backward pass

is the latest date by which all immediately following activities must be started for the project to be completed on time. As with activity-on-node networks, we assume that the latest finish date for the project is the same as the earliest finish date – that is, we wish to complete the project as early as possible.

Figure 6.28 illustrates our network and Table 6.4 the activity table after carrying out the backward pass – as with the forward pass, event dates are recorded on the diagram and activity dates on the activity table.

Identifying the critical path   The critical path is identified in a way similar to that used in activity-on-node networks. We do, however, use a different concept, that of *slack*, in identifying the path. Slack is the difference between the earliest date and the latest date for an event – it is a measure of how late an event may be without affecting the end date of the project. The critical path is the path joining all nodes with a zero slack (Figure 6.29).

Table 6.4 The activity table following the backward pass

Activity	Duration (weeks)	Earliest start date	Latest start date	Earliest finish date	Latest finish date	Total float
A	6	0	2	6	8	
B	4	0	3	4	7	
C	3	6	8	9	11	
D	4	4	7	8	11	
E	3	4	7	7	10	
F	10	0	0	10	10	
G	3	10	10	13	13	
H	2	9	11	11	13	

The critical path is the longest path through the network.

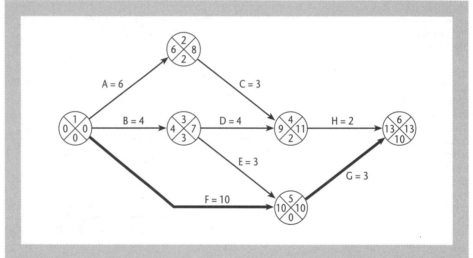

Figure 6.29   The critical path

6.17   Conclusion

In this chapter, we have discussed the use of the critical path method and precedence networks to obtain an ideal activity plan. This plan tells us the order in which we should execute activities and the earliest and latest we can start and finish them.

These techniques help us to identify which activities are critical to meeting a target completion date.

In order to manage the project we need to turn the activity plan into a schedule that will specify precisely when each activity is scheduled to start and finish. Before we can do this, we must consider what resources will be required and whether or not they will be available at appropriate times. As we shall see, the allocation of resources to an activity may be affected by how we view the importance of the task and the risks associated with it. In the next two chapters we look at these aspects of project planning before we consider how we might publish a schedule for the project.

6.18   Further exercises

1. Draw an activity network using either activity-on-node or activity-on-arrow network conventions for each of the following projects:
   - getting married;
   - choosing and purchasing a desktop computer;
   - organizing and carrying out a survey of users' opinions of an information system.

2. If you have access to a project planning application, use it to produce a project plan for the IOE maintenance group accounts project. Base your plan on that used for Exercise 6.2 and verify that your application reports the same information as you calculated manually when you did the exercise.

3. Based on your answer to Exercise 6.2, discuss what options Amanda might consider if she found it necessary to complete the project earlier than day 104?

CHAPTER 7

Risk management

Objectives

When you have completed this chapter you will be able to:

- identify the factors putting a project at risk;
- categorize and prioritize action for risk elimination or containment;
- quantify the likely effects of risk on project time-scales.

7.1 Introduction

In Chapter 3 we considered project evaluation, including assessment of the risk of the project not delivering the expected benefits. In that chapter we took a high-level view of the risks associated with the project as would be the case very early in the project's life cycle.

In this chapter we are concerned with a more detailed evaluation: the identification of possible problems that could cause the project to run late or over budget and with the identification of the steps that can be taken to avoid those problems or minimize their effects.

The identification of the hazards and possible problems, the evaluation of their importance and the drawing up of plans to monitor and deal with those problems is known as risk management.

The allocation of resources is discussed in the next chapter. Staff motivation is covered in Chapter 11.

Risk management is not, however, restricted to the material in this chapter. There is a continuum between the early risk evaluation described in Chapter 3 and those described in this chapter – some of the techniques described here will be useful in those early stages and vice versa. The risk of an activity running over time is likely to depend, at least in part, on who is doing or managing it – the evaluation of risk, the allocation of staff to activities and the management and motivation of the project team are therefore closely connected.

Project monitoring is the subject of Chapter 9.

It must also be emphasized that risk management is not a one-off activity. It must start at the very conception of the project and continue throughout its life. Possible threats to a project, and the likelihood of those threats occurring will change over time; some hazards will occur and require the invocation of contingency plans; monitoring threats may give an early warning of their occurrence.

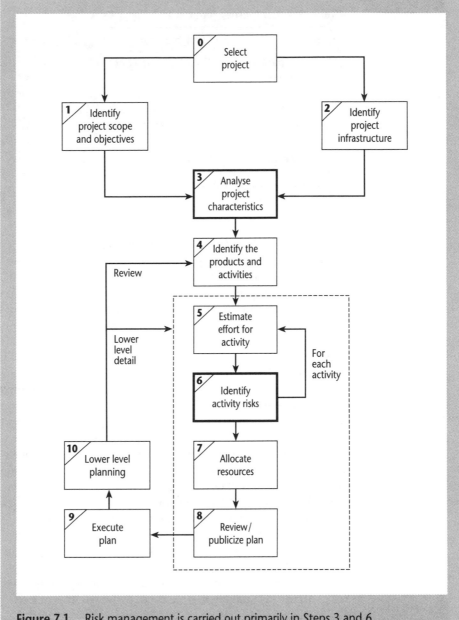

Figure 7.1 Risk management is carried out primarily in Steps 3 and 6

7.2 The nature of risk

A risk is something that may or may not happen. If it does happen then it is likely to jeopardize the success of the project. Risk is associated with uncertainty, but we do not call all uncertain events or outcomes 'risks'. We normally reserve the word 'risk' to describe non-desirable events or outcomes – beneficial occurrences are normally called 'opportunities'.

Table 7.1 Car journey hazards

Hazard	Likely problem	Action plan
Unusually bad traffic congestion	Could miss start of interview	Listen to traffic reports on radio Plan alternative routes before starting out
Flat tyre	Could miss interview or be late	Ensure spare tyre is usable and inflated
Car breakdown or accident	Probably would miss interview entirely	No action plan

In discussing risks it is important to distinguish between specific, risk-laden *events* that may occur, which we will, to be more precise, call 'hazards' and their *outcomes*, which we will call 'problems'. Problems, when they occur will, if we do not have successful contingency plans, put the success of the project at risk.

Imagine, for a moment, that we are planning an important car journey where it is important to arrive on time – a job interview, perhaps. Three of the many hazards that we might consider before setting out are listed in Table 7.1 along with possible consequences and action plans.

Although we will have taken account of normal traffic conditions in estimating our journey time, we might regard unusually bad traffic congestion to be well within the bounds of possibility and it would therefore be prudent to take some action to avoid this hazard occurring. We could therefore plan to get up a little early and listen to the traffic reports on the radio. Armed with the current traffic reports and a set of alternative routes we are in a good position to avoid any unusual traffic congestion. We therefore have an avoidance plan by which we hope to avoid the hazard if it should occur.

Having a flat tyre during the journey is fairly unlikely, but it costs little to check the spare tyre the day before we set out and doing so will ensure that, should we have a puncture, we can change the tyre with a minimum of delay. The time taken to change the tyre may cause us to be a little late in arriving, but our plan has minimized the likely effect.

A major breakdown or accident would be pretty disastrous and, were such a hazard to occur, it is unlikely that we could arrive on time or even, perhaps, on the right day. However, we might consider such an eventuality very unlikely so it is a risk we are willing to accept if we are to travel by car.

For each of these three hazards we have identified a resulting problem – the problem that we might be late or, in the worst case, so late that we never effectively arrive. By considering that problem we can, perhaps, come up with a further plan to mitigate its seriousness. We could, for example, take a mobile phone and, if, at some stage on the journey, it looks as if we are going to be late, we can phone ahead to apologize and even make arrangements for a later interview. This problem-oriented plan also has the advantage that it may help should a totally unforeseen hazard occur.

Even in this simple example we can see that the identification of risks and drawing up plans to deal with them can be quite complex. We have one strategy for avoiding a hazard, one for minimizing the possible problem caused by a hazard and, in another case, we have adopted a 'no action' strategy – that is, accepting that the problem may occur and, if it does, we will live with the consequences. We have also adopted a further problem-oriented plan for mitigating the effects of the immediate result of most hazards which might occur (even some hazards we have not considered). In doing this we have implicitly or explicitly assessed the likelihood of each hazard occurring, the seriousness of each hazard, the cost or difficulty of adopting an action plan, the likely effectiveness of each action plan and the ultimate cost of a problem arising.

From this small example we can see that, in order to deal with risk in anything but the very smallest project, we need a set of tools and techniques for identifying and assessing risk and it is that which is the concern of the rest of this chapter.

7.3 Types of risk

For the purpose of identifying and managing those risks that may cause a project to overrun its timescale or budget, it is convenient to identify three types of risk:

- those caused by the inherent difficulties of estimation;
- those due to assumptions made during the planning process;
- those of unforeseen (or at least unplanned) events or hazards occurring.

Estimation errors

Improved quality control should make it easier to predict the time required for program and system testing.

Some tasks are harder to estimate than others because of the lack of experience of similar tasks or because of the inherent nature of the task. Producing a set of user manuals is reasonably straightforward and, given that we have carried out similar tasks previously, we should be able to estimate with some degree of accuracy how long the task will take and how much it will cost. On the other hand, the time required for program testing and debugging might be difficult to predict with a similar degree of accuracy – even if we have written similar programs in the past.

See Chapter 5 for methods of estimation.

Estimation can be improved by analysing historic data for similar activities and similar systems. Keeping records comparing our original estimates with the final outcome will reveal the type of tasks that are difficult to estimate correctly.

Planning assumptions

At every stage during planning, assumptions are made which, if not valid, may put the plan at risk. Our activity network, for example, is likely to be built on the assumption of using a particular design methodology – which may be subsequently changed. We generally assume that, following coding, a module will be tested and then integrated with others – we might not plan for module testing showing up the need for changes in the original design but, in the event, it might happen.

At each stage in the planning process, it is important to list explicitly all of the assumptions that have been made and identify what effects they might have on the plan if they are inappropriate.

Eventualities

Some eventualities might never be foreseen and we can only resign ourselves to the fact that unimaginable things do, sometimes, happen. They are, however, very rare. The majority of unexpected events can, in fact, be identified – the requirements specification might be altered after some of the modules have been coded, the senior programmer might take maternity leave, the required hardware might not be delivered on time. Such events do happen from time to time and, although the likelihood of any one of them happening during a particular project may be relatively low, they must be considered and planned for.

7.4 Managing risk

The objective of risk management is to avoid or minimize the adverse effects of unforeseen events by avoiding the risks or drawing up contingency plans for dealing with them.

There are a number of models for risk management, but most are similar, in that they identify two main components – *risk analysis* and *risk management*. An example of an often-used model is that in Figure 7.2, which shows a task breakdown structure for what Barry Boehm calls *risk engineering*.

- *Risk identification* consists of listing all of the risks that can adversely affect the successful execution of the project. We discuss this in more detail in Section 7.5 which we call 'hazard identification' to emphasize the fact that we must start by identifying the primary causes of risk.

- *Risk estimation* consists of assessing the likelihood and impact of each hazard. We discuss this in more detail in Section 7.6 under the broader topic of risk analysis.

This is based on the breakdown presented by Barry Boehm in his *Tutorial on Software Risk Management*, IEEE Computer Society, 1989.

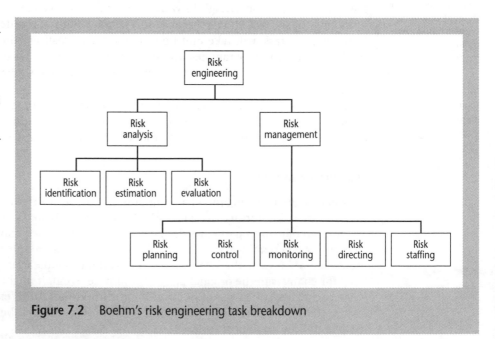

Figure 7.2 Boehm's risk engineering task breakdown

- *Risk evaluation* consists of ranking the risks and determining risk aversion strategies. We discuss this in Section 7.6 on hazard analysis and Section 7.7 where we discuss strategies for risk aversion.

- *Risk planning* consists of drawing up contingency plans and, where appropriate, adding these to the project's task structure. With small projects, risk planning is likely to be the responsibility of the project manager, but medium or large projects will benefit from the appointment of a full-time risk manager.

- *Risk control* concerns the main functions of the risk manager in minimizing and reacting to problems throughout the project. This function will include aspects of quality control in addition to dealing with problems as they occur.

- *Risk monitoring* must be an ongoing activity, as the importance and likelihood of particular risks can change as the project proceeds. Risk monitoring is discussed in Chapter 9.

- *Risk directing* and *risk staffing* are concerned with the day-to-day management of risk. Risk aversion and problem-solving strategies frequently involve the use of additional staff and this must be planned for and directed.

Whatever task model or whichever techniques are used, risk management will not be effective unless all project staff are risk-oriented and are provided with an environment where they can freely discuss the risks that might affect a project. All too often, team members who identify potential risks at an early stage are seen as having a negative attitude.

Dwayne Phillips, *The Project Manager's Handbook*, IEEE Computer Society, 1998.

Writing about attitudes to risk, Dwayne Phillips remarks that '*I have seen a room get suddenly quiet when someone brings up a "concern"* ' but says that '*pretending that problems will not occur will not prevent them*'. For effective risk management, it is important that the project team are encouraged to identify and discuss risks as early as possible in the project's life.

This is not necessarily easy – there will be cases where identifying risks to a project or activity may be close to admitting a personal deficiency or inability to deal with a challenge. In large organizations or with large projects, it is possible that risk management and, in particular, risk analysis will be carried out by a separate team not otherwise associated with the project team. Where this is not the case it is important that risk identification and analysis is seen as a positive activity encouraged by management. Handled in the correct way it can become a team-building activity – handled in the wrong way it can be a recipe for team members to avoid confronting potential hazards until it is too late to avoid the consequent problems.

The techniques described in the rest of this chapter describe how risks can be identified and quantified and are designed to provide a framework that engenders a positive attitude to the analysis and management of project risks. Above all, the techniques are designed to increase risk visibility.

7.5 Hazard identification

The first stage in any risk assessment exercise is to identify the hazards that might affect the duration or resource costs of the project. A hazard is an event that might occur and will, if it does occur, create a problem for the successful completion of the project. In identifying and analysing risks, we can usefully distinguish between the cause (or hazard), its immediate effect (the problem that it creates) and the risk that it will pose to the project.

For example, the illness of a team member is a *hazard* that might result in the *problem* of late delivery of a component. The late delivery of that component is likely to have an effect on other activities and might, particularly if it is on the critical path, put the project completion date at *risk*.

A common way of identifying hazards is to use a checklist listing all the possible hazards and factors that influence them. Typical checklists list many, even hundreds, of factors and there are, today, a number of knowledge-based software products available to assist in this analysis.

Some hazards are *generic risks* – that is, they are relevant to all software projects and standard checklists can be used and augmented from an analysis of past projects to identify them. These will include risks such as misunderstanding the requirements or key personnel being ill. There will also be *specific risks* that are relevant to an individual project and these are likely to be more difficult to identify without an involvement of the members of the project team and a working environment that encourages risk assessment.

The categories of factors that will need to be considered include the following:

Some of these issues have been addressed in Chapter 4.

Application factors   The nature of the application – whether it is a simple data processing application, a safety-critical system or a large distributed system with real-time elements – is likely to be a critical factor. The expected size of the application is also important – the larger the system, the greater is the likelihood of errors and communication and management problems.

The effect of staff experience was considered in Chapter 5 on effort estimation.

Staff factors   The experience and skills of the staff involved are clearly major factors – an experienced programmer is, one would hope, less likely to make errors than one with little experience. We must, however, also consider the appropriateness of the experience – experience in coding small data processing modules in Cobol may be of little value if we are developing a complex real-time control system using C++.

Such factors as the level of staff satisfaction and the staff turn-over rates are also important to the success of any project – demotivated staff or key personnel leaving unexpectedly have caused many a project to fail.

Project factors   It is important that the project and its objectives are well defined and that they are absolutely clear to all members of the project team and all key stakeholders. Any possibility that this is not the case will pose a risk to the success of the project. Similarly, an agreed and formal quality plan must be in place and adhered to by all participants and any possibility that the quality plan is inadequate or not adhered to will jeopardize the project.

Project methods   Using well-specified and structured methods (such as PRINCE 2 and SSADM) for project management and system development will decrease the risk of delivering a system that is unsatisfactory or late. Using such methods for the first time, though, may cause problems and delays – it is only with experience that the benefits accrue.

Hardware/software factors   A project that requires new hardware for development is likely to pose a higher risk than one where the software can be developed on existing (and familiar) hardware. Where a system is developed on one type of hardware or software platform to be used on another there might be additional (and high) risks at installation.

Changeover factors   The need for an 'all-in-one' changeover to the new system poses particular risks. Incremental or gradual changeover minimizes the risks involved but is not always practical. Parallel running can provide a safety net but might be impossible or too costly.

Supplier factors   The extent to which a project relies on external organizations that cannot be directly controlled often influences the project's success. Delays in, for example, the installation of telephone lines or delivery of equipment may be difficult to avoid – particularly if the project is of little consequence to the external supplier.

Environment factors   Changes in the environment can affect a project's success. A significant change in the taxation regulations could, for example, have serious consequences for the development of a payroll application.

Health and safety factors   While not generally a major issue for software projects (compared, say, to civil engineering projects), the possible effects of project activities on the health and safety of the participants and the environment should be considered. BS 6079 states that 'every project should include an audit of these specific risks before work starts' and that 'audit updates should be scheduled as part of the overall project plan'.

Exercise 7.1   Brigette finds that Brightmouth HE College does not have a project hazard checklist or questionnaire and decides to produce her own for the payroll project. List at least one question that she might include under each of the above headings.

Although some factors might influence the project as a whole, it is necessary to consider them individually for each activity – a key member of staff being ill during fact-finding might, for example, be far less serious than a similar absence during user training. Within a PRINCE 2 environment it can be appropriate to list the factors for each of the products identified in the product breakdown structure.

Identification of project-specific risks should normally involve the entire project team and many organizations use risk or hazard identification forms such as the one illustrated in Figure 7.3. During the initial hazard identification activity each member of the team may be required to submit at least one form for each activity with which they are involved – if there are no envisaged problems then the form is marked 'no problems'. Additionally they may also be used as routine risk notification forms throughout the project's life – either on a periodic basis or as and when team members identify potential hazards.

Ideally these reports would be submitted directly to management and discussed openly at team planning meetings. In organizations where there is not a healthy, well-developed risk awareness culture, however, it may be beneficial to allow for anonymous submission of hazard reports.

7.6 Hazard analysis

Having identified the hazards that might affect our project we need some way of assessing their importance. Some will be relatively unimportant (for example, the risk that some of the documentation is delivered a day late), whereas some will be of major significance (such as the risk that the software is delivered late). Some are quite likely to occur (it is quite likely, for example, that one of the software developers in a team will take a few days' sick leave during a lengthy project), whereas others are relatively unlikely (hardware failure causing loss of completed code, perhaps).

Clearly we cannot plan for every conceivable hazard so we need to prioritize hazards according to some measure of seriousness. For small projects we may need only to use a small set of relatively easy to assess hazard properties such as those given in the hazard identification form (Figure 7.3). We could, for example, rank the hazards and deal with them as shown in Table 7.2.

Even with large projects we might use such a ranking method as an initial analysis but, with a large number of hazards, a more discriminatory ordering method is required. The most favoured method of ranking is to calculate the *risk exposure* for each hazard as a measure of the importance of the risk.

Risk exposure

These terms are common but not universal – you might come across alternative terms.

The probability of a hazard occurring is known as the *risk likelihood*; the effect that the resulting problem will have on the project, if it occurs, is known as the *risk impact* and the importance of the risk is known as the *risk value* or *risk exposure*. The risk value is calculated as:

$$\text{risk exposure} = \text{risk likelihood} \times \text{risk impact}$$

Expected costs and benefits were used in cost–benefit analysis in Chapter 3.

Ideally the risk impact is estimated in monetary terms and the likelihood assessed as a probability. In that case the risk exposure will represent an expected cost in the same sense that we calculated expected costs and benefits when discussing cost–benefit analysis. The risk exposures for various risks can then be compared with each other to assess the relative importance of each risk and they can be directly compared with the costs and likelihoods of success of various contingency plans.

However, estimation of these costs and probabilities is likely to be difficult, subjective, time-consuming and costly. In spite of this, it is valuable to obtain some quantitative measure of risk likelihood and impact because, without these, it is difficult to compare or rank risks in a meaningful way. Moreover, the effort put into obtaining a good quantitative estimate can provide a deeper and valuable understanding of the problem.

Many risk managers use a simple scoring method to provide a quantitative measure for assessing each risk. Some just categorize likelihoods and impacts as high, medium or low, but this form of ranking does not allow the calculation of a risk exposure. A better and popular approach is to score the likelihood and impact on a scale of, say, 1 to 10 where the hazard that is most likely to occur receives a score of 10 and the least likely a score of 1.

Ranking likelihoods and impacts on a scale of 1 to 10 is relatively easy, but most risk managers will attempt to assign scores in a more meaningful way such that, for example, a likelihood scoring 8 is considered twice as likely as one with a score of 4.

Hazard identification form

Project ID:_____
Hazard ID:_____
Date:_____

Likelihood	Timeframe	Impact
Likely ($p > 50\%$) ☐	Near ☐	Critical ☐
Unlikely ($p < 50\%$) ☐	Far ☐	Significant ☐
		Insignificant ☐

Statement of hazard

Potential affects

Recommendation for dealing with hazard / problem (optional)

Figure 7.3   Hazard identification form

Table 7.2 Hazard ranking

Priority	Criteria	Action
1	Any critical hazard	Take immediate action
2	Significant, likely and near-term	Initiate risk planning procedures
3	Significant, likely and far-term	Get more information and take to next review meeting
4	Significant but unlikely	Get more information about likelihood and reassess
5	Insignificant	Keep under review

Impact measures, scored on a similar scale, must take into account the total risk to the project. This must include the following potential costs:

● the cost of delays to scheduled dates for deliverables;

● cost overruns caused by using additional or more expensive resources;

● the costs incurred or implicit in any compromise to the system's quality or functionality.

Table 7.3 Part of Amanda's risk exposure assessment

Hazard		Likelihood	Impact	Risk exposure
R1	Changes to requirements specification during coding	1	8	8
R2	Specification takes longer than expected	3	7	21
R3	Significant staff sickness affecting critical path activities	5	7	35
R4	Significant staff sickness affecting non-critical activities	10	3	30
R5	Module coding takes longer than expected	4	5	20
R6	Module testing demonstrates errors or deficiencies in design	1	10	10

Table 7.3 illustrates part of Amanda's risk value assessment. Notice that the hazard with the highest risk value might not be the one that is most likely nor the one with the greatest potential impact.

Prioritizing the risks

Managing risk involves the use of two strategies:

● reducing the risk exposure by reducing the likelihood or impact;

● drawing up contingency plans to deal with the risk should it occur.

Exercise 7.2 Consider Amanda's risk exposure analysis shown in Table 7.3 and add some of the hazards that you considered when answering Exercise 7.1.

Estimate values for the likelihood and impact of each of these items and calculate their risk exposures.

Rank each of your risks according to their risk exposure and, assuming that Amanda does not have the time or resources to deal with all of them, try to categorize each of them as high, medium or low priority.

Any attempt to reduce a risk exposure or put a contingency plan in place will have a cost associated with it. It is therefore important to ensure that this effort is applied in the most effective way and we need a way of prioritizing the risks so that the more important ones can receive the greatest attention.

Risk exposures based on scoring methods must be treated with some caution. Amanda's assessment shown in Table 7.3 does not indicate, for example, that risk R5 is twice as important as R6. Nor can it be taken as necessarily meaning that R2 is more important than R5. In the first case, this is because we cannot interpret the risk exposure values quantitatively because they are based on a non-cardinal scoring method. In the second case, the exposure values are far too close for us to be able to distinguish between them – particularly in view of the somewhat approximate and subjective way in which Amanda is likely to have assessed the likelihoods and, perhaps to a lesser extent, the impacts.

The risk exposures will, however, allow us to obtain an approximate ranking in order of importance. Considering just the risks in Table 7.3, R3 and R4 are, on this basis, clearly the most important and we could classify them as being high risk concerns. There is a significant difference between the exposure scores of these two and one with the next highest exposure, R2. R2 and R5 have similar scores and might be thought of as medium priority risks. The two remaining risks, R1 and R6 have quite low exposure values and can therefore be classified as low risk items.

In practice, there are generally other factors, in addition to the risk exposure value, that must also be taken into account when prioritizing risks.

Classifying risks into these three categories is clearly not always as easy as in this example although, in practice, risks do frequently cluster and break points are often quite distinct.

- *Confidence of the risk assessment*   Some of our risk exposure assessments will be relatively poor. Where this is the case, there is a need for further investigation before action can be planned.

- *Compound risks*   Some risks will be dependent on others. Where this is the case, they should be treated together as a single risk.

- *The number of risks*   There is a limit to the number of risks that can be effectively considered and acted on by a project manager. We might therefore wish to limit the size of the prioritized list.

Risk reduction leverage

Some risks, once recognized, can be reduced or avoided immediately with very little cost or effort and it is sensible to take action on these regardless of their risk value. For other risks we need to compare the estimated costs of taking action with the expected benefits of reducing the risk and then to direct our efforts to where they will have greatest effect

The RRL is used as a factor in prioritizing risks and for evaluating alternative courses of action in dealing with a particular risk.

The most popular method for doing this is to calculate the *risk reduction leverage* (*RRL*) using the equation

$$RRL = \frac{RE_{before} - RE_{after}}{risk\ reduction\ cost}$$

where RE_{before} is the original risk exposure value, RE_{after} is the expected risk exposure value after taking action and the *risk reduction cost* is the cost of implementing the risk reduction action.

Risk reduction costs must be expressed in the same units as risk values – that is, expected monetary values or score values. Risk reduction costs represent the expected cost or effort of putting the risk reduction plan into action.

The difference, $RE_{before} - RE_{after}$, is a measure of the effectiveness of our risk reduction plan in reducing the impact or likelihood of the hazard, or both. Larger values of *RRL* indicate most cost-effective risk reduction plans.

If the values used to calculate *RRL* are expected monetary v~~
greater than one indicates that we can expect to gain from i.
reduction plan because the expected reduction in risk exposu.
cost of the plan. Do not forget, though, that the word 'expect~
used in the same way as when we were discussing cost–benefit
Chapter 3 – that is, consistently implementing plans which an
unity would, in the long term, be beneficial.

In most practical situations, because of the difficulty and cost of estimating monetary values, we would score the various risk reduction plans using the same scoring method as was used for scoring the impacts. In this case the RRL can only be used as a ranking method – the higher the RRL the more cost-effective or worthwhile will be the risk reduction plan.

7.7 Risk planning and control

Broadly, there are five strategies for planning for risk reduction and controlling problems should hazards occur.

- *Hazard prevention* Some hazards can be prevented from occurring or their likelihood reduced to insignificant levels. The risk of key staff being unavailable for meetings can be minimized by early scheduling, for example.

- *Likelihood reduction* Some risks, while they cannot be prevented, can have their likelihoods reduced by prior planning. The risk of late changes to a requirements specification can, for example, be reduced by prototyping. Prototyping will not eliminate the risk of late changes and will need to be supplemented by contingency planning.

- *Risk avoidance* A project can, for example, be protected from the risk of overrunning the schedule by increasing duration estimates or reducing functionality.

- *Risk transfer* The impact of some risks can be transferred away from the project by, for example, contracting out or taking out insurance.

- *Contingency planning* Some risks are not preventable and contingency plans will need to be drawn up to reduce the impact should the hazard occur. A project manager should draw up contingency plans for using agency programmers to minimize the impact of any unplanned absence of programming staff.

In Section 7.5 we mentioned the use of checklists for hazard identification. Many of these generic checklists, as well as listing common generic hazards, list typical actions for risk reduction. The checklist in Table 7.4 is based upon an often-quoted list produced by Barry Boehm.

Exercise 7.3 For each of the risks listed in Table 7.3, identify actions that Amanda might take to reduce their likelihood or impact.

7.8 Evaluating risks to the schedule

We have seen that not all risks can be eliminated – even those that are classified as avoidable or manageable can, in the event, still cause problems affecting activity durations. By identifying and categorizing those risks, and in particular, their likely effects on the duration of planned activities, we can assess what impact they are likely to have on our activity plan.

We will now take a look at two methods for assessing the effects of these uncertainties on the project schedule, PERT and Monte Carlo simulation.

This top ten list of software risks is based on one presented by Barry Boehm in his *Tutorial on Software Risk Management*, IEEE Computer Society, 1989.

Table 7.4 Software projects risks and strategies for risk reduction

Risk	Risk reduction techniques
Personnel shortfalls	Staffing with top talent; job matching; teambuilding; training and career development; early scheduling of key personnel
Unrealistic time and cost estimates	Multiple estimation techniques; design to cost; incremental development; recording and analysis of past projects; standardization of methods
Developing the wrong software functions	Improved project evaluation; formal specification methods; user surveys; prototyping; early users' manuals
Developing the wrong user interface	Prototyping; task analysis; user involvement
Gold plating	Requirements scrubbing; prototyping; cost–benefit analysis; design to cost
Late changes to requirements	Stringent change control procedures; high change threshold; incremental prototyping; incremental development (defer changes)
Shortfalls in external supplied components	Benchmarking; inspections; formal specifications; contractual agreements; quality assurance procedures and certification
Shortfalls in externally performed tasks	Quality assurance procedures; competitive design or prototyping; teambuilding; contract incentives
Real-time performance shortfalls	Simulation; benchmarking; prototyping; tuning; technical analysis
Development technically too difficult	Technical analysis; cost–benefit analysis; prototyping; staff training and development

Using PERT to evaluate the effects of uncertainty

PERT was developed to take account of the uncertainty surrounding estimates of task durations. It was developed in an environment of expensive, high-risk and state-of-the-art projects – not that dissimilar to many of today's large software projects.

The method is very similar to the CPM technique (indeed many practitioners use the terms PERT and CPM interchangeably) but, instead of using a single estimate for the duration of each task, PERT requires three estimates.

PERT (program evaluation and review technique) was published in the same year as CPM. Developed for the Fleet Ballistic Missiles Program, it is said to have saved considerable time in development of the Polaris missile.

- *Most likely time*: the time we would expect the task to take under normal circumstances. We shall denote this by the letter m.

- *Optimistic time*: the shortest time in which we could expect to complete the activity, barring outright miracles. We shall use the letter a to denote this.

- *Pessimistic time*: the worst possible time allowing for all reasonable eventualities but excluding 'acts of God and warfare' (as they say in most insurance exclusion clauses). We shall denote this by b.

PERT then combines these three estimates to form a single expected duration, t_e, using the formula

$$t_e = \frac{a + 4m + b}{6}$$

Exercise 7.4

Table 7.5 provides additional activity duration estimates for the network shown in Figure 6.14. There are new estimates for a and b and the original activity duration estimates have been used as the most likely times, m. Calculate the expected duration, t_e, for each activity.

Using expected durations

The expected durations are used to carry out a forward pass through a network; using the same method as the CPM technique. In this case, however, the calculated event dates are not the earliest possible dates, but are the dates by which we expect to achieve those events.

Exercise 7.5

Before reading further, use your calculated expected activity durations to carry out a forward pass through the network (Figure 6.14) and verify that the project duration is 13.5 weeks.

What does an expected duration of 13.5 weeks mean in terms of the completion date for the project?

The PERT network illustrated in Figure 7.4 indicates that we expect the project to take 13.5 weeks. In Figure 7.4 we have used an activity-on-arrow network as this form of presentation makes it easier to visually separate the estimated activity data (expected durations and, later, their standard deviations) from the calculated data (expected completion dates and target completion dates). The method can, of course, be equally well supported by activity-on-node diagrams.

Unlike the CPM approach, the PERT method does not indicate the earliest date by which we could complete the project but the expected (or most likely) date. An advantage of this approach is that it places an emphasis on the uncertainty of the real world. Rather than being tempted to say 'the completion date for the project is . . .' we are led to say 'we expect to complete the project by . . .'.

It also focuses attention on the uncertainty of the estimation of activity durations. Requesting three estimates for each activity emphasizes the fact that we are not certain what will happen – we are forced to take into account the fact that estimates are approximate.

Activity standard deviations

This standard deviation formula is based on the rationale that there are approximately six standard deviations between the extreme tails of many statistical distributions.

A quantitative measure of the degree of uncertainty of an activity duration estimate may be obtained by calculating the standard deviation s of an activity time, using the formula

$$s = \frac{b - a}{6}$$

The activity standard deviation is proportional to the difference between the optimistic and pessimistic estimates, and can be used as a ranking measure of the degree of uncertainty or risk for each activity. The activity expected durations and standard deviations for our sample project are shown in Table 7.6.

The likelihood of meeting targets

The main advantage of the PERT technique is that it provides a method for estimating the probability of meeting or missing target dates. There might be only a single target date – the project completion – but we might wish to set additional intermediate targets.

Suppose that we must complete the project within 15 weeks at the outside. We expect it will take 13.5 weeks but it could take more or, perhaps, less. In addition, suppose that activity C must be completed by week 10, as it is to be carried out by a member of staff who is scheduled to be working on another project and that

Table 7.5 PERT activity time estimates

Activity	Optimistic (a)	Most likely (m)	Pessimistic (b)
		Activity durations (weeks)	
A	5	6	8
B	3	4	5
C	2	3	3
D	3.5	4	5
E	1	3	4
F	8	10	15
G	2	3	4
H	2	2	2.5

Even number	Target date
Expected date	Standard deviation

The PERT event labelling convention adopted here indicates event number and its target date along with the calculated values for expected time and standard deviation.

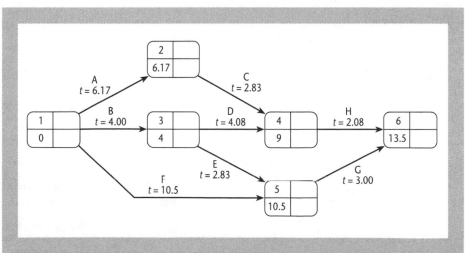

Figure 7.4 The PERT network after the forward pass

Table 7.6 Expected times and standard deviations

	Activity durations (weeks)				
Activity	Optimistic (a)	Most likely (m)	Pessimistic (b)	Expected (t_e)	Standard deviation (s)
A	5	6	8	6.17	0.50
B	3	4	5	4.00	0.33
C	2	3	3	2.83	0.17
D	3.5	4	5	4.08	0.25
E	1	3	4	2.83	0.50
F	8	10	15	10.50	1.17
G	2	3	4	3.00	0.33
H	2	2	2.5	2.08	0.08

event 5 represents the delivery of intermediate products to the customer. These three target dates are shown on the PERT network in Figure 7.5.

The PERT technique uses the following three-step method for calculating the probability of meeting or missing a target date:

● calculate the standard deviation of each project event;
● calculate the z value for each event that has a target date;
● convert z values to a probabilities.

Calculating the standard deviation of each project event

The square of the standard deviation is known as the variance. Standard deviations may not be added together but variances may.

Standard deviations for the project events can be calculated by carrying out a forward pass using the activity standard deviations in a manner similar to that used with expected durations. There is, however, one small difference – to add two standard deviations we must add their squares and then find the square root of the sum. Exercise 7.6 illustrates the technique.

Exercise 7.6

The standard deviation for event 3 depends solely on that of activity B. The standard deviation for event 3 is therefore 0.33.

For event 5 there are two possible paths, B + E or F. The total standard deviation for path B + E is $\sqrt{(0.33^2 + 0.50^2)} = 0.6$ and that for path F is 1.17; the standard deviation for event 5 is therefore the greater of the two, 1.17.

Verify that the standard deviations for each of the other events in the project are as shown in Figure 7.5.

Calculating the z values

The z value is calculated for each node that has a target date. It is equivalent to the number of standard deviations between the node's expected and target dates. It is calculated using the formula

$$z = \frac{T - t_e}{s}$$

where t_e is the expected date and T the target date.

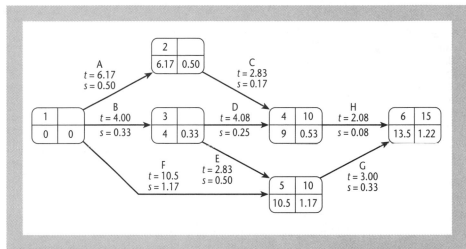

Figure 7.5 The PERT network with three target dates and calculated event standard deviations

Exercise 7.7

The z value for event 4 is $(10 - 9.00)/0.53 = 1.8867$.

Calculate the z values for the other events with target dates in the network shown in Figure 7.5.

Converting z values to probabilities

A z value may be converted to the probability of not meeting the target date by using the graph in Figure 7.6.

Exercise 7.8

The z value for the project completion (event 6) is 1.23. Using Figure 7.6 we can see that this equates to a probability of approximately 11%, that is, there is an 11% risk of not meeting the target date of the end of week 15.

Find the probabilities of not achieving events 4 or 5 by their target dates of the end of week 10.

What is the likelihood of completing the project by week 14?

The advantages of PERT

We have seen that by requesting multivalued activity duration estimates and calculating expected dates, PERT focuses attention on the uncertainty of forecasting. We can use the technique to calculate the standard deviation for each task and use this to rank them according to their degree of risk. Using this ranking, we can see, for example, that activity F is the one regarding which we have greatest uncertainty, whereas activity C should, in principle, give us relatively little cause for concern.

If we use the expected times and standard deviations for forward passes through the network we can, for any event or activity completion, estimate the probability of meeting any set target. In particular, by setting target dates along the critical path, we can focus on those activities posing the greatest risk to the project's schedule.

This graph is the equivalent of tables of z values, also known as standard normal deviates, which may be found in most statistics textbooks

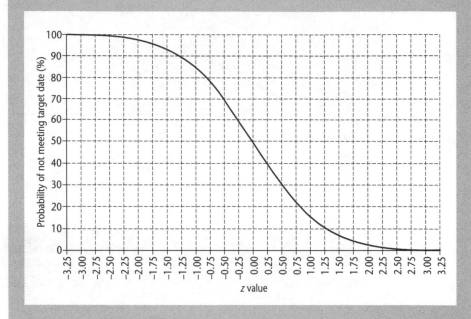

Figure 7.6 The probability of obtaining a value within z standard deviations of the mean for a normal distribution

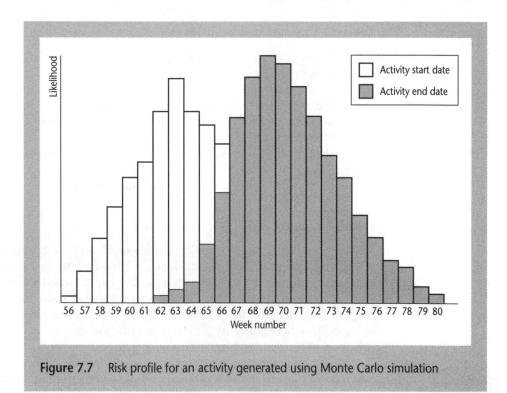

Figure 7.7 Risk profile for an activity generated using Monte Carlo simulation

Monte Carlo simulation

Monte Carlo simulation was also discussed in Section 3.7 in the context of project evaluation.

As an alternative to the PERT technique, and to provide a greater degree of flexibility in specifying likely activity durations, we can use Monte Carlo simulation techniques to evaluate the risks of not achieving deadlines. The basis of this technique involves calculating activity completion times for a project network a large number of times, each time selecting estimated activity times randomly from a set of estimates for each activity. The results are then tabulated, summarized or displayed as a graph such as that shown in Figure 7.7.

Activity duration estimates can be specified in a variety of forms, depending upon the information available. If, for example, we have historic data available about the durations of similar activities, we might able to specify durations as a probability distribution. With less information available we should, at least, be able to provide three time estimates as used by PERT.

The calculation required for this is clearly extensive as we may have to carry out the forward pass through the network many hundreds of times before obtaining a representative selection of possible completion times. Fortunately there are a number of packages available for carrying out Monte Carlo simulation. Some will exchange data with project scheduling applications and some interface to standard spreadsheet software. The majority of these packages will apply Monte Carlo risk analysis to cost and resource as well as duration estimates.

7.9 Conclusions

In this chapter, we have seen how to identify and manage the risks that might affect the success of a project. Risk management is concerned with assessing and prioritizing risks and drawing up plans for addressing those risks before they become problems.

This chapter has also described techniques for estimating the effect of risk on the project's activity network and schedule.

Many of the risks affecting software projects can be reduced by allocating more experienced staff to those activities that are affected. In the next chapter we consider the allocation of staff to activities in more detail.

7.10 Further exercises

1. Identify five risks that might affect the success of the Brightmouth College payroll project and suggest strategies that Brigette might consider for dealing with each of them.

2. The list of risks and risk reduction strategies in Table 7.4 is concerned with generic risks for software projects. What additional risks, in addition to those itemized in Table 7.3, can you identify that would be specific to Amanda's IOE accounts project?

3. List the major risks that might affect your next programming assignment and identify strategies for minimizing each of those risks.

4. If you have access to a project planning computer application find out whether or not it supports the PERT methods described in this chapter.

CHAPTER 8

Resource allocation

Objectives

When you have completed this chapter you will be able to:

- identify the resources required for a project;
- make the demand for resources more even throughout the life of a project;
- produce a work plan and resource schedule.

8.1 Introduction

In Chapter 6, we saw how to use activity network analysis techniques to plan *when* activities should take place. This was calculated as a time-span during which an activity should take place – bounded by the earliest start and latest finish dates. In Chapter 7 we used the PERT technique to forecast a range of expected dates by which activities would be completed. In both cases these plans took no account of the availability of resources.

In this chapter we shall see how to match the activity plan to available resources and, where necessary, assess the efficacy of changing the plan to fit the resources. Figure 8.1 shows where resource allocation is applied in Step Wise.

In general, the allocation of resources to activities will lead us to review and modify the ideal activity plan. It may cause us to revise stage or project completion dates. In any event, it is likely to lead to a narrowing of the time-spans within which activities may be scheduled.

The final result of resource allocation will normally be a number of schedules including:

These schedules will provide the basis for the day-to-day control and management of the project. These are described in Chapter 9.

- *activity schedule* indicating the planned start and completion dates for each activity;
- *resource schedule* showing the dates on which each resource will be required and the level of that requirement;
- *cost schedule* showing the planned cumulative expenditure incurred by the use of resources over time.

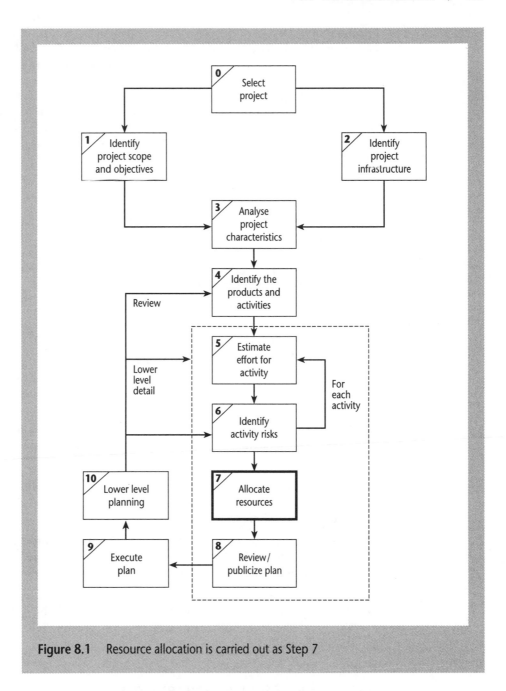

Figure 8.1   Resource allocation is carried out as Step 7

8.2 The nature of resources

A resource is any item or person required for the execution of the project. This covers many things – from paper clips to key personnel – and it is unlikely that we would wish to itemize every resource required, let alone draw up a schedule for their use! Stationery and other standard office supplies, for example, need not normally be the concern of the project manager – ensuring there is always an adequate supply is the role of the office manager. The project manager must concentrate on those resources where there is a possibility that, without planning, they might not be sufficiently available when required.

Some resources, such as a project manager, will be required for the duration of the project whereas others, such as a specific software developer, might be required for a single activity. The former, while vital to the success of the project, does not require the same level of scheduling as the latter. Individual programmers, for example, might be committed to working on a number of projects and it will be important to book their time well in advance.

In general, resources will fall into one of seven categories.

- *Labour*   The main items in this category will be members of the development project team such as the project manager, systems analysts and software developers. Equally important will be the quality assurance team and other support staff and any employees of the client organization who might be required to undertake or participate in specific activities.

- *Equipment*   Obvious items will include workstations and other computing and office equipment. We must not forget that staff also need basic equipment such as desks and chairs.

- *Materials*   Materials are items that are consumed, rather than equipment that is used. They are of little consequence in most software projects but can be important for some – software that is to be widely distributed might, for example, require supplies of floppy disks to be specially obtained.

- *Space*   For projects that are undertaken with existing staff, space is normally readily available. If any additional staff (recruited or contracted) should be needed then office space will need to be found.

- *Services*   Some projects will require procurement of specialist services – development of a wide area distributed system, for example, requires scheduling of telecommunications services.

The cost of money as a resource is a factor taken into account in DCF evaluation.

- *Time*   Time is the resource that is being offset against the other primary resources – project timescales can sometimes be reduced by increasing other resources and will almost certainly be extended if they are unexpectedly reduced.

- *Money*   Money is a secondary resource – it is used to buy other resources and will be consumed as other resources are used. It is similar to other resources in that it is available at a cost – in this case interest charges.

8.3   Identifying resource requirements

The first step in producing a resource allocation plan is to list the resources that will be required along with the expected level of demand. This will normally be done by considering each activity in turn and identifying the resources required. It is likely, however, that there will also be resources required that are not activity specific, but are part of the project's infrastructure (such as the project manager) or required to support other resources (office space, for example, might be required to house contract software developers).

Amanda has produced a precedence network for the IOE project (Figure 8.2) and used this as a basis for a resource requirements list, part of which is shown in Table 8.1. Notice that, at this stage, she has not allocated individuals to tasks but has decided on the type of staff that will be required. The activity durations assume that they will be carried out by 'standard' analysts or software developers.

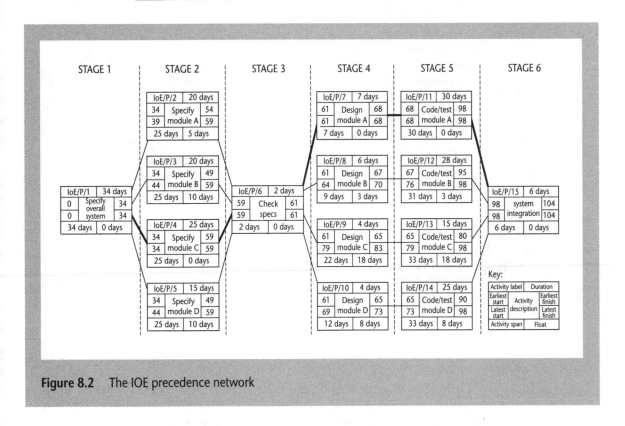

Figure 8.2   The IOE precedence network

At this stage, it is necessary that the resource requirements list be as comprehensive as possible – it is better that something is included that may later be deleted as unnecessary than to omit something essential. Amanda has therefore included additional office space as a possible requirement, should contract software development staff be recruited.

8.4   Scheduling resources

Having produced the resource requirements list, the next stage is to map this onto the activity plan to assess the distribution of resources required over the duration of the project. This is best done by representing the activity plan as a bar chart and using this to produce a resource histogram for each resource.

Table 8.1 Part of Amanda's resource requirements list

Stage	Activity	Resource	Days	Quantity	Notes
ALL		Project manager	104 F/T		
1	All	Workstation	34		Check software availability
	IoE/P/1	Senior analyst	34 F/T		
2	All	Workstation	–	3	1 per person would be ideal
	IoE/P/2	Analyst–designer	20 F/T		
	IoE/P/3	Analyst–designer	15 F/T		
	IoE/P/4	Analyst–designer	25 F/T		
	IoE/P/5	Analyst–designer	15 F/T		Could use analyst–programmer
3	All	Workstation	2 F/T		
	IoE/P/6	Senior analyst*	2 F/T		
4	All	Workstation	–	3	As stage 2
	IoE/P/7	Analyst–designer	7 F/T		
	IoE/P/8	Analyst–designer	6 F/T		
	IoE/P/9	Analyst–designer	4 F/T		
	IoE/P/10	Analyst–designer	4 F/T		
5	All	Workstation	–	4	1 per programmer
	All	Office space	–		If contract programmers used
	IoE/P/11	Programmer	30 F/T		
	IoE/P/12	Programmer	28 F/T		
	IoE/P/13	Programmer	15 F/T		
	IoE/P/14	Programmer	25 F/T		
6	All	Full machine access	–		Approx. 16 hours for full system test
	IoE/P/15	Analyst–designer	6 F/T		

*In reality, this would normally be done by a review involving all the analysts working on stage 2.

Figure 8.3 illustrates Amanda's activity plan as a bar chart and a resource histogram for analyst–designers. Each activity has been scheduled to start at its earliest start date – a sensible initial strategy, since we would, other things being equal, wish to save any float to allow for contingencies. Earliest start date scheduling, as is the case with Amanda's project, frequently creates resource histograms that start with a peak and then tail off.

Changing the level of resources on a project over time, particularly personnel, generally adds to the cost of a project. Recruiting staff has costs and even where staff are transferred internally, time will be needed for familiarization with the new project environment.

The resource histogram in Figure 8.3 poses particular problems in that it calls for two analyst–designers to be idle for eleven days, one for six days and one for two days between the specification and design stage. It is unlikely that IOE would have another project requiring their skills for exactly those periods of time and this raises the question as to whether this idle time should be charged to Amanda's project. The ideal resource histogram will be smooth with, perhaps an initial build-up and a staged run-down.

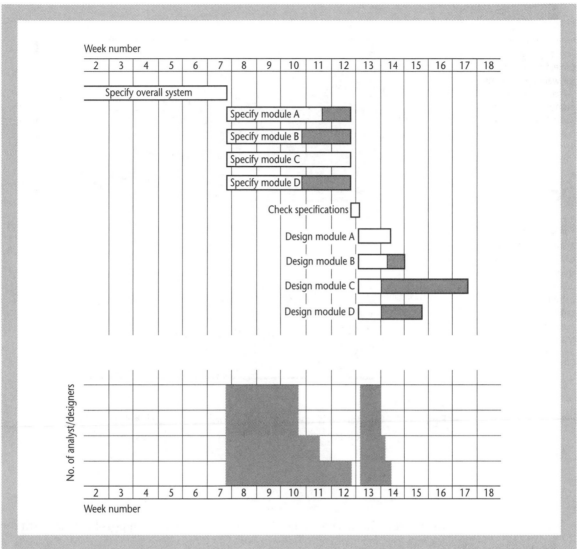

Figure 8.3 Part of Amanda's bar chart and resource histogram for analyst–designers

White rectangles indicate when an activity is scheduled and shaded rectangles the total float.

An additional problem with an uneven resource histogram is that it is more likely to call for levels of resource beyond those available. Figure 8.4 illustrates how, by adjusting the start date of some activities and splitting others, a resource histogram can, subject to constraints such as precedence requirements, be smoothed to contain resource demand at available levels. The different letters represent staff working on a series of module testing tasks, that is, one person working on task A, two on tasks B and C, etc.

In Figure 8.4, the original histogram was created by scheduling the activities at their earliest start dates. The resource histogram shows the typical peaked shape caused by earliest start date scheduling and calls for a total of nine staff where only five are available for the project.

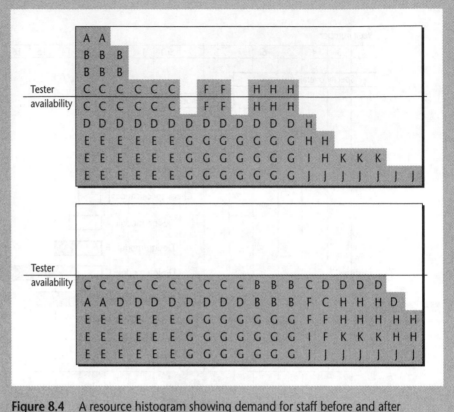

Figure 8.4   A resource histogram showing demand for staff before and after smoothing

By delaying the start of some of the activities, it has been possible to smooth the histogram and reduce the maximum level of demand for the resource. Notice that some activities, such as C and D, have been split. Where non-critical activities can be split they can provide a useful way of filling troughs in the demand for a resource, but in software projects it is difficult to split tasks without increasing the time they take.

Some of the activities call for more than one unit of the resource at a time – activity F, for example, requires two programmers, each working for two weeks. It might be possible to reschedule this activity to use one programmer over four weeks although that has not been considered in this case.

Exercise 8.1   Amanda has already decided to use only three analyst–designers on the project in order to reduce costs. Her current resource histogram, however, calls for four during both stage 2 and stage 4. Suggest what she might do to smooth the histogram and reduce the number of analyst–designers required to three.

In practice, resources have to be allocated to a project on an activity-by-activity basis and finding the 'best' allocation can be time consuming and difficult.

As soon as a member of the project team is allocated to an activity that activity acquires a scheduled start and finish date and the team member becomes unavailable for other activities for that period. Thus, allocating a resource to one activity limits the flexibility for resource allocation and scheduling of other activities.

It is therefore helpful to prioritize activities so that resources can be allocated to competing activities in some rational order. The priority must always be to allocate resources to critical path activities and then to those activities that are most likely to affect others. In that way, lower priority activities are made to fit around the more critical, already scheduled activities.

Of the various ways of prioritizing activities, two are described below:

- **Total float priority**   Activities are ordered according to their total float, those with the smallest total float having the highest priority. In the simplest application of this method, activities are allocated resources in ascending order of total float. However, as scheduling proceeds, activities will be delayed (if resources are not available at their earliest start dates) and total floats will be reduced. It is therefore desirable to recalculate floats (and hence reorder the list) each time an activity is delayed.

- **Ordered list priority**   With this method, activities that can proceed at the same time are ordered according to a set of simple criteria. An example of this is Burman's priority list, which takes into account activity duration as well as total float:

P. J. Burman, *Precedence Networks for Planning and Control*, McGraw-Hill, 1972.

1. shortest critical activity;
2. critical activities;
3. shortest non-critical activity;
4. non-critical activity with least float;
5. non-critical activities.

Unfortunately, resource smoothing, or even containment of resource demand to available levels, is not always possible within planned timescales – deferring activities to smooth out resource peaks often puts back project completion. Where that is the case, we need to consider ways of increasing the available resource levels or altering working methods.

Exercise 8.2

Amanda finds that, with only three analyst–designers the specification of module D (see Figure 8.3) will have to be deferred until after the specification of module B and this will add five days to the overall project duration (making 109 in total). She had hoped to have the project completed within 100 days and this is a further disappointment. She therefore decides to have another look at her activity plan.

You will remember that early on she decided that she should check all of the specifications together (activity IoE/P/6) before allowing design to start. It is now apparent that this is causing a significant bottleneck and delaying module D will only exacerbate the problem. She therefore decides on a compromise – she will check the specifications for modules A, B and D together but will then go ahead with their design without waiting for the module C specification. This will be checked against the others when it is complete.

She redraws her precedence network to reflect this, inserting the new activity of checking the module C specification against the others (activity IoE/P/6a). This is shown in Figure 8.5. Draw a new resource histogram to reflect this change.

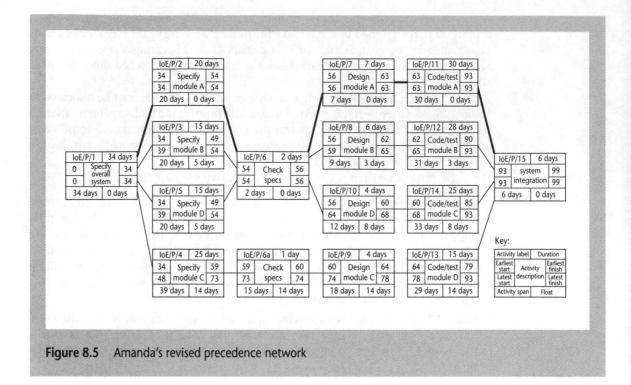

Figure 8.5   Amanda's revised precedence network

8.5   Creating critical paths

Scheduling resources can create new critical paths. Delaying the start of an activity because of lack of resources will cause that activity to become critical if this uses up its float. Furthermore, a delay in completing one activity can delay the availability of a resource required for a later activity. If the later one is already critical then the earlier one might now have been made critical by linking their resources.

Amanda's revised schedule, which still calls for four analyst–designers, but only for a single day, is illustrated in the solution to Exercise 8.2 (check it in the back of the book if you have not done so already). Notice that in rescheduling some of the activities she has introduced additional critical activities. Delaying the specification of module C has used up all of its float – and that of the subsequent activities along that path! Amanda now has two critical paths – the one shown on the precedence network and the new one.

In a large project, resource-linked criticalities can be quite complex – a hint of the potential problems may be appreciated by looking at the next exercise.

Exercise 8.3   Amanda decides to delay the specification of module C for a further day to ensure that only three analyst–designers will be required. The relevant part of her revised bar chart and resource histogram are shown in Figure 8.6.

Which activities will now be critical?

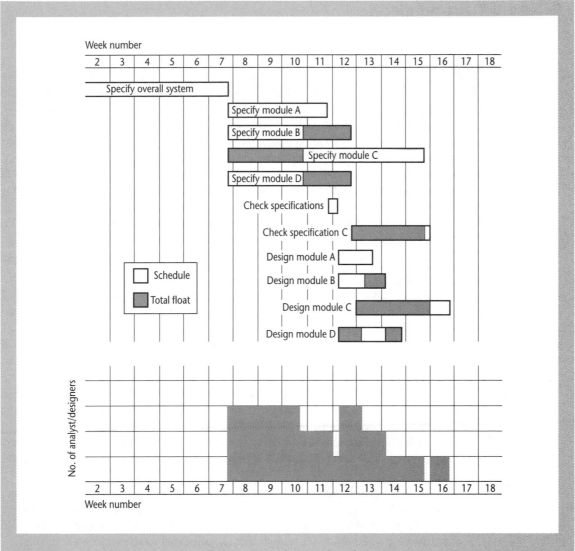

Figure 8.6 Amanda's project scheduled to require three analyst–designers

8.6 Counting the cost

The discussion so far has concentrated on trying to complete the project by the earliest completion date with the minimum number of staff. We have seen that doing this places constraints on when activities can be carried out and increases the risk of not meeting target dates.

Alternatively, Amanda could have considered using additional staff or lengthening the overall duration of the project. The additional costs of employing extra staff would need to be compared to the costs of delayed delivery and the increased risk of not meeting the scheduled date. The relationship between these factors is discussed later in this chapter.

8.7 Being specific

Allocating resources and smoothing resource histograms is relatively straight-forward where all resources of a given type can be considered more or less equivalent. When allocating labourers to activities in a large building project we need not distinguish among individuals – there are likely to be many labourers and they may be treated as equals so far as skills and productivity are concerned.

This is seldom the case with software projects. We saw in Chapter 5 that, because of the nature of software development, skill and experience play a significant part in determining the time taken and, potentially, the quality of the final product. With the exception of extremely large projects it makes sense to allocate individual members of staff to activities as early as possible, as this can lead us to revise our estimate of their duration.

In allocating individuals to tasks, a number of factors need to be taken into account.

- *Availability* We need to know whether a particular individual will be available when required. Reference to the departmental work plan determines this, but the wise project manager will always investigate the risks that might be involved – earlier projects might, for example, over-run and affect the availability of an individual.

Reappraisal of the critical path and PERT or Monte Carlo risk analysis might need to be carried out in parallel with staff allocation.

- *Criticality* Allocation of more experienced personnel to activities on the critical path often helps in shortening project durations or at least reduces the risk of overrun.
- *Risk* We saw how to undertake activity risk assessment in the previous chapter. Identifying those activities posing the greatest risk, and knowing the factors influencing them, helps to allocate staff. Allocating the most experienced staff to the highest risk activities is likely to have the greatest effect in reducing over-all project uncertainties. More experienced staff are, however, usually more expensive.
- *Training* It will benefit the organization if positive steps are taken to allocate junior staff to appropriate non-critical activities where there will be sufficient slack for them to train and develop skills. There can even be direct benefits to the particular project since some costs may be allocated to the training budget.
- *Team building* The selection of individuals must also take account of the final shape of the project team and the way they will work together. This and additional aspects of personnel management are discussed in Chapter 11.

Exercise 8.4

Amanda has decided that, where possible, whoever writes the specification for a module should also produce the design, as she believes this will improve the commitment and motivation of the three analyst–designers, Belinda, Tom and Daisy.

She has decided that she will use Tom, a trainee analyst–designer, for the specification and design of module D as both of these activities have a large float compared to their activity span ($^6/_{21}$ and $^9/_{13}$ of their span respectively). Since the specification and design of module C are on the critical path, she decides to allocate both of these tasks to Belinda, a particularly experienced and capable member of staff.

Having made these decisions she has almost no flexibility in how she assigns the other specification and design activities. Work out from the activity bar chart produced as part of the solution to Exercise 8.2 (shown in Figure 8.6) whom she assigns to which of the remaining specification and design activities.

8.8 Publishing the resource schedule

In allocating and scheduling resources we have used the activity plan (a precedence network in the case of the examples in this chapter), activity bar charts and resource histograms. Although good as planning tools, they are not the best way of publishing and communicating project schedules. For this we need some form of work plan. Work plans are commonly published either as lists or charts such as that illustrated in Figure 8.7. In this case Amanda has chosen not to include activity floats (which could be indicated by shaded bars) as she fears that one or two members of the team might work with less urgency if they are aware that their activities are not critical.

Notice that, somewhat unusually, it is assumed there are no public holidays or other non-productive periods during the 100 days of the project and that none of the team has holidays for the periods they are shown as working.

Amanda has also made no explicit allowance for staff taking sick leave.

Amanda now transfers some of the information from the work schedule to her precedence network. In particular, she amends the earliest start dates for activities and any other constraints (such as revised latest finish dates where resources need to be made available) that have been introduced. A copy of her revised precedence network is shown in Figure 8.8 – notice that she has highlighted all critical activities and paths.

8.9 Cost schedules

It is now time to produce a detailed cost schedule showing weekly or monthly costs over the life of the project. This will provide a more detailed and accurate estimate of costs and will serve as a plan against which project progress can be monitored.

Calculating cost is straightforward where the organization has standard cost figures for staff and other resources. Where this is not the case, then the project manager will have to calculate the costs.

In general, costs are categorized as follows:

- *Staff costs* These will include staff salaries as well as the other direct costs of employment such as the employer's contribution to social security funds, pension scheme contributions, holiday pay and sickness benefit. These are commonly charged to projects at hourly rates based on weekly work records completed by staff. Note that contract staff are usually charged by the week or month – even when they are idle.

- *Overheads* Overheads represent expenditure that an organization incurs, which cannot be directly related to individual projects or jobs including space rental, interest charges and the costs of service departments (such as personnel). Overhead costs can be recovered by making a fixed charge on development departments (in which case they usually appear as a weekly or monthly charge for a project), or by an additional percentage charge on direct staff employment costs. These additional charges or oncosts can easily equal or exceed the direct employment costs.

- *Usage charges* In some organizations, projects are charged directly for use of resources such as computer time (rather than their cost being recovered as an overhead). This will normally be on an 'as used' basis.

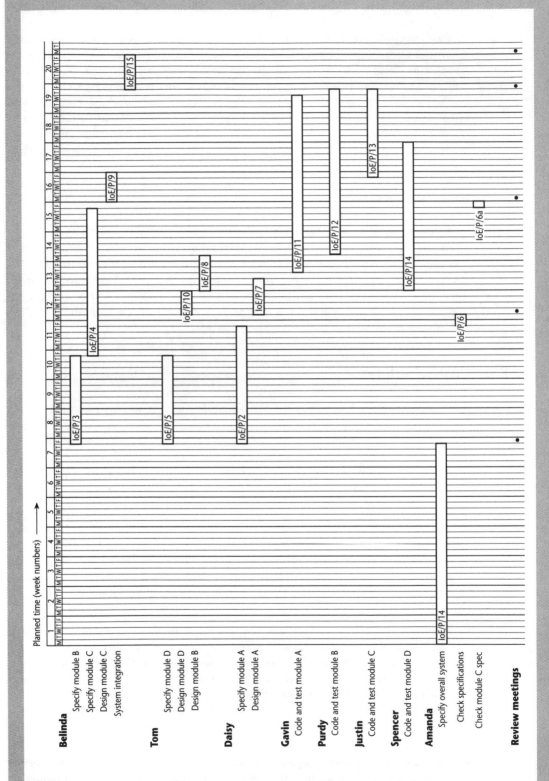

Figure 8.7 Amanda's work schedule

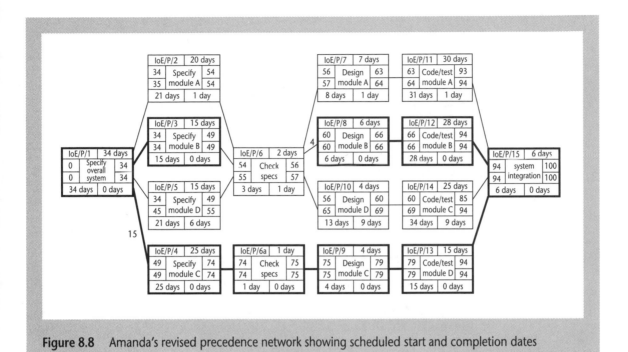

Figure 8.8 Amanda's revised precedence network showing scheduled start and completion dates

Table 8.2 Staff costs (including oncosts)
for Amanda's project team

Staff member	Daily cost (£)
Amanda	300
Belinda	250
Tom	175
Daisy	225
Gavin	150
Purdy	150
Justin	150
Spencer	150

Exercise 8.5

Amanda finds that IOE recovers some overheads as oncosts on direct staff costs although others are recovered by charging a fixed £200 per day against projects. Staff costs (including overheads) are as shown in Table 8.2. In addition to the commitments in the work plan (Figure 8.7) Amanda estimates that, in total, she will have spent an additional 10 days planning the project and carrying out the post-project review.

Calculate the total cost for Amanda's project on this basis. How is the expenditure spread over the life of the project?

Figure 8.9 shows the weekly costs over the 20 weeks that Amanda expects the project to take. This is a typical *cost profile* – building up slowly to a peak and then tailing off quite rapidly at the end of the project. Figure 8.10 illustrates the

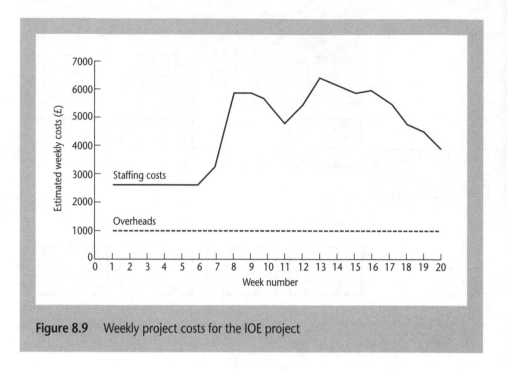

Figure 8.9 Weekly project costs for the IOE project

cumulative cost of the project and it is generally this that would be used for cost control purposes.

8.10 The scheduling sequence

Going from an ideal activity plan to a costed schedule can be represented as a sequence of steps, rather like the classic waterfall life-cycle model. In the ideal world, we would start with the activity plan and use this as the basis for our risk assessment. The activity plan and risk assessment would provide the basis for our resource allocation and schedule from which we would produce cost schedules.

In practice, as we have seen by looking at Amanda's project, successful resource allocation often necessitates revisions to the activity plan, which, in turn, will affect our risk assessment. Similarly, the cost schedule might indicate the need or desirability to reallocate resources or revise activity plans – particularly where that schedule indicates a higher overall project cost than originally anticipated.

The interplay between the plans and schedules is complex – any change to any one will affect each of the others. Some factors can be directly compared in terms of money – the cost of hiring additional staff can be balanced against the costs of delaying the project's end date. Some factors, however, are difficult to express in money terms (the cost of an increased risk, for example) and will include an element of subjectivity.

While good project planning software will assist greatly in demonstrating the consequences of change and keeping the planning synchronized, successful project scheduling is largely dependent upon the skill and experience of the project manager in juggling the many factors involved (Figure 8.11).

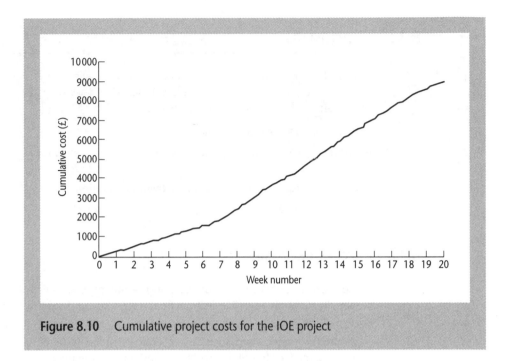

Figure 8.10 Cumulative project costs for the IOE project

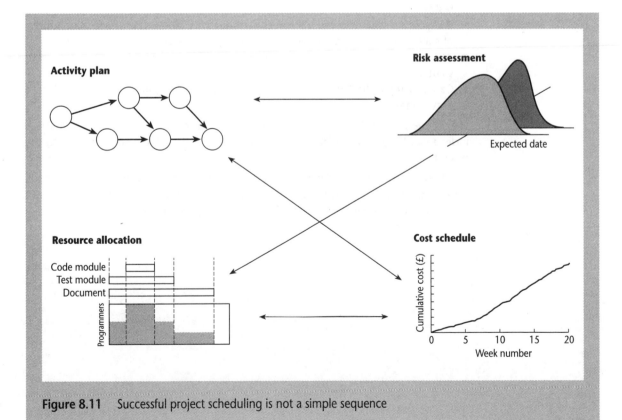

Figure 8.11 Successful project scheduling is not a simple sequence

8.11 Conclusion

In this chapter we have discussed the problems of allocating resources to project activities and the conversion of an activity plan to a work schedule. In particular, we have seen the importance of the following:

- identifying all the resources needed;
- arranging activity starts to minimize variations in resource levels over the duration of the project;
- allocating resources to competing activities in a rational order of priority;
- taking care in allocating the right staff to critical activities.

8.12 Further exercises

1. Burman's priority ordering for allocating resources to activities takes into account the activity duration as well as its total float. Why do you think this is advantageous?

2. If you have access to project planning software use it to produce an activity plan for Amanda's project and include the staff resource requirements for each activity. Explore the facilities of your software and answer the following questions:

   - Can you set up resource types and ask the application to allocate individuals to tasks?
   - Will your software allow you to specify productivity factors for individual members of staff so that the duration of an activity depends upon who is carrying it out?
   - Will your software carry out resource smoothing or provide a minimum cost solution?
   - Can you replicate Amanda's resource schedule (see Figure 8.7) – or produce a better one?

3. On a large project it is often the responsibility of a team leader to allocate tasks to individuals. Why might it be unsatisfactory to leave such allocations entirely to the discretion of the team leader?

4. In scheduling her project, Amanda ignored the risks of absence due to staff sickness. What might she have done to estimate the likelihood of this occurring and how might she have taken account of the risk when scheduling the project?

Monitoring and control

9.1 Introduction

Once work schedules have been published and the project is under way, attention must be focused on ensuring progress. This requires monitoring of what is happening, comparison of actual achievement against the schedule and, where necessary, revision of plans and schedules to bring the project as far as possible back on target.

In earlier chapters we have stressed the importance of producing plans that can be monitored – for example, ensuring that activities have clearly defined and visible completion points. We will discuss how information about project progress is gathered and what actions must be taken to ensure a project meets its targets.

The final part of this chapter discusses how we can deal with changes that are imposed from outside – namely, changes in requirements.

9.2 Creating the framework

Exercising control over a project and ensuring that targets are met is a matter of regular monitoring, finding out what is happening, and comparing it with current targets. If there is a mismatch between the planned outcomes and the actual ones then either replanning is needed to bring the project back on target or the target will have to be revised. Figure 9.1 illustrates a model of the project control cycle and shows how, once the initial project plan has been published, project control is a continual process of monitoring progress against that plan and, where necessary, revising the plan to take account of deviations. It also illustrates the important steps that must be taken after completion of the project so that the experience gained in any one project can feed into the planning stages of future projects, thus allowing us to learn from past mistakes.

See Chapter 11 for a discussion of software quality.

In practice we are normally concerned with departures from the plan in four dimensions – delays in meeting target dates, shortfalls in quality, inadequate functionality, and costs going over target. In this chapter we are mainly concerned with the first and last of these.

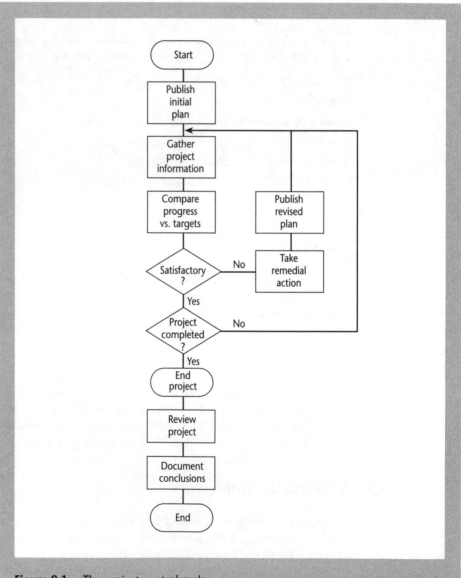

Figure 9.1 The project control cycle

Responsibility

The overall responsibility for ensuring satisfactory progress on a project is often the role of the *project steering committee* or *project board*. Day-to-day responsibility will rest with the project manager and, in all but the smallest of projects, aspects of this can be delegated to team leaders.

The concept of a reporting hierarchy was introduced in Chapter 1.

Figure 9.2 illustrates the typical reporting structure found with medium and large projects. With small projects (employing around half a dozen or fewer staff) individual team members usually report directly to the project manager, but in most cases team leaders will collate reports on their section's progress and forward summaries to the project manager. These, in turn, will be incorporated into project-level reports for the steering committee and, via them or directly, progress reports for the client.

Reporting may be oral or written, formal or informal, or regular or ad hoc and some examples of each type are given in Table 9.1. While any effective team leader or project manager will be in touch with team members and available to discuss problems, any such informal reporting of project progress must be complemented by formal reporting procedures – and it is those we are concerned with in this chapter.

Assessing progress

Progress assessment will normally be made on the basis of information collected and collated at regular intervals or when specific events occur. Wherever possible, this information will be objective and tangible – whether or not a particular report has been delivered, for example. However, such end-of-activity deliverables might not occur sufficiently frequently throughout the life of the project. Here progress assessment will have to rely on the judgement of the team members who are carrying out the project activities.

In a PRINCE 2 environment, there is a Project Assurance function reporting to the Project Board and independent of the Project Manager.

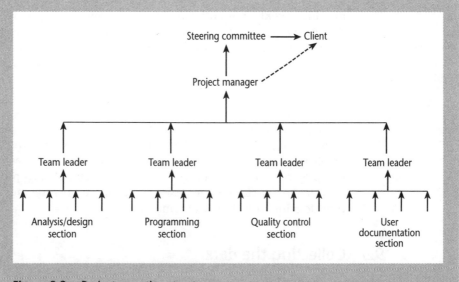

Figure 9.2   Project reporting structures

Table 9.1 Categories of reporting

Report type	Examples	Comment
Oral formal regular	Weekly or monthly progress meetings	While reports may be oral, formal written minutes should be kept
Oral formal ad hoc	End-of-stage review meetings	While largely oral, likely to receive and generate written reports
Written formal regular	Job sheets, progress reports	Normally weekly using forms
Written formal ad hoc	Exception reports, change reports	
Oral informal ad hoc	Canteen discussion, social interaction	Often provides early warning; must be backed up by formal reporting

Setting checkpoints

The PRINCE 2 standard described in Appendix A has its own terminology.

It is essential to set a series of checkpoints in the initial activity plan. Checkpoints may be:

- regular (monthly, for example);
- tied to specific events such as the production of a report or other deliverable.

Taking snap-shots

The frequency with which the managers need to receive information about progress will depend upon the size and degree of risk of the project or that part of the project under their control. Team leaders, for example, need to assess progress daily (particularly when employing inexperienced staff) whereas project managers may find weekly or monthly reporting appropriate. In general, the higher the level, the less frequent and less detailed the reporting needs to be.

Short, Monday morning team progress meetings are a common way of motivating staff to meet short-term targets.

There are, however, strong arguments in favour of formal weekly collection of information from staff carrying out activities. Collecting data at the end of each week ensures that information is provided while memories are still relatively fresh and provides a mechanism for individuals to review and reflect upon their progress during the past few days.

Major, or project-level, progress reviews will generally take place at particular points during the life of a project – commonly known as *review points* or *control points*. PRINCE 2, for example, designates a series of checkpoints where the status of work in a project or for a team is reviewed. At the end of each project Stage, PRINCE 2 provides for an End Stage Assessment where an assessment of the project and consideration of its future are undertaken.

9.3 Collecting the data

As a rule, managers will try to break down long activities into more controllable tasks of one or two weeks' duration. However, it will still be necessary to gather information about partially completed activities and, in particular, forecasts of how much work is left to be completed. It can be difficult to make such forecasts accurately.

Exercise 9.1

A software developer working on Amanda's project has written the first 250 lines of a Cobol program that is estimated to require 500 lines of code. Explain why it would be unreasonable to assume that the programming task is 50% complete.

How might you make a reasonable estimate of how near completion it might be?

Where there is a series of products, partial completion of activities is easier to estimate. Counting the number of record specifications or screen layouts produced, for example, can provide a reasonable measure of progress.

In some cases, intermediate products can be used as in-activity milestones. The first successful compilation of a Cobol program, for example, might be considered a milestone even though it is not the final product of the activity code and test.

Partial completion reporting

Many organizations use standard accounting systems with weekly time sheets to charge staff time to individual jobs. The staff time booked to a project indicates the work carried out and the charges to the project. It does not, however, tell the project manager what has been produced or whether tasks are on schedule.

It is therefore common to adapt or enhance existing accounting data collection systems to meet the needs of project control. Weekly time sheets, for example, are frequently adapted by breaking jobs down to activity level and requiring information about work done in addition to time spent. Figure 9.3 shows a typical example of such a report form, in this case requesting information about likely slippage of completion dates as well as estimates of completeness.

Asking for estimated completion times can be criticized on the grounds that frequent invitations to reconsider completion dates deflects attention away from the importance of the originally scheduled targets and can generate an ethos that it is acceptable for completion dates to slip.

Risk reporting

One popular way of overcoming the objections to partial completion reporting is to avoid asking for estimated completion dates, but to ask instead for the team members' estimates of the likelihood of meeting the planned target date.

There are a number of variations on the traffic-light technique. The version described here is in use in IBM and is described in A. Down, M. Coleman and P. Absolon, *Risk Management for Software Projects*, McGraw-Hill, 1994.

One way of doing this is the traffic-light method. This consists of the following steps:

● identify the key (first level) elements for assessment in a piece of work;

● break these key elements into constituent elements (second level);

● assess each of the second level elements on the scale *green* for 'on target', *amber* for 'not on target but recoverable', and *red* for 'not on target and recoverable only with difficulty';

● review all the second level assessments to arrive at first level assessments;

● review first and second level assessments to produce an overall assessment.

Weekly timesheets are a valuable source of information about resources used.

They are often used to provide information about what has been achieved. However, requesting partial completion estimates where they cannot be obtained from objective measures encourages the 99% complete syndrome – tasks are reported as on time until 99% complete, and then stay at 99% complete until finished.

Time Sheet

Staff __John Smith__   Week ending __26/3/99__

Rechargeable hours

Project	Activity code	Description	Hours this week	% complete	Scheduled completion	Estimated completion
P21	A243	Code mod A3	12	30	24/4/99	24/4/99
P34	B771	Document take-on	20	90	1/4/99	29/3/99

Total recharged hours	32

Non-rechargeable hours

Code	Description	Hours this week	Comment & authorization
z99	Day in lieu	8	Authorized by RB

Total non-rechargeable hours	8

Figure 9.3   A weekly time sheet and progress review form

For example, Amanda decides to use a version of the traffic-light method for reviewing activities on the IOE project. She breaks each activity into a number of component parts (deciding, in this case, that a further breakdown is unnecessary) and gets the team members to complete a return at the end of each week. Figure 9.4 illustrates Justin's completed assessment at the end of week 16.

Traffic-light assessment highlights only risk of non-achievement; it is not an attempt to estimate work done or to quantify expected delays.

Following completion of assessment forms for all activities, the project manager uses these as a basis for evaluating the overall status of the project. Any critical activity classified as amber or red will require further consideration and often leads to a revision of the project schedule. Non-critical activities are likely to be considered as a problem if they are classified as red, especially if all their float is likely to be consumed.

Note that this form refers only to uncompleted activities. Justin would still need to report activity completions and the time spent on activities.

Activity Assessment Sheet

Staff ___Justin___

Ref: IoE/P/13   **Activity:** Code & test module C

Week number	13	14	15	16	17	18		
Activity summary	G	A	A	R				

Component								Comments
Screen handling procedures	G	A	A	G				
File update procedures	G	G	R	A				
Housekeeping procedures	G	G	G	A				
Compilation	G	G	G	R				
Test data runs	G	G	G	A				
Program documentation	G	G	A	R				

Figure 9.4   A traffic-light assessment of IoE/P/13

9.4 Visualizing progress

Having collected data about project progress, a manager needs some way of presenting that data to greatest effect. In this section, we look at some methods of presenting a picture of the project and its future. Some of these methods (such as Gantt charts) provide a static picture, a single snapshot, whereas others (such as timeline charts) try to show how the project has progressed and changed through time.

The Gantt chart

One of the simplest and oldest techniques for tracking project progress is the Gantt chart. This is essentially an activity bar chart indicating scheduled activity dates and durations frequently augmented with activity floats. Reported progress is recorded on the chart (normally by shading activity bars) and a 'today cursor' provides an immediate visual indication of which activities are ahead or behind schedule. Figure 9.5 shows part of Amanda's Gantt chart as at the end of Tuesday of week 17. *Code & test module D* has been completed ahead of schedule and *code & test module A* appears also to be ahead of schedule. The coding and testing of the other two modules are behind schedule.

Henry Gantt
(1861–1919) was an
industrial engineer
interested in the
efficient organization
of work.

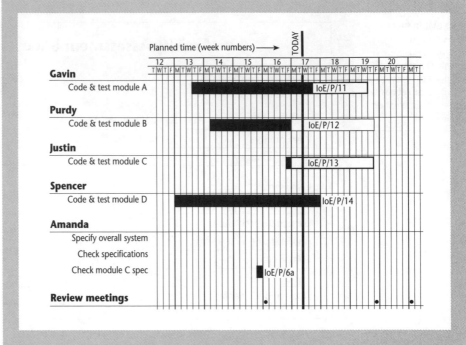

Figure 9.5 Part of Amanda's Gantt chart with the 'today cursor' in week 17

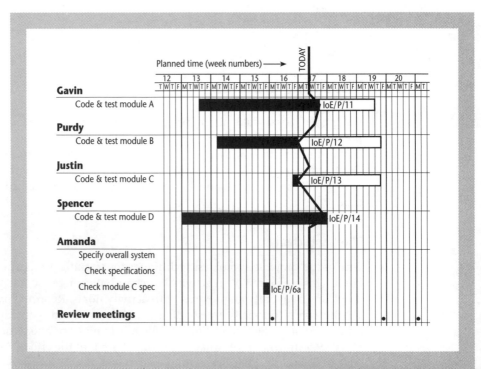

Figure 9.6 The slip chart emphasizes the relative position of each activity

The slip chart

A slip chart (Figure 9.6) is a very similar alternative favoured by some project managers who believe it provides a more striking visual indication of those activities that are not progressing to schedule – the more the slip line bends, the greater the variation from the plan. Additional slip lines are added at intervals and, as they build up, the project manager will gain an idea as to whether the project is improving (subsequent slip lines bend less) or not. A very jagged slip line indicates a need for rescheduling.

Ball charts

A somewhat more striking way of showing whether or not targets have been met is to use a ball chart as in Figure 9.7. In this version of the ball chart, the circles indicate start and completion points for activities. The circles initially contain the original scheduled dates. Whenever revisions are produced these are added as second dates in the appropriate circle until an activity is actually started or completed when the relevant date replaces the revised estimate (in bold italic in Figure 9.7). Circles will therefore contain only two dates, the original and most recent target dates, or the original and actual dates.

Where the actual start or finish date for an activity is later than the target date, the circle is coloured red (dark grey in Figure 9.7) – where an actual date is on time or earlier than the target then the circle is coloured green (light grey in Figure 9.7).

Such charts are frequently placed in a prominent position and the colour coded balls provide a constant reminder to the project team. Where more than one team is working in close proximity, such a highly visible record of achievement can encourage competitiveness between teams.

David Youll in *Making Software Development Visible*, Wiley, 1990, describes a version of the ball chart using three sets of dates and part-coloured balls.

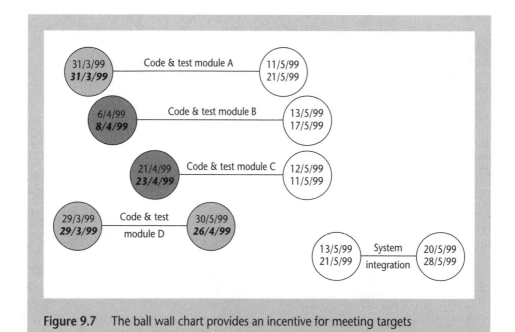

Figure 9.7 The ball wall chart provides an incentive for meeting targets

Another advantage of ball charts over Gantt and slip charts is that they are relatively easy to keep up to date – only the dates and possibly colours need to be changed, whereas the others need to be redrawn each time target dates are revised.

The timeline

One disadvantage of the charts described so far is that they do not show clearly the slippage of the project completion date through the life of the project. Knowing the current state of a project helps in revising plans to bring it back on target, but analysing and understanding trends helps to avoid slippage in future projects.

The timeline chart is a method of recording and displaying the way in which targets have changed throughout the duration of the project.

Figure 9.8 shows a timeline chart for Brigette's project at the end of the sixth week. Planned time is plotted along the horizontal axis and elapsed time down the

Brigette's timeline chart contains only the critical activities for her project; ● indicates actual completion of an activity.

For the sake of clarity, the number of activities on a timeline chart must be limited. Using colour helps to distinguish activities, particularly where lines cross.

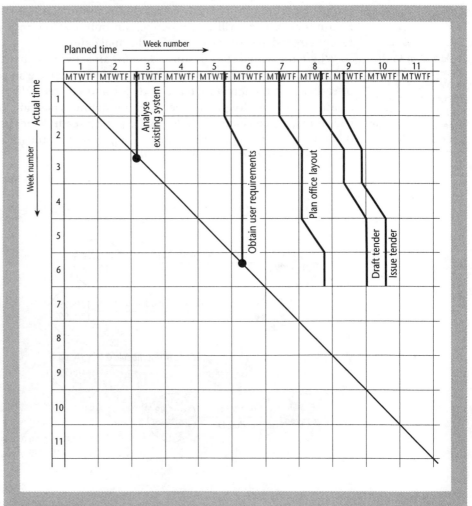

Figure 9.8   Brigette's timeline chart at the end of week 6

vertical axis. The lines meandering down the chart represent scheduled activity completion dates – at the start of the project *analyse existing system* is scheduled to be completed by the Tuesday of week 3, *obtain user requirements* by Thursday of week 5, *issue tender*, the final activity, by Tuesday of week 9, and so on.

At the end of the first week Brigette reviews these target dates and leaves them as they are – lines are therefore drawn vertically downwards from the target dates to the end of week 1 on the actual time axis.

At the end of week 2, Brigette decides that *obtain user requirements* will not be completed until Tuesday of week 6 – she therefore extends that activity line diagonally to reflect this. The other activity completion targets are also delayed correspondingly.

By the Tuesday of week 3, *analyse existing system* is completed and Brigette puts a blob on the diagonal timeline to indicate that this has happened. At the end of week 3 she decides to keep to the existing targets.

At the end of week 4 she adds another three days to *draft tender* and *issue tender*.

Note that, by the end of week 6, two activities have been completed and three are still unfinished. Up to this point she has revised target dates on three occasions and the project as a whole is running seven days late.

Exercise 9.2

By the end of week 8 Brigette has completed planning the office layout but finds that drafting the tender is going to take one week longer that originally anticipated.

What will Brigette's timeline chart look like at the end of week 8?

If the rest of the project goes according to plan, what will Brigette's timeline chart look like when the project is completed?

The timeline chart is useful both during the execution of a project and as part of the post-implementation review. Analysis of the timeline chart, and the reasons for the changes, can indicate failures in the estimation process or other errors that might, with that knowledge, be avoided in future.

9.5 Cost monitoring

Expenditure monitoring is an important component of project control. Not only in itself, but also because it provides an indication of the effort that has gone into (or at least been charged to) a project. A project might be on time, but only because more money has been spent on activities than originally budgeted. A cumulative expenditure chart such as that shown in Figure 9.9 provides a simple method of comparing actual and planned expenditure. By itself it is not particularly meaningful – Figure 9.9 could, for example, illustrate a project that is running late or one that is on time, but has shown substantial costs savings! We need to take account of the current status of the project activities before attempting to interpret the meaning of recorded expenditure.

Cost charts become much more useful if we add projected future costs calculated by adding the estimated costs of uncompleted work to the costs already incurred. Where a computer-based planning tool is used, revision of cost schedules is generally provided automatically once actual expenditure has been recorded. Figure 9.10 illustrates the additional information available once the revised cost schedule is included – in this case it is apparent that the project is behind schedule and over budget.

Project costs may be monitored by a company's accounting system. By themselves, they provide little information about project status.

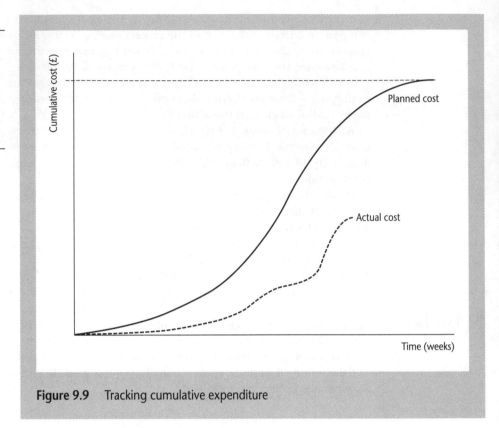

Figure 9.9 Tracking cumulative expenditure

9.6 Earned value

Earned value analysis, also known as budgeted cost of work performed, is recommended by a number of agencies including the US and Australian departments of defence. It is also recommended in BS 6079.

Earned value analysis has gained in popularity in recent years and may be seen as a refinement of the cost monitoring discussed in the previous section. Earned value analysis is based on assigning a 'value' to each task or work package (as identified in the WBS) based on the original expenditure forecasts. The assigned value is the original budgeted cost for the item and is known as the *baseline budget* or *budgeted cost of work scheduled* (BCWS). A task that has not started is assigned the value zero and when it has been completed, it, and hence the project, is credited with the value of the task. The total value credited to a project at any point is known as the *earned value* or *budgeted cost of work performed* (BCWP) and this can be represented as a value or as a percentage of the BCWS.

Where tasks have been started but are not yet complete, some consistent method of assigning an earned value must be applied. Common methods in software projects are:

● *the 0/100 technique*   where a task is assigned a value of zero until such time that it is completed when it is given a value of 100% of the budgeted value;

● *the 50/50 technique*   where a task is assigned a value of 50% of its value as soon as it is started and then given a value of 100% once it is complete;

● *the milestone technique*   where a task is given a value based on the achievement of milestones that have been assigned values as part of the original budget plan.

Project costs augmented by project monitoring can be used to generate forecasts of future costs.

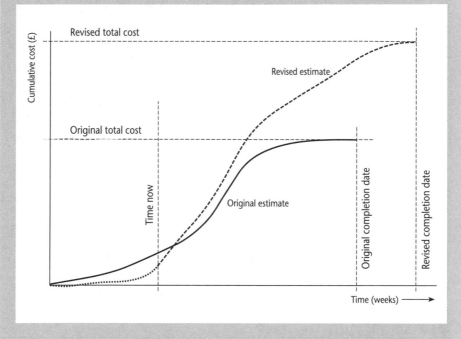

Figure 9.10 The cumulative expenditure chart can also show revised estimates of cost and completion date

Of these, we prefer the 0/100 technique. The 50/50 technique can give a false sense of security by over-valuing the reporting of activity starts. The milestone technique might be appropriate for activities with a long duration estimate but, in such cases, it is better to break that activity into a number of smaller ones.

The baseline budget

The first stage in setting up an earned value analysis is to create the *baseline budget*. The baseline budget is based on the project plan and shows the forecast growth in earned value through time. Earned value may be measured in monetary values but, in the case of staff-intensive projects such as software development, it is common to measure earned value in person-hours or work-days. Amanda's baseline budget, based on the schedule shown in Figure 8.7, is shown in Table 9.2 and diagrammatically in Figure 9.11. Notice that she has based her baseline budget on work-days and is using the 0/100 technique for crediting earned value to the project.

Amanda's project is not expected to be credited with any earned value until day 34, when the activity *specify overall system* is to be completed. This activity was forecast to consume 34 person-days and it will therefore be credited with 34 person-days earned value when it has been completed. The other steps in the baseline budget chart coincide with the scheduled completion dates of other activities.

Table 9.2 Amanda's baseline budget calculation

Task	Budgeted work-days	Scheduled completion	Cumulative work-days	% cumulative earned value
Specify overall system	34	34	34	14.35
Specify module B	15	49	} 64	27.00
Specify module D	15	49		
Specify module A	20	54	84	35.44
Check specifications	2	56	86	36.28
Design module D	4	60	90	37.97
Design module A	7	63	97	40.93
Design module B	6	66	103	43.46
Check module C spec	1	70	104	43.88
Specify module C	25	74	129	54.43
Design module C	4	79	133	56.12
Code & test module D	25	85	158	66.67
Code & test module A	30	93	188	79.32
Code & test module B	28	94	} 231	97.47
Code & test module C	15	94		
System integration	6	100	237	100.00

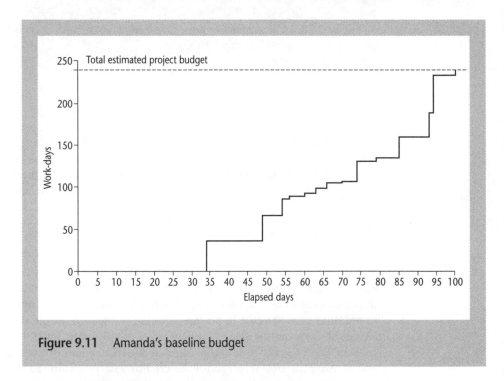

Figure 9.11   Amanda's baseline budget

Monitoring earned value

Having created the baseline budget, the next task is to monitor earned value as the project progresses. This is done by monitoring the completion of tasks (or activity starts and milestone achievements in the case of the other crediting techniques).

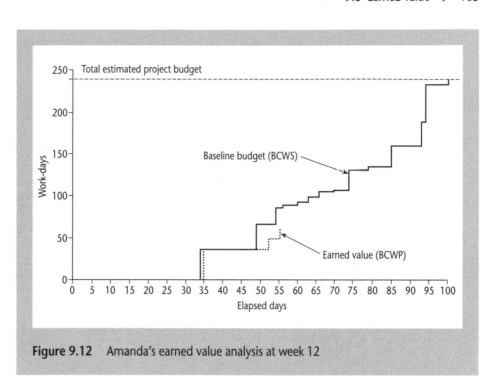

Figure 9.12 Amanda's earned value analysis at week 12

Exercise 9.3 Figure 9.12 shows Amanda's earned value analysis at the start of week 12 of the project. The earned value (BCWP) is clearly lagging behind the baseline budget, indicating that the project is behind schedule.

By studying Figure 9.12, can you tell exactly what has gone wrong with her project and what the consequences might be?

As well as recording BCWP, the actual cost of each task can be collected as *actual cost of work performed*, ACWP. This is shown in Figure 9.13, which, in this case, records the values as percentages of the total budgeted cost.

Figure 9.13 also illustrates the following performance statistics, which can be shown directly or derived from the earned value chart.

Budget variance This can be calculated as ACWP − BCWS and indicates the degree to which actual costs differ from those planned.

Schedule variance The schedule variance is measured in cost terms as BCWP − BCWS and indicates the degree to which the value of completed work differs from that planned. Figure 9.13 also indicates the schedule variance in time, which indicates the degree to which the project is behind schedule.

Cost variance This is calculated as BCWP − ACWP and indicates the difference between the budgeted cost and the actual cost of completed work. It is also an indicator of the accuracy of the original cost estimates.

Performance ratios Two ratios are commonly tracked: the *cost performance index* (CPI = BCWP/ACWP) and the *schedule performance index* (SPI = BCWP/BCWS).

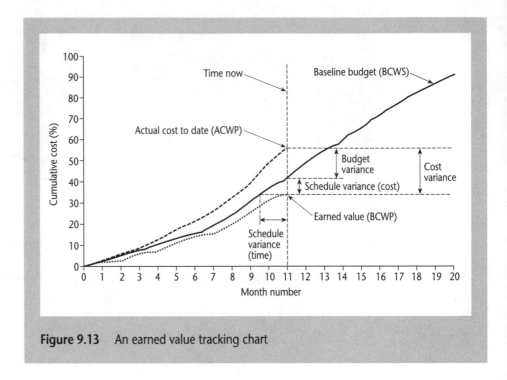

Figure 9.13 An earned value tracking chart

They can be thought of as a 'value-for-money' indices. A value greater than one indicates that work is being completed better than planned whereas a value of less than one means that work is costing more than and/or proceeding more slowly than planned.

In the same way that the expenditure analysis in Figure 9.9 was augmented to show revised expenditure forecasts, we can augment the simple earned value tracking chart with forecasts as illustrated in Figure 9.14.

Earned value analysis has not yet gained universal acceptance for use with software development projects, perhaps largely because of the attitude that, whereas a half-built house has a value reflected by the labour and materials that have been used, a half-completed software project has virtually no value at all. This is to misunderstand the purpose of earned value analysis, which, as we have seen, is a method for tracking what has been achieved on a project – measured in terms of the budgeted costs of completed tasks or products.

9.7 Prioritizing monitoring

So far we have assumed that all aspects of a project will receive equal treatment in terms of the degree of monitoring applied. We must not forget, however, that monitoring takes time and uses resources that might sometimes be put to better use!

In this section we list the priorities we might apply in deciding levels of monitoring.

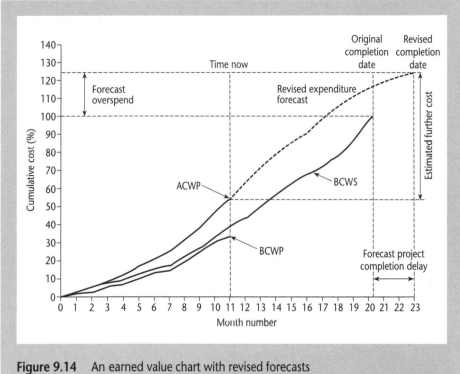

Figure 9.14 An earned value chart with revised forecasts

- *Critical path activities*   Any delay in an activity on the critical path will cause a delay in the completion date for the project. Critical path activities are therefore likely to have a very high priority for close monitoring.

Free float is the amount of time an activity may be delayed without affecting any subsequent activity.

- *Activities with no free float*   A delay in any activity with no free float will delay at least some subsequent activities even though, if the delay is less than the total float, it might not delay the project completion date. These subsequent delays can have serious effects on our resource schedule as a delay in a subsequent activity could mean that the resources for that activity will become unavailable before that activity is completed because they are committed elsewhere.

- *Activities with less than a specified float*   If any activity has very little float it might use up this float before the regular activity monitoring brings the problem to the project manager's attention. It is common practice to monitor closely those activities with less than, say, one week free float.

PERT and the significance of activity duration variance was described in Chapter 7.

- *High-risk activities*   A set of high-risk activities should have been identified as part of the initial risk profiling exercise. If we are using the PERT three-estimate approach we will designate as high risk those activities that have a high estimated duration variance. These activities will be given close attention because they are most likely to overrun or overspend.

- *Activities using critical resources*   Activities can be critical because they are very expensive (as in the case of specialized contract programmers). Staff or other resources might be available only for a limited period, especially if they are controlled outside the project team. In any event, an activity that demands a critical resource requires a high level of monitoring.

9.8 Getting the project back to target

A contingency plan should, of course, already exist as a result of the risk analysis methods described in Chapter 7.

Almost any project will, at one time or another, be subject to delays and unexpected events. One of the tasks of the project manager is to recognize when this is happening (or, if possible, about to happen) and, with the minimum delay and disruption to the project team, attempt to mitigate the effects of the problem. In most cases, the project manager tries to ensure that the scheduled project end date remains unaffected. This can be done by shortening remaining activity durations or shortening the overall duration of the remaining project in the ways described in the next section

The schedule is not sacrosanct – it is a plan that should be adhered to so long as it is relevant and cost-effective.

It should be remembered, however, that this might not always be the most appropriate response to disruptions to a plan. There is little point in spending considerable sums in overtime payments in order to speed up a project if the customer is not overly concerned with the delivery date and there is no other valuable work for the team members once this project is completed.

There are two main strategies to consider when drawing up plans to bring a project back on target – shortening the critical path or altering the activity precedence requirements.

Shorten the critical path

The overall duration of a project is determined by the current critical path, so speeding up non-critical path activities will not bring forward a project completion date.

Extolling staff to 'work harder' might have some effect, although frequently a more positive form of action is required, such as increasing the resources available for some critical activity. Fact-finding, for example, might be speeded up by allocating an additional analyst to interviewing users. It is unlikely, however, that the coding of a small module would be shortened by allocating an additional programmer – indeed, it might be counterproductive because of the additional time needed organizing and allocating tasks and communicating.

Resource levels can be increased by making them available for longer. Thus, staff might be asked to work overtime for the duration of an activity and computing resources might be made available at times (such as evenings and weekends) when they might otherwise be inaccessible.

Time/cost trade-off: there is a general rule that timescales can be shortened by buying more (or more expensive) resources; sometimes this is true.

Where these do not provide a sufficient solution, the project manager might consider allocating more efficient resources to activities on the critical path or swapping resources between critical and non-critical activities. This will be particularly appropriate with staff – an experienced programmer should be significantly more productive than a more junior member of the team.

By such means we can attempt to shorten the timescale for critical activities until such time as either we have brought the project back to schedule or further efforts prove unproductive or not cost-effective. Remember, however, that shortening a critical path often causes some other path, or paths, to become critical (see Section 6.14).

Reconsider the precedence requirements

If attempting to shorten critical activities proves insufficient, the next step is to consider the constraints by which some activities have to be deferred pending completion of others. The original project network would most probably have been drawn up assuming 'ideal' conditions and 'normal' working practices. It might be that, to avoid the project delivering late, it is now worth questioning whether as yet unstarted activities really do have to await the completion of others. It might, in a particular organization, be 'normal' to complete system testing before commencing user training. In order to avoid late completion of a project it might, however, be considered acceptable to alter 'normal' practice and start training earlier.

One way to overcome precedence constraints is to subdivide an activity into a component that can start immediately and one that is still constrained as before. For example, a user handbook can be drawn up in a draft form from the system specification and then be revised later to take account of subsequent changes.

If we do decide to alter the precedence requirements in such a way, it is clearly important to be aware that quality might be compromised and to make a considered decision to compromise quality where needed. It is equally important to assess the degree to which changes in work practices increase risk. It is possible, for example, to start coding a module before its design has been completed. It would normally, however, be considered foolhardy to do so since, as well as compromising quality, it would increase the risk of having to redo some of the coding once the final design had been completed and thus delay the project even further.

9.9 Change control

So far in this chapter, we have assumed that the nature of the tasks to be carried out has not changed. A project leader like Amanda or Brigette might find, however, that requirements are modified because of changing circumstances or because the users get a clearer idea of what is really needed. The payroll system that Brigette is implementing might, for instance, need to be adjusted if the staffing structure at the college is reorganized.

Other, internal, changes will crop up. Amanda might find that there are inconsistencies in the program specifications that become apparent only when the programs are coded, and these would result in amendments to the specifications.

Careful control of these changes is needed because an alteration in one document often implies changes to other documents and the system products based on that document. The Product Flow Diagrams that have been explained in Chapter 2 indicate relationships between the products of a project where this is the case.

Exercise 9.4　A change in a program specification will normally be carried through into changes to the program design and then changed code. What other products might need to be modified?

Configuration librarian's role

BS EN ISO 9001:2000 requires that a formal change control procedure be in place.

Control of changes and documentation ought to be the responsibility of someone who may variously be named the configuration librarian, the configuration manager or project librarian. Among this person's duties would be:

- the identification of all items that are subject to change control;
- the establishment and maintenance of a central repository of the master copies of all project documentation and software products;
- the setting up and running of a formal set of procedures to deal with changes;
- the maintenance of records of who has access to which library items and the status of each library item (e.g. whether under development, under test or released).

It will be recalled that it was suggested that the setting up of change control procedures might be one of the first things that Brigette might want to do at Brightmouth College.

Change control procedures

A simple change control procedure for operational systems might have the following steps.

1. One or more users might perceive a need for a modification to a system and ask for a change request to be passed to the development staff.

2. The user management consider the change request and if they approve it pass it to the development management.

3. The development management delegate a member of staff to look at the request and to report on the practicality and cost of carrying out the change. They would, as part of this, assess the products that would be affected by the change.

4. The development management report back to the user management on the findings and the user management decide whether, in view of the cost quoted, they wish to go ahead.

5. One or more developers are authorized to take copies of the master products that are to be modified.

6. The copies are modified. In the case of software components this would involve modifying the code and recompiling and testing it.

7. When the development of new versions of the product has been completed the user management will be notified and copies of the software will be released for user acceptance testing.

8. When the users are satisfied that the products are adequate they will authorize their operational release. The master copies of configuration items will be replaced.

Exercise 9.5   The above steps relate to changes to operational systems. How could they be modified to deal with systems under development?

Changes in scope of a system

This is sometimes called scope creep.

A common occurrence with IS development projects is for the size of the system gradually to increase. One cause of this is changes to requirements that are requested by users.

Exercise 9.6   Think of other reasons why there is a tendency for scope creep.

The scope of a project needs to be carefully monitored and controlled. One way is to re-estimate the system size in terms of SLOC or function points at key milestones.

9.10 Conclusions

In this chapter we have discussed the requirements for the continual monitoring of projects and the need for making progress visible. Among the important points to emerge were:

- planning is pointless unless the execution of the plan is monitored;
- activities that are too long need to be subdivided to make them more controllable;
- ideally, progress should be measured through the delivery of project products;
- progress needs to be shown in a visually striking way, such as through ball charts, in order to communicate information effectively;
- costs need to be monitored as well as elapsed time;
- delayed projects can often be brought back on track by shortening activity times on the critical path or by relaxing some of the precedence constraints.

9.11 Further exercises

1. Take a look at Amanda's project schedule shown in Figure 8.7. Identify those activities scheduled to last more than three weeks and describe how she might monitor progress on each of them on a fortnightly or weekly basis.

2. Amanda's Gantt chart at the end of week 17 (Figure 9.5) indicates that two activities are running late. What effect might this have on the rest of the project? How might Amanda mitigate the effects of this delay?

3. Table 9.2 illustrates Amanda's earned value calculations based on work-days. Revise the table using monetary values based on the cost figures that you used in Exercise 8.5. Think carefully about how to handle the costs of Amanda as project manager and the recovered overheads and justify your decisions about how you treat them.

4. If you have access to project planning software, investigate the extent to which it offers support for earned value analysis. If it does not do so directly, investigate ways in which it would help you to generate a baseline budget (BCWS) and track the earned value (BCWP).

5. Describe a set of change control procedures that would be appropriate for Brigette to implement at Brightmouth College.

CHAPTER 10

Managing contracts

Objectives

When you have completed this chapter you will be able to:

- understand the advantages and disadvantages of using goods and services brought in from outside the organization;
- distinguish the different types of contract;
- follow the stages needed to negotiate an appropriate contract;
- outline the contents of a contract for goods and services;
- plan the evaluation of a proposal or product;
- administer a contract from its signing until the final acceptance of project completion.

10.1 Introduction

In the Brightmouth College scenario, the management of the college have made a decision to obtain their software from an external supplier. Given the range of payroll software on the market and their own limited capability for developing new and reliable software, this would seem sensible. Meanwhile at IOE, Amanda has available, at least in theory, a team of software developers who are employees of IOE. However, the demand for software design and construction effort will fluctuate, rising when a new project is initiated and trailing off as it is completed. In-house developers could thus have periods of intense pressure when new projects are being developed, interspersed by periods of relative idleness. The IOE management might therefore decide that it would be more cost-effective to get an outside software house to carry out the new development while a reduced group of in-house software development staff remain busy maintaining and giving support to the users of existing systems.

The buying in of both goods and services, rather than 'doing it yourself', is attractive when money is available but other, less flexible, types of resource, especially staff time, are in short supply. However, there are hazards for organizations who adopt this policy. Many of these potential dangers arise from the fact that considerable staff time and attention will still be needed to manage a contracted-out project successfully. Although the original motivation for contracting out might have been to reduce management effort, it is essential that customer

It is not unusual for a major organization to spend 6 to 12 months and 40% of the total acquisition and implementation budget on package evaluation with major customer service and support applications (Demian Martinez, 'Decision Drivers Inc.', *Computing*, 23 July 1998).

organizations such as Brightmouth College and IOE find time to make clear their exact requirements at the beginning of the planned work, and also to ensure that the goods and services that result are in fact what are actually required.

Also, it need hardly be said that potential suppliers are more likely to be flexible and accommodating before any contract has been signed than they will be afterwards – especially if the contract is for a fixed price. All this points to the need for as much forethought and planning with an acquisition project as with an internal development project.

It was, for example, reported that two consortia led by Sema and EDS respectively had spent £4 million over two years bidding for a UK government project to renew the IT infrastructure in the prison service – the final job was estimated as being worth £350 million (*Computing*, 13 August 1998).

Note that the bargaining position of the customer will be much stronger if their business is going to be very valuable. If you are buying a cut-price computer game from a local store, you are unlikely to be able to negotiate variations on the supplier's standard contract of sale! (Indeed, because of the inequality of the parties in such circumstances, such sales are subject to special consumer protection laws). It is reasonable for potential suppliers to weigh up carefully the time and money they are willing to spend responding to a customer's initial request, as there is no guarantee of their obtaining the final contract.

In the remainder of this chapter, we will first discuss the different types of contract that can be negotiated. We will then follow through the general steps that ought to be followed when placing a contract. The issues that ought to be considered when drafting a contract are then examined. We conclude by describing some of the things that need to be done while the contract is actually being executed.

10.2 Types of contract

The external resources required could be in the form of *services*. A simple example of this could be using temporary staff on short-term contracts to carry out some project tasks. At Brightmouth College, Brigette could use temporary staff to type into the computer system the personnel details needed to set up the payroll standing data for the new system, while at IOE a decision might be made to carry out the required system building in-house, but to augment the permanent staff with contract programmers for the duration of the project. A more far-reaching use of external services would be for the contractor not only to supply the new system, but to also operate it on the customer's behalf. For example, it might well be worth Brightmouth College abandoning the idea of buying a package and instead getting a payroll services agency to carry out all the payroll work on their behalf.

On the other hand, the contract could be placed for the supply of a *completed software application*.

This could be:

- a *bespoke* system, that is, a system that is created from scratch specifically for one customer;
- *off-the-shelf*, which you buy 'as is' – this is sometimes referred to as *shrink-wrapped* software;
- *customized off-the-shelf* (COTS) software – this is a basic core system, which is modified to meet the needs of a particular customer.

Exercise 10.1 Which of the three system options (that is, bespoke, off-the-shelf or COTS) might Amanda consider with regard to the IOE maintenance group accounts system? What factors would she need to take into account?

David Bainbridge's *Introduction to Computer Law*, Pitman, 3rd edn, 1996 is highly recommended as a guide to the legal aspects of IT contracts.

The section on ways of assessing supplier payments draws heavily on material from Paul Radford and Robyn Lawrie of Charismatek Software Metrics, Melbourne, Australia.

Where equipment is being supplied then, in English law, this may be regarded as a contract for the supply of *goods*. In the case of the supply of software this may be regarded as supplying a service (to write the software) or the granting of a *licence* (or permission) to use the software, which remains in the ownership of the supplier. These distinctions will have legal implications.

Another way of classifying contracts is by the way that the payment to suppliers is calculated. We will look at:

- fixed price contracts;
- time and materials contracts;
- fixed price per delivered unit contracts,

Fixed price contracts

As the name implies, in this situation a price is fixed when the contract is signed. The customer knows that, if there are no changes in the contract terms, this is the price to be paid on the completion of the work. In order for this to be effective, the customer's requirement has to be known and fixed at the outset. In other words, when the contract is to construct a software system, the detailed requirements analysis must already have been carried out. Once the development is under way, the customer will not be able to change their requirements without renegotiating the price of the contract.

The advantages of this method are the following:

- *Known customer expenditure*   If there are few subsequent changes to the original requirements, the customer will have a known outlay.
- *Supplier motivation*   The supplier has a motivation to manage the delivery of the system in a cost-effective manner.

The disadvantages include the following:

- *Higher prices to allow for contingency*   The supplier absorbs the risk for any errors in the original estimate of product size. To reduce the impact of this risk, the supplier will add a margin when calculating the price to be quoted in a tender.
- *Difficulties in modifying requirements*   The need to change the scope of the requirements sometimes becomes apparent as the system is developed – this can cause friction between the supplier and customer.
- *Upward pressure on the cost of changes*   When competing against other potential suppliers, the supplier will try to quote as low a price as possible. If, once the contract is signed, further requirements are put forward, the supplier is in a strong position to demand a high price for these changes.
- *Threat to system quality*   The need to meet a fixed price can mean that the quality of the software suffers.

Time and materials contracts

With this type of contract, the customer is charged at a fixed rate per unit of effort, for example, per staff-hour. At the start of the project, the supplier normally provides an estimate of the overall cost based on their current understanding of the customer's requirements, but this is not the basis for the final payment.

The advantages of this approach are the following:

- *Ease of changing requirements*   Changes to requirements are dealt with easily. Where a project has a research orientation and the direction of the project changes as options are explored, then this can be an appropriate method of calculating payment.

- *Lack of price pressure*   The lack of price pressure can allow better quality software to be produced.

The disadvantages of this approach are:

- *Customer liability*   The customer absorbs all the risks associated with poorly defined or changing requirements.

- *Lack of incentives for supplier*   The supplier has no incentive to work in a cost-effective manner or to control the scope of the system to be delivered.

Because the supplier appears to be given a blank cheque, this approach does not normally find favour with customers. However, the employment of contract development staff, in effect, involves this type of contract.

Fixed price per unit delivered contracts

Function point counting was discussed in Chapter 5.

This is often associated with function point (FP) counting. The size of the system to be delivered is calculated or estimated at the outset of the project. The size of the system to be delivered might be estimated in lines of code, but FPs can be more easily and reliably derived from requirements documents. A price per unit is also quoted. The final price is then the unit price multiplied by the number of units. Table 10.1 shows a typical schedule of prices.

The company who produced this table, RDI Technologies of the United States, in fact charge a higher fee per FP for larger systems. For example, a system to be implemented contains 2,600 FPs. The overall charge would be 2,000 × $967, plus 500 × $1,1019, plus 100 × $1,058.

One problem that has already been noted is that the scope of the system to be delivered can grow during development. The software supplier might first carry out the system design. From this design, an FP count could be derived. A charge could then be made for design work based on the figures in the 'Function design cost per FP' column. This, if the designed system was counted at 1,000 FPs, would be 1,000 × $242 = $242,000. If the design were implemented, and the actual software

This table comes from D. Garmus and D. Herron, *Measuring The Software Process*, Prentice-Hall, 1996.

Table 10.1 A schedule of charges per function point

Function point count	Function design cost per FP	Implementation cost per FP	Total cost per FP
Up to 2,000	$242	$725	$967
2,001–2,500	$255	$764	$1,019
2,501–3,000	$265	$793	$1,058
3,001–3,500	$274	$820	$1,094
3,501–4,000	$284	$850	$1,134

constructed and delivered, then the additional $1,000 \times \$725 = \$725,000$ would be charged. If the scope of the system grows because the users find new requirements, these new requirements would be charged at the combined rate for design and implementation. For example, if new requirements amounting to 100 extra FPs were found, then the charge for this extra work would be $\$967 \times 100 = \$96,700$.

Exercise 10.2 A system to be designed and implemented is counted as comprising 3,200 FPs. What would be the total charge according to the schedule in Table 10.1?

The advantages of this approach are as follows.

- *Customer understanding* The customer can see how the price is calculated and how it will vary with changed requirements.
- *Comparability* Pricing schedules can be compared.
- *Emerging functionality* The supplier does not bear the risk of increasing functionality.
- *Supplier efficiency* The supplier still has an incentive to deliver the required functionality in a cost-effective manner (unlike with time and materials contracts).
- *Life-cycle range* The requirements do not have to be definitively specified at the outset. Thus the development contract can cover both the analysis and design stages of the project.

The disadvantages of this approach are as follows.

> The impact of late changes will be further discussed in Chapter 12 on Software quality.

- *Difficulties with software size measurement* Lines of code can easily be inflated by adopting a verbose coding style. With FPs, there can be disagreements about what the FP count should really be: in some cases, FP counting rules might be seen as unfairly favouring either the supplier or customer. Users, in particular, will almost certainly not be familiar with the concept of FPs and special training might be needed for them. The solution to these problems might be to employ an independent FP counter.
- *Changing requirements* Some requested changes might affect existing trans-actions drastically, but not add to the overall FP count. A decision has to be taken about how to deal with these changes. A change made late in the development cycle will almost certainly require more effort to implement than one made earlier.

To reduce the last difficulty, one suggestion from Australia has been to vary the charge depending on the point at which they have been requested – see Table 10.2.

Exercise 10.3 A contract stipulates that a computer application is to be designed, constructed and delivered at a cost of $600 per FP. After acceptance testing, the customer asks for changes to some of the functions in the system amounting to 500 FPs and some new functions which amount to 200 additional FPs. Using Table 10.2, calculate the additional charge.

In addition to the three payment methods above, there are other options and permutations of options. For instance, the implementation of an agreed specifi-cation could be at a fixed price, with provision for any additions or changes to the requirements to be charged for on a per FP basis. Another example could be where the contractor has to buy in large amounts of equipment, the price of which might fluctuate through no fault of the contractor. In this case it is possible to negotiate a contract where the final price contains a fixed portion for labour plus an amount that depends on the actual cost of a particular component used.

Exercise 10.4

It is easy to see why passing on fluctuations in equipment costs can be advantageous to the contractor. However, is there any advantage to the customer in such an arrangement?

An underlying problem with software can once again be seen when the questions of contractual obligations and payment are considered – namely its relative invisibility and its flexibility. These mean that system size and consequently development effort tends to be very difficult to judge. If contractors are realistically to quote firm prices for work, the tasks they are asked to undertake must be carefully constrained. For example, it would be unrealistic for a contractor to be asked to quote a single price for all the stages of a development project: how can they estimate the construction effort needed when the requirements are not yet established? For this reason it will often be necessary to negotiate a series of contracts, each covering a different part of the system development life cycle.

Another way of categorizing contracts, at least initially, is according to the approach that is used in contractor selection:

This categorization is based on European Union regulations.

- open;
- restricted;
- negotiated.

GATT stands for 'General Agreement on Trade and Tariffs'. The specific part of GATT that is relevant here is the Agreement on Government Procurement. GATT covers the European Union and also several other countries including the United States and Japan.

Open tendering process

In this case, any supplier can bid to supply the goods and services. Furthermore, all bids that are compliant with the original conditions laid down in the *invitation to tender* must be considered and evaluated in the same way as all the others. With a major project where there are lots of bids and the evaluation process is time-consuming, this can be an expensive way of doing things.

In recent years, there has been a global movement towards removing artificial barriers that hamper businesses in one country supplying goods and services in another. Examples of this are the drives by bodies such GATT and the European Union to ensure that national governments and public bodies do not limit the

The table comes from the draft Acquisition of Customized Software policy document, published by the Department of State Development, Victoria, 1996.

Table 10.2 Examples of additional charges for changed functionality

	Pre-acceptance testing handover	Post-acceptance testing handover
Additional FPs	100%	100%
Changed FPs	130%	150%
Deleted FPs	25%	50%

granting of contracts to their fellow nationals without good reason. One element of this is the laying down of rules about how tendering processes should be carried out. In certain circumstances, these demand that an open tendering process be adopted.

Restricted tendering process

In this case, there are bids only from suppliers who have been invited by the customer. Unlike the open tendering process, the customer may at any point reduce the number of potential suppliers being considered. This is usually the best approach to be adopted. However, it is not without risk: where the resulting contract is at a fixed price, the customer assumes responsibility for the correctness and completeness of the requirements specified to the prospective suppliers. Defects in this requirements documentation sometimes allow a successful bidder sub-sequently to claim for additional payments.

Negotiated procedure

There are often, however, some good reasons why the restricted tendering process might not be the most suitable in some particular sets of circumstances. Say, for example, that there is a fire that destroys part of an office, including IT equipment. The key concern here is to get replacement equipment up and running as quickly as possible and there is no time to embark on a lengthy tendering process. Another situation might be where a new software application had been successfully built and implemented by an outsider, but the customer decides to have some extensions to the system. As the original supplier has staff who have complete familiarity with the existing system, it might once again be inconvenient to approach other potential suppliers via a full tendering process.

In these cases, an approach to a single supplier might be justified. However, it takes little imagination to realise that approaching a single supplier can open the customer up to charges of favouritism and should be done only where there is a clear justification.

10.3 Stages in contract placement

We are now going to discuss the typical stages in awarding a contract.

This discussion assumes that a feasibility study has already provisionally identified the need for the intended software.

David Bainbridge, *ibid.*, page 135.

Requirements analysis

Before potential suppliers can be approached, you need to have a clear set of requirements. Two points need to be emphasized here. The first is that it is easy for this step to be skimped where the user has many day-to-day pressures and not much time to think about future developments. In this situation, it can be useful to bring in an external consultant to draw up a requirements document. Even here, users and their managers need to look carefully at the resulting requirements document to ensure that it accurately reflect their needs. As David Bainbridge has pointed out: *'the lack of, or defects in, the specification are probably the heart of most disputes resulting from the acquisition of computer equipment and software'*.

Table 10.3 Main sections in a requirements document

Section name

1. Introduction
2. A description of any existing systems and the current environment
3. The customer's future strategy or plans
4. System requirements
   - mandatory
   - desirable
5. Deadlines
6. Additional information required from potential suppliers

The requirements document might typically have sections with the headings shown in Table 10.3. This requirements document is sometimes called an *operational requirement* or *OR*.

Chapter 12 on Software Quality discusses how aspects of quality can be measured.

The requirements define carefully the *functions* that need to be carried out by the new application and all the necessary *inputs* and *outputs* for these functions. The requirements should also state any *standards* with which there should be compliance, and the existing systems with which the new system needs to be compatible. As well as these functional requirements, there will also need to be operational and quality requirements concerning such matters as the required response times, reliability, usability and maintainability of the new system.

In general, the requirements document should state *needs* as accurately as possible and should avoid technical specifications of possible solutions. The onus should be placed on the potential suppliers to identify the technical solutions that they believe will meet the customer's stated needs. After all, they are the technical experts who should have access to the most up-to-date information about current technology.

Each requirement needs to be identified as being either *mandatory* or *desirable*.

- *Mandatory* If a proposal does not meet this requirement, the proposal is to be immediately rejected. No further evaluation would be required.

- *Desirable* A proposal might be deficient in this respect, but other features of the proposal could compensate for it.

One suggestion is that the weighting between product criteria and supplier criteria when selecting software ought to be 50 : 50 (Demian Martinez, 'Decision Drivers Inc.', *Computing*, 23 July 1998).

For example, in the case of the Brightmouth College payroll acquisition project, Brigette might identify as a mandatory requirement that any new system should be able to carry out all the processes previously carried out by the old system. However, a desirable feature might be that the new payroll software should be able to produce accounting details of staff costs in an electronic format that can be read directly by the college's accounting computer system.

Among the other details that should be included in the requirements document to be issued to potential suppliers would be requests for any information needed to help us judge the standing of the organization itself. This could include financial reports, references from past customers and the CVs of key development staff.

Evaluation plan

Having drawn up a list of requirements, we now need to draw up a plan of how the proposals that are submitted are to be evaluated. The situation will be slightly different if the contract is for a system that is to be specially written as opposed to an off-the-shelf application. In the latter case, it is the system itself that is being evaluated while in the former situation it is a proposal for a system.

First, a means of checking that all the mandatory requirements have been met needs to be identified. The next consideration is of how the desirable requirements can be evaluated. The problem here is weighing the value of one quality against another. The ISO 9126 standard, which is discussed in the chapter on software quality, can be used to decide that one system has more 'quality' than another, but if there is a difference in price between the two, we need to be able to estimate whether the increase in quality is worth the additional price. Hence *value for money* is often the key criterion. For example, we mentioned above an instance where the existence of an accounting link file was identified as a desirable requirement in the case of the Brightmouth College payroll acquisition project. Could a financial value be placed on this? If we were to cost clerical effort at £20 an hour and we knew that four hours of clerical effort a month went into entering staffing costs into the accounting computer system, we could conclude that over a four year period (£20 an hour × 4 hours a month × 48 months), or £3,840, would be saved. If system A has this feature and costs £1,000 more than system B, which does not, then this would seem to give system A an advantage. If, however, system A cost £5,000 more than B, the picture would be different.

Some of these issues were touched on in Chapter 3 on project evaluation.

It needs to be stressed that the costs to be taken into account are those for the whole of the lifetime of the proposed system, not just the costs of acquiring the system. Also, where the relationship with the supplier is likely to be ongoing, the supplier organization needs to be assessed as well as its products.

Exercise 10.5

One desirable feature sought in the Brightmouth College payroll is the ability to raise staff to the next point in their salary scale automatically at the beginning of each payroll year. At present, the new scale points have to be input clerically and then be checked carefully. This takes about 20 hours of staff effort each year, which can be costed at £20 an hour. System X has this feature, but system Y does not. System X also has a feature which can automatically produce bar charts showing payroll expenditure per department. Such a report currently has to be produced twice a year by hand and on each occasion takes about 12 hours effort to complete. With system Y, changes to department names can be carried out without any coding effort, whereas in the case of system X, the supplier would charge a minimum of £300 to do this. The college authorities estimate that there is 50% chance that this could occur during the expected four-year lifetime of the system. System X costs £500 more than system Y. On the basis of this information which system appears to give better value for money?

Invitation to tender

Having produced the requirements and the evaluation plan, it is now possible to issue the invitation to tender to prospective suppliers. Essentially, this will be the requirement document with a supporting letter, which may have additional information about how responses to the invitation are to be lodged. A deadline will be specified and it is hoped that by then a number of proposals with price quotations will have been received.

In English law, for a contract to exist there must be an offer on one side that must be accepted by the other side. The invitation to tender is not an offer itself, but an invitation for prospective suppliers to make an offer.

Certain new problems now emerge. The requirements that have been laid down might be capable of being satisfied in a number of different ways. The customer needs to know not only a potential supplier's price, but also the way in which they intend to satisfy the requirements – this will be particularly important where the contract is to build a new system from scratch.

In some relatively straightforward cases, it would be enough to have some post-tender clarification and negotiation to resolve issues in the supplier's proposal. With more complex projects a more elaborate approach may be needed. One way of getting the detail of the suppliers' proposals elaborated is to have a two stage tendering process.

This approach is recommended by the CCTA in the United Kingdom.

In the first stage, technical proposals are requested from potential suppliers who do not necessarily quote any prices at this stage. Some of these proposals can be dismissed out of hand as not being able to meet the mandatory requirements. With the remaining ones, discussions may be held with representatives of the suppliers in order to clarify and validate the technical proposals. The suppliers may be asked to demonstrate certain aspects of their proposals. Where short-comings in the proposal are detected, the supplier may be given the opportunity to remedy these.

The result of these discussions could be a *Memorandum of Agreement* (MoA) with each prospective supplier. This is an acceptance by the customer that the proposed solution (which might have been modified during discussions) offered by the supplier satisfactorily meets the customer's requirement.

In the second stage, tenders are invited from all the suppliers who have signed individual Memoranda of Agreement. The tender would incorporate the MoA and would be concerned with the financial terms of a potential contract.

If a design has to be produced as part of the proposal made by a supplier in response to an invitation to tender, a difficulty would be that the supplier would have to do a considerable amount of detailed design work with only a limited prospect of being paid for it. One way of reducing this burden is for the customer to choose a small number of likely candidates who will be paid a fee to produce design proposals. These can then be compared and the final contract for construction awarded to the most attractive proposal.

ISO 12207 is described in Appendix D

The ISO 12207 has a rather different approach. Once a contract for software construction is signed, the supplier develops a design, which then has to be agreed by the customer.

Evaluation of proposals

This needs to be done in a methodical and planned manner. We have already mentioned the need to produce an evaluation plan, which will describe how each proposal will be checked to see whether it meets each requirement. This reduces risks of requirements being missed and ensures that all proposals are treated consistently. Otherwise, there is a risk that a proposal might be unfairly favoured because of the presence of a feature that was not requested in the original requirement.

It will be recalled that an application could be either bespoke, off-the-shelf, or customized. In the case of off-the-shelf packages, it would be the software itself that would be evaluated and it might be possible to combine some of the evaluation with acceptance testing. With bespoke development it would be a proposal that is evaluated, while COTS may involve elements of both. Thus different planned approaches would be needed in each case.

The process of evaluation may include:

- scrutiny of the proposal documents;
- interviewing suppliers' representatives;
- demonstrations;
- site visits;
- practical tests.

The proposal documents provided by the suppliers can be scrutinized to see whether they contain features satisfying all the original requirements. Clarification might need to be sought over certain points. Any factual statements made by a supplier imply a legal commitment on their part if it influences the customer to offer the contract to that supplier. It is therefore important to get a written, agreed, record of these clarifications. The customer may take the initiative here by keeping notes of meetings and then writing afterwards to the suppliers to get them to confirm the accuracy of the notes. A supplier might, in the final contract document, attempt to exclude any commitment to any representations that have been made in pre-contract negotiations – the terms of the contract need to be scrutinized in this respect.

Where the delivered product is to be based on an existing product it might be possible to see a demonstration. A danger with demonstrations is that they can be controlled by the supplier and as a passive observer it is often difficult to maintain full attention for more than, say, half-an-hour. Because of this, the customer should produce a schedule of what needs to be demonstrated, ensuring that all the important features are seen in operation.

With off-the-shelf software, it should be possible to have actual access to the application. For example, a demonstration version, which closes itself down after 30 days, might be available. Once again a test plan is needed to ensure that all the important features are evaluated in a complete and consistent manner. Once a particular package emerges as the most likely candidate, it needs to be carefully investigated to see whether there are any previously unforeseen factors that might invalidate this choice.

A frequent problem is that while an existing application works well on one platform with a certain level of transactions, it does not work satisfactorily on the platform that the customer has or at the level of throughput that it would be subjected to in the customer's work environment. Demonstrations will not generally reveal this problem. Visits to operational sites already using the system will be more informative in this respect. In the last resort a special volume test could be conducted.

| Exercise 10.6 | How would you evaluate the following aspects of a proposal? |

1. The usability of an existing software application.
2. The usability of a software application that is yet to be designed and constructed.
3. The maintenance costs of hardware to be supplied.
4. The time taken to respond to requests for software support.
5. Training.

Where substantial sums of money are involved, legal advice on the terms of the contract is essential.

Eventually a decision will be made to award the contract to one of the suppliers. One of the central reasons for using a structured and, as far as possible, objective approach to evaluation is to be able to demonstrate that the decision has been made impartially and on merit. In most large organizations, placing a contract involves the participation of a second party within the organization, such as a contracts department, who can check that the correct procedures have been carried out. Also the final legal format of a contract will almost certainly require some legal expertise.

In any case, not only should the successful candidate be notified, but the unsuccessful candidates should also be told of the decision. This is not simply a matter of courtesy: under GATT or EU rules, there is a legal requirement to do this in certain circumstances. It makes dealing with unsuccessful bidders easier if they can be given clear and objective reasons why their proposals did not find favour.

10.4 Typical terms of a contract

In a textbook such as this, it is not possible to describe all the necessary content of contracts for IT goods or services. It is possible, however, to outline some of the major areas of concern.

Definitions

The terminology used in the contract document may need to be defined, for example, who is meant by the words 'client' and 'supplier'.

Form of agreement

For example, is it a contact of sale, a lease, or a licence? Also, can the subject of the contract, such as a licence to use a software application, be transferred to another party?

Goods and services to be supplied

Equipment and software to be supplied   This includes an actual list of the individual pieces of equipment to be delivered, complete with the specific model numbers.

Services to be provided   This covers such things as:

- training;
- documentation;
- installation;
- conversion of existing files;
- maintenance agreements;
- transitional insurance arrangements.

Ownership of the software

Who has ownership of the software? There are two key issues here: firstly, whether the customer can sell the software to others and, secondly, whether the supplier can sell the software to others. Where off-the-shelf software is concerned, the supplier often simply grants a licence for you to use the software. Where the software is being written specially for a customer, then that customer will normally wish to ensure exclusive use of the software – they may object to software which they hoped would give them a competitive edge being sold to their rivals. They could do this by acquiring the copyright to the software outright or by specifying that they should have *exclusive use* of the software. This would need to be written into the contract. Where a core system has been customized by a supplier, then there is less scope for the customer to insist on exclusive use.

Where software is written by an employee as part of a contract of employment, it is assumed that the copyright belongs to the employer. Where the customer organization has contracted an external supplier to write software, the contract needs to make clear who is going to retain the copyright – it cannot, in this case, be automatically assumed it is the customer. The customer might have decided to take over responsibility for maintenance and further development once the software is delivered and in this case will need access to the source code. In other cases, where the customer does not have an adequate in-house maintenance function, the supplier can retain the source code, and the customer will have to approach the supplier for any further changes. There are many potential dangers with this, not the least being that the supplier could go out of business. An *escrow agreement* can be included in the contract so that up-to-date copies of the source code are deposited with a third party. In the United Kingdom, the National Computing Centre provide an escrow service.

Environment

Where physical equipment is to be installed, the demarcation line between the supplier's and customer's responsibilities with regard to such matters as accommodation and electrical supply needs to be specified. Where software is being supplied, the compatibility of the software with the existing hardware and operating system platforms would need to be confirmed.

Customer commitments

Even when work is carried out by external contractors, a development project still needs the participation of the customer. The customer will have to provide accommodation for the suppliers and perhaps other facilities such as telephone lines.

Acceptance procedures

Some customers find that specially written or modified software is not thoroughly tested by the supplier before delivery. Some suppliers seem to think that it is cheaper to get the customer to do the testing for them!

Good practice would be to accept a delivered system only after it has undergone user acceptance tests. This part of the contract would specify such details as the time that the customer will have to conduct the tests, deliverables upon which the acceptance tests depend and the procedure for signing off the testing as completed.

Standards

This covers the standards with which the goods and services should comply. For example, a customer can require the supplier to conform to the ISO 12207 standard relating to the software life cycle and its documentation (or, more likely, a customized sub-set of the standard). Within the European Union, government customers with contracts for projects above a certain threshold value must, by law, ensure that the work conforms to certain standards.

Project and quality management

The arrangements for the management of the project must be agreed. Among these would be frequency and nature of progress meetings and the progress information to be supplied to the customer. The contract could require that appropriate ISO 9000-series standards be followed. The ISO 12207 standard provides for the customer to have access to quality documentation generated internally by the supplier, so that the customer can ensure that there is adherence to standards.

Timetable

This provides a schedule of when the key parts of the project should be completed. This timetable will commit both the supplier and the customer. For example, the supplier might be able to install the software on the agreed date only if the customer makes the hardware platform available at that point.

Price and payment method

Obviously the price is very important! What also needs to be agreed is when the payments are to be made. The supplier's desire to be able to meet costs as they are incurred needs to be balanced by the customer's requirement to ensure that goods and services are satisfactory before parting with money.

Miscellaneous legal requirements

This is the legal small print. Contracts often have clauses that deal with such matters as the legal jurisdiction that will apply to the contract, what conditions would apply to the sub-contracting of the work, liability for damage to third parties, and liquidated damages. *Liquidated damages* are estimates of the financial losses that the customer would suffer if the supplier were to fall short of their obligations. It is worth noting that under English law, the penalties laid down in penalty clauses must reflect the actual losses the customer would suffer and cannot be unrealistic and merely punitive. Even this limitation will not be enough in some cases as far as the supplier is concerned. As computer systems assume increasingly critical roles in many organizations and in safety-critical systems can even be life-threatening in the case of malfunction, the possible consequential damage could be very great. Suppliers will not unnaturally try to limit this kind of liability. The courts (in England and Wales) have tended to look critically at such attempts at limiting liability, so that suppliers will, in the case of major contracts, take out insurance to cover such liabilities.

If there is a dispute, resorting to litigation, while being lucrative to the lawyers involved, is both time-consuming and expensive. An alternative is to agree that disputes be settled by *arbitration*. This requires that any dispute be referred to an expert third party whose decision as to the facts of the case is binding. Even this procedure is seldom quick and inexpensive and another option is *alternative dispute resolution* where a third party acts as a mediator who has only an advisory capacity and attempts to broker an agreement between the two sides.

10.5 Contract management

We now need to consider the communications between the supplier and the customer while the work contracted for is being carried out. It would probably suit all concerned if the contractor could be left to get on with the work undisturbed. However, at certain *decision points*, the customer needs to examine work already done and make decisions about the future direction of the project. The project will require representatives of the supplier and customer to interact at many points in the development cycle – for example, users need to be available to provide information needed to carry out effective detailed interface design.

This interaction, or other external factors, often leads to changes being needed, which effectively vary the terms of the contract and so a careful change control procedure is needed. Each of these topics will now be tackled in a little more detail.

Chapter 4 discusses incremental delivery.

When the contract is being negotiated, certain key points in the project can be identified where customer approval is needed before the project can proceed. For example, a project to develop a large system can be divided into increments. For each increment there could be an interface design phase, and the customer needs to approve the designs before the increment is built. There could also be a decision point between increments.

For each decision point, the deliverables to be presented by the suppliers, the decisions to be made by the customer and the outputs from the decision point all need to be defined. These decision points have added significance if payments to the supplier are based on them. Not only the supplier but also the customer has responsibilities with respect to these decision points – for example, the supplier should not be unnecessarily delayed while awaiting customer approval of some interim deliverable.

Where work is contracted out there will be a general concern about the quality of that work. The ISO 12207 standard envisages the possibility of there being agents, employed independently of the supplier or customer, who will carry out verification, validation and quality assurance. It also allows for joint reviews of project processes and products, the nature of which needs to be clearly agreed when the contract is negotiated, otherwise the supplier might claim unwarranted interference in their work.

As the system is developed a need to change certain of the requirements often emerges. As noted earlier, essentially, this is varying the terms of the contract. Oral evidence is not normally admissible to contradict, add to, or vary the terms of a written contract, so that agreed changes need to be documented properly. An effective change control procedure is therefore needed to record requests for changes, along with the supplier's agreement to them and any fees for the additional work.

It could happen that the supplier does not meet one or more of their legal obligations. This might be through no fault of theirs, if, for example, the customer has caused the delay by being tardy in giving the necessary approvals for inter-mediate products. If no action is taken when the default occurs, this can be taken to imply that the customer in fact condones the failure and this can lead to the loss of a right to legal redress. The customer should therefore protect their legal rights by officially notifying the supplier as soon as possible that the failure has been recognized. It will be recalled that under English law any claim for liquidated damages should be based on actual losses. From the point where the default occurs, the customer needs to keep an accurate record of the actual losses incurred as a result of the default including any consequential losses.

10.6 Acceptance

When the work has been completed, the customer needs to take action to carry out acceptance testing. The contract might put a time limit on how long acceptance testing can take, so the customer must be organized to carry out this testing before the time limit for requesting corrections expires.

We have already noted that some software houses are rather cursory with their pre-acceptance testing: the implication seeming to be that they would rather the users spent their time on testing than they themselves. This imposition can be reduced by asking to approve the supplier's internal test plans. An associated pitfall is that once the main development work is completed, the supplier not unnaturally wants to reallocate the most productive staff to other projects. The customer can find that all their problem reports are being dealt with by relatively junior members of the supplier's staff, who might not be familiar with all aspects of the delivered system.

Part or all of the payment to the supplier will depend on this acceptance testing. Sometimes part of the final payment will be retained for a period of operational running and is eventually paid over if the levels of reliability are as contracted for. There is usually a period of warranty during which the supplier should fix any errors found for no charge. The supplier might suggest a very short warranty period of say 30 days. It is in the customer's interests to negotiate a more realistic period of say at least 120 days.

10.7 Summary

Some of the key points in this chapter have been:

- the successful contracting out of work requires considerable amounts of management time;
- it is easier to gain concessions from a supplier before a contract is signed than afterwards;
- alternative proposals need to be evaluated as far as possible by comparing costs over the whole lifetime of the system rather than just the acquisition costs;
- a contract will place obligations on the customer as well as the supplier;
- contract negotiation should include reaching agreement on the management of the supplier–customer relationship during the execution of the project.

10.8 Further exercises

1. At IOE, the management are considering 'out-sourcing' the maintenance accounting system, that is, getting an outside specialist organization to take over the operation,

maintenance and support activities associated with the system. Write a short memorandum to management outlining the advantages and disadvantages of such a re-organization.

2. In each of the following cases discuss whether the type of application software to be adopted would be most likely to be bespoke, off-the-shelf or COTS.

   (a) A college requires a student fees application. It is suggested that the processes required in the application are similar to those of any billing system with some requirements that are peculiar to the administration of higher education.

   (b) A computer-based application is needed at IOE to hold personnel details of staff employed.

   (c) A national government requires a system that calculates, records and notifies individual tax-payers about income tax charges.

   (d) A hospital needs a knowledge-based system to diagnose the causes of eye complaints.

3. The schedule of charges per function point shown in Table 10.1 has higher rates for larger systems. Give arguments explaining why this might be justified and also arguments against.

4. Table 10.2 has a charge of 25% and 50% of the normal rate for deleting transactions from an application. This seems to be rather high for simply removing code. What work would be involved in deleting functionality that could justify this cost?

5. Assume that IOE has decided on a COTS solution that will replace the whole of the existing maintenance accounting system rather than simply plugging in additional modules to deal with groups accounts. Write a memorandum that Amanda could send to IOE's legal department outlining the important provisions that a contract to supply this system should have.

Managing people and organizing teams

Objectives

When you have completed this chapter you will be able to:

- identify some of the factors that influence people's behaviour in a project environment;
- select and induct new staff into a project;
- increase staff motivation;
- improve group working;
- use the most appropriate leadership styles;
- appreciate the characteristics of the various team structures;
- take steps to reduce unnecessary stress and threats to health and safety.

11.1 Introduction

We are going to examine some of the problems that Amanda and Brigette could meet when dealing with members of their teams. Where possible we will see whether the writers on organizational behaviour (OB) can provide advice.

There will be three main concerns: staff selection, staff development and staff motivation.

We will look at how the project leader can encourage effective group working and decision making while giving purposeful leadership where needed. As part of the concern for the well-being of team members some attention will be paid to stress and other issues of health and safety.

The issues raised in this chapter have impacts at all stages of project planning and execution, but in particular at the following points (see also Figure 11.1).

- Some objectives can address health and safety during the project (Step 1).
- Although the project leader may have little control over organizational structure they need to be aware of its implications (Step 2).

209

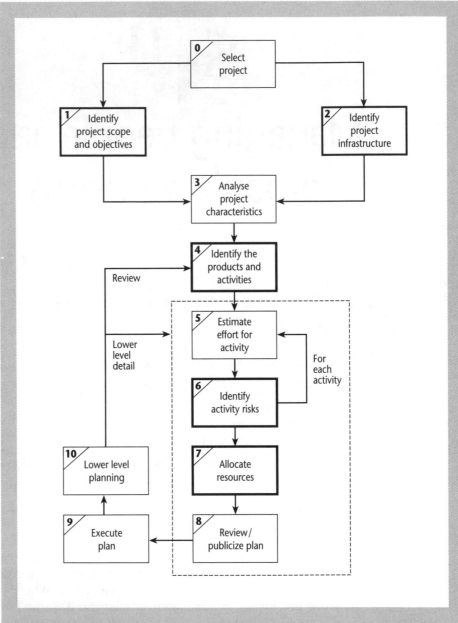

Figure 11.1 Some places in the Step Wise framework where staffing concerns are important

- The scope and nature of activities can be set in a way that will enhance staff motivation (Step 4).
- Many risks to project success relate to staffing (Step 6).
- The qualities of individual members of staff should be taken into account when allocating staff to activities (Step 7).

11.2 Understanding behaviour

People with practical experience of projects invariably identify the handling of people as an important aspect of project management. What people like Amanda and Brigette want to know is whether the effective and sensitive management of staff comes only from experience or whether expert advice can help.

The discipline of organizational behaviour (OB) has evolved theories that try to explain people's behaviour. These theories are often structured 'If A is the situation then B is likely to result'. Attempts are made to observe behaviour where variables for A and B are measured and a statistical relationship between the two variables sought. Unlike physical science it is rarely, if ever, the case that it can be said that B *must* always follow A.

In the real world there will be a wide range of influences on a situation, many invisible to the observer. It is therefore difficult to decide which set of research findings is relevant. A danger is that we end up with a set of maxims which is little better than superstitions. However, by examining these issues people can become more sensitive and thoughtful about them.

J. Arnold, C. L. Cooper and I. T. Robertson, *Work Psychology*, Pitman, 1998 is a good general text on these topics.

In what follows we will be making references to workers in the OB field such as Taylor, McGregor and Herzberg. Rather than overwhelming the reader with references, we recommend the reader who is interested in exploring this topic further to look at some of the books in the Further Reading section at the back of the book. Where we have given references these tend to be for works related specifically to an IT environment.

11.3 Organizational behaviour: a background

The roots of studies in OB can be traced back to work done in the late 19th and early 20th centuries by Frederick Taylor. Taylor attempted to analyse the most productive way of doing manual tasks. The workers were then trained to do the work in that way.

Taylor had three basic objectives:

Frederick Winslow Taylor, 1856–1915, is regarded as the father of 'scientific management' of which OB is a part.

- to select the best person for the job;
- to instruct them in the best methods;
- to give incentives in the form of higher wages to the best workers.

'Taylorism' is often represented as crude and mechanistic. However, a concern for identifying best practice is valid. In the world of software development, the growth of structured methods is an example of an emphasis on best practice. Both Amanda and Brigette will be concerned that tasks are carried out in the proper way. More contentious is Taylor's emphasis on the exclusively financial basis of staff motivation, although Amanda and Brigette will find many colleagues who hold Taylor's view on the importance of 'performance-related pay'. Unfortunately, Amanda and Brigette are likely to have very little control over the financial rewards of their staff. However, they should be encouraged by findings that motivation rests not just on such rewards.

The research that obtained these findings was done at the Hawthorne Works of Western Electric in Chicago, hence the 'Hawthorne Effect'.

During the 1920s, OB researchers discovered, while carrying out a now famous set of tests on the conditions under which staff worked best, that not only did a group of workers for whom conditions were improved increase their work-rates, but also a control group for whom conditions were unchanged. Simply showing a concern for what workers did increased productivity. This illustrated how the state of mind of the worker influenced their productivity.

The cash-oriented view of work of some managers can thus be contrasted with a more rounded vision of the person in their place of work. The two attitudes were labelled Theory X and Theory Y by Donald McGregor.

Theory X holds that:

- the average human has an innate dislike of work;

- there is a need therefore for coercion, direction and control;

- people tend to avoid responsibility.

Theory Y, on the other hand, holds that:

A 'reward' does not have to be a financial reward – it could be something like a sense of achievement.

- work is as natural as rest or play;

- external control and coercion are not the only ways of bringing about effort directed towards the company's ends;

- commitment to objectives is a function of the rewards associated with their achievement;

- the average human can learn to accept and further seek responsibility;

- the capacity to exercise imagination and other creative qualities is widely distributed.

One way of judging whether a manager espouses Theory X or Theory Y is to observe how their staff react when the boss is absent: if there is no discernible change then this is a Theory Y environment; if everyone visibly relaxes, it is a Theory X environment! McGregor's distinction between the two theories also draws attention to the way that expectations influence behaviour. If a manager (or teacher) assumes that you are going to work diligently and do well, you are likely to try to meet their expectations.

11.4 Selecting the right person for the job

B. W. Boehm considered the quality of staff the most important influence on productivity when constructing the COCOMO software cost model (Chapter 5).

P. M. Cheney, 'Effects of individual characteristics, organizational factors and task characteristics on computer programmer productivity and job satisfaction', *Information and Management*, 7, 1984.

Taylor stressed the need for the right person for the job. Many factors, such as the use of software tools and methodologies, affect programming productivity. However, one of the biggest differences in software development performance is between individuals. As early as 1968 a comparison of experienced professional programmers working on the same programming task found a ratio, in one case, of $1:25$ between the shortest and longest time to code the program and, more significantly perhaps, of $1:28$ for the time taken to debug it. Amanda and Brigette should therefore be rightly concerned to get the best possible people working for them.

What sort of characteristics should they be looking for? Is an experienced programmer better than a new graduate with a first class mathematics degree? It is dangerous to generalize but looking at behavioural characteristics the American researcher Cheney found that the most important influence on programmer productivity seemed to be experience. Mathematical aptitude had quite a weak influence in comparison.

Amanda and Brigette will want staff who can communicate well with each other and with users. Unfortunately, the American researchers Couger and Zawacki

J. D. Couger and
R. A. Zawacki 'What
motivates DP
professionals?',
Datamation, 24,
1978.

found that information systems (IS) professionals seemed to have much weaker 'social needs' than people in other professions. They quote Gerald Weinberg: 'If asked, most programmers probably say they prefer to work alone where they wouldn't be disturbed by other people.' We see many who are attracted to writing software, and are good at it, but do not make good managers later in their careers.

Later surveys, however, have *not* found significant differences between IS and other staff. An explanation of this could be that IS has become broader and less purely technical in recent years.

The recruitment process

R. Meredith Belbin,
Team roles at work,
Butterworth-
Heinemann, 1993.

It must be stressed that often project leaders have little choice about the people who will make up their team – they have to make do with the 'materials that are to hand'. Recruitment is often an organizational responsibility: the person recruited might, over a period of time, work in many different parts of the organization.

Meredith Belbin usefully distinguishes between *eligible* and *suitable* candidates. *Eligible* candidates have a curriculum vitae (CV) which shows, for example, the 'right' number of years in some previous post and the 'right' paper qualifications. *Suitable* candidates can actually do the job well. A mistake is to select an eligible candidate who is not in fact suitable. Suitable candidates who are not officially eligible can, on the other hand, be ideal candidates as once in post they are more likely to remain loyal. Belbin suggests we should try to assess actual skills rather than past experience and provide training to make good minor gaps in expertise. It seems to us to show that policies that avoid discrimination on the grounds of race, gender, age or irrelevant disabilities can be not just socially responsible, but also a shrewd recruitment strategy.

A general approach might be the following.

- *Create a job specification* Advice is often needed as there could be legal implications in an official document. However, formally or informally, the requirements of the job should be documented and agreed.
- *Create a job holder profile* The job specification is used to construct a profile of the person needed to carry out the job. The qualities, qualifications, education and experience required would be listed.
- *Obtain applicants* Typically, an advertisement would be placed, either within the organization or outside in the trade or local press. The job holder profile would be examined carefully to identify the medium most likely to reach the largest number of potential applicants at least cost. For example, if a specialist is needed it would make sense to advertise in the relevant specialist journal. The other principle is to give enough information in the advertisement to allow an element of self-elimination. By giving the salary, location, job scope and any essential qualifications, the applicants will be limited to the more realistic candidates.

A standard form
which lists each
selection criterion and
the degree to which
the candidate meets it
should be used to
ensure a consistent
and fair approach.

- *Examine CVs* These should be read carefully and compared to the job holder profile – nothing is more annoying for all concerned than when people have CVs which indicate clearly they are not eligible for the job and yet are called for interview.
- *Interviews, etc.* Selection techniques include aptitude tests, personality tests, and the examination of samples of previous work. Any method must test specific qualities detailed in the job holder profile. Interviews are the most commonly

used method. It is better if there is more than one interview session with an applicant and with each session there should not be more than two interviewers as a greater number reduces the possibility of follow-up questions and discussion. Some formal scoring system for the qualities being judged should be devised and interviewers should then decide scores individually which are then compared. An interview might be of a technical nature where the practical expertise of the candidate is assessed, or of a more general nature. In the latter case, a major part of the interview could be evaluating and confirming statements in the CV – for example time gaps in the education and employment history would be investigated, and the precise nature of previous jobs would need to be explored.

● *Other procedures*　References will need to be taken up where necessary, and a medical examination might be needed.

| **Exercise 11.1** | A new analyst/programmer is to be recruited to work in Amanda's team at IOE. The intention is to recruit someone who already has some experience. Make a list of the types of activities that the analyst/programmer should be capable of carrying out that can be used as the basis for a job specification. |

11.5　Instruction in the best methods

> Decisions will need to be made about whether a newcomer can more effectively pick up technical expertise on the job or on formal training courses.

This is the second concern that we have taken from Taylor. When new members of the team are recruited, the team leader will need to plan their induction into the team very carefully. Where a project is already well under way, this might not be easy. However, the effort should be made – it should pay off as the new recruit will become a fully effective member of the team more quickly.

The team leader should be aware of the need to assess continually the training needs of their team members. Just as you formulate a user requirement before considering a new system, and a job holder profile before recruiting a member of staff, so a *training needs profile* ought to be drawn up for each staff member when considering specific courses. Some training might be provided by commercial training companies. Where money is tight, alternative sources of training should be considered, but training should not be abandoned. It could just be a team member finding out about a new software tool and then demonstrating it to colleagues. Of course the nice thing about external courses is talking to colleagues from other organizations – but attending meetings of your local branch of one of the IS/IT professional associations can serve the same purpose.

The methods learnt need, of course, to be actually applied. Reviews and inspections help to ensure this.

11.6　Motivation

> Piece-rates are where workers are paid a fixed sum for each item they produce. Day-rates refer to payment for time worked.

The third of Taylor's concerns was that of motivating people to work. We are going to look at some models of motivation.

The Taylorist model

Taylor's viewpoint is reflected in the use of piece-rates in manufacturing industries and sales bonuses amongst sales forces. Piece-rates can cause difficulties if a new system will change work practices. If new technology improves productivity, adjusting piece-rates to reflect this will be a sensitive issue. Usually, radical changes in work practices have to be preceded by a move from piece-rates to day-rates.

Even where work practices are stable and output can be easily related to reward, people paid by the amount they produce will not automatically maximize their output in order to maximize their income. The amount of output will often be constrained by 'group norms', informal, even unspoken, agreements among colleagues about the amount to be produced.

Rewards based on piece-rates need to relate directly to work produced. Where a computer application is being developed, it is difficult to isolate and quantify work done by an individual, as system development and support is usually a team effort. As one member of staff in a study of software support work said:

'This support department does well because we're a team, not because we're all individuals. I think it's the only way the support team can work successfully.'

In this kind of environment, a reward system that makes excessive distinctions between co-workers could damage morale and productivity. Organizations sometimes get around this problem by giving bonuses to project team members at the end of a successful project, especially if staff have 'volunteered' considerable unpaid overtime to get the project completed.

Group norms are discussed further under group decision making.

Quoted by Wanda J. Orlikowski in *Groupware & teamwork*, Claudio U. Ciborra (ed.), Wiley, 1996.

Exercise 11.2

A software development department wants to improve productivity by encouraging the reuse of existing software components. It has been suggested that this could be encouraged through financial rewards. To what extent do you think this could be done?

Maslow's hierarchy of needs

The motivation of individuals varies. Money is a strong motivator when you are broke. However, as the basic need for cash is satisfied, other motivators are likely to emerge. Abraham Maslow, an American psychologist, suggested a hierarchy of needs. As a lower level of needs is satisfied then gradually a higher level of needs emerges. If these are then satisfied, yet another level of will emerge. Basic needs include food, shelter and personal safety. The highest level need, according to Maslow, is the need for 'self-actualization', the feeling that you are completely fulfilling your potential.

In practice, people are likely to be motivated by different things at different stages of their life. For example, salary increases, while always welcome, probably have less impact on the more mature employee who is already relatively well paid, than on a lowly paid trainee. Older team members might place more value on qualities of the job such as being given autonomy which shows respect for their judgement and sense of responsibility.

Some individual differences in motivation relate simply to personality differences. Some staff have 'growth needs' – they are interested in their work and want to develop their work roles – while others simply see the job as a way of earning a living.

However, salary level can be important to staff approaching retirement because the amount of pension paid can depend on it.

Exercise 11.3

Newspapers often report on the vast sums of money that are paid to the top executives of many companies. Does this mean that these people are at a low level in the Maslow hierarchy of motivation? Do they really need all this money to be motivated? What do you think that the significance of these salaries really is?

Herzberg's two-factor theory

Some things about a job can make you dissatisfied. If the causes of this dissatisfaction are removed, this does not necessarily make the job more exciting. Research into job satisfaction by Herzberg and his associates found two sets of factors about a job:

- *Hygiene or maintenance factors* which can make you dissatisfied if they are not right, for example, the level of pay or the working conditions.

- *Motivators* which make you feel that the job is worthwhile, like a sense of achievement or the challenge of the work itself.

Brigette, at Brightmouth College, might be in an environment where it is difficult to compete with the high level of maintenance factors that can be provided by a large organization like IOE, but the smaller organization with its closer contact with the users might be able to provide better motivators.

Exercise 11.4 Identify three incidents or times when you felt particularly pleased or happy about something to do with your work or study. Identify three occasions when you were particularly dissatisfied with your work or study. Compare your findings with those of your colleagues and try to identify any patterns.

The expectancy theory of motivation

Amanda and Brigette need to be aware of how the day-to-day ups and downs of system development affect motivation. A model of motivation developed by Vroom and his colleagues illustrates this. It identifies three influences on motivation:

- *Expectancy*: the belief that working harder will lead to a better performance.

- *Instrumentality*: the belief that better performance will be rewarded.

- *Perceived value*: of the resulting reward.

Motivation will be high when all three factors are high. A zero level for any one of the factors can remove motivation.

Imagine trying to get a software package supplied by a third party to work. You realize that you will never get it to work because of a bug, and you give up. No matter how hard you work you will not be able to succeed (*zero expectancy*).

You are working on a package for a user and, although you think you can get it to work, you discover that the user has started employing an alternative package and no longer needs this one. You will probably feel you are wasting your time and give up (*zero instrumentality*).

Given that the users really do want the package, your reward might simply be the warm feeling of helping your colleagues and their gratitude. If, in fact, when the users employ the package, all they do is complain and hold you responsible for shortcomings, then you might avoid getting involved if they later ask for help implementing a different package (*low perceived value of reward*).

11.7 The Oldham–Hackman job characteristics model

Managers should group together the elements of tasks to be carried out so that they form meaningful and satisfying assignments. Oldham and Hackman suggest that the satisfaction that a job gives is based on five factors. The first three factors make the job 'meaningful' to the person who is doing it are:

- *skill variety*: the number of different skills that the job holder has the opportunity to exercise;
- *task identity*: the degree to which your work and its results are identifiable as belonging to you;
- *task significance*: the degree to which your job has an influence on others.

The other two factors are:

- *autonomy*: the discretion you have about the way that you do the job;
- *feedback*: the information you get back about the results of your work.

Oldham and Hackman also noted that the job holders' personal growth needs influenced their perception of the job as did the working environment. Some writers have pointed out that if people are happy with their work for other reasons, they are likely to rate it higher on the Oldham–Hackman dimensions anyway. Thus it might be that cause and effect are reversed.

In practical terms, activities should be designed so that, where possible, staff follow the progress of a particular product and feel personally associated with it.

Methods of improving motivation

To improve motivation the manager might therefore do the following:

- *Set specific goals*: these goals need to be demanding and yet acceptable to staff. Involving staff in the setting of goals helps to gain acceptance for them.
- *Provide feedback*: not only do goals have to be set, but staff have to have regular feedback about how they are progressing.
- *Consider job design*: jobs can be altered to make them more interesting and give staff more feeling of responsibility.

Two measures are often used to enhance job design – *job enlargement* and *job enrichment*.

Job enlargement and job enrichment are based on the work of F. Herzberg.

- *Job enlargement*: the person doing the job carries out a wider variety of activities. It is the opposite of increasing specialization. For example, a programmer in a maintenance group might be given responsibility for specifying minor amendments as well as carrying out the actual code changes. Couger and Zawacki found that programmer/analysts had higher job satisfaction than programmers.
- *Job enrichment*: the job holder carries out tasks that are normally done at a managerial or supervisory level. With programmers in a maintenance team, they might be given authority to accept requests for changes which involve less than five days' work without the need for their manager's approval.

11.8 Working in groups

A problem with major software projects is that they always involve working in groups, and many people attracted to software development find this difficult.

Formal groups can be either the departmental groupings seen on organization hierarchy diagrams reflecting the formal management structure, or *task groups* which carry out specific tasks. Task groups might call on people from different departments and would usually be disbanded once the task was completed.

11.9 Becoming a team

Simply throwing people together will not immediately enable them to work together as a team. Group feelings develop over time. It is suggested that teams go through five basic stages of development:

This classification is associated with B. W. Tuckman and M. A. Jensen.

- *Forming*: the members of the group get to know each other and try to set up some ground rules about behaviour.
- *Storming*: conflicts arise as various members of the group try to exert leadership and the group's methods of operation are being established.
- *Norming*: conflicts are largely settled and a feeling of group identity emerges.
- *Performing*: the emphasis is now on the tasks at hand.
- *Adjourning*: the group disbands.

Sometimes specific team-building exercises can be undertaken. Some organizations, for example, send their management teams off on outdoor activities. Without going to these lengths, Amanda and Brigette might devise some training activities which promote team building.

R. Meredith Belbin *Management Teams: Why They Succeed Or Fail*, Heinemann, 1981, contains a self-assessment questionnaire which can help identify to which role a person is best suited.

Valuable research examined the best mix of personalities in a project team. Belbin studied teams working together on management games. He initially tried putting the most able people who into one group. Surprisingly, these élite teams tended to do very badly – they argued a lot and as a result important tasks were often neglected.

Belbin came to the conclusion that teams needed a balance of different types of people.

In *Team Roles at Work*, Butterworth-Heinemann, 1993, Belbin suggests that 'co-ordinator' and 'implementer' are better descriptions than 'chair' and 'team worker'. A new role is added: the 'specialist', the 'techie' who likes to acquire knowledge for its own sake.

- *The chair*: not necessarily brilliant leaders but they must be good at running meetings, being calm, strong but tolerant.
- *The plant*: someone who is essentially very good at generating ideas and potential solutions to problems.
- *The monitor-evaluator*: good at evaluating ideas and potential solutions and helping to select the best one.
- *The shaper*: rather a worrier, who helps to direct the team's attention to the important issues.
- *The team worker*: skilled at creating a good working environment, e.g. by 'jollying people along'.
- *The resource investigator*: adept at finding resources in terms of both physical resources and information.
- *The completer-finisher*: concerned with completing tasks.
- *The company worker*: a good team player who is willing to undertake less attractive tasks if they are needed for team success.

A person can have elements of more than one type. On the other hand, about 30% of the people examined by Belbin could not be classified at all! To be a good team member you must be able to:

- time your interventions, e.g. not overwhelm the others in the team;
- be flexible;
- be restrained;
- keep the common goals of the team in mind all the time.

Group performance

The IBM manager was quoted by Angelo Failla in 'Technologies for Co-ordination in a Software Factory' in *Groupware & Teamwork*, C. U. Ciborra (ed.), Wiley, 1996.

Are groups more effective than individuals working alone? Given the preference of many people attracted to software development for working on their own, this is an important question. In many projects, judgements need to be made about which tasks are best carried out collectively and which are best delegated to individuals. As one manager at IBM said: '*Some work yields better results if carried out as a team while some things are slowed down if the work is compartmentalized on an individual basis*'. Part of the answer lies in the type of task being undertaken.

One way of categorizing group tasks is into:

- additive tasks;
- compensatory tasks;
- disjunctive tasks;
- conjunctive tasks.

Additive tasks mean the efforts of each participant are added to get the final result, e.g. a gang clearing snow. The people involved are interchangeable.

Code reviews could be seen as an example of a compensatory task.

With *compensatory tasks* the judgements of individual group members are pooled so that the errors of some are compensated for by the inputs from others. For example, individual members of a group are asked to provide estimates of the effort needed to produce a piece of software and the results are then averaged. In these circumstances group work is generally more effective than the efforts of individuals.

With *disjunctive tasks* there is only one correct answer. The effectiveness of the group depends on:

- someone coming up with the right answer;
- the others recognizing it as being correct.

Here the group can only be as good as its best member – and could be worse!

Conjunctive tasks are where progress is governed by the rate of the slowest performer. Software production where different staff are responsible for different modules is a good example of this. The overall task is not completed until all participants have completed their part of the work. In this case co-operative attitudes are productive: the team members who are ahead can help the meeting of group objectives by assisting those who are behind.

The source of the quotation is the paper by Failla that is cited above.

With all types of collective task, but particularly with additive ones, there is a danger of *social loafing*, where some individuals do not make their proper contribution. This can certainly occur with student group activities, but is not unknown in 'real' work environments. As one software developer has commented: '*[The contribution made to others] is not always recognized. Nor is the lack of any contributions . . . nobody points out those who fail to make any contributions. Like when there's somebody with vital skills and you ask him for help, but he doesn't provide it'.*

Exercise 11.5 Social loafing is a problem that students often encounter when carrying out group assignments. What steps can participants in a group take to encourage team members to 'pull their weight' properly?

11.10 Decision making

Before we can look more closely at the effectiveness with which groups can make decisions we need to look in general terms at the decision-making process.

Decisions can be categorized as being:

Many of the techniques in Chapter 3 are attempts to make decision making more structured.

- *structured*: generally relatively simple, routine decisions where rules can be applied in a fairly straightforward way;
- *unstructured*: more complex and often requiring a degree of creativity.

Another way of categorizing decisions is by the amount of *risk* and *uncertainty* that is involved.

Some mental obstacles to good decision making

Many of the techniques in Chapter 3 on project selection are based on the rational-economic model.

So far we have rightly stressed a structured, rational, approach to decision making. Many management decisions in the real world, however, are made under pressure and based on incomplete information. We may have to accept the role of intuition in such cases, but be aware of some mental obstacles to effective intuitive thinking, for example:

- **Faulty heuristics**   Heuristics or 'rules of thumb' can be useful but there are dangers:
  - they are based only on information that is to hand which might be misleading;
  - they are based on stereotypes, such as accepting a Welshman into a male voice choir without an audition because of the 'well-known fact' that the Welsh are a great singing nation.
- **Escalation of commitment**   This refers to the way that once you have made a decision it is increasingly difficult to alter it even in the face of evidence that it is wrong.
- **Information overload**   It is possible to have too much information so that you 'cannot see the wood for the trees'.

Group decision making

A different type of participatory decision making might occur when end-users are consulted about the way a projected computer system is to operate.

There might be occasions when Amanda at IOE, for instance, might want to consult with her whole project team. With a project team different specialists and points of view can be brought together. Decisions made by the team as a whole are more likely to be accepted than those that are imposed.

Assuming that the meetings are genuinely collectively responsible and have been properly briefed, research would seem to show that groups are better at solving complex problems when the members of the group have complementary skills and expertise. The meeting allows them to communicate freely and to get ideas accepted.

Groups deal less effectively with poorly structured problems needing creative solutions. Brainstorming techniques can help groups in this situation, but research shows that people often come up with more ideas individually than in a group. Where the aim is to get the involvement of end-users of a computer system, then prototyping and participatory approaches such as JAD might be adopted.

Joint Application Development was discussed in Chapter 4.

Obstacles to good group decision making

Amanda could find that group decision making has disadvantages: it is time consuming; it can stir up conflicts within the group; and decisions can be unduly influenced by dominant personalities.

Conflict can, in fact, be less than might be expected. Experiments have shown that people will modify their personal judgements to conform to *group norms*, which are the common attitudes developed by a group over time.

Once established group norms can survive many changes of membership in the group.

You might think that this would moderate the more extreme views that some in the group might hold. In fact, people in groups sometimes make decisions that carry more risk than when they make the decision on their own. This is known as the *risky shift*.

Measures to reduce the disadvantages of group decision making

One method of making group decision making more efficient and effective is by training members to follow a set procedure. The *Delphi technique* endeavours to collate the judgements of a number of experts without actually bringing them face to face. Given a problem, the following procedure is carried out:

- the co-operation of a number of experts is enlisted;
- the problem is presented to the experts;
- the experts record their recommendations;
- these recommendations are collated and reproduced;
- the collected responses are recirculated;
- the experts comment on the ideas of others and modify their recommendations if so moved;
- if the leader detects a consensus then the process is stopped, otherwise the comments are recirculated to the experts.

The big problem with this approach used to be that although the experts could be geographically dispersed the process was time consuming.

Exercise 11.6 What developments in information technology would be of particular assistance to use of the Delphi technique?

11.11 Leadership

When Amanda and Brigette first took on project management responsibilities, one of their private anxieties might well have been that staff would not take them seriously. Leadership is generally taken to mean the ability to influence others in a group to act in a particular way to achieve group goals. A leader is not necessarily a good manager or vice versa as managers have other roles such as organizing, planning and controlling.

Authorities on this subject have found it difficult to agree a list of the common characteristics of good leaders. It would, however, seem safe to say that they seem to have a greater need for power and achievement and have more self-control and more self-confidence than others.

Leadership is based on the idea of authority or power although leaders do not necessarily have much formal authority. Power may either come from the person's position (*position* power), from person's individual qualities (*personal* power) or may be a mixture of the two. Position power has been further analysed into:

> These ideas are associated with the work of J. R. P. French and B. H. Raven.

- *coercive* power, the ability to force someone to do something by threatening punishment;
- *connection* power, which is based on having access to those who have power;
- *legitimate* power, which is based on a person's title conferring a special status;
- *reward* power, where the holder gives rewards to those who carry out tasks to his or her satisfaction.

Personal power, on the other hand, can be further analysed into:

- *expert* power, which comes from being the person who is able to do a specialized task;
- *information* power, where the holder has exclusive access to information;
- *referent* power, which is based on the personal attractiveness of the leader.

Exercise 11.7

What kinds of power (as defined above) would the following people have?

(i) An internal auditor looking at the payroll system at Brightmouth College.

(ii) A consultant who is called in to advise International Office Equipment about ways of improving software development productivity.

(iii) The principal of Brightmouth College who has told staff that they must accept a new contract or face the sack.

(iv) Brigette in respect to the users of the college payroll system.

(v) Amanda in respect of the people in the project team developing the group maintenance accounts application.

Leadership styles

Amanda and Brigette might be initially concerned about establishing their personal authority. Balanced against this is the need to involve the staff in decision making in order to make the best use of expertise and to gain commitment. Amanda and Brigette will need to judge when they must be authoritative and insist on things and when they must be more flexible and tolerant. Amanda, for example, might decide to be very democratic when formulating plans, but once the plans have been agreed, to insist on a very disciplined execution of the plan. Brigette, on the other hand, might find at Brightmouth College that she alone has the technical expertise to make some decisions, but, once she has briefed staff, they expect to be left alone to get on with the job as they see fit.

Attempts have been made to measure leadership styles on two axes: directive vs. permissive and autocratic vs. democratic:

This approach is associated with Rensis Likert.

● *directive autocrat*: makes decisions alone, close supervision of implementation;
● *permissive autocrat*: makes decisions alone, subordinates have latitude in implementation;
● *directive democrat*: makes decisions participatively, close supervision of implementation;
● *permissive democrat*: makes decisions participatively, subordinates have latitude in implementation.

It should be emphasized that there is no one best style of management – it depends on the situation.

Another axis used to measure management styles has been on the degree to which a manager is *task-oriented*, that is, the extent to which the execution of the task at hand is paramount, and the degree to which the manager is concerned about the people around them (*people-oriented*). It is perhaps not surprising that subordinates appear to perform best with managers who score highly in *both* respects.

Work environments vary with the amount of control exerted over work. Some jobs are routine and predictable (e.g. dealing with batched computer output). Others are driven by outside factors (e.g. a help desk) or are situations where future direction is uncertain (e.g. at the early stages of a feasibility study). With a high degree of uncertainty subordinates will seek guidance from above and welcome a task-oriented management style. As uncertainty is reduced, the task-oriented manager is likely to relax becoming more people-oriented and this will have good results. People-oriented managers are better where staff can control the work they do, without referring matters to their line managers. It is then argued that if control becomes even easier the people-oriented manager will be tempted to get involved in more task-centred questions with undesirable results.

Research also shows that where team members are relatively inexperienced, a task-oriented approach is most effective. As group members mature, consideration for their personal needs and aspirations becomes more valued. Where maturity is very high then there is no need for a strong emphasis on either of these approaches.

Exercise 11.8 What in your view would be the most appropriate management style when dealing with the following subordinates?

(i)   At Brightmouth College, a former member of the local authority who has dealt with the college payroll for several years and who has been employed by the college to set up and manage the new payroll section.

(ii) At IOE, a new trainee analyst programmer who has just joined Amanda's group.

(iii) At IOE, a very experienced analyst programmer in their 40s, who was recruited into the software development department some time ago from the accounts department and who has been dealing with system support for the old maintenance accounts system that is now being revised.

11.12 Organizational structures

Formal versus informal structures

While organizational structures can have an enormous impact on the way a project is conducted, it is something which project leaders such as Amanda at IOE might find they can do little to change.

The *formal* structure is expressed in the staff hierarchy chart. It is basically concerned with *authority*, about who has which boss. It is backed by an *informal* structure of contacts and communication that grows up spontaneously between members of staff during the course of work. When the unexpected happens it is often this system that takes over. Over time the advantages and disadvantages of different organizational structures tend to even out – the informal organization gets built up and staff find unofficial ways of getting around the obstacles posed by the formal structure.

Hierarchical approach

The 'traditional' management structure is based on the concept of the *hierarchy* – each member of staff has only one manager, while a manager will have responsibility for several members of staff. Authority flows from the top down through the structure. A traditional concern has been with the *span of control* – the number of people that a manager can effectively control.

Staff versus line

Staff in organizations can often be divided into *line* workers who actually produce the end product and support *staff* who carry out supporting roles. In some organizations which produce software for the market or as a component of a larger product which is sold, the software specialists might be seen as part of the line. In a financial organization, on the other hand, the information systems department would probably be seen as part of the support staff.

Departmentalization

Differentiation concerns the organizations are departmentalized. This might be based on staff specialisms, product lines, categories of customer or geographical location, for example.

Software development is usually organized using either a *functional* or a *task-oriented* approach. With functional departmentalization, systems analysts could be put in a separate group to the programmers. The programmers would act as a pool from which resources are drawn for particular tasks. With a task-oriented approach the programmers and systems analysts are grouped together in project teams. The project team could be gathered to implement a specific long-term project or could exist on a permanent basis to service the needs of a particular set of users.

Programme management which is discussed in Appendix C can facilitate better sharing of staff between projects.

The functional approach can lead to a more effective use of staff. Programmers can be allocated to jobs on a need basis and be released for other work when the task is completed. For instance, in a project team there are bound to be periods of greater and lesser coding activity and programmers could experience times when they are under-utilized. The functional organization will also make it easier for programmers to have a career which is technically oriented – there will probably be a career structure within the programming department which allows programmers to rise without changing their specialism. This type of organization should also encourage the interchange of new technical ideas between technical staff and the promulgation of company-wide standards.

However, having separate departments could lead to communication problems, especially if a developer is unfamiliar with an application area. There will also be problems with software maintenance – here it is helpful to have programmers who have built up a familiarity with particular parts of the application software. Users often prefer the established project team approach because they will have a group dedicated to their needs and will not find themselves in the position of always having to fight other departments for development resources. The project team structure tends to favour a pattern of career progression where programmers eventually become systems analysts.

A third method of departmentalization is based on life-cycle phase. Here there are separate teams for development and maintenance. Some staff can concentrate on developing new systems with few interruptions while other teams, more oriented towards service and support, deal with maintenance.

Some organizations have attempted to get the best of all worlds by having a *matrix* structure. In this case the programmer would have two managers: a project leader who would give them day-to-day direction about the work in hand and a programming manager who would be concerned about such things as career development.

Egoless programming

G. M. Weinberg, *The Psychology of Computer Programming*, Van Nostrand Reinhold, 1971.

In the early days of computer development, managers tended to think of the programmer as communing mysteriously with the machine. The tendency was for programmers to see programs as being an extension of themselves and to feel over-protective towards them. The effects of this on the maintainability of programs can be imagined. Gerald Weinberg made the then revolutionary suggestion that programmers and programming team leaders should read other people's programs. Programs would become in effect the common property of the programming group and programming would become 'egoless'. Peer code reviews are based on this idea. Weinberg's ideal programming team was a decentralized group freely communicating within itself.

Chief programmer teams

Brooks' *Mythical Man-Month* has already been referred to. He was in charge of the huge team that created the operating system for the IBM 360 range.

The larger the development group the slower it will get because of the increased communication. Thus, large time-critical projects call for a more formalized, centralized structure. Brooks pointed out the need for design consistency when producing a large complex system and how this is difficult with a large number of people involved in producing a piece of software. He suggested reducing the number of people actually creating software, but making these programmers as productive as possible by giving them as much support as possible.

The result was the *chief programmer* team. The chief programmer defines the specification, and designs, codes, tests and documents the software. There is also a *copilot*, with whom the chief programmer can discuss problems and who writes some code. They are supported by an *editor* to write up the documentation drafted by the chief programmer, a *program clerk* to maintain the actual code, and a *tester*. The general idea is that this team is under the control of a single unifying intellect.

The chief programmer concept was used on the influential *New York Times* data-bank project where many aspects of structured programming were tried out. In this case each chief programmer managed a senior level programmer and a program librarian. Additional members could be added to the team on a temporary basis to deal with particular problems or tasks.

The problem with this kind of organization is getting hold of really outstanding programmers to carry out the chief programmer role. There are also the dangers of information overload on the chief programmer and the potential for staff dissatisfaction among those who are there simply to minister to the needs of the superstar chief programmers.

The new *extreme programming* concepts have inherited many of these ideas. Here software development by pairs of developers is advocated – this seems to be a new version of the chief programmer/co-pilot relationship.

Extreme programming was discussed in Chapter 4.

11.13 Stress

Quoted in *Death March*, Edward Yourdon, Prentice-Hall 1997.

Projects are about overcoming obstacles and achieving objectives. Almost by definition both the project manager and team members will be under pressure. An American project manager is quoted as saying: '*Once a project gets rolling, you should expect members to be putting in at least 60 hours a week. . . . The project leader must expect to put in as many hours as possible . . .*'

Some pressure is actually healthy. Boredom can make many jobs soul-destroying. Beyond a certain level of pressure, however, the quality of work decreases and health can be affected. There is good evidence that productivity and the quality of output goes down when more than about 40 hours a week are worked. As long ago as 1960 it was found in a US study that people under 45 years of age who worked more than 48 hours a week had twice the risk of death from coronary heart disease.

Many software developers are expected to work overtime on projects for no additional payment. In these cases, a fall in productivity is more than compensated for by the fact that the work is effectively free to the employer.

Clearly, it is sometimes necessary to put in extra effort to overcome some temporary obstacle or to deal with an emergency, but if overtime working becomes a way of life then there will be longer term problems.

Good project management can reduce the reliance on overtime by the more realistic assessment of effort and elapsed time needed, based on careful recording and analysis of the performance of previous projects. Good planning and control will also help to reduce 'unexpected' problems generating unnecessary crises.

Stress can be caused by *role ambiguity* when staff do not have a clear idea of the objectives that their work is supposed to be fulfilling, what is expected of them by others and the precise scope of their responsibilities. The project manager could clearly be at fault in these instances.

Role conflict can also heighten stress. This is where the person is torn between the demands of two different roles. The parent of young children might be torn between the need to look after a sick child and the need to attend an important meeting to win new business.

Some managers claim to be successful through the use of essentially bullying tactics to push projects through. They need to create crises in order to justify the use of such tactics. This, however, is the antithesis of professional project management which aims at a rational, orderly and careful approach to the creation of complex products.

11.14 Health and safety

Professional Issues in Software Engineering (3rd edn), M. F. Bott *et al*, Taylor and Francis, 2000, explores these issues in greater depth.

Health and safety issues are more prominent in construction and other heavy engineering projects than in IT development. Sometimes, however, the implementation of office systems requires the creation of physical infrastructure which can have inherent physical dangers. The IT infrastructure could, for example, be installed in a building where construction work is still going on.

In this section we are not addressing general concerns relating to the safety of IT equipment of which any organization using such equipment would need to be aware. Nor are we discussing the safety of products created by the software development process. We are focusing briefly on the health and safety issues that relate to the conduct of a project.

Various pieces of legislation govern safety policy and the details of these can be consulted in the appropriate literature. In the United Kingdom, legislation requires organizations employing more than five employees to have a written *safety policy* document. A project manager should be aware of the contents of the document that applies to the environment in which the project is to be undertaken.

As far as the project manager is concerned, safety objectives, where appropriate, should be treated like any other project objectives, such as the level of reliability of the completed application or the overall cost of the project. The management of safety should therefore be embedded in the general management of the project.

Responsibility for safety must be clearly defined at all levels. Some points that will need to be considered include:

- top management must be committed to the safety policy;
- the delegation of responsibilities for safety must be clear;
- job descriptions should include definitions of duties related to safety;
- those to whom responsibilities are delegated must understand the responsibilities and agree to them;
- there should be deployment of a safety officer and the support of experts in particular technical areas;
- there should be consultation on safety;
- there should be an adequate budgeting for safety costs.

Safety procedures must be brought to the attention of employees and appropriate training be given where needed.

This is a very cursory glimpse at some of the issues in this area. For a fuller treatment, the specialized literature should be consulted.

11.15 Conclusion

Some of the important points that have been made in this chapter are:

- people may be motivated by money, but they are motivated by other things as well;
- both staff selection and the identification of training needs should be done in an orderly, structured, way where requirements are clearly defined first;

- thoughtful job design can increase staff motivation;
- consideration should be given, when forming a new project team, to getting the right mix of people and to planning activities which will promote team building;
- group working is more effective with some types of activity than others;
- different styles of leadership are needed in different situations;
- the people who need to communicate most with each other should be grouped together organizationally;
- undue pressure on staff can have short-term gains, but is harmful to both productivity and personal health in the longer term;
- project objectives should include, where appropriate, those relating to health and safety.

11.16 Further exercises

1. An organization has detected low job satisfaction in the following departments:
    - the system testing group;
    - the computer applications help desk;
    - computer batch input.

    How could these jobs be redesigned to give more job satisfaction?

2. In Exercise 11.1, a job specification was requested.
    (a) Write a job holder profile of the sort of person who would be able to fulfil the specification in terms of qualities, qualifications, previous education and experience.
    (b) For each element in the job holder profile that you have produced in (a) above describe ways of finding out whether an applicant has met the requirement.

3. To what extent is the Belbin approach to balanced teams compatible with having chief programmer teams?

4. If you have been involved recently in a group activity or project, try to categorize each participant according to the Belbin classification. Were there any duplications or gaps in any of the roles? Did this seem to have any impact on progress?

5. Three different mental obstacles to good decision making were identified in the text: faulty heuristics, escalation of commitment and information overload. What steps do you think can be taken to reduce the danger of each of these?

6. In Exercise 11.8, the management style most appropriate for each of three different situations was asked for. Go back and consider how you as a manager would respond to each of these three situations in terms of practical things to do or avoid.

Software quality

Objectives

When you have completed this chapter you will be able to:

- explain the importance of software quality to software users and developers;
- define the qualities of good software;
- design methods of measuring the required qualities of software;
- monitor the quality of the processes in a software project;
- use external quality standards to ensure the quality of software acquired from an outside supplier;
- develop systems using procedures that will increase their quality.

12.1 Introduction

While quality is generally agreed to be 'a good thing', in practice the quality of a system can be a vague, undefined, attribute. We therefore need to define precisely what qualities we require of a system. However, this is not enough – we need to judge objectively whether a system meets our quality requirements and this needs measurement. This would be of particular concern to someone like Brigette at Brightmouth College in the process of selecting a package.

For someone, like Amanda at IOE, developing software, waiting until the system exists before measuring it would be leaving things rather late. She would want to forecast the likely quality of the final system while it was still under development, and also to make sure that the development methods used were likely to produce that quality. This leads to a slightly different emphasis – rather than concentrating on the quality of the final system, a potential customer for software might try to check that the suppliers were using the best methods.

This chapter examines these issues.

12.2 The place of software quality in project planning

Quality will be of concern at all stages of project planning and execution, but will be of particular interest at the following points in the Step Wise framework (Figure 12.1).

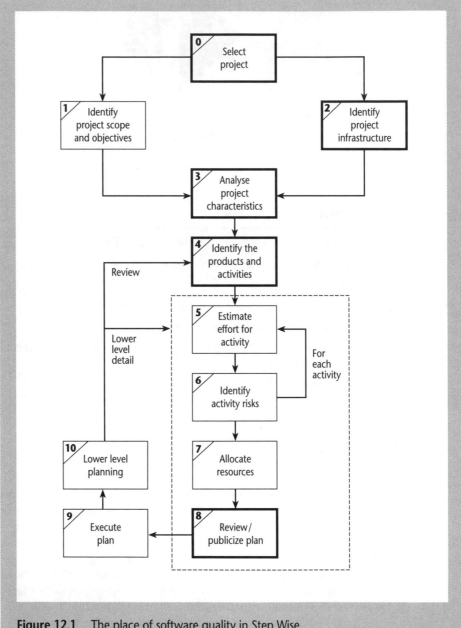

Figure 12.1 The place of software quality in Step Wise

- *Step 1: Identify project scope and objectives* Some objectives could relate to the qualities of the application to be delivered.

- *Step 2: Identify project infrastructure* Within this step, activity 2.2 identifies installation standards and procedures. Some of these will almost certainly be about quality.

- *Step 3: Analyse project characteristics* In activity 3.2 ('Analyse other project characteristics – including quality based ones') the application to be implemented will be examined to see if it has any special quality requirements. If, for example, it is extremely safety critical then a whole range of additional activities could be added such as *n*-version development where a number of teams develop versions of the same software which are then run in parallel with the outputs being cross-checked for discrepancies.

- *Step 4: Identify the products and activities of the project* It is at this point that the entry, exit and process requirements are identified for each activity. The nature of these requirements is described later in this chapter.

- *Step 8: Review and publicize plan* At this stage the overall quality aspects of the project plan are reviewed.

12.3 The importance of software quality

We would expect quality to be a concern of all producers of goods and services. However, the special characteristics of software, and in particular its intangibility and complexity, make special demands.

- *Increasing criticality of software* The final customer or user is naturally anxious about the general quality of software, especially its reliability. This is increasingly the case as organizations become more dependent on their computer systems and software is used more and more in areas which are safety critical, for example to control aircraft.

The intangibility of software presents particular problems – see Frederick P. Brooks, 'No Silver Bullet: Essence and Accidents of Software Engineering', *IEEE Computer*, April 1987.

- *The intangibility of software* This makes it difficult to know whether a particular task in a project has been completed satisfactorily. The results of these tasks can be made tangible by demanding that the developer produce 'deliverables' that can be examined for quality.

- *Accumulating errors during software development* As computer system development is made up of a number of steps where the output from one step is the input to the next, the errors in the earlier deliverables will be added to those in the later steps leading to an accumulating detrimental effect. In general, the later in a project that an error is found the more expensive it will be to fix. In addition, because the number of errors in the system is unknown the debugging phases of a project are particularly difficult to control.

For these reasons quality management is an essential part of effective overall project management.

12.4 Defining software quality

Quality is a rather vague term and we need to define carefully what we mean by it. For any software system, there should be three specifications:

- a *functional specification* describing what the system is to do – methodologies such as SSADM are primarily concerned with this;

- a *quality (or attribute) specification* concerned with how well the functions are to operate;

- a *resource specification* concerned with how much is to be spent on the system.

James A. McCall, 'An introduction to software quality metrics', J. D. Cooper & M. J. Fisher (eds.), *Software Quality Management*, Petrocelli, New York 1978.

Exercise 12.1

At Brightmouth College, Brigette has to select the best off-the-shelf payroll package for the college. How should she go about this in a methodical manner?

One element of the approach could be the identification of criteria against which payroll packages are to be judged. What might these criteria be? How could you check the extent to which packages match these criteria?

One attempt to identify specific product qualities that are appropriate to software has been that of James A. McCall. He grouped software qualities into three sets of quality factors:

● product operation qualities;
● product revision qualities;
● product transition qualities.

The definitions below are those given by McCall, but the reader may come across others. These are not all-bracing: sometimes other qualities might be of interest.

The ISO 9126 standard presents an alternative set which is described later.

Product operation quality factors

● *Correctness* The extent to which a program satisfies its specifications and fulfils the user's objectives.
● *Reliability* The extent to which a program can be expected to perform its intended function with required precision.
● *Efficiency* The amounts of computer resources required by the software.
● *Integrity* The extent to which access to software or data by unauthorized persons can be controlled.
● *Usability* The effort required to learn, operate, prepare input and interpret output.

The relationship between any two quality factors may be:

● *indifferent* – the presence of one quality has no effect on the other;
● *complementary* – the presence of one quality would suggest the presence of the other;
● *conflicting* – the presence of one quality is likely to reduce the presence of the other.

Product revision quality factors

● *Maintainability* The effort required to locate and fix an error in an operational program.
● *Testability* The effort required to test a program to ensure it performs its intended function.
● *Flexibility* The effort required to modify an operational program.

Product transition quality factors

● *Portability* The effort required to transfer a program from one hardware configuration and/or software system environment to another.
● *Reusability* The extent to which a program can be used in other applications.
● *Interoperability* The effort required to couple one system to another.

Exercise 12.2

Look at McCall's list of quality factors. Identify examples of pairs that are (a) indifferent, (b) complementary, and (c) conflicting.

McCall's software quality factors reflect the external view of software that users would have. For instance, usability would be a key concern of users. These quality

The same software quality criterion may apply to more than one of the software quality factors.

Table 12.1 Software quality criteria

Quality factor	Software quality criteria
Correctness	Traceability, consistency, completeness
Reliability	Error tolerance, consistency, accuracy, simplicity
Efficiency	Execution efficiency, storage efficiency
Integrity	Access control, access audit
Usability	Operability, training, communicativeness, input/output volume, input/output rate
Maintainability	Consistency, simplicity, conciseness, modularity, self-descriptiveness
Testability	Simplicity, modularity, instrumentation, self-descriptiveness
Flexibility	Modularity, generality, expandability, self-descriptiveness
Portability	Modularity, self-descriptiveness, machine independence, software system independence
Reusability	Generality, modularity, software system independence, machine independence, self-descriptiveness
Interoperability	Modularity, communications commonality, data commonality

factors have to be translated into internal factors of which the developers would be aware – *software quality criteria* (Table 12.1).

Exercise 12.3

The same software quality criteria often appear for more than one software quality factor. What is the significance of this?

Measures may be:

- *relative quantity measures* where an attempt is made to quantify the presence of the quality, or
- *binary measures* where the quality is deemed either to be present or not present.

Some writers use the term *metric* interchangeably with measure. Software measurement specialists would, however, maintain that there is a technical difference between the two terms.

Defining quality is not enough. If we are to judge whether a system meets our requirements we need to be able to measure its qualities. For each criterion, one or more measures have to be invented which assess the degree to which the quality is present.

A good measure must be able to relate the number of units to the maximum possible in the circumstances. The maximum number of faults in a program, for example, is related to the size of the program so a measure of faults per thousand lines of code is more helpful than *total faults in a program* as a means of judging the quality of a program.

Trying to find measures for a particular quality helps to clarify what that quality really is. What is being asked is, in effect, *'how do we know when we have been successful?'* Answering this allows the quality objectives to be communicated widely.

The measures may be *direct* where we can measure the quality directly or *indirect* where the thing being measured is not the quality itself but an indicator that the quality is present. By identifying measures the management are setting targets for project team members so care has to be taken that an improvement in the measured quality is always meaningful. For example, the number of errors found in program inspections could be counted. This count could, of course, be improved by allowing more errors to go through to the inspection stage rather than eradicating them earlier – which is not quite the point!

In general, the user of software would be concerned with measuring what McCall called *quality factors* while the developers would be concerned with *quality criteria*.

The following should be laid down for each quality:

- *scale*: the unit of measurement;
- *test*: the practical test of the extent to which the attribute quality exists;
- *worst*: the worst acceptable value;
- *plan*: the value that it is planned to achieve;
- *best*: the best value that appears to be feasible (the 'state of the art' limit); this would be a level that is known to have been achieved elsewhere;
- *now*: the value that applies currently.

When drafting *quality specifications* a quality criterion might be broken down into sub-criteria. Take the quality criterion 'communicativeness' which contributes to 'usability'. One aspect of this might be the ease of understanding of the menu structure, that is, how easy it is to find the command to carry out some function. Another aspect of communicativeness would be how informative the error messages were, while another would be the clarity of the 'help' pages.

Exercise 12.4 Suggest quality specifications for a word processing package. Give particular attention to the way that practical tests of these attributes could be conducted.

12.5 ISO 9126

Over the years, various lists of software quality characteristics have been put forward such as those of McCall, described above, and of Boehm. A difficulty has been the lack of agreed definitions of the qualities of good software. The term 'maintainability' has been used, for example, to refer to the ease with which an error can be located and corrected in a piece of software, and also in a wider sense to include the ease of making any changes. For some 'robustness' has meant the software's tolerance of incorrect input, while for others it has meant the ability to change program code without introducing unexpected errors. ISO 9126 standard was published in 1991 to tackle the question of the definition of software quality. This 13 page document was designed as a foundation upon which further, more detailed, standards could be built.

ISO 9126 identifies six software quality characteristics:

- *functionality*, which covers the functions that a software product provides to satisfy user needs;
- *reliability*, which relates to the capability of the software to maintain its level of performance;
- *usability*, which relates to the effort needed to use the software;
- *efficiency*, which relates to the physical resources used when the software is executed;
- *maintainability*, which relates to the effort needed to the make changes to the software;
- *portability*, which relates to the ability of the software to be transferred to a different environment.

ISO 9126 suggests sub-characteristics for each of the primary characteristics. It is indicative of the difficulties of gaining widespread agreement that these sub-characteristics are outside the main standard and are provided for 'information only'. They are useful as they clarify what is meant by the main characteristics.

Characteristic	Sub-characteristics
Functionality	Suitability
	Accuracy
	Interoperability
	Compliance
	Security

Compliance refers to the degree to which the software adheres to application-related standards or legal requirements. Typically these could be auditing requirements.

Interoperability and *security* are good illustrations of the efforts of ISO 9126 to clarify terminology. 'Interoperability' refers to the ability of the software to interact with other systems. The framers of ISO 9126 have chosen this word rather than *compatibility* because the latter causes confusion with the characteristic referred to by ISO 9126 as 'replaceability' (see below).

Characteristic	Sub-characteristics
Reliability	Maturity
	Fault tolerance
	Recoverability

Maturity refers to the frequency of failure due to faults in a software product, the implication being that the more the software has been used, the more faults will have been uncovered and removed. It is also interesting to note that *recoverability* has been clearly distinguished from *security* which describes the control of access to a system.

Characteristic	Sub-characteristics
Usability	Understandability
	Learnability
	Operability

Understandability is a pretty clear quality to grasp, although the definition 'attributes that bear on the users' efforts for recognizing the logical concept and its applicability' in our view actually makes it less clear!

Note how *learnability* is distinguished from *operability*. A software tool could be easy to learn but time-consuming to use because, say, it uses a large number of nested menus. This might be fine for a package used intermittently, but not where the system is used for many hours each day. In this case *learnability* has been incorporated at the expense of *operability*.

Characteristic	Sub-characteristics
Efficiency	Time behaviour
	Resource behaviour
Maintainability	Analysability
	Changeability
	Stability
	Testability

Analysability is the quality that McCall called *diagnosability*, the ease with which the cause of a failure can be determined. *Changeability* is the quality that others have called *flexibility*: the latter name is perhaps a better one as *changeability* has a slightly different connotation in plain English – it might implies that the suppliers of the software are always changing it!

Stability, on the other hand, does not mean that the software never changes: it means that there is a low risk of a modification to the software having unexpected effects.

Characteristic	Sub-characteristics
Portability	Adaptability
	Installability
	Conformance
	Replaceability

Conformance, as distinguished from *compliance*, relates to those standards that have a bearing on portability. The use of a standard programming language common to many software/hardware environments would be an example of *conformance*. *Replaceability* refers to the factors that give 'upwards compatibility' between old software components and the new ones. *Downwards* compatibility, is specifically excluded from the definition.

ISO 9126 provides guidelines for the use of the quality characteristics. Variation in the importance of different quality characteristics depending on the type of product is stressed. Thus reliability will be of particular concern with safety critical systems while efficiency will be important for some real time systems. For interactive end-user systems, the key quality might be usability. Once the requirements for the software product have been established, the following steps are suggested:

Quality metrics selection   Measurements which correlate to the characteristics of each quality have to be identified. No specific guidance is given by ISO 9126 on the applicability of various measurements.

Ratings level definition   The metrics used must be mapped onto scales that indicate the degree to which the requirements have been satisfied. For example, in one application 'time behaviour' in the sense of response time might be important. For a key transaction, actual response times might be mapped onto quality scores thus:

response time (seconds)	quality score
<2	5
2–3	4
4–5	3
6–7	2
8–9	1
>9	0

Assessment criteria definition   The way that the quality scores are combined to give an overall view of the product has to be defined. The software product has now to be evaluated by measuring its qualities, converting them to quality scores or ratings, and summarizing the ratings to obtain an overall judgement. ISO 9126 does not specify how this has to be done, only that some method must be devised.

Margin notes:

For example, a new version of a word processing package might read the documents produced by previous versions, but previous versions not be able to read documents created by the new version.

The problem here is to map an objective measurement onto an indicator of customer satisfaction which is subjective.

Table 12.2 Quality rating scores

product quality	importance rating (a)	product A		product B	
		quality score (b)	weighted score (a × b)	quality score (c)	weighted score (a × c)
Usability	3	1	3	3	9
Efficiency	4	2	8	2	8
Maintainability	2	3	6	1	2
Overall			17		19

One approach recognizes some quality rating levels as mandatory. If a product fails to reach a mandatory rating level, it must be rejected regardless of how good it might otherwise be. Other characteristics might be desirable but not essential. A rating in the range 1–5, say, could be assigned to reflect how important they are. Above we have shown how time behaviour in a particular product can be awarded a quality score on a scale 0–5. The scores for the more or less important qualities can be given due weight by multiplying each one by its importance weighting. These weighted scores can then be summed to obtain an overall score for the product. The scores for various products can then be ordered to get a initial scale of preferences. For example, the quality of two products might be compared on usability, efficiency and maintainability. The importance of each of these qualities might be rated as 3, 4 and 2 respectively, out of a possible maximum of 5. Quality tests might result in the scores shown in Table 12.2.

An attempt was made to use the ISO 9126 standard to define the qualities needed in the software to control an unmanned station in the Antarctic which performed scientific experiments that were to be monitored and controlled by satellite link from Italy. It emerged that the qualities required varied from component to component within the system and that therefore quality definition at the level of the overall application was not appropriate. The researchers also found that the most important quality for this application was *availability* which was a mixture of the ISO 9126 top level qualities of reliability and maintainability – separating the two elements was in practice difficult.

12.6 Practical software quality measures

Below are some ways that might be used to measure particular qualities. It is emphasized that the measures are illustrations only and are certainly not definitive! Each project needs to devise its own measures to meet its specific needs. The measures described relate to the final software products of a project.

Reliability

This might be measured in terms of:

- *availability*: the percentage of a particular time interval that a system is usable;
- *mean time between failures*: the total service time divided by the number of failures;

- *failure on demand*: the probability that a system will not be available at the time required or the probability that a transaction will fail;
- *support activity*: the number of fault reports that are generated.

Exercise 12.5

IOE maintenance group accounts system has been installed, and is normally available to users from 8.00 am until 6.00 pm from Monday to Friday. Over a four-week period the system was unavailable for one whole day because of problems with a disc drive and was not available on two other days until 10.00 in the morning because of problems with overnight batch processing runs.

What were the availability and the mean time between failures of the service?

Maintainability

Maintainability can be seen from two different perspectives. The user will be concerned with the *elapsed time* between a fault being detected and it being corrected, while the programming management will be concerned about the *effort involved*.

This is closely related to flexibility, the ease with which the software can be modified. The main difference is that before an amendment can be made, the fault has to be diagnosed. Maintainability can therefore be seen as flexibility plus a new quality *diagnosability* defined as the average time to diagnose a fault.

Extendibility

This is a component of the more general quality of flexibility. It can be defined as the productivity needed to incorporate a new feature into an existing system expressed as a percentage of the normal productivity when developing the software from scratch.

CASE STUDY EXAMPLES

The original IOE maintenance billing system comprised 5000 SLOC and took 400 work-days to implement. An amendment to the core system caused by the introduction of group accounts has led to 100 SLOC being added which took 20 work-days to implement, thus:

productivity for the original system
= 5000/400
= 12.5 SLOC/staff-day

productivity for the amendment
= 100/20
= 5 SLOC/staff-day

extendibility
= 5/12.5 × 100
= 40%

12.7 Product versus process quality management

The measurements described above can only be taken once the system is operational. It could then be too late to remedy problems. What would be more

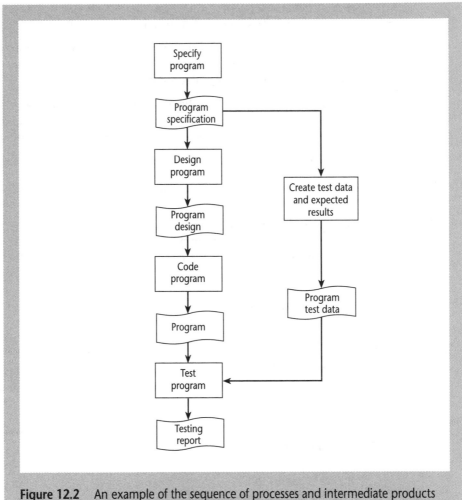

Figure 12.2 An example of the sequence of processes and intermediate products

helpful to someone such as Amanda at IOE are measurements taken during development which can help control what the final application will be like.

The system development process is made up of a number of activities that are linked together so that the output from one activity is the input to the next (Figure 12.2). Thus program testing will depend on there being a program to test which will be the deliverable from the program coding stage. Errors can enter the process at any stage. They can either be introduced because of a defect in the way a process is carried out, as when a programmer makes a mistake in the logic of their program, or because information has not been passed clearly and unambiguously between stages.

Errors that creep in at the early stages are more expensive to correct at later stages for the following reasons.

- The later the error is found the more rework at more stages of development will be needed. An error in the specification found in testing will mean rework at all the stages between specification and testing.

This model should already be very familiar from the discussion of precedence networks where the dependence of one or more activities on the completion of one or more preceding activities is taken into account.

- The general tendency is for each successive stage of development to be more detailed and less able to absorb change.

Errors should therefore be eradicated by careful examination of the deliverables of each stage before they are passed on to the next. To do this, the following *process requirements* should be specified for each activity.

> These requirements may be laid out in installation standards, or a *Software Quality Plan* may be drawn up for the specific project if it is a major one.

- *Entry requirements* which have to be in place before an activity can start. An example would be that a comprehensive set of test data and expected results be prepared and approved before program testing can commence.
- *Implementation requirements* which define how the process is to be conducted. In the testing phase, for example, it could be laid down that whenever an error is found and corrected, all test runs must be repeated, even those that have previously been found to run correctly.
- *Exit requirements* which have to be fulfilled before an activity is deemed to have been completed. For example, for the testing phase to be recognized as being completed, all tests will have to have been run successfully with no outstanding errors.

Exercise 12.6 In what cases might the entry conditions for one activity be different from the exit conditions for another activity that immediately precedes it?

Exercise 12.7 Amanda at IOE already has a quality manual that she can consult. Brigette at Brightmouth College has to specify her own entry and exit requirements. What might she specify as the entry and exit requirements for the process *code program* shown in Figure 12.2?

12.8 External standards

BS EN ISO 9001:2000

> The British standard for Quality Management systems was previously called BS 5750. ISO 9001:2000 replaces a previous, 1994, standard.

At IOE, a decision might have been made to use an outside contractor to produce the maintenance group accounts sub-system rather than develop the software in-house. As a client using the services of an outside contractor it would be concerned that the contractor follows the best quality practices. It is now common to include in contracts terms covering the types of technique that a contractor will use. Various national and international standards bodies, including the British Standards Institution (BSI) in the United Kingdom, have inevitably got involved in the creation of standards for quality management systems. The British standard is now called BS EN ISO 9001:2000, which is identical to the international standard, ISO 9001:2000. Standards such as ISO 9000 series try to ensure that a monitoring and control system to check quality is in place. They are concerned with the certification of the development process, not of the end-product as in the case of crash helmets and electrical appliances with their familiar kite-marks. The ISO 9000 series govern quality systems in general terms and not just those in the software development environment.

ISO 9000 describes the fundamental features of a quality management system (QMS) and defines the terminology used. ISO 9001 describes how a QMS can be applied to the creation of products and the provision of services. ISO 9004 applies to ISO 9000 to process improvement.

There has been some controversy over the value of these standards. Stephen Halliday, writing in *The Observer*, had misgivings that these standards are taken by many customers to imply that the final product is of a certified standard although as Halliday says: '*It has nothing to do with the quality of the product going out of the gate. You set down your own specifications and just have to maintain them, however low they may be*'. It has also been suggested that obtaining certification can be an expensive and time-consuming process which can put smaller, but still well-run, businesses at a disadvantage. Finally, there has been a concern that a preoccupation with certification might distract attention from the real problems of producing quality products.

Putting aside these reservations, let us examine how the standard works. A primary task is to identify those things which are to be the subject of quality requirements. Having defined the requirements, a system must be put in place which checks that the requirements are being fulfilled and that corrective action is being taken where necessary.

An overview of BS EN ISO 9001:2000 QMS requirements

Remember that these standards are designed for all kinds of production – not just software development.

The standard is built on a foundation of the following principles:

- understanding by an organization of the needs of their customers so that they can meet, or even exceed, those requirements;
- leadership to provide the unity of purpose and direction needed to achieve quality objectives;
- involvement of staff at all levels;
- a focus on the individual processes carried out which create intermediate or deliverable products and services;
- a focus on the systems of interrelated processes that create delivered products and services;
- continuous improvement of processes;
- decision-making based on factual evidence;
- building mutually beneficial relationships with suppliers.

The way that these principles are applied is through cycles which involve the following activities:

1. Determining the needs and expectations of the customer.
2. Establishing a *quality policy*, that is, a framework with which allows the organization's objectives in relation to quality to be defined. The actual objectives can then be established.
3. Design the *processes* which will create the products (or deliver the services) which will have the qualities implied in the organization's quality objectives.
4. Allocate responsibilities for meeting these requirements for each element of each process.
5. Ensure that adequate resources are available for the proper execution of these processes.
6. Devise methods of measuring the effectiveness and efficiency of each process in contributing to the organization's quality objectives.

7. Collect measurements.

8. Identify any discrepancies between the actual measurements and the target values.

9. Analyse the causes of discrepancies and action to take to eliminate these causes.

The procedures above should be designed and executed in such a way that there is continual improvement. They should, if carried out properly, lead to an effective QMS. More detailed ISO 9001 requirements include:

- *Documentation* of objectives, procedures (in the form of a *quality manual*), plans, and records relating to the actual operation of processes. The documentation must be subject to a change control system that ensures that it is current. Essentially one needs to be able to demonstrate to an outsider that the QMS exists and is actually adhered to.

- *Management responsibility* – the organization needs to show that the QMS and the processes that produce goods and services that conform to the quality objectives are actively and properly managed.

- *Resources* – an organization must ensure that adequate resources, including appropriately trained staff and appropriate infrastructure, are applied to the processes.

- *Production* should be characterized by:
  - planning;
  - determination and review of customer requirements;
  - effective communications between the customer and supplier being established;
  - design and development subject to planning, control and review;
  - requirements and other information upon which the design is based being adequately and clearly recorded;
  - design outcomes being verified, validated and documented in a way that provides sufficient information for those who have to use the designs; changes to the designs should be properly controlled;
  - where components are purchased, there should be adequate measures to specify and evaluate their quality;
  - production of goods and the provision of services should be under controlled conditions – these conditions include the adequate provision of information, work instruction, equipment, measurement devices, and post-delivery activities;
  - measurement – to demonstrate products conform to standards, and the QMS is effective, and to improve the effectiveness of processes that create products or services.

Exercise 12.8

One of the processes involved in developing software is system testing and any subsequent modifications to the application in the light of errors found. If a software development organization were to attempt to conform to BS EN ISO 9001:2000, how might this affect system testing?

Exercise 12.9

Bearing in mind the criticisms of BS EN ISO 9001 that have been mentioned, what precautionary steps could a project manger take where some work of which the quality is important is to be contracted out to a supplier with certification?

Capability process models

See H. S. Watts, *Managing the Software Process*, Addison-Wesley, New York, 1989.

Rather than just checking that a system is in place to detect faults, a customer might wish to check that a supplier is using software development methods and tools which are likely to produce good quality software. A customer might feel more confident, for instance, if they know that their software supplier is using structured methods. In the United States, an influential *capability maturity model* (CMM) has been developed at the Software Engineering Institute (SEI), a part of the Carnegie-Mellon University. This attempts to place organizations producing software at one of five levels of process maturity which indicate the sophistication and quality of their software production practices. These levels are defined as follows:

The SEI originally developed CMM for the US Department of Defense who wanted to be able to assess the capability of contractors from whom they procured software.

- *Level 1: Initial* The procedures followed tend to be haphazard. Some projects might be successful, but this tends to be because of the skills of particular individuals including project managers. The is no level 0 and so any organization would be at this level by default.

- *Level 2: Repeatable* Organizations at this level will have basic project management procedures in place. However, the way individual tasks are carried out will depend largely on the person doing it.

- *Level 3: Defined* The organization has defined the way that each task in the software development life cycle should be done.

- *Level 4: Managed* The products and processes involved in software development are subject to measurement and control.

- *Level 5: Optimizing* Improvement in procedures can be designed and implemented using the data gathered from the measurement process.

For each of the levels, apart from the default level 1, *key process areas* (KPAs) have been identified as distinguishing the current level from the lower ones. These are listed in the Table 12.3.

The assessment is done by a team of assessors coming into the organization and interviewing key staff about their practices using a standard questionnaire to capture the information. A key objective is not just to assess, but to recommend specific actions to bring the organization up to a higher level.

Table 12.3 CMM Key process areas

Level	Key process areas
1. Initial	Not applicable
2. Managed	Configuration management, quality assurance, sub-contract management, project tracking and oversight, project planning
3. Defined	Peer reviews, inter-group coordination, software product engineering, integrated software management, training programme, organization process definition and focus
4. Managed	Quality management, process measurement and analysis
5. Optimizing	Process change management, technology innovation, defect prevention

Bootstrap also caters for ratings between the major levels, e.g. at 2.6 which indicates that the project is better than level 2, but not yet up to a level 3 standard.

A criticism has been made of the approach that it is unrealistic to try to assess an organization as a whole – in reality there will be major differences between the way that individual projects are conducted. *Bootstrap*, which is a European initiative along the same lines as CMM, does allow assessment to be done at a project level.

Assessing software products

The concern in the last two sections has been with the assessment of organizations and the processes that they use to produce software, but many purchasers of software, including project managers contemplating the purchase of software tools may be more directly worried about the quality of the software product itself. Compilers for some programming languages, for example, are subject to certification. Much progress, however, has still to be made in this area.

12.9 Techniques to help enhance software quality

So far in this chapter we have looked at the steps a customer might take to ensure the quality of software produced by an outside supplier. We now need to look at what techniques a project team might wish to employ to help them improve their own software development processes. Three main themes emerge.

Gerald Weinberg, *The Psychology of Computer Programming*, Van Nostrand Reinhold, 1971.

- *Increasing visibility*   A landmark in this movement towards making the software development process more visible was the advocacy by the American software guru, Gerald Weinberg, of 'egoless programming'. Weinberg encouraged the simple practice of programmers looking at each other's code.

- *Procedural structure*   At first programmers were more or less left to get on with writing the programs although there might be some general guidelines. Over the years there has been the growth of methodologies where every process in the software development cycle has carefully laid down steps.

The creation of an early working model of a system may still be useful as the creation of prototypes shows.

- *Checking intermediate stages*   It seems inherent in human nature to push forward quickly with the development of any engineered object until a 'working' model, however imperfect, has been produced which can then be 'debugged'. One of the elements of the move towards quality practices has been to put emphasis on checking the correctness of work at its earlier, conceptual, stages.

We are now going to look at some specific techniques in more detail. The push towards more visibility has been dominated by the increasing use of walkthroughs, inspections and reviews. The movement towards more procedural structure inevitably leads to discussion of structured programming techniques and to its later manifestation in the ideas of 'clean-room' software development.

The interest in the dramatic improvements made by the Japanese in product quality has led to much discussion of the quality techniques they have adopted such as the use of quality circles and these will be looked at briefly. Some of these ideas are variations on the theme of inspection and clean-room development, but they are seen from a slightly different angle.

Inspections

The principle of inspection can be extended to any document produced at any stage of the development process. For instance, test cases need to be reviewed – their production is usually not a high-profile task even though errors can get through to operational running because of their poor quality.

Inspection means that when a piece of work is completed, copies of the work are distributed to co-workers who then examine the work noting defects. A meeting is then held to discuss the work and a list of defects requiring rework is produced. The work to be examined could be, for instance, a program listing that is free of compilation errors.

Our own experience of using this technique has been that:

- it is a very effective way of removing superficial errors;
- it motivates developers to produce better structured and self-explanatory software because they know that other people will be criticizing it;
- it helps spread good programming practices as the participants discuss the advantages and disadvantages of specific pieces of code;
- it can enhance team spirit.

> The main problem is maintaining the commitment of participants to a thorough examination of the work they have been allocated after the novelty value of reviews has worn off.

The item will usually be reviewed by colleagues who are involved in the same area of work, so that programmers, for example, will have their work reviewed by fellow programmers. However, to reduce the problems of incorrect communication between different stages there may be representatives from the stages that precede and follow the one which produced the work under review.

> See M. E. Fagan's article 'Design and code inspections to reduce errors in program development', *IBM Systems Journal*, 15(3).

IBM have put the review process on a more structured and formal basis, and produced statistics to show its effectiveness. A Fagan inspection (named after the IBM employee who pioneered the technique) is a more formalized procedure which is led, not by the author of the work, but by a specially trained 'moderator'.

The general principles behind the Fagan method

- Inspections are carried out on all major deliverables.
- All types of defect are noted – not just logic or function errors.
- Inspections can be carried out by colleagues at all levels except the very top.
- Inspections are carried out using a pre-defined set of steps.
- Inspection meetings do not last for more than two hours.
- The inspection is led by a *moderator* who has had specific training in the technique.
- The other participants have defined roles. For example, one person will act as a *recorder* and note all defects found and another will act as *reader* and take the other participants through the document under inspection.
- Checklists are used to assist the fault-finding process.
- Material is inspected at an optimal rate of about 100 lines an hour.
- Statistics are maintained so that the effectiveness of the inspection process can be monitored.

Exercise 12.10

This exercise needs to be done in groups. Select for review a small program that has been written by one of your colleagues.

Choose a moderator, a reader and a recorder for the group. Spend about 20 minutes examining listings of the program individually and then come together to review the code jointly.

Structured programming and clean-room software development

E. W. Dijkstra in 1968 wrote a letter to a learned computing journal which was entitled 'Go To Statement Considered Harmful'. This unfortunately led to the common idea that structured programming was simply about not using GO TOs.

One of the people most closely associated with the origins of structured pro-gramming is Dijkstra. In the late 1960s, software was seen to be getting more complex while the capacity of the human mind to hold detail remained limited. It was also realized that it was impossible to test any substantial piece of software completely – there were just too many possible combinations of inputs. Testing, at best, could prove the presence of errors, not their absence. It was suggested by Dijkstra and others that, because of this, the only way that we could reassure ourselves about the correctness of software was by actually looking at the code.

The way to deal with complex systems, it was contended, was to break them down into components which were of a size for the human mind to comprehend. For a large system there would be a hierarchy of components and sub-components. For this decomposition to work properly, each component would have to be self-contained with only one entry and exit point.

The ideas of structured programming were further developed into the ideas of clean-room software development by people such as Harlan Mills of IBM. With this type of development there are three separate teams:

- a *specification team* which obtains the user requirements and also a *usage profile* estimating the volume of use for each feature in the system;
- a *development team* which develops the code but which does no machine testing of the program code produced;
- a *certification team* which carries out testing.

The incremental approach was discussed in Chapter 4.

Any system is produced in increments each of which should be capable of actual operation by the end user. The development team does no debugging; instead, all software has to be verified by them using mathematical techniques. The argument is that software which is constructed by throwing up a crude program which then has test data thrown at it and a series of hit-and-miss amendments made to it until it works is bound to be unreliable.

The certification team carry out the testing which is continued until a statistical model shows that the failure intensity has been reduced to an acceptable level.

Formal methods

The section on clean-room development mentioned the use of mathematical verification techniques. These techniques use unambiguous, mathematically-based, specification languages of which Z and VDM are examples. They are used to define *pre-conditions* and *post-conditions* for each procedure. Pre-conditions define the allowable states, before processing, of the various items of data upon which a procedure is to work. The post-conditions define the state of those data items after the procedure has been executed. Because the mathematical notation is precise, a specification expressed in this way should be unambiguous. It should also be possible to prove mathematically (in much the same way that at school you learnt to prove Pythagoras' theorem) that a particular algorithm will work on the data defined by the pre-conditions in such a way as to produce the post-conditions. It need hardly be pointed out that in many cases this will be more easily said than done. In fact structured programming can be seen as an attempt to analyse a program structure into small, self-contained, procedures that will be amenable to this formal verification approach.

Software quality circles

Much interest has been shown in Japanese software quality practices. The aim of the 'Japanese' approach is to examine and modify the activities in the development process in order to reduce the number of errors that they have in their end-products. Testing and Fagan inspections can assist the removal of errors – but the same types of error could occur repeatedly in successive products created by a process. By uncovering the source of errors, this repetition can be eliminated

Staff are involved in the identification of sources of errors through the formation of *quality circles*. These can be set up in all departments of an organization including those producing software where they are known as software quality circles (SWQC).

A quality circle is a group of four to ten volunteers working in the same area who meet for, say, an hour a week to identify, analyse and solve their work-related problems. One of their number is the group leader and there could be an outsider, a *facilitator*, who can advise on procedural matters. In order to make the quality circle work effectively training needs to be given.

Problem solving by quality circles

The steps that the circle go through in solving problems are:

(a) identify a list of problems;

(b) select one problem to solve;

(c) clarify the problem;

(d) identify and evaluate the causes;

(e) identify and evaluate the solutions;

(f) decide on a solution;

(g) develop an implementation plan;

(h) present the plan to management;

(i) implement the plan;

(j) monitor the plan;

(k) consider wider applicability of solution;

(l) restart from (b).

Exercise 12.11

What are the important differences between a quality circle and a review group?

People may feel inhibited from contributing ideas to a group and brainstorming can help to reduce this inhibition.

A number of specific techniques characterize quality circles, the most prominent of which is *brainstorming*. A subject or problem for which ideas are needed is nominated and the group then suggest as many ideas as possible. As ideas are suggested they are written down on a flip-chart. Other members of the group do not, at this stage, make any comments or criticisms of any suggestions made. At the end of the session the group go through the ideas listed and put similar ideas together and combine overlapping ideas. Typically this technique would be used to generate the initial list of problems or a list of possible solutions to a particular problem.

Also associated with quality circles is the compilation of *most probable error lists*. For example, at IOE, Amanda might find that the maintenance group accounts project is being delayed because of errors in the requirements specifications. The project team could be assembled and spend some time producing a list of the most common types of error that occur in requirements specifications. This is then used to identify actions which can reduce the occurrence of each type of error. They might suggest, for instance, that test cases be produced at the same time as the requirements specification and that these test cases should be dry run at an inspection. Another result might be a checklist for use when conducting inspections of requirement specifications.

Exercise 12.12	This exercise has to be carried out as a group. Select a particular area of common experience where problems have arisen in the past. For example, if you are a group of students you could use the course or module you are undertaking, or a recent assignment that you have just completed. By means of a brainstorming session, identify all the problems that the participants have had. At the end of the brainstorming session, group together similar problems and combine overlapping ones.

The problems needing crisis management are often technical in nature. Quality circles can encourage problem-solving activity at lower levels of the organization and prevent crises occurring as their causes are tackled.

The effectiveness of quality circles

For quality circles to work there must be full support for them at all levels of management. First-line management might feel threatened by them as they might appear to undermine their authority. After all, problem solving is one of their main tasks. The proponents of quality circles see them as a way of giving management more time for planning and development. Any manager will have to devote time to 'fire-fighting' dealing with *ad hoc* crises, and this can detract from longer term activities which will be able to improve the effectiveness of the organization.

12.10 Quality plans

Some organizations produce *quality plans*. These, in essence, show how the standard quality procedures and standards that should be laid down in an organization's *quality manual* will actually be applied to a particular project. If an approach to planning such as Step Wise has been followed, quality-related activities and requirements should have been dealt with by the main planning process and a separate quality plan would not be required. However, where software is being produced for an external customer then their quality assurance staff might require the equivalent of a quality plan to make sure that the delivered products are likely to be of high quality. A quality plan might also be required as a kind of checklist that all quality issues have been dealt with by the planning process. In this case most of the content will be references to various other documents.

A quality plan might have entries for:

This contents list is based on a draft IEEE standard for software quality assurance plans.

- purpose – scope of plan;
- list of references to other documents;
- management, including organization, tasks and responsibilities;
- documentation to be produced;
- standards, practices and conventions;

- reviews and audits;
- testing;
- problem reporting and corrective action;
- tools, techniques and methodologies;
- code, media and supplier control;
- records collection, maintenance and retention;
- training;
- risk management – the methods of risk management that are to be used,

12.11 Conclusions

Important points to remember about software quality include the following:

- Quality by itself is a vague concept and practical quality requirements have to be carefully defined.
- There have to be practical ways of testing for the relative presence or absence of a quality.
- Most of the qualities that are apparent to the users of software can only be tested for when the system is completed.
- Ways of checking during development the likely quality of the final system are therefore needed.
- Some quality enhancing techniques concentrate on testing the products of the development process while others try to evaluate the quality of the development processes used.

12.12 Further exercises

1. McCall suggests that simplicity, modularity, instrumentation and self-descriptiveness are software quality criteria, i.e. internal characteristics that promote the external quality of testability.

   (a) Explain what is meant by each of the four criteria above.
   (b) Describe possible measures for each of the criteria.
   (c) Describe practical ways in which the measures could be assessed.

2. Discuss how meaningful the following measurements are.

   (a) The number of error messages produced on the first compilation of a program.
   (b) The average effort to implement changes requested by users to a system.
   (c) The percentage of lines in program listings that are comments.
   (d) The number of pages in a requirements document.

3. How might you measure the effectiveness of a user manual for a software package? Consider both the measurements that might be applicable and the procedures by which the measurements might be taken.

4. What might the entry, implementation and exit requirements be for the process *design program structure*?

5. Identify a task that you do as part of your everyday work. For that task identify entry, process and exit requirements.

6. What BS EN ISO 9001 requirements have a bearing on the need for an effective configuration management system?

Small projects

13.1 Introduction

Many of the readers of this book are students who will have to plan their own projects that they will have to carry out as part of their course of studies. In some cases, these will be undertaken for an external client. In other cases, a piece of software, perhaps of an experimental nature, is to be produced where there is no identifiable client, apart from a project tutor. Although the projects that are carried out for 'real' clients are more convincing tests of the student, they are in many ways more risky than the purely academic ones.

One of the problems that students face when planning projects is applying techniques that they have learnt on software project planning courses and that were designed for much larger scale projects than their own. In this chapter we present an outline of how students should set out their plans. It is based on a structure that we have recommended to our own students over the years. It contrasts with the material in Appendix A on PRINCE 2, which is designed to support the management of large projects. The overall Step Wise approach is still applicable to the planning of your project – but the techniques used at the different steps of the planning process will need to be carefully chosen as appropriate to the scaled-down application.

13.2 Some problems with student projects

Note that here we are discussing a practical application of the risk identification and avoidance policies.

There are some problems or risks that seem particularly to affect student projects.

Use of unfamiliar tools

Very often students will be using a new software tool (for example, an application builder in a Windows environment) that they have not used before. Clearly, time

251

will need to be allocated in the project plan to learning the package. When trying to formulate plans, because of their ignorance of the software tool, students might have difficulties estimating how long tasks will take. There will also be risks that unexpected technical problems will halt or delay the project's progress. Students often have other things on their minds, such as examinations, in the period leading up to the start of the project, but the risks of technical problems will be reduced if they are able to try out the software tools at this point.

If you are really keen to learn about and use a new tool, you might consider framing the objectives of the project to include an evaluation of the tool. Technical difficulties then become transformed from being obstacles to being interesting data.

Uncertain design requirements

Many project assignments require students to demonstrate a careful analysis and design process and then to build at least part of the application. Until the analysis has been done, it can be difficult to plan exactly how design and software building is to be executed.

Two points are worth making here. The first is that the structure of the project is going to be dictated to a large extent by the amount of time available.

Say that you have ten weeks in which to carry out a project that involves analysing user requirements, designing a new system and building it. It is not a bad idea to start planning on the basis of doing the project in nine weeks in order to allow for slippage. Working backwards from the end, of those nine weeks, it might be decided that the last two should be reserved for testing and evaluation. This might seem an excessive amount of time to some students, but with most assessment schemes your project is likely to gain really good marks if you can demonstrate that it is of good quality and that you have evaluated it carefully. You might decide to allocate proportions of the remaining first seven weeks to analysis, design and system building so that you get the following skeleton schedule:

- *weeks 1–2*: analysis;
- *week 3*: design;
- *weeks 4–7*: system building;
- *weeks 8–9*: testing and evaluation;
- *week 10*: contingency.

The actual breakdown will vary, depending on the circumstances of your particular project. A very well-structured problem area means that you can spend less time on analysis, while, on the other hand, if you know the software building tools that you are going to use, you might decide to reduce the time for analysis in favour of devoting more effort to a more sophisticated operator interface.

In Chapter 6 we discussed the practice of design to cost, that is, designing the system to fit the resources available to build it.

The second point, and one that we have already emphasized, is that you should be prepared to delay planning a particular phase of a project in detail until more information becomes available. When you have completed your analysis phase at the end of the second week in the above plan, you should be in a much better position to plan the design and system building phases in more detail – you will know, for example, what the main transactions are going to be in an information systems application. You should also be in a position to cut down the scope of the application to fit the time available to build it!

Incomplete systems

In Chapter 4 we discussed the incremental approach which is relevant here.

Sometimes students simply run out of time and so do not have a working system to demonstrate. In the case of student projects, it is a good idea to try to arrange things so that you have something, even if it is not much, to demonstrate from a relatively early stage of the project. In the skeleton plan described above, it would not be a bad idea to have certain features of the application up and running after the first week or so of system building. Having these 'in the bag' so to speak, you can go on and add new functions or features, secure in the knowledge that at any point you will have at least something to demonstrate. You might find that you can even break the work down into increments to give you something similar to the following:

- *weeks 1–2*: analysis;
- *week 3*: design increment 1;
- *week 4*: build/test increment 1;
- *week 5*: design increment 2;
- *week 6*: build/test increment 2;
- *week 7*: design increment 3;
- *week 8*: build/test increment 3;
- *week 9*: evaluate complete system;
- *week 10*: writing up/contingency.

If something went wrong so that increment 3 could not be completed on time, you would still have increments 1 and 2 to demonstrate and in your project evaluation report you could describe your proposed design for increment 3.

In the skeleton plan above, we have allocated week 10 for writing up. As a general rule, it is best to try to write up as much of your project as you can as you go along. It will not save you any time if you leave it and you will be able to write more clearly and fully about your analysis process, for example, while it is still clear in your mind. Pausing to do this writing should also help you to reflect on what you are doing and help you consider coolly what needs to be done next.

Lack of commitment from clients

In most cases, where a project is for an external client, the student will not be being paid. The advantage of this is that the outside organization might be attracted to the chance of having a free resource and take on a project for a student about whose capabilities they know little or nothing. The danger is that because the resource is free, there will be little commitment from the client to the project. If they had to pay for the work, they would think more carefully about whether they really needed the work before agreeing to the project and they would pay attention to getting value for money.

There is no such thing as a completely free project, even when the student's efforts are free. The student might need access to hardware and software facilities to be provided by the client and even where this is not the case, the client needs to be prepared to give up some spare time to discuss requirements and to evaluate intermediate results. It has to be said that sometimes clients can let students down as far as this is concerned. Our advice to students would be to try to get to know your client thoroughly before the project starts. Try, for instance, to meet all the people in the organization who will be affected by your work before you actually get going on the project. Show a copy of your initial project plan to the clients and get them to comment on it. Arrange beforehand to have regular meetings with them to discuss progress.

13.3   Content of a project plan

We discuss below what should be in your project planning document. It is suggested that the plans for small projects being done for outside clients should follow this format. Specific course requirements (for example, learning objectives) are not covered.

1   Introduction

In the introduction to any document, it is always a good idea to explain briefly what the document is and why it has been produced. The introduction to the project plan should also include:

- identity of client – that is, the organization or department for whom the work is to be done;
- short description of project – not more than two or three brief lines;
- identity of the project authority – the person or persons within the client organization who will have authority over the project's direction. It is essential that such an authority be identified.

2   Background

This includes:

- relevant information about the client's business;
- descriptions of the existing software/hardware environment;
- circumstances or problems leading to the current project;
- work already carried out in the area of the project;
- stakeholders in the projects, in other words, all those who will be affected by the project or who have some other interest in it.

3   Objectives of the project

These might already have been defined in a terms of reference (TOR) document. If so, then it can be attached as an appendix to the plan.

   The objectives must define what is to be achieved and the method of measuring the extent of that achievement. One problem with small projects conducted by students is that the project's success is evaluated in course terms soon after its completion, whereas the project's true value to the users will take much longer to emerge (if ever!). As this document is in part for the benefit of the client, the objectives from the client's viewpoint should have the emphasis here.

   Students sometimes have problems distinguishing between their personal objectives and those of the project. The project objectives are those that are held

Objectives and goals were discussed in Chapter 1.

in common between the client and the developer in relation to the project. For example, a university student could be producing a timetabling system for a local school. The creation of this timetabling system would be a project objective shared by the developer (the student) and the client (the school). The student will also have a personal objective of getting a good grade that is not shared by the school (although they will usually be sympathetic to it). From the viewpoint of the student's personal objectives the creation of the timetabling system is seen as a sub-objective, or goal, a step on the way to achieving the overarching objective of getting the good grade.

Where there are several objectives, an order of priority should be given to them if this is possible.

4   Constraints

It is convenient to merge this into the project objectives, above. Constraints include:

- externally imposed time scales;
- legal requirements;
- specific standards;
- limitations on the people who can be approached for information.

5   Methods/technology to be used

These might have already have been laid down for you, or it might be that part of the project will involve the selection of the most appropriate technologies and methods. In other cases, you need to specify the general approach you will take – for instance that you are going to use a structured systems analysis and design method (like SSADM), or a soft system methodology (like SSM) approach. In a small project it is unlikely that you will have time for a full structured analysis/design approach and you might decide to use a subset of the techniques – this should be specified.

The methods selected will, of course, govern much of what will go into Section 6 below on project products and Section 7 on activities. When discussing prototypes, we emphasized that a prototype should always be a tool for learning or clarifying something (for instance, the best interface for the user). If you claim you are producing a prototype, you must be prepared to define learning objectives for the prototype, a method of evaluation and an analysis of what has been learnt.

If you are developing software, the choice of software tools should be stated in this section.

Some justification of the decisions made here should be given, as they can be crucial to the success of the project.

The training and other resource requirements (perhaps the need to purchase a particular package) that result from the decisions should be noted.

6   Project products

This is a list of all the products or deliverables that the project will produce, such as software modules, documentation, user guides and reports.

Intermediate products, such as design documents, should be included.

7 Activities

The drawing up of a Product Flow Diagram helps to bridge between the product list and the activity plan – see Chapter 2.

This is a list of the main activities that the project will involve. There must be activities to produce all the products listed in Section 6. Also, in general, each activity should result in some deliverable: avoid tasks like 'familiarization with departmental procedures' in favour of 'documentation of departmental procedures'. In identifying activities, new interim products will often be discovered.

For each activity, define:

- *pre-requisites*: what has to be done before this activity can start;
- *dependent activities*: activities that need this one to be completed first;
- *estimated time/effort*: this may be a range of values;
- *quality checks*: details of how you are going to verify and validate the product of the activity.

PERT or Gantt charts may be used, but are often not needed.

8 Resources

This includes staff time, accommodation and hardware/software requirements.

9 Risk analysis

Identify the main things that can be seen as possibly going wrong. Typically this might include:

- unavailability of resources (as with a delay in getting a software package);
- unavailability of key client personnel;
- technical problems (such as software bugs).

Roughly a probability of 2 means 2 chances out of 10 of it occuring

A priority can be given to each risk by allocating a *probability rating* (1–10) and a seriousness of *impact rating* (1–10). Multiplying the two together gives an overall score for priority purposes.

For the most serious risks (those with the highest scores), *preventive* measures to reduce or remove the risk should be specified. For example, in order to prevent problems with the unavailability of key client personnel, meetings must be arranged with them at the planning stage and holiday plans could be ascertained. In some cases *contingency* measures that can be undertaken once the risk has actually materialized are more appropriate.

13.4 Conclusions

In this chapter, we have tried to show how some of the broader issues of project planning that have been covered elsewhere in the book can be related to the kind of task a student might be asked to undertake as a project. On the other hand, a student undertaking a substantial industrial placement might be involved in a project team undertaking a large project and using a method such as PRINCE 2, described in Appendix A, to control the project.

Important points to remember include:

- take care when using techniques or tools that are completely new to you in a project;
- you will have to adjust the scope of your project to fit the time available;
- take steps to maintain the commitment of the client to your 'free' project;
- recognize the distinction between the project objectives and your personal objectives;
- avoid planning activities for which there is no tangible result – such as 'familiarization'.

PRINCE 2 – an overview

A.1 Introduction to PRINCE 2

The CCTA is the Central Computer and Telecommunications Agency, which, among other things, recommends standards for UK government IT projects. It is the owner of PRINCE. PRINCE® is the CCTA's registered trademark.

Large organizations can have a number of software and other projects being executed at the same time. Some of these might use external suppliers of products and services. In such an environment it would be helpful if the procedures by which each project were run were standardized rather than having to be continually reinvented. However, each project will make different demands on management: some, for example, might be more technically challenging, or might affect particularly critical areas of the business or might involve larger numbers of different types of users. Because the adoption of a management method is not cost-free, the degree of control that will be cost-effective will vary from project to project. Hence any standard approach should incorporate mechanisms to tailor management procedures and structures to suit localized needs. In the UK, the government has sponsored, through the CCTA, a set of such procedures, called PRINCE, which has, after several years, been revised as PRINCE 2.

PRINCE stands for 'PRojects IN Controlled Environments'.

The precursor to PRINCE was a project management method called PROMPT, which suffered from the defect that it was not flexible enough to deal adequately with all types of project. This was followed by the first version of PRINCE, which was designed primarily for an IT development environment so that, for example, it was made to have a good fit with SSADM. It soon became apparent, however, that the method was applicable to projects outside the strictly IT domain and PRINCE 2 makes no specific references to IT development.

It is now possible to take examinations in PRINCE 2 and to be thus recognized as a PRINCE practitioner.

A.2 The components of PRINCE 2

The method does not claim to cover all aspects of project management. It has the following components:

- organization;
- planning;
- controls;

- stages;
- management of risk;
- quality;
- configuration management;
- change control.

The following list provides a convenient structure that we will use to explain PRINCE 2:

- techniques;
- organization;
- documentation;
- procedures.

This appendix will not explore the supplementary techniques where the PRINCE 2 manual lays down some basic requirements. We do not describe these areas in detail since there is sufficient material elsewhere in this book. They include:

- risk management;
- quality management;
- configuration management;
- change control.

Below, we will outline the general approach to planning that PRINCE 2 advocates. It will be noted that PRINCE 2, compared, for example, to SSADM, is rather light in its description of techniques. It is stronger in its rules for the project management structures that should be adopted. In our view, its main focus is on the project as an information system. Project management information is identified and the procedures by which the various elements of this information are created, processed and used are described at some length. This project information is mainly associated with the delivery of *products*, in a controlled environment, resulting in benefits to the business.

A.3 PRINCE planning technique

The Step Wise approach was outlined in Chapter 2, while risk was discussed in Chapter 7.

Figure A.1 shows the stages in the planning process that are suggested by PRINCE 2. The first of these – *Design a plan* – is essentially deciding what kind of information is to go into the plan, particularly at what level of detail the plan is to be drawn. The remaining steps are very similar to the Step Wise approach to planning that was outlined in Chapter 2, except that in the Step Wise approach the risk analysis was carried out immediately after the estimation of effort for each activity. This was because in our view risk identification follows on naturally from estimation: you work out how long you think it will take to do an activity and then you consider what factors could work to make that estimate incorrect. Also, the identification of risks can lead to new activities' being introduced to avoid the risks occurring and this is conveniently done before the schedule is put together by allocating resources. However, the Step Wise approach is not necessarily at odds with PRINCE 2 as PRINCE 2 does emphasize the iterative nature of risk analysis.

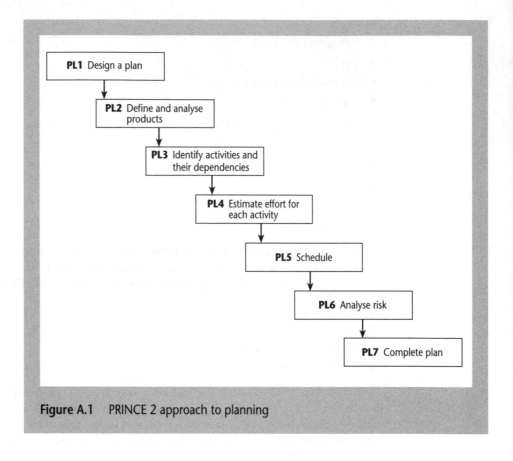

Figure A.1   PRINCE 2 approach to planning

Like Step Wise, PRINCE 2 is very product-based. In the second planning phase, PL2 in Figure A.1, all the business products, plus the management and quality documents needed to control their delivery, are identified.

This sequence of steps can be used in several places in the PRINCE 2 procedural framework to produce a variety of different types of plan.

A.4 PRINCE 2 project organization

PRINCE identifies roles rather than jobs. Depending on the circumstances, a role could, in fact, be carried out by more that one person, or a single person could assume more than one role.

PRINCE 2 is based on the perception that the project will involve *users* of the products of the project, on the one hand, and *suppliers* of goods and services needed by the project on the other. While the users and suppliers could in fact belong to the same organization, for management and control purposes the two sides need to be carefully distinguished. Furthermore, on the customer side, two management roles exist. Any development project is carried out, not for its own sake, but to do something useful for the customer organization. The *Executive* role has the responsibility of ensuring that the project continues to meet these business requirements. A danger, for example, is that development costs might grow in such a way that they exceed any benefits of the completed project. The customer side will also, of course, contain the community who will actually use the completed system on a day-to-day basis. Although we have talked about the supplier and customer sides, it could also be argued that the suppliers who will provide the system and the users who will operate it need to cooperate together to ensure that the operational system provides the benefits sought after by their customer, the 'Executive'.

PRINCE 2 specifies that the three roles of *Executive, Supplier* and *User* are represented on a *Project Board* which has overall accountability for the success of the project and responsibility for the commitment of resources.

The senior staff carrying out the respective roles will be responsible officers within their respective organizations and the oversight of the project will probably be only one of many responsibilities. Hence, the task of managing the project on a day-to-day basis will be delegated by the Project Board to a *Project Manager*. On a large project it could be necessary for the Project Manager to delegate the managing of certain aspects of the project to specialist *Team Managers*.

Conscientious and motivated staff will inevitably focus on meeting user requirements and give a lower priority to dealing with what they might see as project management 'red tape'. It could even be that the Project Manager with the daily burden of pushing the project forward might not be immune to this. However, this 'red tape' is needed to ensure that the project remains under control and that it continues to meet its business justification. Thus, some assurance is needed, independent of project management, that project management procedures are being properly followed. The ultimate responsibility for this assurance resides with the Project Board, but in practice detailed project assurance could be carried out by staff, independent of the team executing the project, who report to the Project Board members. Different types of project assurance specialists might be employed to ensure the business justification of the project is maintained, that the users' needs are being met and that the necessary technical requirements are being adhered to by the suppliers.

> Note that we have followed the convention of indicating specific PRINCE 2 terms by initial capital letters, Project Board, for example. All these terms are as in the PRINCE 2 manual, which has Crown copyright.

Project support

> The Project Board, Project Manager, Team Leaders and project assurance and support staff are known collectively in PRINCE 2 as the Project Management Team.

The Project Manager can require day-to-day support with the administration of the project. This might involve such tasks as processing time sheets or updating a computer-based project management tool such as Microsoft Project. It could be convenient for one group within an organization to supply this support to a number of projects. A key member of the project support team will be the Configuration Librarian, who will keep track of the latest versions of the products and documents generated by the project.

A.5 Project Stages

It is sensible to divide large projects into more manageable segments. PRINCE 2 caters for this through the idea of *Stages*. These are subsets of the project activities and are managed as a sequence of individual units. Normally, the Project Manager will, at any one time, be authorized by the Project Board to execute only the current Stage. The Project Manager will be able to start the next Stage only when the Project Board has met to give its approval for the plans for that Stage. The end of a Stage signals a decision point when the Project Board will review the progress to date and reassure itself that the project is still viable from a business point of view – in particular, that the expected benefits are still likely to justify the projected costs.

The typical system development life cycle contains a number of phases, where each phase makes use of different specialist techniques. These technical phases might be the typical steps outlined in Chapter 1: requirements analysis and specification, logical design, physical design, build, testing and installation. It is convenient in many cases for the management Stages specified by PRINCE 2 to be mapped onto these technical phases, but the PRINCE 2 standards are at pains to stress that it is not always convenient to do this – for instance the project might be more manageable if more than one technical phase were combined to create a Stage.

As will be explained in more detail in Section A.8 on 'Starting a project', at the beginning of a project a *Project Plan* will be created which will give the envisaged Stages. Only the first of these Stages will need to have a detailed *Stage Plan* immediately available. For the later stages, it is better to complete the detailed Stage Plan just a little while before the Stage is due to start. In that way, the Stage Plan can take account of a more complete picture of the project: at the beginning of the project, for example, it would be impossible to plan the system building stage in detail when the system requirement has not yet been clearly defined.

Once the Stage has been authorized and its execution has been embarked upon, the Project Board should not need to meet as long as any deviations from planned time and cost are only minor and are within laid-down project tolerances. It should be sufficient for members of the Project Board to receive regular reports from the Project Manager. If these tolerances are likely to be exceeded, then the Project Manager has a responsibility to produce an Exception Report for the Project Board. If the problems are serious enough to undermine the Stage Plan, then the Project Manager might then be required to produce a modified Stage Plan, or more properly an Exception Plan, which the Project Board will need to approve formally. In extreme circumstances the Project Board might at this point to decide to terminate the project prematurely.

A.6 Project procedures

Table A.1 lists the main project management processes for which PRINCE 2 lays down procedures to deal with the various events that the Project Management Team might encounter.

The levels of staff who are involved with each of the groups of project management processes in Table A.1 are indicated in Figure A.2. The general planning process PL is not shown as this can take place at various times and places for different reasons. For example, it could take place during the 'Initiating a project' (IP) process to create the Project Plan, or during 'Managing stage boundaries' (SB) when a Stage Plan for the next Stage is constructed or when an Exception Plan needs to be produced.

Table A.1 Major PRINCE 2 processes

PRINCE Id	Major processes
SU	Starting up a project
IP	Initiating a project
DP	Directing a project
CS	Controlling a stage
MP	Managing product delivery
SB	Managing stage boundaries
CP	Closing a project
PL	Planning

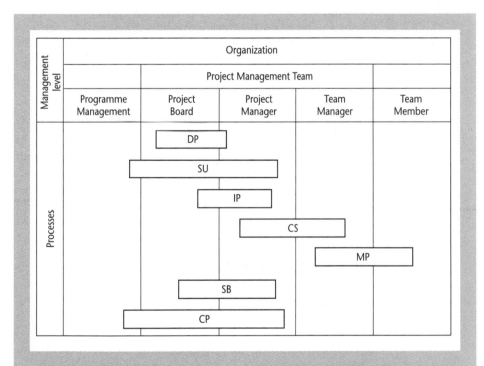

Figure A.2 Project management roles (see Table A.1 for key)

A.7 Directing a project

The main points where the Project Board have to be active are covered by the DP processes – *Directing a project*. These points are:

● authorizing initiation – agreeing to the start of detailed planning of a project;

● authorizing a project – agreeing, after the planning has been completed, that the project can go ahead;

- authorizing a Stage or Exception Plan;
- giving *ad hoc* direction;
- closing a project.

A.8 Starting up a project

With the first version of PRINCE there were sometimes difficulties knowing at which point the project had really started. The separate processes of Start Up and Initiation could avoid this.

As we noted in Chapter 3, the decision to undertake a project does not spring out of thin air. Where a customer organization has a coherent strategy, it is likely that there will be a layer of *programme management* where the 'programme' is a group of projects that are coordinated to meet an integrated set of business requirements. The current project could therefore be triggered by the programme managers. In any case, PRINCE 2 envisages that the project cycle will be sparked by some kind of *Project Mandate*, which will identify the customer and the general subject of the project. The PRINCE 2 Start Up process is essentially concerned with getting into a position where detailed planning of the proposed project can begin. As a starting point, this will need the recruitment of people to the various roles in the Project Management Team. The Project Mandate, which could be a rather insubstantial or imprecise document might need to be refined and expanded into a *Project Brief*, which defines the objectives of the project. Based on this, the general technical approach to be adopted to meet these objectives needs to be decided upon and documented in the *Project Approach*. The kinds of issue raised in Chapter 4 will need to be considered at this point. This could involve decisions about whether an off-the-shelf package can be bought or whether a bespoke package is required, and, if so, whether its development is to be carried out 'in-house' or by external contractors. All these activities lead to the formulation of a general plan of how the detailed planning is to be carried out.

A.9 Initiating the project

Having completed the Start Up Process, the Project Board can now decide that there are sufficient grounds to go on to more detailed planning. This begins with the consideration of a *Project Quality Plan*. Despite what some books suggest, quality levels do have cost implications. Different projects will have different quality requirements – faults in a college timetabling system are annoying but do not have the same consequences as the failure of a system controlling the flight of a passenger aeroplane. These quality requirements will have an effect on the activities that will have to be scheduled and the resources that will have to be found. This Project Quality Plan, plus the information in the Project Brief and Project Approach documents, now allow a *Project Plan* to be drafted. This will contain:

- the major products to be created;
- the main activities to be undertaken;
- project risks and their counter-measures;
- effort requirements;
- timescales;
- key decision points.

We now have a much clearer idea of the overall cost of the project than we did at the time of the original Project Mandate. The business case can now be reviewed to see whether the proposed project is still viable. The reliability of the business case will depend on the validity of the assumptions upon which it is based. The possibility that particular assumptions are incorrect is assessed and documented in a *Risk Log*. The final parts of project initiation are specifying how the project is to be controlled in terms of reporting and decision-making responsibilities and the setting up of project files.

The culmination of Initiating a Project is the putting together of a *Project Initiation Document*, which brings together the documentation generated by the Start Up and Initiation processes. If the Project Board can approve this document then the first proper Stage of the project can start.

A.10 Controlling a Stage

Once a Stage has been initiated, the Project Manager should be able to get on with the direction of the Stage without having to organize regular formal meetings with the Project Board.

Table A.2 shows the actions that the Project Manager might have to carry out while the Stage is being executed and for which the originators of PRINCE 2 have laid down procedural guidelines.

The Project Manager will have to authorize *Work Packages* (CS1), tasks that have to be carried out to create the products that should be the desired outcome of the project, such as software modules. On a substantial project, these authorizations will be passed not directly to the people who will do the work but to Team Managers.

Once the work has been authorized, the Project Manager will then need to find out how that work is progressing (CS2). This involves the kinds of task touched on in Chapter 9 on project control. For instance, progress information will have to be gathered to see if tasks are likely to be completed on time; feedback on recent quality-checking activities will also be needed to ensure that apparent progress is not being made by releasing products before they are really ready. Eventually, for each Work Package the Project Manager will be informed that the work can be signed-off as completed (CS9). This progress data will be used to add actual

Table A.2 PRINCE 2 processes when controlling a Stage

PRINCE ID	Controlling Stages (CS) processes
CS1	Authorize Work Package
CS2	Assess progress
CS3	Capture Project Issues
CS4	Examine Project Issues
CS5	Review Stage status
CS6	Report highlights
CS7	Take corrective action
CS8	Escalate project issue
CS9	Receive completed Work Package

completion dates to the details of planned activities that have been recorded in the Stage Plan.

A major part of a Project Manager's job during the execution of a Stage is bound to be 'fire-fighting' – dealing with the unexpected problems that are certain to occur. PRINCE 2 lays down a procedure (CS3 *Capturing project issues*) to ensure that these 'issues' are properly recorded. The 'issues' could be changes to requirements, changes to the environment such as new legal obligations, and other problems that might or might not have been foreseen by the risk analysis for the project. All these issues should be logged. Another PRINCE 2 procedure (CS4) is designed to ensure that all these issues are dealt with in an effective way. Outcomes can include a *Request for Change* to modify the user requirement or an *Off-Specification*, which records known and accepted errors and omissions in the product to be delivered.

The process of assessing progress (CS2) requires the Project Manager to look at the individual strands of work going on in his or her area of responsibility. PRINCE 2 envisages a separate but related activity where having gathered this progress information and also any outstanding Project Issues, the Project Manager checks the health of the Stage as a whole (CS5). In particular, the Project Manager will want to be reassured that the project as a whole is still progressing within its *tolerances*, the boundaries within which the Project Manager is allowed to manoeuvre without having to obtain clearance from the Project Board. One outcome of CS5 could be the carrying out of corrective action (CS7) that might include authorizing new Work Packages to deal with specific problems. Where work is progressing so that Project Issues are being kept under control and the Stage is within tolerances, then it will be enough to communicate progress to the Project Board by means of *Highlight reports* (CS6). In some cases the Project Manager might feel unable to progress with a matter without guidance from higher management and will request advice. Where activities have taken longer than planned or have taken up more resources than were budgeted so that the Project Manager is in danger of having to act outside the tolerances laid down in the Stage Plan, the Project Manager might have to 'escalate' a particular issue (CS8) by drafting an *Exception Report* to be considered by the Project Board. This should not only explain why the Stage has gone adrift from its original plan, but also detail possible options for recovering the situation and make a specific recommendation to the Project Board.

A.11 Managing product delivery

The processes described in 'Controlling a Stage' all assume that the work needed to complete a Stage is under the direct control of the Project Manager. Of course, it could be the case that, as described in Chapter 10 on contract management, some of the work is to be carried out by third party suppliers, that is, by an external organization that is not the primary supplier in direct contact with the customer, but a sub-contractor who carries out work on behalf of the supplier. These sub-contractors might not be using PRINCE 2. Hence the situation could need careful handling and PRINCE 2 provides some guidelines to help this – see Table A.3.

Once the Project Manager has authorized a Work Package (CS1), as described in the 'Controlling a Stage' section, the person who is to be responsible for the execution of the Work Package needs to check the requirements of the Work Package to ensure that there is common understanding on what exactly is to be

Table A.3 PRINCE 2 processes when managing product delivery

PRINCE Id	Managing product delivery (MP) processes
MP1	Accept Work Package
MP2	Execute Work Package
MP3	Deliver Work Package

Table A.4 PRINCE processes when managing stage boundaries

PRINCE ID	Managing stage boundaries
SB1	Planning a Stage
SB2	Updating the Project Plan
SB3	Updating the project business case
SB4	Updating the Risk Log
SB5	Reporting a Stage End
SB6	Producing an Exception Report

delivered, the constraints that might apply to the work and the requirements of any interfaces with other work (MP1). The Team Manager who is accepting the work must be confident that the targets can be realistically achieved. This could involve working out a *Team Plan* detailing how the work is to be done.

Once the work has been accepted, work can start on executing the Work Package (MP2). As this could be done by a sub-contractor who does not use PRINCE 2, PRINCE 2 lays down the general requirement that the responsible Team Manager should have the information ready to hand to report back to the Project Manager on progress as laid down in the authorized Work Package document. Finally, the need to define and agree the process by which completed Work Packages are handed over to the Project Manager is identified (MP3).

A.12 Managing stage boundaries

The transition from one Stage to another will involve the processes shown in Table A.4.

A key PRINCE 2 principle is to avoid too detailed planning at too early a stage. At the beginning of the project, for instance, the overall Project Plan is produced, but the more detailed Stage Plan is only produced for the first Stage. Towards the end of a Stage, the detailed plan for the next Stage can be mapped out as a clearer idea of the project requirements emerges (SB1). The creation of the Stage Plan for the next Stage could show up inadequacies in the overall Project Plan, which might need to be updated. For example, the design Stage of a project might reveal that the functionality of the system is greater than was foreseen when the first Project Plan was produced. More time might therefore be needed at the build Stage and this needs to be reflected in the Project Plan (SB2).

More time needed at build Stage will almost certainly mean that the date by which the project will be finally completed will be put back. This will lead to increasing development costs and the deferment of any income from the implemented system. At this point we need a process that checks that the project is still viable, that is, that the benefits of the delivered system will still outweigh the costs (SB3).

The situation with regard to risks might also have changed and this too needs to be reviewed (SB4). For example, as the project moves from design to build, some risks will disappear – if users were heavily involved in a design phase based around prototyping, a risk such as the non-availability of users for prototype evaluation will no longer be applicable and can be struck out. Other risks might, however, have materialized – a new version of the software building tool to be used could have been imposed by the organization and there is the possibility that developers might have technical difficulties adapting to the new product.

When all these things have been done, the new Stage will still need to wait for the successful completion of the last Stage. When this happens, the Project Manager can report the completion of the Stage (SB5) and the approval of the Project Board for the new Stage Plan can be requested.

A.13 Closing the project

PRINCE 2 divides the closing of a project into three separate processes:

- decommissioning a project (CP1);
- identifying follow-on actions (CP2);
- evaluating the project (CP3).

One follow-on action will be to plan for the Post Project Review which evaluates the effectiveness of the installed system after a set period of operation.

Decommissioning is mainly ensuring that all the loose ends are tied up. All Project Issues should either have been resolved or have been recorded as requiring *Follow-on Actions*. All the planned project products should have been accepted by the client and the requested operational and maintenance arrangements should be in place. Project files will have to be stored away into an archive and all parties involved should be notified that the project is now closed. PRINCE 2 does not specify that team members and key users should have a celebratory drink, but now might be the time to consider this. Decommissioning might have been caused by an *ad hoc* direction (DP4) to terminate a project prematurely as it is no longer required and in this case a wake could be more appropriate.

In organizations where development resources are scarce, there might appear to be little time available to reflect on practice and to dwell on past mistakes. However, if this is not done, time will be wasted in dealing with recurrent problems. PRINCE 2 recognizes this by specifying that at this point a *Project End Report* should be produced, documenting the extent to which the project has met the objectives set out in the Project Initiation Document, and also a *Lessons Learnt Report*, which should make suggestions about how problems could be avoided in future projects.

BS 6079:1996 – an overview

B.1 Introduction

Both as individuals and as organizations, we are continually exchanging goods and services – this is very much the basis of the commercial world we know today. This free exchange would be impeded unless on the whole there were a basic trust and common expectations about the nature and quality of the products involved and the processes by which those products had been created. To this end, business communities and governments have worked to produce standards. An important part of this has been the definition of agreed terminology so that we have a clear idea of what is meant by particular terms.

We would hope that standards are reasonably precise and unambiguous while being flexible enough to deal with the vagaries of the real world. It would also be hoped that standards would reflect accepted current best practice. A desirable feature of such standards would be some kind of accreditation of qualified practitioners so that customers for a product or service could know that they were dealing with someone competent in the particular area of expertise.

The British Standards Institution has had a leading role in the United Kingdom in this field and in 1996 published BS 6079 'Guide to project management'. While this 49-page document may have some claim to approach being a 'standard' because it reflects what the compilers of the document feel is current best practice, it is really, as its name suggests, a set of guidelines that are often couched in general terms of broad advice. In many ways it is like a general essay on project management.

Adrian Dooley, 'BS 6079 A base for the future?', *Project Manager Today*, 9(4), pp. 12–13, April 1997.

The advantage of its being in the form of a British Standard, as Adrian Dooley has pointed out, is that this can give these broad, but important, project management principles more credibility in some quarters of the business community. A disadvantage of this format, in our view, is that apart from other BSI standards, the project manager reading this text is given no information about where further guidance on the techniques described can be obtained.

Pippa Newman, 'PRINCE 2 The method for the next millennium', pp. 14–15 of the same issue of *Project Manager Today* as above.

A key question is how this standard fits in with the other UK standard PRINCE 2 or even why two separate standards are necessary. It is emphasized by the promoters of these two standards that they are not meant to be competitors. Pippa Newman, a CCTA Associate involved with promoting PRINCE 2 has written of PRINCE 2 that *'one of its major roles is to provide a means by which the British Standard can be implemented'*. As will be seen, this could imply a degree of coordination between the developers of the two approaches that is not evident when the two documents are closely studied. One of the reasons for the differences in the two approaches might be their different origins – although PRINCE 2 is now meant for a rather wider context, its origins are in IT/IS development, while BS 6079 has more of a hard engineering background. However, once again, as Adrian Dooley commented:

With a bit of work an organisation could be consistent with both. The biggest problem is the need to harmonise the differing terminologies used by the two approaches. As someone who is keen to see project management develop as a mature discipline, I feel terribly frustrated by the lack of consistency in the profession. Why is it that the two bodies developing tools to promote better project management, both funded by the government, producing their respective documents at about the same time, cannot work closely together to agree consistent terminology at even the simplest level?

Some of the differences between PRINCE 2 and BS 6079 are summarized in Table B.1.

Table B.1 Comparison of PRINCE 2 and BS 6079

Topic	PRINCE 2	BS 6079
Main focus	Procedures	Techniques
Definition of project	Temporary organization to deliver a business product	Covers the *whole* system life cycle
Project organization	Supplier vs. Customer focus	Functional departments vs. project team
Project authority	Project Board	Sponsor
Stage organization	Detailed planning done by Stage	Concept of phases/milestones matches Stages – but no focus on incremental planning at phase level
Planning method	Product-driven (Product Breakdown Structures)	Task-driven (Work Breakdown Structures)
Work definitions	Product descriptions in the plan – turned into Work Packages by Project Manager	Statements of Work (SOW) in the plan
Techniques	Only minimal reference to techniques (such as to Activity Networks)	Detailed descriptions of techniques like Earned Value Analysis
Supporting techniques	Configuration, quality and risk management	Those for PRINCE 2, plus financial control and procurement
Financial control	Cost control not dealt with in detail	Financial control dealt with more fully

The main elements of project management dealt with by BS 6079 are:

- the project life cycle;
- project organization;
- the planning process;
- project control;
- supporting techniques.

We will now look at each of these in turn.

The project life cycle

BS 6079 sees a 'project' in terms different from those of PRINCE 2. It uses the word to refer to the whole of the system life cycle from the initial idea right through the system's operation to final decommissioning. The BS 6079 definition of project is similar to the view of a 'project' used in Chapter 3, when the cash projections for alternative 'projects' were calculated. When developing information systems, however, the development project is more usually seen as starting after the feasibility study has established that the project appears to be worthwhile and finishing when the system is handed over for operation. In fact, it is possible to treat individual phases within that project as projects in their own right. As it happens, despite the BS 6079 definition of project, most of the BS 6079 guidelines for planning and control are compatible with the information systems development view of the project being completed at system hand-over.

Figure B.1 illustrates the main project phases as seen by BS 6079. Note that 'implementation' in this context means 'implementation of the project plan'. Information systems developers often use the term 'implementation' to refer merely to the installation of the system once it has been developed. A further interesting point is that while the standard recommends the equivalent of the PRINCE 2 Project End and Lessons Learnt Reports, no mention is made of the Post Implementation Review, or Post Project Review as it is now called.

Project organization

BS 6079 does not have PRINCE 2's emphasis on the Supplier–Customer relationship. Neither is the concept of a Project Board or steering committee presented. The focus of attention is on the project as a set of activities that cut across the normal functional structures of most organizations. A heavy emphasis is put on the desirability of a matrix management structure, where staff belong to a particular functional group in the longer term but may be allocated from time to time to multi-disciplinary teams that have been given the responsibility for achieving the objectives of a particular project.

It can be argued that the need to create an environment for successful projects, which can take time, is an important message for the perceived readership of BS 6079.

One usually expects standards to be applicable fairly immediately, but the writers of BS 6079 warn that it might take an organization three to five years to move from a totally functional to a matrix organization. Rather surprisingly for a document that is supposed to be focused on project management, there is a section on the broader topic of how to bring about organizational change. This is an

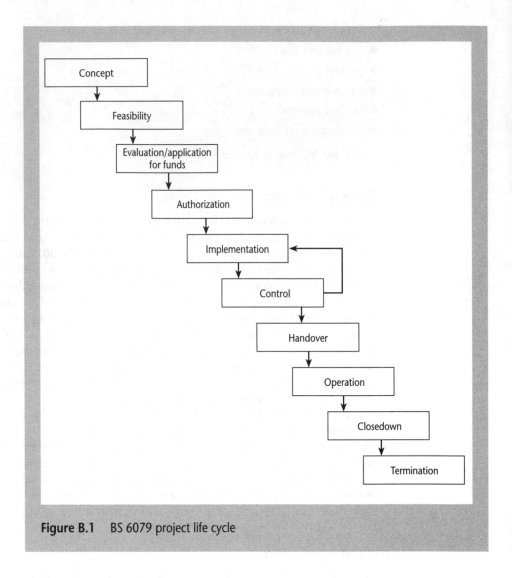

Figure B.1 BS 6079 project life cycle

example of where a reference to a fuller treatment in another text would have been useful.

The other management role that BS 6079 emphasizes is that of *task owners*. Each task that is identified as needing doing in a project requires an owner, someone who will be accountable for its successful completion. Figure B.2 shows the relationships among the different project roles as envisaged in BS 6079.

B.2 The planning process

According to BS 6079, a plan should have five main elements:

- introduction;
- commitment acceptance;

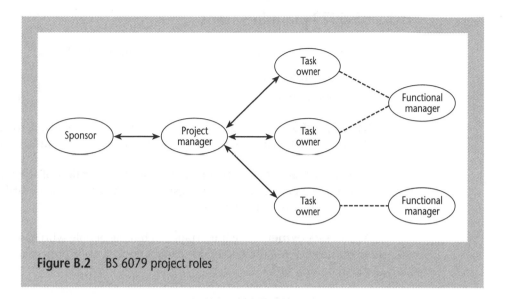

Figure B.2   BS 6079 project roles

- work breakdown structure;
- schedule;
- statements of work.

The terms 'Work Breakdown Structure' and 'Statement of Work' (SOW) will be explained later in this section.

One of the major differences between BS 6079 and PRINCE 2 is that while PRINCE 2 advocates a product-driven approach to planning, where the products the project has to create are initially identified, BS 6079 uses an activity-based approach, featuring a *Work Breakdown Structure* (WBS), right from the beginning.

The standard does not put the same heavy emphasis on a Stage structure for projects as PRINCE 2. Passing references are, however, made to having project phases with milestones between the phases where there would be critical reviews of the progress that has been made and where decisions would be made about the continuing viability of the project. However, basing planning cycles on these phases, as PRINCE 2 does, is not suggested.

Apart from the WBS, the other important element in project documentation, according to this standard, is the *Statement of Work* (SOW), which combines elements of PRINCE 2's Product Description and Work Package. A SOW is created for each element in the WBS. These documents contain sections that cover such details as:

- summary of requirements;
- task ownership;
- key deliverables and their delivery dates;
- task dependencies;
- cost breakdown;
- risk assessment;
- performance criteria;
- progress reporting arrangements.

BS 6079 does mention a 'product-based WBS' which equates to a PRINCE 2 'Product Breakdown Structure', but does not use Product Flow Diagrams.

B.3 BS 6079 planning steps

The major BS 6079 planning steps are summarized below:

Obtain project authorization;

Establish project organization.

Develop WBS It is suggested that it is useful to produce a cross-reference table showing which activities are the responsibility of which parts of the organization.

Analyse project tasks This includes the identification of the task owner, of the way that the performance of the task is to be measured, its criticality to the project, its cost elements and any risks.

Assign task owner The importance of having people who have responsibility and accountability for the successful completion of each project task is very strongly stressed in BS 6079.

Develop the statements of work

Monte Carlo simulation was discussed briefly in Chapter 7.

Balance time, cost, integrity of specification and risk This is where the planner tries out different options for allocating effort and timescale targets to activities to see what the likely consequences would be. Although Monte Carlo simulation is not mentioned by name, its possible use is implied.

Obtain commitments to do project tasks Task owners are asked to agree formally and commit themselves to the relevant tasks. Before the task owners can do this, they will need to quantify the resources that will be needed and to match this requirement against available resources, reserving the selected resources for use in the project.

Finalize agreements

B.4 Project control

Project control in BS 6079 is considered under the three distinct headings of change control, financial control and progress monitoring.

Change control BS 6079 recognizes that it is essential to have a formal mechanism to control changes, but while the requirements of such an administrative system are outlined, it does not specify any detailed steps. A major change can call for the planning cycle to be re-executed.

Financial control BS 6079 makes more specific references to financial control than PRINCE 2. The need is recognized for a process whereby the expenditure by the sponsoring organization on the project can be allocated to annual budgets. As time passes and progress is made, arrangements must be in place for the required funding to be released. Even with the best regulated projects, circumstances can require additional expenditure for unforeseen contingencies and a management reserve ought to be available for this.

Monitoring progress   The BS 6079 emphasis on financial control is seen once again in the requirement that the project manager has a prime responsibility to report actual costs compared to planned costs. Task owners are required to pass on to the project manager revised estimates of the overall cost and projected completion dates for each task for which they have responsibility.

The compilers of BS 6079 clearly had a very strong preference for earned value analysis and the method is given considerable space in the standards document.

Not only does the project manager receive reports of progress from task owners, but he or she should warn the task owners of any external threats to their areas of activity. A report of a delay by one task owner can require the owners of tasks dependent upon the delayed task to be warned.

The need for risks to be continually assessed is stressed. Risk assessment techniques based on statistical probability are recommended.

The need for project managers to motivate and, if needs be, negotiate with, task owners is recognized by the document. Thus having good communications is stressed, and readers are warned that specifying additions to requirements is easier before a contract is signed than afterwards!

Earned value analysis has been described in Section 9.6.

The kind of risk management techniques that BS 6079 recommends have been discussed in Chapter 7.

B.5   Supporting techniques

It will be recalled that PRINCE 2 described the basic requirements for some supporting techniques, in particular, change and configuration management, quality management and risk management. BS 6079 adopts a similar approach but adds procurement and financial control.

With regard to procurement, the different organizational arrangements for making purchases for a project are outlined. For example, the buyers might belong to a centralized group or might be dedicated to the specific projects. The key role of purchase order documents as a control mechanism is highlighted. The need to have some way of identifying trustworthy and qualified vendors, perhaps by maintaining a list of preferred vendors who have a satisfactory track record, is described in the BS 6079 document. The document also warns of the need to have in place procedures to expedite external work and to ensure the satisfactory standard of delivered work through inspections.

The section on financial control illustrates quite nicely the differences in approach between BS 6079 and PRINCE 2. In the BS 6079 document, two very specific quantitative techniques are described in some detail, namely the calculation of the net present value of a potential project and the analysis of the earned value of a project currently being executed. PRINCE 2 tends to avoid describing detailed technical data manipulation, with some notable exceptions to do with core planning methods, and concentrates on the necessary administrative procedures that need to be in place.

Programme management

C.1 What is programme management?

In Chapter 1 we described a spectrum of collaborative work, ranging from well-understood, routine jobs to speculative ventures probing the unknown. We identified undertakings that fell between the two extremes as being most susceptible to effective project management. The 'project' was seen as a cohesive and tightly coordinated cluster of activities directed towards the accomplishment of some well-defined objective. These projects are more likely to be successful when there is single-minded – perhaps even obsessive – focus on pushing them through. However, the business world does not always allow this luxury. Often managers have to be concerned with a number of projects at the same time.

Such a group of projects could be a *programme* of projects, and the discipline which organizes and controls such programmes is *programme management*. The US spelling of 'program' is used in the United Kingdom to denote a unit of software. It is convenient to use the UK spelling, 'programme' to distinguish a programme of projects from a software program.

> Unfortunately, American books do not take advantage of this convenient distinction between 'program' and 'programme'.

C.2 Varieties of programme management

Programmes can exist in different forms:

Strategic programmes

There may be several projects which together implement a single strategy. For example, two organizations are to be merged. This might involve the creation of unified payroll and accounting applications, the physical reorganization of offices, training, new organizational procedures, re-creating a corporate image through advertising and so on. Many of these activities could be treated as projects in their own right, but they would need to be coordinated as a programme.

Business cycle programmes

The collection of projects that an organization undertakes within a particular planning cycle is sometimes referred to as a *portfolio*. Many organisations have a fixed budget for IT development. Decisions have to be made about the portfolio of projects that are to be implemented within a single accounting period. Often finance is allocated on a yearly basis. If expenditure on one project is delayed to a later year, this could release resources for some other project. On the other hand, if a project absorbs more resources than expected, this could be at the expense of some other project. Planners need to have some way of assessing the comparative value and urgency of projects within a portfolio. Often this is straightforward because external circumstances – such as the adoption of the euro – force the priorities. Where the relative merits of the needs of different groups of users need to be balanced, priority-setting can become very political.

Often the projects in the portfolio have to compete for a share of a common pool of resources, such as teams of software developers. The allocation of available staff between projects poses particular problems which will be discussed in the next section.

Infrastructure programmes

Some organizations have very integrated information systems. Other organizations, such as local government bodies, can have various departments which have distinct, relatively self-contained, systems. In a local authority, one department might have responsibilities for the maintenance of highways, another for rubbish collection, another for education and so on. These distinct activities will probably require distinct databases and information systems. However, other applications, such as those to do with accounting, may cross over these boundaries. In such a situation, the central IT function will have responsibility for setting up and maintaining the IT infrastructure, including the networks, work-stations and servers, upon which these distinct applications run. A uniform infrastructure would allow the sharing of applications between departments where that was desirable, and would make life easier for the central IT function, as it would allow the bulk purchasing of equipment and the development of expertise for standard products. In these circumstances, a programme would refer to the activities of identifying a common IT infrastructure and its implementation and maintenance.

Research and development programmes

Truly innovative companies, especially those that are trying to develop new products for the market, are well aware that projects will vary in terms of their risk of failure and the potential returns that they might eventually reap. Some development projects will be relatively safe, and result in the final planned product, but that product might not be radically different from existing ones on the market. Other projects might be extremely risky, but the end result, if successful, could be a revolutionary technological break-through that meets some pressing but previously unsatisfied need.

Alan Webb, 'When project management doesn't work', *Project Manager Today*, May 2001.

An example of this is described by Alan Webb. In 1968, Dupont reviewed a range of long-term research projects that they were developing and tried to forecast which ones would create products that would be profitable in 30 years' time. Thirty years later, it was possible to see how far they had been correct. A few had been very successful, but many had led to dead-ends. A company like Dupont needs to create and maintain a portfolio of projects which are a mixture of 'safe projects' with relatively low returns and some riskier projects that might fail, but if successful

Warren McFarlan's 'Portfolio approach to information systems', *Harvard Business Review*, September/October 1981, pp. 142–150, introduced the portfolio concept to information systems.

would generate handsome profits which will off-set the losses on the failures. Clearly, if a company gets this balance wrong it could get into serious difficulties.

The risks associated with an innovative project will fluctuate. Research work may lead to technological break-throughs or to the discovery of insurmountable problems, so the portfolio of projects needs to be reviewed on a regular basis.

Innovative partnerships

Some technological developments, if handled properly, benefit whole industries. The development of the internet and the World Wide Web is an example. Often, technological products can only be exploited if they inter-operate with other products. The joke about the invention of the first telephone not being as important as the invention of the second comes to mind. Companies therefore often come together to work collaboratively on new technologies in a 'pre-competitive' phase. Separate projects in different organizations need to be coordinated and this might be done as a programme.

C.3 Managing the allocation of resources within programmes

We are now going to examine in more detail programmes where resources have to be shared between concurrent projects. Typically, an IT department has pools of particular types of expertise, such as software developers, database designers, network support staff and these might be called upon to participate in a number of projects which can be going on at the same time.

The comparison is based on G. Reiss, *Programme Management Demystified*, Chapman Hall, 1996.

In these circumstances, programme managers will have concerns about the optimal use of specialist staff. These concerns can be contrasted with those of project managers – see Table C.1.

The project managers are said to have an 'impersonal relationship' with resource types because, essentially, they require a competent systems analyst and who fills that role does not matter. The programme manager has a number of individual systems analysts under his or her control whose deployment has to be planned.

We can see that when a project is planned, at the stage of allocating resources, programme management will be involved. Some activities in the project might have to be delayed until the requisite technical staff are freed from work on other

Table C.1 Programme managers versus project managers

Programme manager	*Project manager*
Many simultaneous projects	One project at a time
Personal relationship with skilled resources	Impersonal relationship with resource type
Need to maximize utilization of resources	Need to minimize demand for resources
Projects tend to be similar	Projects tend to be dissimilar

projects. Where expensive technical staff are employed full time, you would want to avoid them having short periods of intense activity interspersed with long periods of idleness during which they are still being paid. It is most economic when the demand for work is evenly spread from month to month.

As we know from Chapter 9 on monitoring and control, when a project is executed, activities can take longer (or sometimes even less) than planned. Delays can mean that specialist staff are prevented from moving on to their next project. Hence it can be seen that programme management needs to be concerned with the continual monitoring of the progress of projects.

An example of programme management of this type is the footwear designers, Overland Group Services Limited. A typical project for this company involves:

- a shoe design to a brief provided by the client;
- obtaining approval of the design;
- creating a prototype of the shoe;
- setting up production for the shoe with a manufacturer.

The details of the example are taken from 'Overland and beyond' by Fiona Powell in *Project Manager Today*, April 2000.

Typically the company might have 20 of these projects to manage at the same time. Louisa Hazlett, a project coordinator, is quoted as saying *'we are a small team and so the only way we are going to do this is to use what we've got. . . . By tracking our resources we can utilize what we have without increasing overheads or employing more people.'* The software tool, Microsoft Project was used to control individual projects and a companion product, Innate Mult-Project was selected to coordinate the different projects.

Although Overland is not an example from the world of software development, there are many small software development enterprises, such as those concerned with website development, which carry out relatively small projects for a range of outside clients, and who have to coordinate these projects so as to make the best use of staff time.

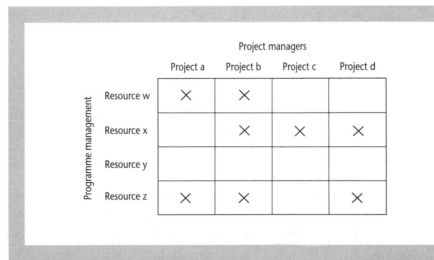

Figure C.1   Projects sharing shared resources

C.4 Strategic programme management

A somewhat different form of programme management is where there is a portfolio of projects that are all contributing to a common objective. Take for example, a business which carries out maintenance work for clients. A customer's interactions with the organization are found to be very variable and inconsistent. For example, the employee who records the customer's requirements is different from the people who actually carry out the work and different again from the clerk who deals with the accounts. Very often a customer has to explain to one company employee a problem that has already been discussed with some other company employee. A business objective might be to present a consistent and uniform front to the client. This objective might require changes to a number of different systems which until now have been largely self-contained. The work to reorganize each individual area could be treated as separate projects, coordinated at a higher level as a programme.

These types of programme are most often needed by large organizations which have a large and complicated organizational structure. Government departments are typical examples and it is not surprising that the CCTA, the United Kingdom government agency which was responsible for the introduction of PRINCE and PRINCE 2 project management standards, has directed its attention to guidelines for effective programme management. The remainder of this appendix is based on the CCTA guidelines.

C.5 Creating a programme

The programme mandate

The CCTA envisages that the planning of a programme will be triggered by the creation of an agreed *programme mandate*. Ideally this should be a formal document with no set form but which should contain:

- what new services or capabilities the programme should deliver;
- how the organization will be improved by being able to use the new services or capability;
- how the programme fits with corporate goals and any other initiatives.

At this point, a *programme director* ought to be appointed to provide leadership for the programme. To be successful, the programme needs a champion who is in a prominent position within the organization. This will signal the seriousness with which the organization takes the programme. The programme director is likely to come from the *sponsoring group* who have identified the need for a programme and have initiated its establishment.

A *programme brief* is now produced which would be the equivalent of feasibility study for the programme. It will have sections containing:

- a preliminary *vision statement* which describes the new capacity that the organization seeks – the 'preliminary' is because this is later elaborated;
- the *benefits* that the programme should create – including when they are likely to be generated and how they might be measured;

- risks and issues;
- estimated costs, timescales and effort.

The vision statement

The programme brief should have given the sponsoring group enough information to decide whether it is worth moving to a more detailed definition of the programme. This would involve a lot of detailed planning work and would justify the setting up of a small team. At this point a *programme manager* who would have day-to-day responsibility for running the programme could well be appointed. The programme manager is likely to be someone with considerable project management experience.

This group can now take the vision statement outlined in the project brief and refine and expand it. It should describe in detail the new capability that the programme will give the organization. If estimates for costs, performance, and service levels cannot be provided, there should at least be an indication of how they might be measured. For example, the headings under which costs will be incurred can be recorded. Similarly, for performance, one might be able to say repeat business will be increased, even if the precise size of the increase cannot be provided.

The blueprint

The achievement of the improved capability described in the vision statement can only come about when changes have been made to the structure and operations of the organization. These are detailed in the *blueprint*. This should contain:

- business models outlining the new processes required;
- organizational structure – including the numbers of staff required in the new systems and the skills they will need;
- the information systems, equipment and other, non-staff, resources that will be needed;
- data and information requirements;
- costs, performance and service level requirements.

To return to the example of the organization which wants to present a consistent interface to its customers: while this aspiration might be stated in the vision statement, the way that it is to be achieved would have to be stated in the blueprint. This might, for example, suggest:

- the appointment of 'account managers' who could act as a point of contact for clients throughout their business transactions with the company;
- a common computer interface allowing the account manager to have access to all the information relating to a particular client or job, regardless of the computer system within which it might reside.

The blueprint will need to be supported by *benefit profiles* which project when the expected benefits will start to be realized following the implementation of the enhanced capability. One principal underpinning of programme management is that the programme should deliver tangible benefits. Because an organization is given the capability to do something, this does not guarantee that the capability will be used to obtain the benefits originally envisaged. For example, as a part of a programme, the marketing department of a travel company might be provided with a database of sales and demographic information which will allow them to target potential customers more accurately. This can then be used to focus sales and promotions more effectively and improve the ratio of sales revenue to advertising costs. However, just because this database is made available does not mean that the marketing staff will make effective use of it. Evidence of the business benefits actually experienced needs to be collected. However, the timing of the benefits needs to be carefully considered. For instance, the business of a travel company is largely seasonal and marketing campaigns might take some time to plan and organize. It follows that the benefits in increased sales and/or lower advertising costs could take some months to become apparent.

The management structure that will be needed to drive this programme forward will need to be planned – see Section C.6 on this aspect.

A preliminary list of the projects that the programme will need in order to achieve its objective will be created as the *programme portfolio*. This will contain an outline schedule to be presented to the sponsoring group with the preliminary estimated timescales for the projects.

Programmes will affect many different groups and individuals in an organization. A major risk is that some of those whose work will be affected by the programme or whose cooperation is needed will not be drawn into the programme effectively. A *stakeholder map* identifying the groups of people with an interest in the project and its outcomes and their particular interests could be drawn up. This can be used to write a *communications strategy* and *plan* showing how the appropriate information flows between stakeholders can be set up and maintained.

We noted back in Chapter 1 that with conventional project planning, it is not usually possible to plan all the phases of a project at the outset, as much of the information needed to produce the detailed plans will not be available until later in the project. It can easily be imagined that this will be even more the case with programmes. However, at the initial programme planning stage, a preliminary plan can be produced containing:

● the project portfolio;
● cost estimates for each project;
● the benefits expected (including the appropriate benefits profile);
● risks identified;
● the resources needed to manage, support and monitor the programme.

The gleaning of this information also allows a *financial plan* to be created. This allows higher management to put in place the budget arrangements to meet the expected costs at the times when they are due to be incurred. The points in the programme will need to be identified when higher management will have to review progress in order to authorize further expenditure.

C.6 The organization to support a programme

Figure C.2 outlines the management structure that the CCTA recommends for the running of a programme.

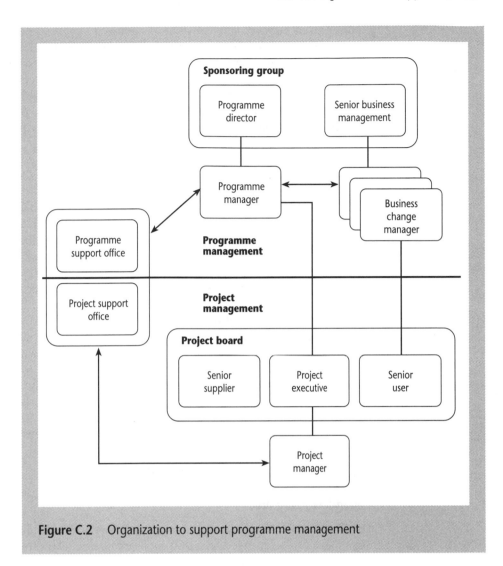

Figure C.2   Organization to support programme management

The *programme director* is a high-level business executive who is most likely to come from one of the organization's major functional areas that hopes to benefit from the programme. Programme directors need to come from a high level in the organization so that they have authority to ensure the programme is progressed effectively. Because of their senior position, and the other responsibilities that make demands upon them, their role will almost certainly be part time.

The *programme manager* will be someone appointed specifically to the job of dealing with the day-to-day running of the programme. The person in this role will ensure that the appropriate detailed plans are created and will monitor the progress of projects in the programme's portfolio. As we noted earlier, the programme manager is likely to have project management experience, but should also be able to understand the business needs of the organization.

Business change managers will also be required. The programme manager could well have an IT or business analysis background and not have a deep understanding of the work of the business departments who will have to bear the brunt of the changes to be brought about by the programme. One or more business change managers should therefore be appointed who understand and have influence in the business areas. They will do such things as advise on the best times to implement change – many businesses are cyclical in nature and a relatively quiet time should be selected during which to implement changes. They would also be responsible for ensuring that the groups they represent are ready to do their part in implementing change, and also that the delivered capability and services are properly exploited to obtain the benefits planned.

There could be a separate *programme assurance* function that reports to the sponsoring group on whether the programme is being implemented in accordance with organizational standards.

Once the programme is under way, progress information will need to be collected from the various projects in the programme's portfolio in order to coordinate them effectively. This involves clerical effort and 'number crunching' which can be supplied by a *programme support office* whose responsibilities are to collect, coordinate, analyse and distribute management information.

PRINCE 2, the CCTA project management guidelines, recommends the establishment of *project support offices,* which carry out similar work, but at a project level. It is sensible in most environments for several projects to share the services of a project support office. From this situation, it is a relatively straight-forward step to make the project support office the programme support office as well – thus we have *programme and project support offices* (PPSOs). As well as collecting progress information, the office can hold and maintain the master copies of programme documentation and can monitor the adherence to project management standards in the individual, constituent, projects of the programme.

C.7 Aids to programme management

Dependency diagrams

There will often be physical and technical dependencies between projects. For example, a project to relocate staff from one building to another might not be able to start until a project to construct a new building has been completed. Dependency diagrams, which are very similar to activity networks at project level, can be used to show these dependencies. Where projects run concurrently in a programme and pass products between one another, the dependency diagrams could become quite complicated.

Earlier in this appendix, we described an example of a programme that resulted from the need to merge to organizations. Figure C.3 shows a dependency diagram for this programme, the constituent parts of which are explained below.

A. *Systems study/design* A project is carried out which examines the various existing IT applications in the two old organizations, analyses their functionality, and makes recommendations about how they are to be combined.

B. *Corporate image design* Independently of Project A, this project is designing the corporate image for the new organization. This would include design of the new logo to be put on company documents.

C. *Build common systems* Once Project A has been completed, work can be triggered on the construction of the new common IT applications.

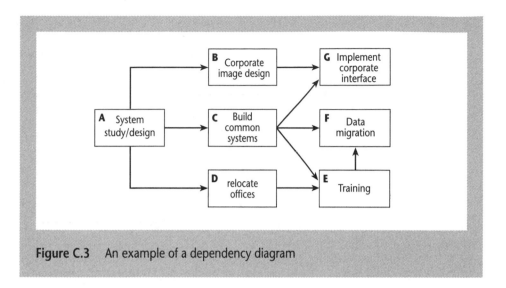

Figure C.3   An example of a dependency diagram

D. *Relocate offices*   This is the project that actually carries out the physical collocation of the staff in the two former organizations. In this scenario, this has to wait until the completion of Project A because that project has examined how the two sets of applications for the previous organizations could be brought together, and this has repercussions on the departmental structure of the new merged organization.

E. *Training*   Once staff have been brought together, perhaps with some staff being made redundant, training in use of the new systems can begin.

F. *Data migration*   When the new joint applications have been developed, and staff have been trained in their use, data can be migrated from existing databases to the new consolidated database.

G. *Implement corporate interface*   Before the new applications can 'go live', the interfaces, including the documentation generated for external customers, must be modified to conform to the new company image.

Delivery planning

The creation of a delivery dependency diagram would typically be a precursor to more detailed programme planning. As part of this planning, *tranches* of project could be defined. A tranche is a group of projects that will deliver their products as one step in the programme. The main criterion for grouping projects into tranches is that the deliverables of each of the projects combine to provide a coherent new capability or set of benefits for the client. An equally pressing consideration will be the need to avoid contention for scarce resources.

Figure C.4 shows how the programme's portfolio of projects can be organized into tranches, each of which delivers some tangible benefits to the user.

At this point, the planning of individual projects can be considered. This could be initiated by the writing of *project briefs*, defining the scope and objectives of each project.

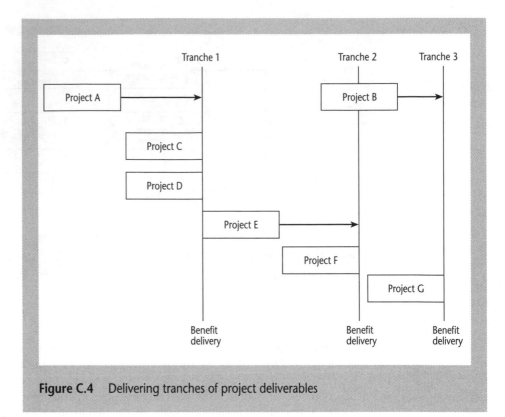

Figure C.4   Delivering tranches of project deliverables

C.8   Benefits management

Thomas K. Landauer's *The Trouble with Computers: Usefulness, Usability and Productivity*, MIT Press, 1995 explores the issues of the 'productivity paradox' in IT.

We have already noted that providing an organization with a capability does not guarantee that the capability will be used to deliver the benefits originally envisaged. This is a very important point, because businesses have become aware of the lack of evidence, in many cases, of the investment in IT increasing the productivity of organizations. Even with *business process re-engineering* (BPR), the radical reorganization of businesses to deliver improvements in efficiency and effectiveness, there are many reported cases where the expected benefits have not materialized.

Benefits management is an attempt to remedy this. It encompasses the identification, optimization and tracking of the expected benefits from a business change in order to ensure that they are actually achieved.

To do this, you must:

● define the expected benefits from the programme;

● analyse the balance between costs and benefits;

● plan how the benefits will be achieved and measured;

● allocate responsibilities for the successful delivery of the benefits;

● monitor the realization of the benefits.

Benefits can be of many different types, including;

- *mandatory compliance*: governmental or European legislation might make certain changes mandatory;
- *quality of service*: an insurance company, for example, might want to settle claims by customers more quickly;
- *productivity*: the same, or even more, work, can be done at less cost in staff time;
- *more motivated workforce*: this might be because of an improved rewards system, or through job enlargement or job enrichment;
- *internal management benefits* (for instance, better decision-making): to take an insurance example, again, better analysis of insurance claims could pinpoint those categories of business which are most risky and allow an insurance company to adjust premiums to reflect this;
- *risk reduction*: the insurance example might also be applicable here, but measures to protect an organization's networks and databases from intrusion and external malicious attack would be even more pertinent;
- *economy*: the reduction of costs, other than those related to staff – procurement policies might be put in place which encourage the consolidation of purchasing in order to take advantage of bulk-buying at discount;
- *revenue enhancement/acceleration*: the sooner bills reach customers the sooner they can pay them;
- *strategic fit*: a change might not directly benefit a particular group within the organization but has to be made in order to obtain some strategic advantage for the organization as a whole.

A change could have more than one of these types of benefits. In fact, benefits are often inter-linked. An example of this is an insurance company which when settling claims for damage to property, introduced a facility whereby it directly arranged for contractors to carry out the remedial work. This improved quality of service for the customer as it saved the trouble of locating a reputable contractor, reduced costs to the insurance company because they could take advantage of the bulk purchase of services and improved staff morale because of the goodwill generated between the insurance company's front-line staff and the customer.

Quantifying benefits

Benefits can be:

- quantified and valued: that is, a direct financial benefit is experienced;
- quantified but not valued: for example, the number of customer complaints is reduced;
- identified but not easily quantified: for example, public approval of the organization in the locality where it is based.

A particular activity might have benefits, but also *disbenefits*. For example, increased sales might mean that more money has to be spent on expensive over-time working.

There can be much controversy over a whether a business change will lead to the particular benefits claimed for it. For example, it might be claimed that a new

Job enlargement and enrichment were discussed in Chapter 11.

company logo will improve staff morale. Some key tests have been suggested in order to sound out whether a putative benefit is likely to be genuine.

- Can you explain in precise terms why this benefit should result from this business change?
- Can you identify the ways in which we will be able to see the consequences of this benefit?
- If the required outcomes do occur, can they be attributed directly to the change, or could other factors explain them?
- Is there any way in which the benefits can be measured?

We have mentioned earlier in this appendix the need to draw up *benefit profiles* which project when and how benefits will be experienced. Specific staff have to be allocated responsibility for ensuring that the planned benefits actually materialize. These will often be the business change managers.

Benefits cannot normally be monitored in a purely project environment because the project will almost certainly have been officially closed before the benefits start to filter through.

In our view, the idea that developers and users are *jointly* responsible for ensuring the delivery of the benefits of projects is a powerful and important one.

APPENDIX D

ISO 12207: an overview

D.1 Introduction

It is stressed that this is only an overview and those using the standard in earnest need to refer to the actual standard itself.

Both PRINCE 2 and BS 6079 originated in the United Kingdom and are designed for any type of project. ISO 12207 differs from these in that, firstly, it is international in standing and, secondly, that it relates specifically to software development.

Broadly speaking, ISO 12207 has as the prime areas of its concern the documentation (or 'software life cycle data' as it calls it) created and used by a software development project and the processes that, during development, will use and update software life cycle data.

D.2 The ISO 12207 approach to software life cycle data

We have chosen to use the term 'documentation' partly to make indexing easier. 'Documentation' could imply paper-based information but, of course, in practice, it could be held in an electronic form.

'Documentation' is an issue that is difficult and important, but at the same time rather unexciting. Software developers and users often complain about the lack of documentation, but when it is available it often remains unread. There could be some justification for this reluctance to read documentation as it might well not be up to date.

One way to look at a software development project is as an information system in its own right. The project is made up of activities, each of which needs to pass information to and from other activities. As with any conventional information system, there needs to be a common database that can be updated and accessed as required. A key factor in the relative success and failure of the project is clearly going to be the effectiveness of this information system.

However, inappropriate documentation can actually be an obstacle to effective working. ISO 12207 focuses attention on the characteristics of good documentation by defining the purpose of good software life cycle data. This data:

- records information about *software products*;
- helps make the product *usable* and *maintainable*;
- defines *processes*;
- *communicates* information;
- records *history*;
- provides *evidence*.

289

The standard lists the characteristics of good documentation as being:

- unambiguous;
- complete;
- verifiable;
- consistent – that is, there are no contradictions within it;
- modifiable;
- traceable – the components from which it is derived are easily identifiable;
- presentable – this means that it is easy to access and view.

The standard recognizes the following generic types of data held by a project:

- requirements – what the system is expected to do;
- design – including details of its structure;
- testing – including test strategy and criteria, test cases and results;
- configuration;
- user – including user manuals;
- management;
- quality – including quality plans and procedures.

IEEE stands for the 'Institute of Electrical and Electronics Engineers', the prestigious US-based organization that has played a key role in setting standards.

The ISO 12207 standard does not specify precise formats for this documentation, but the IEEE, for example, has produced a cross-reference indicating the relevant IEEE standards for each type of document.

D.3 The ISO 12207 approach to software life cycle processes

The processes that, either as a central objective or as a by-product, generate or update life cycle data are particularly the concern of the standard.

It will be recalled from Appendix A and Appendix B that BS 6079 differed from PRINCE 2 in defining, in theory at least, a project as starting with a concept and ending, after the required system had been both built and operated, with its decommissioning. In practice with BS 6079, however, the detailed procedures suggested for project planning and control focused on the development phase.

ISO 12207 identifies the five distinct processes shown in Figure D.1:

- acquisition;
- supply;
- operation;
- maintenance;
- development.

Clearly, maintenance and operation are processes that genuinely belong to the post-implementation phase of a conventional development project. One justification for the inclusion of these post-implementation activities is that sometimes a customer will contract a supplier both to develop a system and operate it on the customer's behalf. Similarly a software house could be responsible contractually both for the construction of a software-based system and its maintenance after

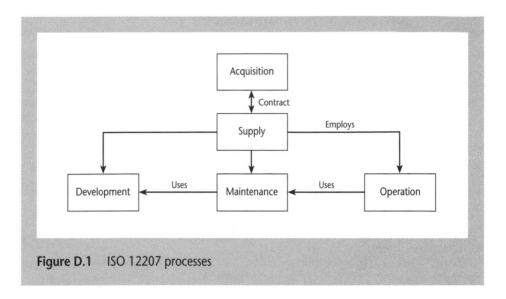

Figure D.1 ISO 12207 processes

Table D.1 ISO 12207 Supporting and organizational processes

Supporting processes	Organizational processes
Documentation	Management
Configuration management	Infrastructure
Quality assurance	Improvement
Verification	Training
Validation	
Joint review	
Audit	
Problem resolution	

installation. Our attention here is given primarily to the acquisition, supply and development processes. It must be stressed once again that this appendix is intended merely to give an overview. Those intending to use the standard 'in anger' must obtain and study the full document.

The acquisition process is the set of procedures that a customer for software (or 'acquirer' in ISO 12207 terminology) will go through in order to obtain that software from an external source. The supply process is the opposite side and is the set of procedures that the supplier should adopt in order to satisfy the acquirer's needs. The supplier might use an existing piece of software or might develop new software, in which case they would need to invoke the development process.

Just as in the case of BS 6079, some supporting processes can be identified. These are listed in Table D.1.

We will now deal briefly with the acquisition, supply, and development processes in turn.

D.4 The acquisition process

A previous discussion in Chapter 10 on contract management has already mentioned ISO 12207 in this context and so we will avoid going into excessive detail here.

Figure D.2 portrays the main activities that compose the acquisition process. The *initiation* activity starts with the description of the 'concept' that the acquirer wishes to make real, or the need that the acquirer wishes to satisfy. The requirements of

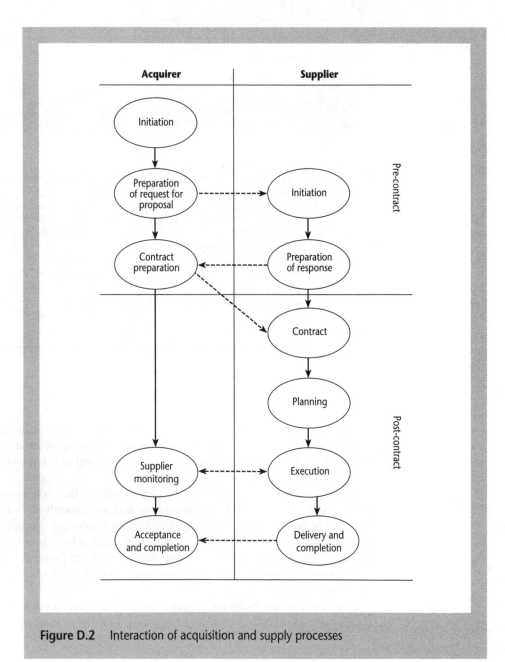

Figure D.2   Interaction of acquisition and supply processes

the system then need to be defined by the acquirer. In fact, the acquiring organization could employ an external source to do this for them, but they would still have the responsibility of approving these requirements.

ISO 12207 distinguishes between system requirements and the software requirements that now have to be analysed and documented – software requirements relate to the distinct software components that will make up the delivered system. Once this has been done, a decision needs to be taken about the best way to acquire the software, for example, whether to make or buy. This is analogous to the 'defining the project approach' (SU4) activity in PRINCE 2.

Having made this decision, the acquirer is now in a position to prepare the acquisition plan, detailing the steps needed to acquire the software, taking account of such matters as who is to be responsible, for example, for any maintenance and support. Any inherent risks need to be considered. It is also important that at this point the criteria for final system acceptance, and the methods by which compliance is to be evaluated, be defined and recorded.

Another name for 'request for proposal' is 'invitation to tender'.

Request for proposal (RFP)   The groundwork has now been done for the production of the *request for proposal* document. This should include sections on the topics listed in Table D.2.

An important activity in the context of ISO 12207 is the tailoring of the standard for a particular project. In some places in the standard, it is stated that certain process requirements should be '*as specified in the contract*'. The precise requirements to be included in the current contract now need to be identified. Depending on the type of product or project, it could be agreed that certain ISO 12207 requirements are to be dropped as not appropriate, while in other cases there could be process requirements above and beyond those in ISO 12207 that need to be documented.

Contract preparation and update   Before you can have a contract, you must have a supplier with whom to have the contract. With this in mind, the criteria to be used in selecting the supplier and the method by which the compliance by potential suppliers with the criteria can be judged have to be set down. Once the preferred supplier has been selected, the final form of the contract between the supplier and acquirer can be negotiated. This often involves some adjustments to the way in which ISO 12207 is to be tailored.

Monitor supplier   This will be done using some of the supporting processes listed in Table D.1, namely joint reviews, audit, verification and validation.

Table D.2 Topics in a request for proposal document

Request for proposal – contents

System requirements
Scope statement
Instructions for bidders
List of software products
Control of sub-contracts
Technical constraints (e.g. the target environment)

Accept completed contract   When the supplier finally delivers the product, the acquirer will conduct acceptance tests and if the specified acceptance criteria are satisfied, the completed software can be signed off as completed.

D.5   The supply process

This process mirrors the acquisition process, but documents the activities that a supplier would need to undertake in response to the request of a acquirer. Figure D.2 outlines the main activities involved. There will be occasions where the sequence of activities is not that shown and yet other occasions when some of the activities will have to be iterated a number of times.

Initiation   The process is started when a potential supplier receives an RFP from an acquirer and the supplier decides to bid for the work.

Preparation of a response   The supplier, after consulting people with various types of expertise, now prepares a response. This should include proposals about how ISO 12207 is to be tailored for the project in view.

Contract   If all goes well, the supplier's proposal will make the right impression and lead to acceptance by the acquirer. The details of the contract are then negotiated and signed.

Planning   The supplier can now draw up a detailed plan of how the work is to be done. The starting point for this will be the requirements as laid down in the RFP. You would normally expect this to include the life cycle approach to be applied by the supplier, as this will influence the points during the project at which consultation between supplier and acquirer is to take place. If the life cycle has not been stipulated, then it should be selected now as a basis for devising the plan. It will have been noted that earlier the acquirer might have considered, as part of the acquisition process, the options of 'make' versus 'buy' and also whether to use in-house or external sources. ISO 12207 now makes provision for the supplier to make a similar choice, and having done this, to develop a plan accordingly. For example, a contractor who is primarily a hardware specialist might use a software house to write the software required as part of a contract.

The general format of the plan is shown in Table D.3.

Execution and control   The plan can now be executed. Depending on whether the contract is for systems development, operation, or maintenance, the ISO 12207 process stipulated for development, operation or maintenance would now be undertaken.

During the execution of the plan, the standard expects the supplier to monitor and control progress and product quality, and to have a mechanism for recording, analysing and resolving the problems that occur. The supplier will also be responsible for passing on requirements that accurately reflect those of the acquirer to any sub-contractors and for ensuring the compliance of sub-contractors with those requirements. The supplier also needs to cooperate fully with any independent verification and validation processes that were laid down in the contract.

Table D.3 Contents of a plan

Topics to be covered by a plan

Project organizational structure
Engineering (i.e. development) environment: including facilities, standards, procedures and tools
Work breakdown structure
Management of quality characteristics
Management of safety, security and other critical requirements
Sub-contractor management
Verification and validation
Acquirer involvement
User involvement
Risk management
Security policy – 'need-to-know' and 'access-to-information' rules
Arrangements for obtaining any regulatory approvals
Scheduling, tracking and reporting
Training

Review and evaluation   The provisions here are mainly to ensure that the supplier allows the acquirer access to the information needed to review the progress of the project, although the precise extent to which the acquirer has a reviewing role and access to supplier documentation has to be specified in the contract.

Delivery and completion   Attention is required in any management plans to the way products are to be delivered and to how any required post-delivery support is to be provided.

D.6   The development process

ISO 12207 sees the development process as being made up of the activities in Figure D.3. Most of the terms used will be familiar to software developers. Some activities address the *system* as a whole – for example, the analysis of user requirements and the overall design of the interacting components that together should meet those requirements ('architecture' design in Figure D.3). Others relate to *software*, which in practice means activities that are repeated for each *software item* in the system. The standard identifies a hierarchy of *software items* in a system that are made up of *components* that, in turn, are made up of *software units*. The software unit is the basic unit of code, but the precise definition of components and items will depend on the circumstances of a particular project. At the same time that these activities are starting, progressing and terminating in the planned sequence in a project, there should be the continuous background operation of supporting activities, such as configuration management and problem resolution – this is represented in Figure D.3 by the 'process implementation' stream.

The structure in Figure D.3 implies a 'waterfall', or in ISO 12207 terms a 'once-through' approach. Figure D.4 and Figure D.5 illustrate how these activities can be

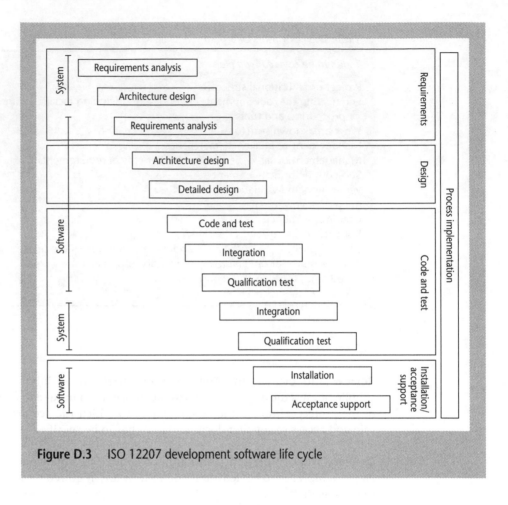

Figure D.3 ISO 12207 development software life cycle

shuffled to fit an incremental or evolutionary approach to a project. Some rather simplistic guidelines are given to help the planner decide which approach to adopt – for example, if the acquirer wants all the system capabilities in the first delivery, an incremental approach would not be advisable!

Guidance as to what should be done for each activity is given and the reader who needs this level of detail really should read the standard itself. The general picture that emerges is that for each activity there should be the following pattern:

- plan;
- do;
- document;
- evaluate.

It is to be hoped that in general the doing and the documenting are going on in parallel, rather than the documentation following the doing as an easily forgotten afterthought. A prime objective of ISO 12207 is to ensure that appropriate and correct data is recorded.

The evaluation procedure following the carrying out of an activity is usually done by means of a joint review, or, where testing has taken place, through audits.

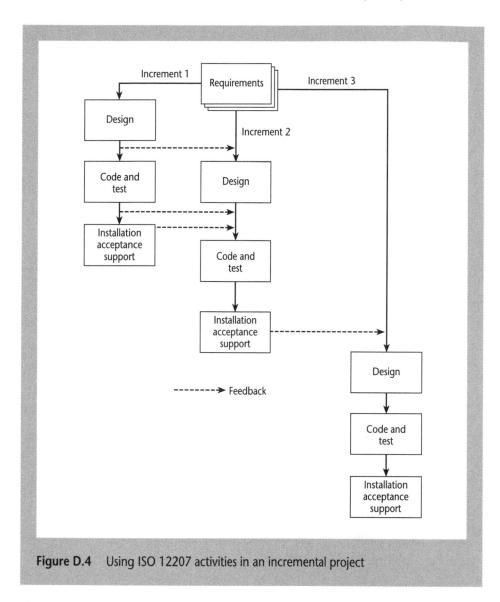

Figure D.4   Using ISO 12207 activities in an incremental project

Reviews can be at a management level where the project is monitored or can be at a technical level where the appropriateness of a particular software product is examined. The technical reviews will look at such considerations as:

● Is the product complete – or are some parts missing?

● Does it comply with the standards and the specification?

● Have all required changes been carried out?

● Is it on schedule?

● Will it be an acceptable basis for the next activity?

● Do the processes used follow those in the plans, schedules, standards and guidelines for this project?

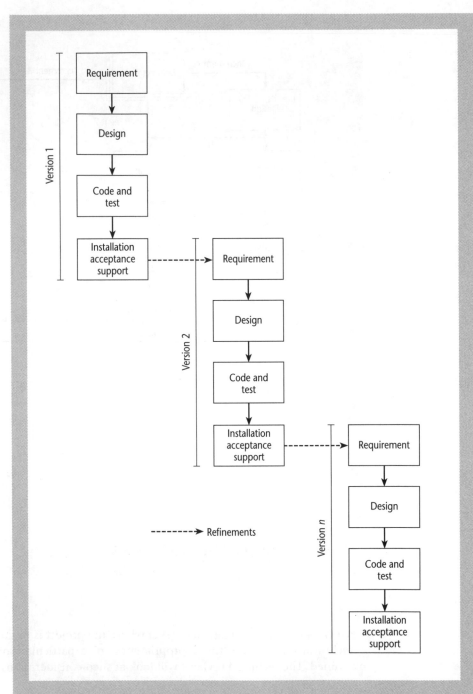

Figure D.5 Using ISO 12207 activities in an evolutionary project

Table D.4 IS 12207 generic acceptance criteria

	Traceability to source documents	Consistency with previous products	Internal consistency	Testability	Test coverage	Conformance to expected results	Appropriate standards and methods	Feasibility of next activity	Operational feasibility	Maintainability
System requirements analysis	✓	✓		✓				✓	✓	✓
System architecture design	✓	✓					✓	✓	✓	✓
Software requirements analysis	✓	✓	✓	✓				✓	✓	✓
Software architecture design	✓	✓	✓				✓	✓	✓	✓
Software detailed design	✓	✓	✓	✓			✓		✓	✓
Software code and test	✓	✓			✓		✓	✓	✓	✓
Software integration	✓	✓	✓		✓	✓	✓	✓	✓	✓
Software qualification test					✓	✓		✓	✓	✓
System integration					✓	✓	✓	✓	✓	✓
System qualification test					✓	✓			✓	✓

In addition, some concerns will relate to the products created by specific activities as Table D.4 shows. The emphasis in many cases on the 'feasibility of operation and maintenance' is worth noting. The software does not only have to meet the acquirer's functional requirements, it needs to work in the planned operating environment and be easy to modify to meet any new requirements. Making these requirements explicit during development is invaluable.

Operation and maintenance processes

As noted earlier, the ISO 12207 standard also prescribes general processes for operation and maintenance. The interested reader is directed to the standard itself for further details of these.

Project Management Bodies of Knowledge

E.1 Introduction

As noted in Appendix A, it is possible to be assessed as a PRINCE 2 practitioner – we have treated this as a specialized qualification in a specific technique rather than a general PM qualification.

The standards and guidelines in the preceding appendices have, to a greater or lesser extent, concentrated on *procedure* – the actions to be taken in specified circumstances. As we noted, one view of the software development process is as an information system in its own right: processes take information from various sources, manipulate and process it to create new products that are used by other processes. It is clearly in the interests of the managers of projects, especially larger ones, to ensure that this is done in an accurate and structured way and standards such as ISO 12207 and PRINCE 2 focus on this aspect.

Correct procedure needs to be supported by professional competence. Administratively, a procedure might be carried out correctly with the appropriate documents recording the decisions made, but if the project manager is not competent the decision that has been conscientiously recorded can still be misjudged and damaging. Competence will stem partly from innate ability, partly from past experience and also from acquired formal knowledge. This appendix will look at some attempts to define the knowledge and/or competencies of the good project manager. In the cases examined, this has been done as a basis for the certification or accreditation of project managers. The review may help readers considering the acquisition of a formal qualification in project management.

E.2 Project Management Institute 'Guide to the Project Management Body of Knowledge'

The Project Management Institute (PMI) was founded in 1969 in the United States and currently has a membership in the region of 80,000 members worldwide. In 1983 it published a *Project Management Body of Knowledge* (PMBOK) which attempted to outline the scope of the knowledge that makes up the Project Management discipline. Since then the PMBOK has been extensively revised and expanded so that the 2000 release, which has the more realistic title of 'A Guide to the Project Management Body of Knowledge', is a mature document.

The PMBOK is based on the concept of bodies of knowledge upon which various professions, such as medicine or law, base their practice. The PMBOK is an attempt to delineate such a body of knowledge for the project management professional. This could be an enormous undertaking and the PMI has made it more manageable by considering only that subset which is generally accepted. Even with this restriction the potential scope is extensive and the fact that the document cannot hope to be all-inclusive is reflected in the word 'guide' in the title.

The objectives of the PMI in producing the PMBOK have been to:

- identify generally accepted project management practice;
- produce a basic reference document;
- identify a common set of terms;
- to act as a basis for training and accreditation.

The compilers of the body of knowledge have therefore defined the scope of 'project management' with some care. Some general management principles and practices have a bearing on projects while others do not. On the other hand there are some project management techniques which relate only to certain technical applications. One example is *software* project management where some material is peculiar to software development, for example the use of function points for effort estimation.

The starting point of PMBOK is a definition of a project as *'a temporary endeavour undertaken to create a unique product or service'* and of project management as *'the application of knowledge, skills, tools and techniques to project activities in order to meet or exceed stakeholder needs and expectations from a project'*. This last definition seems to us to be a little too widely drawn as one can imagine technical activities that could fall within this definition.

The PMBOK is organized into nine key knowledge areas. The PMBOK compilers have experienced a problem that we experienced in structuring this book: the sequence of concerns that a project manager has while planning and executing a project does not map neatly onto the organization of the subject matter. For example, risk management techniques will be called on repeatedly throughout a project.

The problem has been tackled in PMBOK by identifying a set of processes for each phase of a project. A 'process' is defined as *'a set of actions bringing about a result'*. Five groups of process have been identified: initiating, planning, executing, controlling and closing.

Some processes within each group are *core* ones that are often inter-connected so that the output from one process is used by others. In common with most of the approaches that have been discussed in previous appendices there are a number of supporting processes (or *facilitating* processes in PMBOK terminology) such as quality planning and risk identification. For each of the processes, PMBOK defines the inputs, the techniques that may be used and the outputs.

This might seem to be similar to the way PRINCE 2 is organized, but such a comparison would be misleading as the PMBOK describes the components of processes at much higher and more abstract level.

The PMI administer a certification examination (which it is possible to sit, not only in the US, but also in the UK). Once the written examination has been passed, candidates may apply to be assessed for full 'Project Management Professional' (PMP) status. However, in 1998 it was reported that because of the strict criteria

Mark Becker 'The time of the project manager', *Project Manager Today*, January 1998.

concerning the practical experience requirements and the stringent assessment process, the growth in members achieving full PMP status had not been high compared to those taking the examination.

The practical experience requirements are that candidates must either have a university degree and 4,500 hours of experience gained over at least three years, but not more than six years (category A). Candidates without a degree need 7,500 hours of experience within a minimum of the last five years and maximum of eight (category B). There is a four and a half hour, multiple choice examination which is done via a computer system and gives an immediate result. Unlike some other qualifications, there is no oral examination to test verbal skills. From January 2002, a 'Certified Associate Project Manager' (CAPM) qualification is to be introduced requiring only 1500 hours for category A candidates and 3000 for category B.

Once you have your PMP certification you have to obtain 60 professional development credits (PDUs) in each three-year period in order to maintain your certification. The PDUs are 'brownie points' that you earn for such things as attending or providing training events, serving on PMI committees or even providing project management services to your local football club.

The address for the PMI in the United States is:

Project Management Institute
130, South State Road
Upper Darby
PA 19082
USA

The PMI have a website at http://www.pmi.org. There are some chapters of the PMI outside the United States, including in the United Kingdom, but local contact points are best obtained from the PMI centre.

E.3 Australian Institute of Project Management

The roots of the Australian Institute of Project Management go back to the establishment of a Project Managers' Forum in Sydney, New South Wales, in 1976. In 1989, the organization was transformed into the Australian Institute of Project Management which, among other activities to support the professionalism of project management, has undertaken the certification of competent project managers.

The organization has developed sets of competency standards to support the certification of project managers which are recognized as the Australian national standards. An industrial sector or individual enterprise may establish their own standards suitable for their own environment, but these must be consistent with and at least as rigorous as the generic standard.

The AIPM has adopted a definition of a project as 'a unique set of inter-related activities, with defined start and finish times, designed to achieve a common objective'. Project management is defined as 'the integration of project activity through the project life cycle to achieve the delivery of a defined product or service within prescribed constraints of time, budget, scope and quality'.

There are nine functions where competence needs to be shown:

- integration of project activities;
- project scope management;
- project quality management;
- project time management;
- project cost management;
- project risk management;
- project human resources management;
- project contracting/procurement management;
- project communications management.

The Australian Institute for Project Management are the custodians of the *Australian National Competency Standards for Project Management*. The candidate for a qualification at a particular level is issued with a logbook and is assigned an assessor. Assessment of various competencies is carried out by collecting and recording evidence of satisfactory practical performance. This is recorded in the logbook and signed off by the assessor. Eventually the logbook is sent to the Project Management Recognition Council who complete a final validation and approve the award.

The AIPM certify project management specialists at three levels.

- *Qualified Project Practitioner* (QPP) which is at Australian Quality Framework (AQF) level 4 and is for project team specialists who carry out one or more elements of project management as part of their work.

- *Registered Project Manager* (RPM) which is at AQF level 5 and is for those actively involved in the management of a team.

- *Master Project Director* (MPD) which is at AQF level 6 and is for those who are managers of project managers, for example, as a programme manager.

The documentation for these standards are available via WWW from the site at www.aipm.org.au. Enquiries can be addressed to:

Australian Institute of Project Management
Level 9
139 Macquairie Street
Sydney
NSW 2000

E.4 Association for Project Management (APM) Body of Knowledge

The UK-based Association for Project Management have also produced a 'Body of Knowledge'. Although the APM now sets and administers examinations in project management, at the time that the original body of knowledge was formulated, their certification process was based, not on an unseen written examination, but on assessing the practitioner's competence. It is possible to become a Member of the APM by submitting an application form detailing five years of project management experience. If you have less than five years you can become an Associate.

Table E.1 APM key competencies – topics that are not tested in APMP examinations are marked with an asterisk

Section	Sub-section
1. General	1.0 Project management
	1.1 Programme management
	1.2 Project context
2. Strategic	2.0 Project success criteria
	2.1 Strategy/project management plan
	2.2 *Value management**
	2.3 Risk management
	2.4 Quality management
	2.5 Health, safety and environment
3. Control	3.0 Work content and scope management
	3.1 Time scheduling/phasing
	3.2 Resource management
	3.3 Budgeting and cost management
	3.4 Change control
	3.5 Earned value management
	3.6 Information management
4. Technical	4.0 *Design, implementation and hand-over management**
	4.1 *Requirement management**
	4.2 Estimating
	4.3 *Technology management**
	4.4 *Value engineering**
	4.5 *Modelling and testing**
	4.6 Configuration management
5. Commercial	5.0 Business case
	5.1 *Marketing and sales**
	5.2 *Financial management**
	5.3 Procurement
	5.4 *Legal awareness**
6. Organizational	6.0 Life cycle design and management
	6.1 *Opportunity**
	6.2 *Design and development**
	6.3 *Implementation**
	6.4 Hand-over
	6.5 (Post) Project evaluation review
	6.6 Organization structure
	6.7 Organization roles
7. People	7.0 Communication
	7.1 Teamwork
	7.2 Leadership
	7.3 Conflict management
	7.4 Negotiation
	7.5 *Personnel management**

The Certified Project Manager status has a more rigorous procedure. Candidates, who have to be members of the APM, have to submit a curriculum vitae and references. They also have to complete a self-assessment form, where they identify what they consider to be their level of proficiency in various aspects of project management, and produce a précis of a project where they had management responsibilities. These documents are examined and if they are deemed to be satisfactory, a full project report is requested. An interview is also conducted. Those who are successful can use the title Certified Project Manager or MAPM(CPM).

The APM also administers an examination leading to the APMP (APM practitioner) qualification. One part of the examination is a multiple choice paper and the other is a three-hour conventional unseen examination. These examinations are based on the APM Body of Knowledge (BOK) which was updated in January 2000. Table E.1 shows the main topics covered by the BOK. Some elements in the BOK are not covered by the syllabus and these have been indicated by an asterisk. The syllabus adds considerable detail to those parts of the BOK to which it refers. It includes a detailed glossary of project management terms – those of us who have been involved in setting examinations appreciate the need for an agreed and commonly understood set of terms.

The APM body of knowledge is divided into six general topic areas which are broken down into forty-two sub-topics.

Further information can be obtained from:

The Association for Project Management
85 Oxford Road
High Wycombe
Buckinghamshire
HP11 2DX
(http://www.apm.org.uk)

E.5 Information Systems Examination Board Certificate and Diploma in Project Management

A personal interest needs to be declared here as one of the authors has been involved as an examiner and moderator with this body.

In 1998, there were around 3,000 holders of the ISEB Certificate in Project Management.

The Information Systems Examination Board (ISEB) is the wing of the British Computer Society (BCS) which sets and administers examinations to assess professional competence in a number of fields related to information technology and information systems development. These fields include Business Systems Development, IT Service Management, IT Infrastructure Management, System Testing and Project Management. Thus, unlike the qualifications we have already looked at, this is targeted specifically at Information Systems staff.

The aim of the Certificate is to provide an entry level qualification for project management. Candidates must have at least four years' experience in management or in information systems and have attended an accredited course in project management where the candidate's course work will be assessed. They then have to take a three-hour written examination and, if successful, pass an oral examination. There is also an experienced project manager route where the candidate can sit the written and oral examinations without having attended a course.

Table E.2 ISEB Certificate in Project Management – outline of syllabus content

Section	Sub-section	% of course
Overview	Strategy Project management Project life cycle Organization Ethical and legal considerations	5%
Managing plans	Plans Estimating Acceptance of plans Project reviews	17.5%
Managing people and other resources	Skills Project organization Human resource management Technical management Resources other than staff	25%
Managing the development and delivery of project products	Definition of products Control during production Resource management Configuration management and change control Delivery of products Maintenance of documentation Types of documentation	22.5%
Managing quality	Quality management systems Quality standards Quality plans Quality assurance	15%
Managing change	Responding to change Controlling change	7.5%
Managing risk	Risk identification Risk evaluation Risk planning	7.5%

The syllabus is designed to have the capability of being delivered via a two week 80 hour course. The syllabus was updated in October 2001. The revision was partly to clarify the nature of some of the topics, but the need for more flexible project life cycles, for special effort estimation techniques and for links between programme and project management have also been emphasized. An overview of the syllabus is shown in Table E.2.

The ISEB also has a Diploma in Project Management which is designed for practitioners who have the Certificate and eight years' minimum experience. The candidate has to submit five written papers of a minimum of 3,000 words, which they have to complete in their own time, and to make a presentation which is followed by an oral examination.

A recent development at IESB has been the launch of a Programme and Project Support Office (PPSO) qualification with both foundation and advanced examinations.

Details of these qualifications can be obtained from:

Information Systems Examination Board
1 Sanford Street
Swindon
Wiltshire
SN1 1HJ
(http://www.bcs.org.uk)

Answer pointers

Chapter 1

1.1 Examples of projects

The order you put these projects is, of course, to a large degree subjective. Here is one example of a possible ordering.

1. **Building the Channel Tunnel**   Almost everybody puts this one first. The huge scale of the task, the relative novelty of the project, all the different specialisms involved and the international nature of the project make it special.

2. **Writing an operating system**   This is a prime example of a software development project.

3. **Amending a financial computer system to deal with a common European currency**   This project is modifying an existing system rather than creating a new one from scratch. Many software projects have this characteristic and it does not make them any less a software project.

4. **Installing a new version of a word processing package in an organization**   Although no software is being produced or modified, many of the stages that are associated with software projects will be involved and the techniques of software project management would be appropriate.

5. **Investigation into the reasons why a user has a problem with a computer system**   This will have many of the stages common to software projects, although the precise nature of the end result is uncertain at the outset. It could be that the user needs some simple remedial training. On the other hand, it could turn out to be quite a considerable software modification task.

6. **Getting married**   There should be lots of arguments about this one! Some will be reluctant to give a high rating to this because of its personal nature. The degree to which this is 'project-like' will depend very much upon the cultural milieu in which it takes place. Very often it requires a high degree of planning, involves lots of different people and, for most people, is a non-routine operation.

7. **A research project into what makes a good human–computer interface**   Compared to some of the projects above, the objectives of the research project are more open-ended and the idea of a specific client for the end product may be less well-defined. Research projects are in some ways special cases and the

approach to their planning needs a rather different approach, which is outside the scope of this book.

8. **Producing an edition of a newspaper** In some ways this has all the characteristics of a project. There are lots of different people with lots of different specialisms whose work needs to be coordinated in order to produce an end product under very tight time constraints. What argues against this as a typical project is that it is repeated. After a while, everyone knows what he or she each needs to do and most of the problems that arise are familiar and the procedures to deal with them are well defined.

9. **A second year programming assignment for a computing student** This is not being done for a customer, although it could be argued that the tutor responsible for setting and assessing the assignment is, in effect, a surrogate client. Not all the stages of a normal project will be gone through.

1.2 Brightmouth College payroll: Stages of a project

1. **Project evaluation** All the costs that would be incurred by the college if it were to carry out its own payroll processing would need to be carefully examined to ensure it would be more cost effective than letting the local authority carry on providing the service.

2. **Planning** The way that the transfer to local processing is to be carried out needs to be carefully planned with the participation of all those concerned. Some detailed planning would need to be deferred until more information was available, for example, which payroll package was to be used.

3. **Requirements analysis** This is finding out what the users need from the system. To a large extent it will often consist of finding out what the current system does, as it may be assumed that in general the new system is to provide the same functions as the old. The users might have additional requirements, however, or there might even be facilities that are no longer needed.

4. **Specification** This involves documenting what the new system is to be able to do.

5. **Design/coding** As an 'off-the-shelf' package is envisaged, these stages will be replaced by a package evaluation and selection activity.

6. **Verification and validation** Tests will need to be carried out to ensure that the selected package will actually do what is required. This task might well involve parallel running of the old and new systems and a comparison of the output from them both to check for any inconsistencies.

7. **Implementation** This would involve such things as installing the software, setting system parameters such as the salary scales, and setting up details of employees.

8. **Maintenance/support** This will include dealing with users' queries, liaising with the package supplier and taking account of new payroll requirements.

1.3 The nature of an operating system

Many large organizations that are committed to computer-based information systems have specialists responsible for the maintenance of operating systems.

However, as an operating system is primarily concerned with driving the hardware, it is argued that it has more in common with what we have described as embedded systems.

1.4 Brightmouth College payroll: objectives-driven vs. product-driven

This project is really driven by objectives. If in-house payroll processing turns out not to be cost effective, then the project should not try to implement such a solution. Other ways of meeting the objectives set could be considered: for example, it might be possible to contract out the processing to some organization other than the local authority at a lower cost.

1.5 A day in the life of a project manager

Planning:

- staffing requirements for the next year.

Representing the section:

- at the group meeting;
- when communicating with the personnel manager about replacement staff;
- when explaining about the delay to users.

Controlling, innovating, directing:

- deciding what needs to be done to make good the progress that will be lost through temporarily losing a member of staff.

Staffing:

- deciding which member of staff is to do what;
- discussion with personnel about the requirement for temporary staff;
- planning staffing for the next year.

Note: the same activity can involve many different roles.

1.6 Defining objectives

Among the comments and queries that could be made in each case are:

(i) Has the actual time and the amount of the budget been specified somewhere? Deadline and budget constraints normally have to be set against the scope and quality of the functions to be delivered. For example, if the deadline were not achieved, would the customer rather have the full set of functionality at a later date, or an essential sub-set of functions at the deadline?

(ii) 'As few software errors as possible' is not precise. Removing errors requires effort and hence money. Can the developers spend as much money and time as they like if this reduces errors?

(iii) What does 'user-friendly' really mean? How is it measured? Normally 'ease of use' is measured by the time it takes a user to carry out standard operations, and 'ease of learning' by the time it takes for a beginner to become proficient in carrying out standard operations.

(iv) What does 'full' documentation mean? A list of the types of document to be produced, perhaps with an indication of the content layout, would be more useful.

1.7 Brightmouth college payroll: objectives, goals and measures of effectiveness

The original objective might have been formulated as: 'To carry out payroll processing at less cost while maintaining the current scope and quality of services'.

In order to achieve this, sub-objectives or goals will usually have been identified, for example:

- to transfer payroll processing to the college by 1st April;
- to implement in the new system those facilities that exist in the current system less those identified in the initial report as not being required;
- to carry out the implementation of the payroll processing capability within the financial constraints identified in the initial report.

It should be noted that the objectives listed above do not explicitly mention such things as putting into place ongoing arrangements to deal with hardware and software maintenance, security arrangements and so on. By discussing and trying to agree objectives with the various people involved the true requirements of the project can be clarified.

Measures of effectiveness for the sub-objectives listed above might include the following:

- *Date of implementation* Was the new system being used operationally by the agreed date?
- *Facilities* In parallel runs, were all the outputs produced by the old system and also produced by the new system?
- *Costs* How did the actual costs incurred compare with the budgeted costs?

1.8 Brightmouth college payroll: stakeholders

Major stakeholders would include:

- the finance department;
- the personnel department, who would need to supply most of the employee details needed;
- heads of departments, who would need to submit details of hours worked for part-time staff;
- staff, who would naturally be concerned that they are paid correctly;
- site management: the new arrangements may mean that the office layout has to be rearranged physically;
- software and hardware vendors.

One group of stakeholders that might not be readily identified at first is the local government authority and its staff. It might seem strange to list the people who used to do the job, but who are no longer required. The project manager's job will be made a lot easier if their cooperation and help can be obtained. The project manager would do well to sound out tactfully how the local authority staff feel about losing this work. It could be that they are pleased to be shot of the workload and hassle involved! Arrangements that take into account existing local authority staff might be possible. For example, if the college needs to recruit new staff to deal with payroll, it might smooth things to give the job to a member of the local authority staff who already deals with this area.

1.9 Collecting control data

The project seems to have two major components: training and document transfer. If trainers were expected to tour offices giving training, one would expect there to be a schedule indicating when each office was to receive training. The following information about the progress of training might therefore be collected:

- number of offices that had received training – this could be compared against the schedule;
- number of staff that had received training – to ensure staff were attending;
- feedback from staff on the perceived quality of training – for example, by post-training evaluation forms.

For the document transfer aspect, the following might be usefully collected for each office on a regular basis during the transfer process:

- number of documents transferred;
- estimated number of documents still needing to be transferred;
- number of staff hours spent on transferring documents – to monitor the budget and transfer productivity;
- number of staff involved in transfer.

When all the documents had been transferred, performance tests to check response times might be required.

Chapter 2

2.1 External stakeholders in IOE accounts system

The main stakeholders who need to be considered are the IOE customers. It will be worth consulting some representative customers about the layout of the new monthly statement for example.

2.2 Invitation to tender PFD

Figure F.1 illustrates the Product Flow Diagram for invitation to tender for Brightmouth College payroll

2.3 Invitation to tender activity network

Figure F.2 illustrates the activity network for invitation to tender for the Brightmouth College payroll.

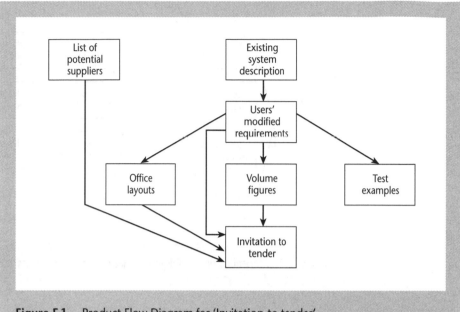

Figure F.1 Product Flow Diagram for 'Invitation to tender'

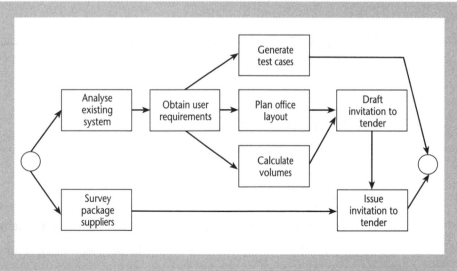

Figure F.2 Brightmouth College payroll project activity network fragment

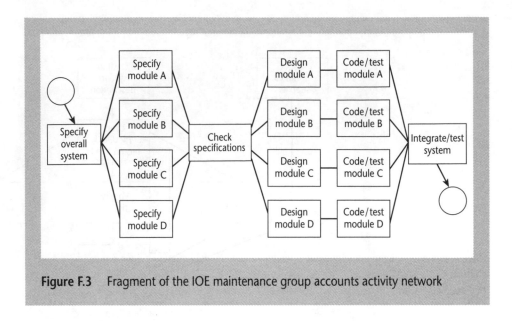

Figure F.3   Fragment of the IOE maintenance group accounts activity network

2.4   Including a checkpoint

Figure F.3 illustrates the inclusion of a checkpoint in Amanda's activity network.

2.5   Quality checks on user requirements

The users will need at least to read and approve the system specification. This might be rather late to make major changes, so user approval of earlier documents such as interview notes would be helpful.

2.6   Step Wise activities

Figure F.4 suggests activities for the different sections of a project plan.

Chapter 3

3.1   Costs and benefits for the Brightmouth College payroll system

Table F.1 lists costs and benefits for the proposed Brightmouth HE College payroll system. It is not comprehensive but illustrates some of the types of items that you should have listed.

3.2   Ranking project cash flows

Obviously you will have your own views about which have the best and worst cash flows. You should, however, have considered the following points: project 2 requires a very large investment compared to its gain – in fact we could obtain £100,000 by undertaking both projects 1 and 3 for a lower cost than project 2. Both projects 1 and 4 produce the bulk of their incomes relatively late in their lives compared with project 3, which produces a steady income over its life.

Section of plan	Step Wise activities
Introduction	
Background	1.3 Identify stakeholders
	2.1 Establish relationship between project and strategic planning
Project objectives	1.1 Identify objectives and measures of effectiveness
	1.4 Modify objectives in the light of stakeholder analysis
Constraints	1.1 Identify objectives and measures of effectiveness
	2.2 Identify installation standards and procedures
Project products	4.1 Identify and describe project products
Methods	3. Analyse project characteristics
	4.2 Document generic product flows (this could help establish a methodology)
Activities to be carried out	4.4 Product ideal activity network
	4.5 Modify ideal activity network
Resources to be used	3.6 Review overall resource estimates
	5.1 Carry out bottom up estimates
	7. Allocate resources
Risks to the project	3.3 Identify high-level project risks
	6. Identify activity risks
	(Note planning – especially 6.3 – should have removed many of the risks initially identified)
Management of the project	1.2 Establish project authority
	1.5 Establish methods of communication with all parties
	2.3 Identify project team organization

Figure F.4   Step Wise activities

3.3   Calculating payback periods

The payback periods for each of the projects will occur during the year indicated: project 1 year 5, project 2 year 5, project 3 year 4 and project 4 year 4 (end).

We would therefore favour project 3 or 4 over the other two. Note that, in reality, with relatively short-term projects such as these we would produce a monthly (or at least quarterly) cash flow forecast and it is therefore likely that project 3 would be seen more clearly to have a shorter payback period than project 4.

3.4   Calculating the return on investment

The return on investments for each of the projects is: project 1: 10%, project 2: 2%, project 3: 10% and project 4: 12.5%. Project 4 therefore stands out as being the most beneficial as it earns the highest return.

3.5   Calculating the net present value

The net present value for each of the projects is calculated as in Table F.2. On the basis of net present value, project 4 clearly provides the greatest return and project 2 is clearly not worth considering.

Table F.1 Costs and benefits for the Brightmouth College payroll system

Category	Cost/benefit
Development costs	Software purchase – software cost plus selection and purchasing cost
	Project team employment costs
Setup costs	Training include costs of trainers and operational staff time lost while training
	Staff recruitment
	Computer hardware and other equipment which might have a residual value at end of projected life
	Accommodation – any new/refurbished accommodation and furniture required to house new system
	Initial systems supplies – purchase of stationery, disks and other consumables
Operational costs	Operations staff – full employment costs
	Stationery – purchase and storage*
	Maintenance and standby – contract or estimation of occurrence costs
	Accommodation including heating, power, insurance etc.*
Direct benefits	Saving on local authority fees
	Later payment – increase interest income through paying salaries later in the month
Indirect benefits	Improved accuracy – assumes that direct costs of correcting current errors that should not occur with a computerized system are known (for example, takes one person one day per week). Note: benefit should measure what can be done with that additional time
Intangible benefits	Improved management information – this should lead to improved decision making but it is very difficult to quantify the potential benefits

*These items, and some other elements, might show corresponding savings or costs through no longer being required. For example, although new office furniture might be required for the new system, the existing furniture might be redeployed or sold.

3.6 Calculating the effect of discount rates on NPV

Table F.3 illustrates the effect of varying discount rates on the NPV. In each case the 'best' project is indicated in bold. In this somewhat artificial example, which project is best is very sensitive to the chosen discount rate. In such a case we must either have a very strong reason to use a particular discount rate or take other criteria into account when choosing among the projects.

3.7 Project evaluation using cost–benefit analysis

Expected sales of £500,000 per year over four years would generate an expected net income of £1.2m (after allowing for annual costs of £200,000) which, by almost any

Table F.2 Calculating the net present value of projects 2, 3 and 4

Year	Discount factor	Discounted cash flow (£)		
		Project 2	Project 3	Project 4
0	1.0000	−1,000,000	−100,000	−120,000
1	0.9091	181,820	27,273	27,273
2	0.8264	165,280	24,792	24,792
3	0.7513	150,260	22,539	22,539
4	0.6830	136,600	20,490	20,490
5	0.6209	186,270	18,627	46,568
NPV		−179,770	13,721	21,662

Table F.3 The effect on net present value of varying the discount rate

Year	Cash flow values (£)		
	Project A	Project B	Project C
0	−8,000	−8,000	−10,000
1	4,000	1,000	2,000
2	4,000	2,000	2,000
3	2,000	4,000	6,000
4	1,000	3,000	2,000
5	500	9,000	2,000
6	500	−6,000	2,000
Net Profit	£4,000	£5,000	£6,000
NPV @ 8%	£2,111	£2,365	**£2,421**
NPV @ 10%	£1,720	**£1,818**	£1,716
NPV @ 12%	**£1,356**	£1,308	£1,070

criteria, would provide a good return on an investment of £750,000. However, if sales are low, and there is a 30% chance of this happening, the company will lose money – it is unlikely that any company would wish to take such a risk knowingly.

This example illustrates one of the basic objections to using this approach for one-off decisions. Were we to repeat the project a large number of times we would expect, *on average*, an income of £500,000 per annum. However, the company is developing this package only once – they can't keep trying in the hope of, on the average, generating a respectable income. Indeed, a severe loss on this project could mean it is the last project they are able to undertake.

Chapter 4

4.1 Classification of systems

(a) A payroll system is a data oriented or information system that is application specific.

(b) The bottling plant system is a process oriented system which contains embedded software.

(c) This looks like an information system that will make heavy use of computer graphics. The plant itself might use control software which might be safety-critical but this is not the subject of the project under consideration.

(d) Project management software tools are often categorized as general packages. There would be a considerable information systems element to them.

(e) This could use an information retrieval package that is a general software package. It is also a strong candidate for a knowledge-based system.

4.2 Identification of risks

The user staff could, arguably, be regarded as a project resource. The writers' view is that it is useful to add a fourth category of risks – those belonging to the *environment* in which the system is to be implemented.

Among the risks that might be identified at Brightmouth College are:

- conflict of views between the finance and personnel departments;
- lack of staff acceptance for the system, especially among personnel staff;
- lack of cooperation by the local authority that used to carry out payroll work;
- lack of experience with running payroll at the college;
- lack of administrative computing expertise at the college;
- possible inadequacy of the chosen hardware;
- changes to the payroll requirements.

4.3 Selection of project approaches

(a) This would appear to be a knowledge-based system that is also safety-critical. Techniques associated with knowledge-based systems could be used for constructing the system. Testing would need to be very carefully conducted. A lengthy parallel run where the system is used to shadow the human decisions made in real cases and the results compared could be considered. Another approach would be to develop two or more systems in parallel so that the advice offered could be cross-checked.

(b) This is an information system that will be on a relatively large scale. An SSADM approach would be justified. When student loans were first introduced there was no existing system and so there might have been some scope for a prototype.

(c) This is an embedded system that is highly safety-critical. Measures that might be adopted to ensure the reliability of the system include:

- use of mathematics-based specification languages to avoid ambiguity;
- developing parallel versions of the same software so that they can be cross-checked;
- statistical control of software testing to allow for the estimation of the reliability of the software.

4.4 Feedback between project review and feasibility study

The review might find that the benefits forecast in the original feasibility study report have not been achieved. 'Corrections' to the existing system might allow those benefits and other ones to be realized. This would lead to a proposal for a new project to modify the installed application.

4.5 Stages of a project where a prototype can be appropriate

(a) A prototype could be useful as part of the feasibility study. A mock-up of an executive information system loaded with current management information could be set up manually and then be tried out by the managers to see how easy and useful they found it.

(b) A prototype could be used to assist in the design of the user dialogues. SSADM allows for prototypes for this purpose as part of its requirement specification module.

(c) A prototype of the most response critical transactions could be made at the physical design stage to see whether Microsoft Access could produce software that gave a satisfactory performance.

Chapter 5

5.1 Calculating productivity rates and using productivity rates to project effort

Tables F.4 and F.5 illustrate productivity rates and estimated project effort.

There would be an under-estimate of 6.9 work-months for project a and an over-estimate of 5.7 for project d.

Table F.4 Productivity rates

Project	Work-months	SLOC	Productivity (SLOC/month)
a	16.7	6,050	362
b	22.6	8,363	370
c	32.2	13,334	414
d	3.9	5,942	1,524
e	17.3	3,315	192
f	67.7	38,988	576
g	10.1	38,614	3,823
h	19.3	12,762	661
i	59.5	26,500	445
Overall	249.3	153,868	617

Table F.5 Estimated effort

Project	Estimated work-months	Actual	Difference
a	6,050/617 = 9.80	16.7	6.90
d	5,942/617 = 9.63	3.9	−5.73

5.2 Course staff costs program – activities required

A list of activities might include:

- obtain user requirements;
- analyse the structure of the data already held;
- design report and write user proposal;
- write test plan;
- write technical specification;
- design software;
- write software;
- test software;
- write operating instruction;
- carry out acceptance testing.

The most difficult tasks to estimate are often those that are most sensitive to the size and the complexity of the software to be produced, in this case the design, writing and testing of the software. Writing the technical specification can also be difficult because of this, but estimating problems tend to be concealed here as deadlines can be met by omitting detail that can be added latter when deficiencies are found.

The duration of activities that are to be carried out by users may also present problems, as this might depend upon their sense of priorities.

5.3 Effort drivers for a student assignment

The most obvious effort driver would seem to be the number of words required. Difficulty factors might include:

- *availability of material*, for example, in the library;
- *familiarity* of the student with the topic;
- *breadth/depth* required, that is, a broad survey of a wide field or an in-depth study of a narrow area;
- *technical difficulty*, that is, some topics are easier to explain than others.

It could be argued that time available is the constraint. The student just does what can be done in the time available (see 'design to cost').

5.4 Calculating Euclidean distance

The Euclidean distance between Project B and the target case

$$= \sqrt{(7 - 5)^2 + (15 - 10)^2}$$
$$= \sqrt{2^2 + 5^2}$$
$$= 5.39$$

Project A is therefore a closer analogy.

5.5   Albrecht function points

The function types are as follows:

External input types	none
External output types	the report, 1
Logical internal file types	the accounting feeder file, 1
External interface file types	payroll file, staff file (timetabling,) courses file (timetabling,) accounting feeder file, 4
External inquiry types	none

Because the accounting feeder file is outgoing, it is counted once as a logical internal file type and once as an external interface file type.

The function points are:

External output types	$1 \times 7 = 7$
Logical internal file types	$1 \times 10 = 10$
External interface types	$4 \times 7 = 28$
Total	45

5.6   Calculation of SLOC from Albrecht function points

Estimated lines of Cobol = $45 \times 91 = 4095$

5.7   Mark II function points

The function types are:

Input data types	6
Entities accessed	1
Output data types	1

Unadjusted function points = $(0.58 \times 6) + (1.66 \times 1) + (0.26 \times 1) = 5.4$.

5.8   SLOC estimate for customer insertion program

Figure F.5 gives an outline program structure. The numbers in circles are our estimates of the lines of Cobol code needed to implement each subprocess in the program. They should add up to 95 SLOC. Note that these do not include data declarations.

5.9   COCOMO estimates

Table F.6 shows a comparison of the actual work-months from Table 5.1 and the COCOMO estimates. It illustrates the need for the calibration of COCOMO to suit local conditions.

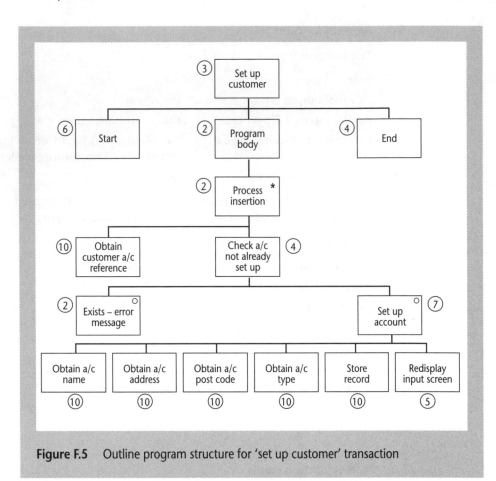

Figure F.5 Outline program structure for 'set up customer' transaction

Table F.6 Comparison of COCOMO estimates and actual effort

SLOC	Actual (work-months)	COCOMO estimates	Difference (work-months)	Difference (%)
6050	16.7	15.9	−0.8	−4.9
8363	22.6	22.3	−0.3	−1.2
13334	32.2	36.4	4.2	13.1
5942	3.9	15.6	11.7	299.7
3315	17.3	8.4	−8.9	−51.2
38988	67.7	112.4	44.7	66.0
38614	10.1	111.2	101.1	1001.5
12762	19.3	34.8	15.5	80.2
26500	59.5	74.9	15.4	25.9

Table F.7 Calculating the development multiplier

Factor	Rating	Multiplier
ACAP	Very high	0.71
AEXP	Low	1.13
PCAP	High	0.80
VEXP	High	0.90
LEXP	Low	1.07

Table F.8 Exponent drivers and ratings for the project

Exponent driver	rating
Precedentedness	3
Development flexibility	0
Architecture/risk resolution	4
Team cohesion	1
Process maturity	4
Total	12

5.10 COCOMO – calculating the development multiplier

Table F.7 shows development effort multipliers (*dem*) for the IOE project.
$$dem = 0.71 \times 1.13 \times 0.80 \times 0.90 \times 1.07 = 0.62$$
final estimate = 4 person-months $\times$ 0.62 = 2.48 staff months

5.11 COCOMO II Maximum size of sf

The maximum possible value for *sf* is:

$$0.91 + 0.01 \times (5 + 5 + 5 + 5 + 5) = 1.16$$

5.12 COCOMO II calculating a scale factor

Table F.8 illustrates the exponent drivers and ratings for this project.
Therefore, $sf = 0.91 + 0.01 \times (3 + 0 + 4 + 1 + 4) = 1.03$

Chapter 6

6.1 Drawing a CPM network

A solution is given in Figure 6.14. If your solution is not exactly the same as this do not worry. Just check that it is *logically* the same and that it follows the precedence network conventions of layout and labelling etc.

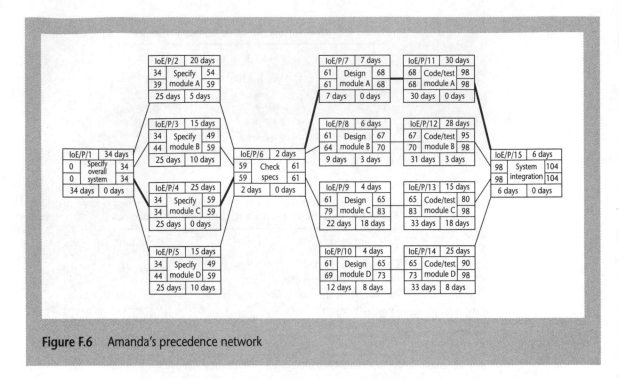

Figure F.6 Amanda's precedence network

Table F.9 Activity floats

Activity	Total float	Free float	Interfering float
A	2	0	2
B	3	0	3
C	2	2	0
D	3	3	0
E	3	3	0
F	0	0	0
G	0	0	0
H	2	2	0

6.2 The precedence network

Figure F.6 illustrates a precedence network for Amanda's project showing an earliest completion date of day 98.

6.3 Calculating activity floats

Free float and interfering float for each of the activities are shown in Table F.9 below. Note that activity A has no free float since any delay in its completion will delay the start of activity C. Activity C, however, has a 2-week free float so long as activity A keeps to time. Float must be regularly monitored as a project progresses since a delay in any activity beyond its free float allowance will eat into the float of subsequent activities.

6.4 Shortening a project duration

Shortening activity F to 8 weeks will bring the project completion date forward to week 11 – that is, it will save 2 weeks on the duration of the project. However, there are now two critical paths, start–F–G–finish and start–A–C–H–finish, so that reducing the duration of activity F any further will not shorten the project duration any further. If we wish to complete the project earlier than week 11 we must save time on both of these critical paths.

6.5 Errors drawing activity networks

(a) Activity D dangles, giving the project two 'end events'. This network should be drawn as below. To aid comparison with the original, the nodes have not been renumbered, although we would normally do so.

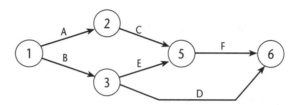

(b) Once again, this network has two end nodes, but in this case the solution is slightly different since we should introduce a dummy activity if we are to follow the standard CPM conventions.

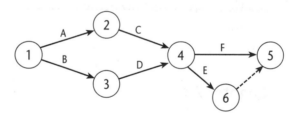

(c) Either this one has a dangle (although, because of the way it is drawn, it is less obvious) or activity E has its arrow pointing in the wrong direction. We need a bit more information before we can redraw this one correctly.

(d) Strictly speaking, there is nothing wrong with this one – it is just badly drawn and the nodes are not numbered according to the standard conventions. It should be redrawn as in the following example.

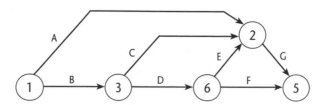

In this diagram the nodes have retained their original numbers (to aid identification) although they should of course be renumbered sequentially from left to right.

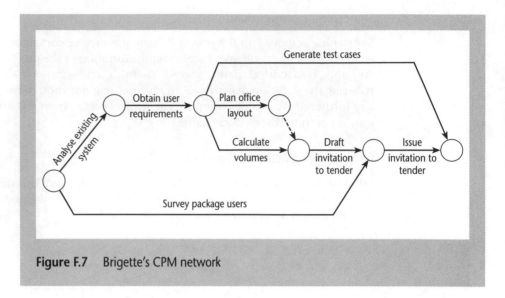

Figure F.7   Brigette's CPM network

(e) This one contains a loop – F cannot start before G has finished, G cannot start before E has finished and E cannot start before G has finished. One of the arrows is wrong! It is probably activity F that is wrong but we cannot be sure without further information.

6.6   Drawing Brigette's activity network as a CPM network

Brigette's payroll CPM network should look like the diagram shown in Figure F.7. If your diagram is not exactly the same as this check that it is logically the same.

Chapter 7

7.1   Brigette's hazard questionnaire

Among the factors that she might consider are the following:

Application factors

- Will the package need to interface with other (existing) systems?
- Are there likely to be large differences between alternative packages?

Staff factors

- Do the staff at the college have experience in evaluating or procuring packages of this type?
- Do the Brightmouth College staff have experience of using similar packages?

Project methods

- Can we use standard methods for this project?
- Does the college have established procedures for this type of project?

Hardware factors

- Will the project involve the purchase of new hardware?
- Will we be able to test candidate packages on the same hardware configuration as we will be operating?

Changeover factors

- Can we run a pilot system before complete changeover?
- Will the master files be convertible from the existing system?

Supplier factors

- Have we experience of purchasing software/hardware from the likely suppliers?
- How well established are the suppliers we are considering?

Environment factors

- Are there any plans for reorganization within the college that could affect the system?
- Are there likely to be any changes in government legislation that could affect the project?

7.2 Amanda's risk prioritization

The risks that you add will clearly depend upon the answers you gave to the previous exercise and you might feel that your assessment of likelihood and impact is somewhat arbitrary. It is best to work in a small group when trying to estimate these figures – where you disagree with your colleagues over a figure then discuss why this is so. For this exercise, the exact numbers that you decide on are not as important as recognizing why you might not agree with each other.

Categorizing risk exposures is discussed in the paragraphs following the exercise and, although you will have more risks than discussed there, you should look for sensible cut-off points along the lines discussed.

7.3 Amanda's risk reductions strategies

The following are illustrative of the actions that Amanda might consider:

- Changes to requirements specification during coding. This risk could be reduced by ensuring the original specification agreed at a senior level and adopting a high change threshold.
- Specification takes longer than expected. Review time estimates or break the activity down into smaller components and estimate each of them. Draw up contingency plans for shortening critical activities later in the project.
- Staff sickness affecting critical activities. Check availability of suitable agency analysts and programmers.
- Staff sickness affecting non-critical activities. Draw up rota of stand-by staff who might be recruited from other projects.
- Module coding takes longer than expected. Scrutinize estimating procedures and compare estimates with similar past projects.

● Module testing demonstrates errors or deficiencies in design. Use more stringent methods to validate design – formal methods or structured walkthroughs could be appropriate.

7.4 Calculating expected activity durations

Table F.10 shows the activity duration estimates from Table 7.5 along with the calculated expected durations, t_e.

7.5 The forward pass to calculate expected completion date

The expected duration and the expected dates for the other project events are shown in Figure 7.4. An expected duration of 13.5 weeks means that we expect the project to be completed half way through week 14, although since this is only an expected value it could finish earlier or later.

7.6 Calculating standard deviations

The correct values are shown in Figure 7.5. Brief calculations for events 4 and 6 are given here.

Event 4:   Path A + C has a standard deviation of $\sqrt{(0.50^2 + 0.17^2)} = 0.53$
Path B + D has a standard deviation of $\sqrt{(0.33^2 + 0.25^2)} = 0.41$
Node 4 therefore has a standard deviation of 0.53.

Event 6:   Path 4 + H has a standard deviation of $\sqrt{(0.53^2 + 0.08^2)} = 0.54$
Path 5 + G has a standard deviation of $\sqrt{(1.17^2 + 0.33^2)} = 1.22$
Node 6 therefore has a standard deviation of 1.22.

7.7 Calculating z values

The z value for event 5 is $\dfrac{10 - 10.5}{1.17} = -0.43$, for event 6 it is $\dfrac{15 - 13.5}{1.22} = 1.23$.

7.8 Obtaining probabilities

Event 4:   The z value is 1.89 which equates to a probability of approximately 3%. There is therefore only a 3% chance that we will not achieve this event by the target date of the end of week 10.

Event 5:   The z value is -0.43 which equates to a probability of approximately 67%. There is therefore a 68% chance that we will not achieve this event by the target date of the end of week 10.

To calculate the probability of completing the project by week 14 we need to calculate a new z value for event 6 using a target date of 14. This new z value is

$$z = \frac{14 - 13.5}{1.22} = 0.41.$$

This equates to a probability of approximately 35%. This is the probability of not meeting the target date. The probability of meeting the target date is therefore 65% (100% $-$ 35%).

Table F.10 Calculating expected activity durations

Activity	Activity durations (weeks)			
	Optimistic (a)	Most likely (m)	Pessimistic (b)	Expected (t_e)
A	5	6	8	6.17
B	3	4	5	4.00
C	2	3	3	2.83
D	3.5	4	5	4.08
E	1	3	4	2.83
F	8	10	15	10.50
G	2	3	4	3.00
H	2	2	2.5	2.08

Chapter 8

8.1 Smoothing resource demand

Smoothing analyst–designer demand for stage 4 is reasonably easy. The design of module D could be scheduled after the design of module C. Stage 2 is more problematic as scheduling the specification of module D to start after the completion of B would delay the project. Amanda might consider doing this if whoever is specifying module A could also be allocated to module D for the last six days – although she may well decide that drafting an extra person into a specification activity is unsatisfactory.

8.2 Drawing a revised resource histogram

If the activities are scheduled at the earliest dates, then the plan still calls for four analyst–designers as shown in Figure F.8. By delaying the start of some activities, however, Amanda is able to ensure that using three analyst–designers are sufficient except for a single day. This is shown in Figure F.9.

Note that if the specification of module C were to be delayed for a further day, the project could be completed with only three analyst–designers, although its completion day would, of course, be delayed.

8.3 Identifying critical activities

The critical path is now as shown in Figure F.10. Note the lag of 15 days against activity IoE/P/4, ensuring that its start is delayed until an analyst/designer is expected to be available.

However, the availability of an analyst/designer for IoE/P/4 is dependent upon IoE/P/3 or IoE/P/5 being completed on time – these two activities are therefore also now critical in the sense that a delay in both of them would delay IoE/P/4, which is on the normal critical path. These two activities, although not on the critical path, are, in that sense, critical.

When activities are scheduled at their earliest start dates, the shaded area of each bar represents the activity's total float.

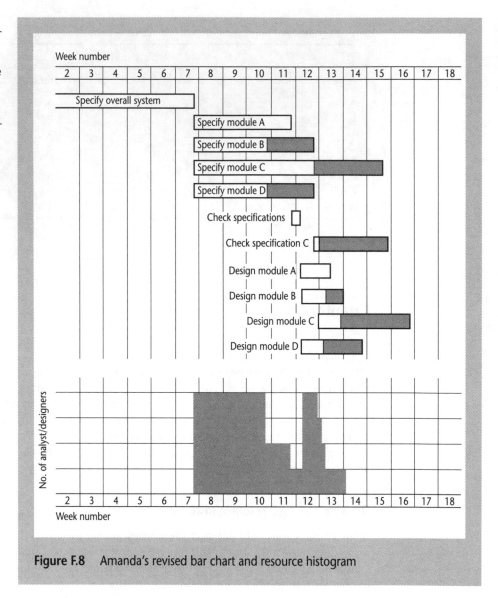

Figure F.8   Amanda's revised bar chart and resource histogram

8.4   Assigning staff to activities

Belinda must specify module B as she will then be available in time to start the specification of module C. This leaves Daisy for the specification and design of module A. Belinda cannot do the design of module B as she will still be working on the module C specification when this needs to be done (6 days between days 56 and 66). This will have to be left to Tom, as he should be free on day 60.

Can you think of any other way in which she might have allocated the three team members to these activities?

Once an activity is scheduled to start later than its earliest date, part of its total float will be 'used up' by that delay. The amount of total float that has been consumed in this way is indicated by the left-hand portion of an activity's shaded bar.

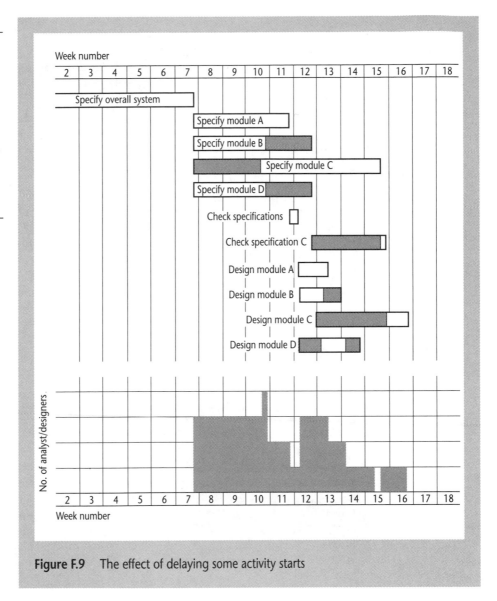

Figure F.9　The effect of delaying some activity starts

8.5　Calculating project costs

The easiest way to calculate the total cost is to set up a table similar to Table F.11.

Calculating the distribution of costs over the life of the project is best done as a per week or per month figure rather than as daily costs. The expenditure per week for Amanda's project is shown as a chart in Figure 8.9.

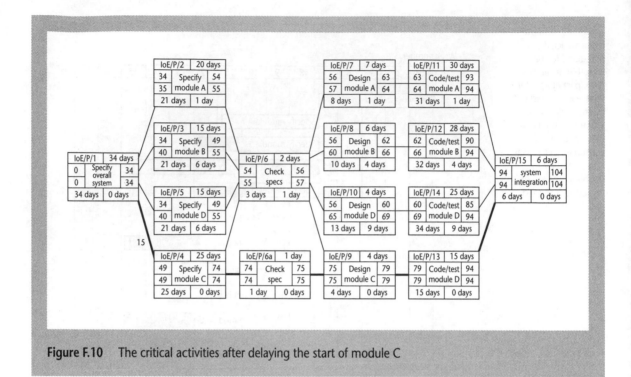

Figure F.10   The critical activities after delaying the start of module C

Table F.11   Calculating the cost of Amanda's project

Analyst	Daily cost (£)	Days required	Cost (£)
Amanda	300	110*	33,000
Belinda	250	50	12,500
Tom	175	25	4,375
Daisy	225	27	6,075
Gavin	150	30	4,500
Purdy	150	28	4,200
Justin	150	15	2,250
Spencer	150	25	3,750
Daily oncost	200	100	20,000
Total			90,650

*This includes 10 days for pre-project planning and post project review.

Chapter 9

9.1   Lines of code as a partial task completion indicator

There are many reasons why the proportion of lines coded is not a good indicator of completeness. In particular, you should have considered the following:

● the estimated total number of lines of code might be inaccurate;

● the lines of code so far written might have been easier, or harder, to write than those to follow;

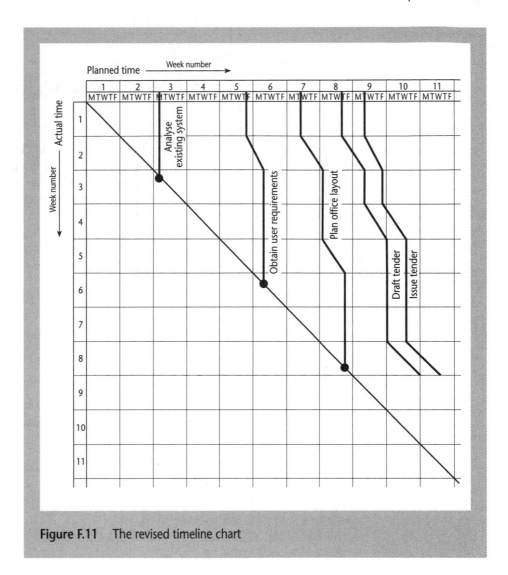

Figure F.11   The revised timeline chart

- a program is not generally considered complete until it has been tested – when 100% of its lines of code have been written a program will still be incomplete until tested.

With more knowledge of what has been done and what is left to complete it might be possible to make a reasonable estimate of completeness. Breaking the development task into smaller sub-tasks such as software design, coding and unit testing might be of some assistance here.

9.2   Revising the timeline chart

At the end of week 8, the scheduled completion dates for drafting and issuing the tender need to be revised – note both need to be changed since they are both on the critical path (Figure F.11).

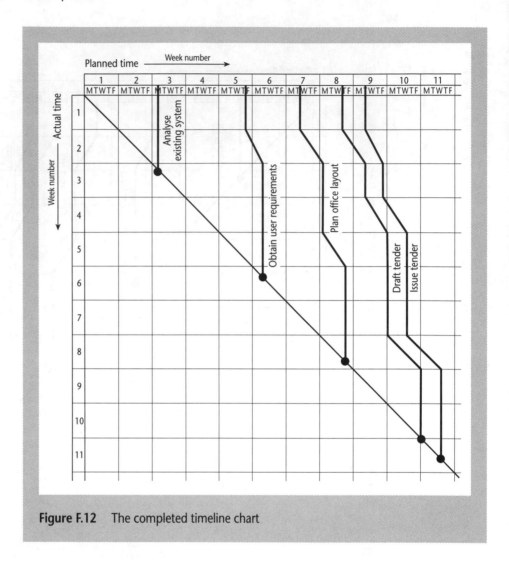

Figure F.12 The completed timeline chart

Subsequently, Brigette needs to show only the completion of each of these two remaining activities on the timeline chart – the project being completed by the Thursday of week 11 (Figure F.12).

9.3 Amanda's earned value analysis

It should be apparent from Figure 9.12 that the initial activity, *specify overall system*, has slipped by one day. It may not be quite so obvious from Figure 9.12 alone what else has happened to her project – inspection of Figure 9.12 and Table 9.2 should, however, make it possible to see that *specify module D* has taken 2 days longer than forecast and *specify module B* has taken 5 days longer. Thus, the project has earned 34 workdays by day 35, 49 workdays by day 52 and 64 workdays by day 55.

From Figure 9.12 it is not possible to deduce the underlying causes of the slippage or to forecast the consequences for the project. The use of earned value analysis for forecasting is described later in Section 9.6.

9.4 The effects of specification changes

Among the items most likely to be affected by the change are test data, expected results and the user handbooks.

9.5 Control procedures for development systems

Stages 1 to 6 will be basically the same except that an estimate on the effect of the project's timescale will need to be included in steps 3 and 4. Step 7 might not be required as system acceptance might not have taken place yet and acceptance testing of the changes will be included in that.

The release of software in step 8 will not be needed if the system is not yet operational, although master copies of products will need to be updated.

9.6 Reasons for scope creep

There can be several different system designs that meet the users' requirements and one may be selected which is more elaborate and involves more processing.

Essential housekeeping and security-driven requirements might become apparent – for example, additional validation of the input to ensure that the database remains consistent.

Chapter 10

10.1 Choice of type of package at IOE

The problem for Amanda at IOE would be that the new maintenance group accounts subsystem would essentially be an extension to and enhancement of the existing maintenance accounting system, so that the interfacing of an off-the-shelf package might involve quite a few difficulties. This seems to indicate that bespoke development is needed. An alternative approach might be to consider replacing the whole of the maintenance accounting system with a new off-the-shelf application.

10.2 Calculation of charges for a project

For the first 2000 FPs	$967 × 2,000	=	$1,934,000
For the next 500 FPs	$1,019 × 500	=	$509,500
For the next 500 FPs	$1,058 × 500	=	$529,000
For the last 200 FPs	$1,094 × 200	=	$218,800
for all 3,200 FPs			$3,191,300

10.3 Calculating the cost of additional functionality

For changed FPs	500 × 600 × (150/100)	=	$450,000
For additional FPs	200 × 600	=	$120,000
Total charge			$570,000

10.4 Advantage to customer of variable cost charges

The supplier will need to quote a price that will include a margin to cater for possible increases in equipment prices. It might turn out that actual prices do not increase as much as was estimated – in the case of IT equipment some prices are likely to go down – but the customer would still have to pay the additional margin. If the contract specifies a fixed charge plus the actual cost of materials and equipment, then the customer in this case would be better off.

10.5 Calculating value for money

System X savings would be £20 × 20 hours × 4 years = £1,600, for the automatic scale point adjustment facility, and £20 × 12 hours × 2 times a year × 4 years = £1,920, for the bar chart production facility. In total the saving for system X would be £3,520.

For System Y, the saving would be £300 × 0.5 (to take account of the probability of change). That is, £150.

Even though System X costs £500 more, it will still give better value for money. Note that discounted cash flow calculations could be applied to these figures.

10.6 Evaluation methods

1. The usability of an existing system could be evaluated by such means as the examination of user handbooks, the observation of demonstrations and practical user trails.

2. This is clearly tricky. One would have to evaluate the methods that the developers intend to use to see whether they adhere to good interface design practice. One might also examine any interface standards that are in use by the supplier.

3. Note that the question focuses on the costs of maintenance, rather than those of reliability. The cost of unexpected maintenance could be reduced, at least for a short time, by passing this risk to the supplier if there is a comprehensive warranty. The warranties provided by suppliers would therefore need to be scrutinized. Discussion with reference sites might also be helpful.

4. Once again guarantees could be put in place by suppliers concerning this. The nature of these guarantees could be examined.

5. Training materials could be examined. The training staff could be interviewed and their CVs examined. Reference sites who have already used the supplier's training services could be approached for their views.

Chapter 11

11.1 Tasks and responsibilities of an analyst/programmer

An analyst/programmer is expected to be able to carry out both analysis and programming tasks. It is likely, however, that the kinds of analysis tasks undertaken will be restricted. They may, for example, do the analysis work for enhancements to existing systems but not of completely new applications. Making this broad assumption, a list of tasks and responsibilities might be as follows:

- carry out detailed investigations of new requirements for existing computer applications;
- analyse the results of investigations and review the solutions to problems experienced, including the estimation of relevant costs;
- prepare systems specifications in accordance with organizational standards;
- conduct appropriate systems testing;
- prepare functional module specifications;
- produce and modify module structure diagrams;
- code and amend software modules;
- carry out appropriate unit testing;
- produce and amend user documentation;
- liaise with users, carrying out appropriate training in the use of computer applications where required.

11.2 Rewarding reuse

A problem here is that the programmers who make most use of reused components will, as a consequence, be producing less code themselves. You also want to encourage programmers to produce software components that other people can use: this might help the productivity of the organization but not that of the current project that they are working on!

You need to have a method, like function point analysis, which measures the functions and features actually delivered to the user. You also need to have some way of measuring the code used in the application that has been taken from elsewhere. Percentage targets of the amount of reused code to new code could be set and staff rewarded if the targets are met. As an alternative, the savings made by reuse could be measured and a profit-sharing scheme could be operated.

Programmers could be encouraged to produce and publish reusable components by a system of royalties for each time a software component is reused.

11.3 Financial incentives for top executives

This exercise was designed to be thought-provoking. Some thoughts that have come out of discussion on this topic are given below.

- To some extent, material wants and, therefore, the motivation to obtain more money to satisfy these wants, can be generated through the marketing and advertising of new types of goods and services – but how likely is this to be at the very top?
- Large salaries are associated with status, esteem and success. It could be that these are the real reward.
- Historically, wealth has been associated with power, such as the ownership of land.

The essential point is that for many people money is not just a means of satisfying material wants.

11.4 High and low motivational incidents

This will obviously depend on individual experiences.

11.5 Social loafing

Among other ideas, the effects of social loafing can be reduced by:

- making the work of each performer individually identifiable;
- involving and interesting group members in the outcome of group efforts;
- rewarding individuals for their contributions to the group effort (rather like sports teams who pick out a 'club player of the year').

11.6 Effect of IT on the Delphi technique

Developments in IT that assist cooperative working, especially the advent of electronic mail and groupware such as Lotus Notes, will cut quite considerably the communication delays involved in the Delphi technique.

11.7 Classification of types of power

More than one type of power can be involved in each case.

i.   Some *expert* power is involved here, but for those who are subject to the audit, the main type of power is *connection* power as the auditor will produce a report that will go to higher management. External auditors often have *coercive* power.

ii.   Here, power will mainly be *expert-* and *information-based*, but as the consultant will report to higher management, *connection* power also exists.

iii.   This sounds pretty *coercive*.

iv.   Brigette has some *connection* power. The technical expertise that is involved in her job means she has some *expert* power. She has little or no *coercive* power as she is not the manger of the staff involved. She might be able to exert some *reward* power on the basis of an informal 'I'll do you a favour if you'll do me a favour' arrangement!

v.   Amanda is unlikely to have direct *coercive* powers although she might be able to institute disciplinary procedures. Through the system of annual reviews common to many organizations, she might have some *reward* power. *Connection* power, through her access to higher management, is also present. Her access to users means she has *information* power. If she brings specific expertise to the project (such as analysis skills) she might have some *expert* power. By acting as a role model that other project team members might want to emulate she may even be displaying *referent* power!

11.8 Appropriate management styles

i.   The clerk will know much more than anyone else about the practical details of the work. Heavy *task-oriented* supervision would therefore not be appropriate. As the clerk is working in a new environment and forging new relationships, a considerable amount of people-oriented supervision/support might be needed initially.

ii. Both task-oriented and people-oriented management would be needed with the trainee.

iii. The experienced maintenance programmer has probably had considerable autonomy in the past. The extensions to the systems could have a considerable, detailed, impact on this person's work. A very carefully judged increase in task-oriented management will be required for a short time.

Chapter 12

12.1 Selection of payroll package for college

(a) Carry out an investigation to find out what the users' requirements really are. This might uncover that there are different sets of requirements for different groups of users.

(b) Organize the requirements into groups relating to individual qualities and attributes. These might be, for example, functionality (the range of features that the software has), price, usability, capacity, efficiency, flexibility, reliability and serviceability.

(c) Some of these requirements will be of an absolute nature. For example, an application will have to hold records for up to a certain maximum number of employees. If it cannot, it will have to be immediately eliminated from further consideration.

(d) In other cases the requirement is relative. Some of the relative requirements are more important than others. A low price is desirable but more expensive software cannot be ruled out straightaway. This can be reflected by giving each of the requirements a rating, a score out of 10, say, for importance.

(e) A range of possible candidate packages needs to be identified. If there are lots of possibilities, an initial screening, for instance, by price, can be applied to reduce the contenders to a manageable shortlist.

(f) Practical ways of measuring the desired qualities in the software have to be devised. In some cases, for example with price and capacity, sales literature or a technical specification can be consulted. In other cases, efficiency for instance, practical trials could be conducted, while in yet other cases a survey of existing users might provide the information required.

(g) It is likely that some software is going to be deficient in some ways, but that this will be compensated by other qualities. A simple way of combining the findings on different qualities is to give a mark out of 10 for the relative presence/absence of the quality. Each of these scores can be multiplied by a score out of 10 for the importance of the quality (see (d)) and the results of all these multiplications can be summed to give an overall score for the software.

12.2 Relationships between pairs of quality factors

● **Indifferent** Usability and reusability would seem to have little bearing on each other in spite of the similarity in their names. (Although it is usually possible to identify at least a tenuous complementary or conflicting relationship between two quality factors if you try hard enough.)

- **Complementary** A program that demonstrated flexibility might also be expected to have a high degree of maintainability.
- **Conflicting** A program can be highly efficient because it exploits the architecture of a particular type of hardware to the full, but not be easy to transfer to another hardware configuration.

12.3 Quality criteria

The presence of the same software quality criterion for more than one software quality factor would indicate that the software quality factors are complementary.

12.4 Possible quality specifications for word processing software

There are many that could be defined and just two examples are given below. One point that may emerge is that the software might be best broken down into a number of different function areas, each of which can be evaluated separately, such as document preparation, presentation, mail merging and so on. For example:

- *quality*: ease of learning;
- *definition*: the time taken, by a novice, to learn how to operate the package to produce a standard document;
- *scale*: hours;
- *test*: interview novices to ascertain their previous experience of word processing. Supply them with a machine, the software, a training manual and a standard document to set up. Time how long it takes them to learn how to set the document up.
- *worst*: 4 hours;
- *planned*: 2 hours;
- *best*: 1 hour;
- *now*: 4 hours;

or

- *quality*: ease of use;
- *definition*: the time taken for an experienced user to produce a standard document;
- *scale*: minutes;
- *test*: time user who has experience of package to produce the standard document;
- *worst*: 45 minutes;
- *planned*: 40 minutes;
- *best*: 35 minutes.

This topic of evaluation is an extensive one and the pointers above leave all sorts of unanswered questions in the air. Readers who wish to explore this area should read one of the more specialist books on the topic.

12.5 Availability and mean time between failures

Each day the system should be available from $18.00 - 8.00$ hours $= 10$ hours.
Over four weeks that should be $10 \times 5 \times 4$ hours $= 200$ hours.
It was unavailable for one day, i.e. 10 hours.
It was unavailable until 10.00 on two other days, $= 4$ hours.
The hours available were therefore $200 - 10 - 4 = 186$ hours.
Availability would therefore be $186/200 \times 100 = 93\%$.

Assuming that three failures are counted, *mean time between failures* would be $186/3 = 62$ hours.

12.6 Entry requirements for an activity different from the exit requirements for another activity that immediately precedes it

It is possible for one activity to start before the immediately preceding activity has been completely finished. In this case, the entry requirement for the following activity has been satisfied, even though the exit requirement of the preceding activity has not. For example, software modules could be used for performance testing of the hardware platform even though there are some residual defects concerning screen layouts.

Another situation where the entry requirements could vary from the preceding exit requirements is where a particular resource needs to be available.

12.7 Entry and exit requirements

- *Entry requirements*   A program design must have been produced that has been reviewed and any rework required by the review must have been carried out and been inspected by the chair of the review group.
- *Exit requirements*   A program must have been produced that has been compiled and is free of compilation errors; the code must have been reviewed and any rework required by the review must have been carried out and been inspected by the chair of the review group.

It should be noted that the review group might use checklists for each type of product reviewed and these could be regarded as further entry/exit requirements.

12.8 Application of BS EN ISO 9001 to system testing

There would need to be a documented procedure that governs system testing.

The quality objective for system testing might be defined as ensuring that the software conforms to the requirements laid down in the user specification.

Processes to ensure this could include documented cross-referencing of test cases to sections of the specification.

The results of executing test cases would need to be recorded and the subsequent remedying of any discrepancies would also need to be recorded.

12.9 Precautionary steps when work is contracted out?

The project manager could check who actually carried out the certification. They could also discover the scope of the BS EN ISO 9001 certification that was awarded.

For example, it could be that certification only applied to the processes that created certain products and not others.

Perhaps the most important point is that the project manager will need to be reassured that the *specification* to which the contractors will be working is an adequate reflection of the requirements of the client organization.

12.10 The important differences between a quality circle and a review group?

The quality circle would be looking at the process in general while the review group would look at a particular instance of a product. The use of review groups alone could be inefficient because they could be removing the same type of defect again and again rather than addressing, as the quality circle does, the task of stopping the defects at their source.

Further reading

General introductory books on project management – not IS specific

Feild, Mike and Laurie Keller, *Project Management*, London, International Thomson Business Press, 1998.

Haynes, Marion E., *Project Management: From Idea to Implementation*, Kogan Page better management skills, London, Kogan Page, 1990.

Haynes, Marion E., *Project Management*, rev. edn, *A Fifty-minute Series Book*, Menlo Park, CA, Crisp Publications, 1996.

Lockyer, Keith and James Gordon, *Project Management and Project Network Techniques*, 6th edn., Financial Times Pitman Publishing, 1996.

Nickson, David, and Suzy Siddons, *Managing Projects*, Made Simple Books; Oxford, Butterworth-Heinemann, 1997.

Weiss, Joseph W. and Robert K. Wysocki, *5-phase Project Management: A Practical Planning & Implementation Guide*, Reading, MA, Addison-Wesley, 1992.

General books on software and IS project management

Bennatan, E. M., *Software Project Management: A Practitioner's Approach*, 2nd edn, London; New York, McGraw-Hill, 1995.

Yeates, Donald and James Cadle, *Project Management for Information Systems*, 2nd edn, London, Pitman Publications, 1996.

Ince, Darrel, Helen Sharp and Mark Woodman, *Introduction to Software Project Management and Quality Assurance*, The McGraw-Hill international series in software engineering, London; New York, McGraw-Hill, 1993.

Other books worth looking at

Brooks, Frederick P., *The Mythical Man-month: Essays on Software Engineering*, anniversary edn, Reading, MA, Addison-Wesley, 1995. The classic exposition of the central issues of software project management from the man who was in charge of the IBM 360 Operating System development project. You should try to look at it at some time.

Kemerer, Chris F. (ed.), *Software Project Management: Readings and Cases*, Chicago, Irwin, McGraw-Hill, 1997. A collection of classic papers on topics such as estimation, risk management, life cycles, re-use and process improvement. Strongly recommended.

Whitten, Neal, *Managing Software Development Projects: Formula for Success*, New York; Chichester, Wiley, 1995.

Strategic planning and programme management

Central Computer and Telecommunications Agency, *Managing Successful Programmes*, The Stationery Office, 1999.

Clare, Chris and Gordon Stuteley, *Information Systems – Strategy to Design*, Tutorial guides in computing and information systems; 7, London, Chapman & Hall, 1995.

Gilb, Tom and Susannah Finzi, *Principles of Software Engineering Management*, Wokingham; Reading, MA, Addison-Wesley, 1988.

Ould, Martyn, *Managing Software Quality and Business Risk*, Wiley series in software engineering practice, New York; Chichester, Wiley, 1999.

Reiss, G., *Programme Management Demystified*, London, Chapman & Hall, 1996.

Project process models

Stapleton, Jennifer, *DSDM Dynamic Systems Development Method*, Wokingham; Reading, MA, Addison-Wesley, 1977.

Beck, Kent, *Extreme Programming Explained: Embrace Change*, Wokingham, Reading, MA, Addison-Wesley, 1999.

Booch, Grady, *Object Solutions: Managing the Object Oriented Project*, Wokingham, Reading, MA, Addison-Wesley, 1996.

Wood, Jane and Denise Silver, *Joint Application Development*, New York Wiley, 1995.

Planning

Bradley, Ken, *PRINCE: A Practical Handbook*, Oxford; Boston, MA, Butterworth-Heinemann, 1993.

Bentley, Colin, *Prince 2: A Practical Handbook*, Computer weekly professional series, Oxford; Boston, MA, Butterworth-Heinemann, 1997.

Harrison, F. L., *Advanced Project Management: A Structured Approach*, Aldershot, Gower, 1992. A general project management book – not just software projects.

Lock, Dennis, *Project Management*, 6th edn, Brookfield, VT, Gower, 1996. An alternative to the Harrison book, it shows some awareness of PRINCE.

Estimation

Boehm, Barry W., *Software Engineering Economics*, Prentice-Hall advances in computing science and technology series, Englewood Cliffs, NJ, Prentice-Hall, 1981.

Along with the Brooks book one of the most frequently cited books on software project management.

Hughes, Bob, *Practical Software Measurement*, London; New York, McGraw-Hill, 2000.

Symons, Charles R., *Software Sizing and Estimating: Mk II FPA (Function Point Analysis)*, *Wiley Series in Software Engineering Practice*, New York; Chichester, Wiley, 1991. A book by the inventor of Mark II function points.

DeMarco, Tom, *Controlling Software Projects: Management, Measurement & Estimation*, New York, Yourdon Press, 1982.

Control and configuration management

Youll, David P., *Making Software Development Visible: Effective Project Control*, Wiley series in software engineering practice, New York; Chichester, Wiley, 1990.

Central Computer and Telecommunications Agency, *Configuration Management*, *IT Infrastructure Library*, London, HMSO, 1990.

CCTA, *Configuration Management Guide*, CCTA, 1989.

Buckle, J. K., *Software Configuration Management*, London, Macmillan, 1982.

Risk

Boehm, Barry W., *Software Risk Management*, Washington, DC, IEEE Computer Society Press, 1989.

Grey, Stephen, *Practical Risk Assessment for Project Management*, Wiley series in software engineering practice, New York; Chichester, Wiley, 1995.

Down, Alex, Michael Coleman and Peter Absolon, *Risk Management for Software Projects*, IBM McGraw-Hill series, London; New York, McGraw-Hill, 1994.

Charette, Robert N., *Software Engineering Risk Analysis and Management*, McGraw-Hill software engineering series, New York, Intertext Publications; McGraw-Hill Book, 1989.

Quality and testing

Humphrey, Watts S., *Managing the Software Process*, repr. 1990 with corrections, SEI series in software engineering, Reading, MA, Addison-Wesley, 1990.

Manns, Tom and Michael Coleman, *Software Quality Assurance*, 2nd edn, Basingstoke, Macmillan, 1996.

Manns, Tom and Michael Coleman, *Software Quality Assurance*, Macmillan computer science series, Basingstoke; Port Washington, NY, Macmillan Education; distributed by Scholium International, 1988.

Daily, K., *Quality Management for Software*, Manchester, NCC Blackwell, 1992.

People management

Arnold, John, Cary Cooper and Ivan Robertson, *Work Psychology: Understanding Human Behaviour in the Workplace*, 3rd edn, London, Pitman, 1998.

DeMarco, Tom and Timothy R. Lister, *Peopleware: Productive Projects and Teams*, 2nd edn, New York, Dorset House, 1999.

Healy, Patrick L., *Project Management: Getting the Job Done on Time and in Budget*, Port Melbourne; Newton, MA, Butterworth-Heinemann, 1997. Although it presents itself as a general book on project management, it is relatively thin on the technical aspects of project planning. However, it makes many useful points about dealing with political and behavioural issues.

Handy, Charles B., *Understanding Organizations*, 4th edn, London, Penguin, 1993. A general book on this topic which is not IS-specific.

Belbin, R. Meredith, *Management Teams: Why They Succeed or Fail*, Oxford; Boston, Butterworth-Heinemann, 1996.

Belbin, R. Meredith, *Team Roles at Work*, Oxford; Boston, MA, Butterworth-Heinemann,1993. This updates but does not replace the 1981 book

Bott, Frank, *Professional Issues in Software Engineering*, 3rd edn, London, Taylor & Francis, 2000.

Project management standards

British Standards Institution, *BS 6079 Guide to Project Management*, London, BSI, 1996.

Central Computer and Telecommunications Agency, *PRINCE 2: [Project Management for Business]*, London, The Stationery Office, 1996.

Project Management Institute and PMI Standards Committee, *A Guide to the Project Management Body of Knowledge*, Upper Darby, PA: Project Management Institute, 1996: obtainable via WWW from http://www.pmi.org.

Contracts

David Bainbridge, *Introduction to Computer Law*, 3rd edn, London, Pitman, 1996.

Index